Collector's Library of Essential Thinkers

HOBBES AND LOCKE ON SOVEREIGNTY

Hobbes and Locke on Sovereignty

Thomas Hobbes:
Leviathan Parts 1 and 2

John Locke:
Second Treatise of Government

The Collector's Library of
ESSENTIAL THINKERS

This edition published in 2005 by
The Collector's Library of Essential Thinkers
an imprint of CRW Publishing Limited
69 Gloucester Crescent, London NW1 7EG

ISBN 1 904919 60 X

1 3 5 7 9 10 8 6 4 2

Typeset in Great Britain by Antony Gray
Printed and bound in China by Imago

Contents

Introduction

If you skim through the selections from Hobbes and Locke contained in this book, you will quickly find that whereas Locke allows – and argues strongly for – the right of subjects to rebel aganst an unjust ruler, Hobbes allows no such right. And if you turn to their lives, you find that Hobbes was a royalist in the English civil war, and had been tutor to the future king Charles II; Locke (though still a schoolboy during the civil war) was a strong supporter of the 'glorious revolution' of 1688, which got rid of the last Stuart king, James II.

Is this, then, another case of philosophers tailoring their philosophy to suit the beliefs they held right from the start? Or is there more to it than that?

Historical background

The seventeenth century, when Hobbes and Locke lived, was the time when the English monarchy stumbled out of the medieval world and into the modern world. The Tudors, in the sixteenth century, had been absolute monarchs. The divine right of kings (or of a queen) was widely accepted; they might have advisers, but there was no requirement that they should follow any advice they were given. However, by the time we get to the eighteenth century, things have changed dramatically. The Hanoverian monarchs are recognisably modern, not medieval. Their rule is constitutional, not absolute.

How did this change come about? Why did what had worked for the Tudors not work for their Stuart successors? There are a number of reasons. The anarchy of the Wars of the Roses became more remote. Stability led to prosperity. As people grew richer, they wanted more say in what was done with the money they contributed to the running of the country. Religion too was a worry. England had become a Protestant country, and the English had painful memories of 'bloody Mary' Tudor, and her attempt to restore Catholicism.

And then the Stuart monarchs were a problem in themselves. James I was a Scot, with a French mother, and England had been at war with with Scotland and France, off and on, for hundreds of years. The Stuarts were closet Catholics, or had strong Catholic sympathies. Above all, they lacked the political nous of the Tudor monarchs. For all their absolutist power, the two Henrys and Elizabeth were shrewd individuals with an acute sense of what people would and would not tolerate. Charles I and James II lacked any such sense.

The civil war (1642–1649)

The war was a conflict over taxation and religion. When Parliament started to challenge the monarch's control over taxation, Charles's reaction was to dismiss Parliament, and rule through advisers. At the same time he set about alienating his natural supporters (among them the Scots) by insisting on uniformity of worship. 1637, for example, was the year when the Pilgrim Fathers, driven by what they saw as religious persecution, set sail for America.

In 1640 a war against the Scots, and the need for additional revenue, compelled Charles to recall Parliament. In return, Parliament called for the execution of the Earl of Strafford, the most competent of Charles's advisers (and the one who would probably have won the coming civil war for Charles in a matter of weeks). The war, when it came, was bitter and divisive. Charles, like the Confederates in the American Civil War, needed to win quickly. His opponents had resources for a long-drawn-out conflict, and he did not. When he failed to win quickly, and still more after he was defeated, he needed to make concessions. His refusal to do so led, eventually, to his execution.

The revolution of 1688

One irony of the civil war is that having won it (for Parliament), Oliver Cromwell then ignored Parliament as comprehensively as Charles had done. He became deeply unpopular, and after his death, the monarchy was restored. Charles II agreed to share power with Parliament, and to continue with the policy of religious toleration – though not for Catholics. The Test Acts stopped Catholics being Members of Parliament or holding high office, but an attempt (in 1683) to bar Catholics (in other words, Charles's younger brother James) from succession to the throne failed.

Just before he died in February 1685, Charles admitted that he was a Catholic, and announced that his brother James was to succeed him. James had enough support to put down a rebellion by the Duke of Monmouth without too much difficulty. But he ignored the Test Acts, and announced his intention of giving Catholics complete religious freedom in England. When the Archbishop of Canterbury objected, James had him arrested.

At this point the House of Commons invited James's daughter Mary and her husband William, Prince of Orange, to come to England. When the English army refused to obey the orders of their Catholic officers, James fled to France. This bloodless coup became known as the Glorious Revolution.

Summary

So the seventeenth-century revolution was a two-part revolution: the first part violent and political – cutting off the king's head to demonstrate the supremacy of parliament); the second part peaceful and prompted mainly by religion – getting rid of a Catholic monarch and inviting Protestants to come and rule instead.

Thomas Hobbes

Hobbes was born in 1588, the year of the Spanish Armada, and lived to the age of 91. He saw the civil war and the Protectorate, the restoration of the monarchy under Charles II, but not the deposition of James II in 1688. He moved in circles where the activities of King and Parliament were much discussed, and he had close ties with the Stuart royal family.

His philosophical work is characterised by strong admiration for scientific method – not so much the experimental science of people like Galileo and Descartes as the deductive science to be found in Spinoza, based on first principles and true definitions. His view of knowledge is modelled on the clarity and deductive power of the proofs of geometry. He insists that terms be accurately defined and relate to concrete experience.

He had little time for scholastic philosophy or religious authority. He was not an atheist, but his materialist metaphysics – as his critics pointed out – makes God's existence difficult to account for. Hobbes always felt vulnerable to accusations of atheism, but he continued to insist that theological disputes must be kept out of politics. Citizens cannot be allowed duties to God that override their duty to obey political authority.

Hobbes was in touch (and nearly always in dispute) with intellectuals in England and abroad. In Descartes' *Objections and Replies*, for example, the first objection is from Hobbes. He was a scientist and mathematician; he wrote on law, religion, metaphysics and epistemology; he is also justly admired for his translation of the Greek historian Thucydides – perhaps the most difficult to translate of all Greek writers. The influence of Thucydides (above all the idea that civil war is an evil to be avoided at whatever cost) is strongly apparent in *Leviathan*.

Leviathan

Hobbes's political ideas are based on the physics and psychology of his day. The chief human impulses, he says, are first of all fear, followed – for those not in poverty or in fear of their lives – by pride and vanity. He wants his science of politics to be a question of rules (as in arithmetic or geometry), not a question of skill (as in tennis).

In *Leviathan* (published in 1651) his greatest fear is social and political chaos, hence his chief aims are order and stability. He ignores ideas such as the law of nature, or divine law. So he emphatically does not support the divine right of kings. He states plainly that it is power which creates law, and not the other way round. Law is law only if it is enforced, so the price of security is a supreme sovereign power. Without that, there is a war of all against all. The true law of nature is self-preservation, which can be achieved only if the citizens make a compact among themselves to transfer their individual power to the 'leviathan' (the ruler), who alone can preserve them in security. Once they have made that compact, they have an unconditional obligation to obey the leviathan they have brought into being.

Such a sovereign power has no supernatural or moral sanction. It need not be an individual (though Hobbes clearly expects it to be). Its authority stems from the people and it ceases to command loyalty only when it can no longer preserve their security. On one thing we should be clear. Hobbes argues for absolute sovereignty, but not for the divine right of kings. The sovereign commands obedience by virtue of being the sovereign, not because the sovereign power is derived from God. Hobbes does not say so, but the same arguments which require obedience of the subject to Charles I also – once Charles has been defeated and Oliver Cromwell has become Protector – require obedience to Oliver Cromwell.

John Locke

Locke's family was Anglican, with Puritan sympathies. His father fought on the side of the Parliamentarians in the Civil War. Locke himself was educated at

Westminster and Christ Church, Oxford, where his interests were science and medicine. He was soon elected a student (fellow) of Christ Church, and in 1660 welcomed the restoration of Charles II to the throne.

Locke taught at Christ Church for a while, but soon turned to medicine. This brought him, by chance, to the notice of Lord Ashley (adviser to Charles II, and later first earl of Shaftesbury). Locke became Ashley's family physician, and also his personal adviser. Ashley stood for constitutional monarchy, a Protestant succession, civil liberty, toleration in religion, the rule of Parliament, and economic expansion – all of which aims were shared by Locke. At Ashley's suggestion, Locke helped draft a constitution for the colony of Carolina, extending freedom of worship to all colonists.

In 1675 Locke departed for France on grounds of ill health, but returned when Shaftesbury became Lord President of the King's Council. There followed the attempt to exclude the Catholic James from the succession, Shaftesbury's dismissal from office and trial for treason, and his flight to Holland (where he died). In 1683 there was a plot to kill Charles II, and Locke, though not directly implicated, in turn fled to Holland. He was expelled, by royal command, from his studentship at Christ Church.

He remained in Holland until the deposition of James II. On his return in 1689, he published the *Essay Concerning Human Understanding*, and in the following year the *Two Treatises of Civil Government*. He retired to the country in 1691, and for the most part remained there, his health deteriorating, until his death in 1704.

The Treatises on Government

Locke defines political power as 'a right of making laws, with penalties of death, and consequently all less penalties for the regulating and preserving of property, and of employing the force of the community in the execution of such laws, and in the defence of the commonwealth from foreign injury, and all this only for the public good.'

The last five words are crucial. The right to government can be forfeited by a ruler who fails to secure the public good. Nor does the individual surrender all his rights when he enters a civil society. He has established his right to property by 'mixing his labour' with things originally given to mankind in common but now made his own by his labour. He has the right to expect political power to be used to preserve his property, in his own person and in his possessions. He also has the right to freedom of thought, speech, and worship. The one right he gives up is the right to judge and punish his fellow man, which was his right in the state of nature. He makes himself subject to the civil law and finds his freedom in voluntary obedience.

To secure this freedom, Locke favoured a mixed constitution and the separation of powers – legislative power in an elected body, and executive power in the monarch. The people are ultimately sovereign, although it is not always clear in Locke's theory where immediate sovereignty lies. But the people always have the right to withdraw their support for the government if it fails to fulfil their trust. This clearly applies to the monarch; it is less clear if it applies to their own elected representatives.

Conclusion

The right of rebellion

Hobbes the royalist goes for the overriding importance of sovereignty. He believed you should obey the sovereign power because the alternative (having no rule of law) was bound to be worse than being ruled by an unjust sovereign. Locke, by contrast, believed there was a right of resistance, and in the last resort a right to overthrow the sovereign. But then, what would you expect him to believe? His father had been a parliamentarian, and Locke himself was opposed to the succession of James II.

Did each of them simply shape his philosophical views to fit his political beliefs? Not necessarily. It is perfectly possible that their political beliefs were the result of their philosophical views, rather than the other way round. Or was it that Hobbes's views were coloured by the violence and cruelty of the Civil War, Locke's by the bloodless revolution of 1688? It was not absurd to present the events of 1688 as the termination of a contract in which one party had failed to carry out its side of the bargain. You couldn't plausibly present 1642–49 in those terms.

Who *was* right?

The influence of Locke has been far greater than that of Hobbes. The belief that there is a contract between rulers and ruled, and that the ruled have the right to rebel if the rulers break that contract, has been a profound influence on Irish nationalism, on the demand for independence in the American colonies, and on the French revolutionaries, to name but three. Does this mean Locke was right and Hobbes was wrong? That is certainly the view most people reading Hobbes or Locke in the developed world would take. But if you are in a position to read books by Hobbes and Locke then you are, by that very fact, part of a biased sample. If you have access to libraries and bookshops, that means you live in a stable society where libraries and bookshops can be taken for granted. The people who might agree with Hobbes (the victims of genocide, or those at the mercy of whichever warlord happens to come through their village this week) do not have the leisure or security to read books, and in any case the books have probably all been burnt some while ago. But if they did have the leisure and security to read them, they might well agree with Hobbes. Any government, they might think, would be better than no government – which is Hobbes's point.

That is all very well, you may say, but does the alternative to a bad government really have to be no government? Why can't it be a better government? To which most people with no recent experience of civil war would say without hesitation that it *is* possible to change a bad government to a better government. It has been done, after all, in England and in France and in America. On the other hand, where civil war is an ever-present threat – as in ancient Greece or parts of modern Africa – it may seem much less obvious that challenging the sovereign power is a good idea.

And finally, it is possible that there is less disagreement between Locke and Hobbes than meets the eye. Hobbes's sovereign power (like Locke's government) does rest on an original contract. And when Locke defends the right of rebellion against a ruler who breaks the contract, it is clear that what he has in mind is the replacement of one orderly regime by another orderly regime, preferably without bloodshed (eg the rule of James II by that of William and Mary). If asked to choose between orderly government and chaos, I suspect that he, like Hobbes, would have chosen orderly government.

TOM GRIFFITH

Further Reading

American Declaration of Independence
Aristotle, *Politics*
Aldous Huxley, *Brave New World*
Locke, *Essay Concerning Human Understanding*
George Orwell, *1984*
Paine, *Rights of Man*
Rousseau, *The Social Contract*
Machiavelli, *The Prince*
Montesquieu, *De l'Esprit des Lois*
Plato, *Republic*

The Selections in this Volume

Leviathan and the *Two Treatises of Government* are perhaps the two most influential and durable works of political theory written in the English language. Parts of them, however, reflect the interests of their time – interests which may not be shared by the modern reader. For this reason, this volume includes Parts 1 and 2 of *Leviathan* ('Of Man' and 'Of Commonwealth') and omits Parts 3 and 4 ('Of a Christian Commonwealth' and 'Of the Kingdom of Darkness'). Of the *Two Treatises of Government* it includes the second treatise. The first treatise is omitted because it consists, essentially, of an attack on the theory of the divine right of kings. In seventeenth century England, with an apparently unending succession of unsatisfactory Stuart monarchs, this was a question of some interest and importance. Today it is not.

LEVIATHAN

(Parts One and Two)

TO MY MOST HONOURED FRIEND MR FRANCIS GODOLPHIN OF *Godolphin*

Honoured Sir – Your most worthy brother Mr Sidney Godolphin, when he lived, was pleased to think my studies something, and otherwise to oblige me, as you know, with real testimonies of his good opinion, great in themselves, and the greater for the worthiness of his person. For there is not any virtue that disposeth a man, either to the service of God, or to the service of his country, to civil society, or private friendship, that did not manifestly appear in his conversation, not as acquired by necessity, or affected upon occasion, but inherent, and shining in a generous constitution of his nature. Therefore, in honour and gratitude to him, and with devotion to yourself, I humbly dedicate unto you this my discourse of Commonwealth. I know not how the world will receive it, nor how it may reflect on those that shall seem to favour it. For in a way beset with those that contend, on one side for too great liberty, and on the other side for too much authority, 'tis hard to pass between the points of both unwounded. But yet, methinks, the endeavour to advance the civil power, should not be by the civil power condemned; nor private men, by reprehending it, declare they think that power too great. Besides, I speak not of the men, but (in the abstract) of the seat of power, (like to those simple and unpartial creatures in the Roman Capitol, that with their noise defended those within it, not because they were they, but there) offending none, I think, but those without, or such within (if there be any such) as favour them. That which perhaps may most offend, are certain texts of Holy Scripture, alleged by me to other purpose than ordinarily they use to be by others. But I have done it with due submission, and also (in order to my subject) necessarily; for they are the outworks of the enemy, from whence they impugn the civil power. If notwithstanding this, you find my labour generally decried, you may be pleased to excuse yourself, and say I am a man that love my own opinions, and think all true I say, that I honoured your brother, and honour you, and have presumed on that, to assume the title (without your knowledge) of being, as I am,

Sir,

Your most humble, and most obedient Servant,

Paris, April 15–25th, 1651

THOMAS HOBBES

The Contents of the Chapters

THE SECOND PART: OF COMMONWEALTH

Author's Introduction

Nature (the art whereby God hath made and governs the world) is by the *art* of man, as in many other things, so in this also imitated, that it can make an artificial animal. For seeing life is but a motion of limbs, the beginning whereof is in some principal part within; why may we not say, that all *automata* (engines that move themselves by springs and wheels as doth a watch) have an artificial life? For what is the *heart*, but a *spring*; and the *nerves*, but so many *strings*; and the *joints*, but so many *wheels*, giving motion to the whole body, such as was intended by the artificer? *Art* goes yet further, imitating that rational and most excellent work of nature, *man*. For by art is created that great Leviathan called a Commonwealth, or State, (in Latin Civitas) which is but an artificial man; though of greater stature and strength than the natural, for whose protection and defence it was intended; and in which, the *sovereignty* is an artificial *soul*, as giving life and motion to the whole body; the *magistrates*, and other *officers* of judicature and execution, artificial *joints*; *reward* and *punishment* (by which fastened to the seat of the sovereignty, every joint and member is moved to perform his duty) are the *nerves*, that do the same in the body natural; the *wealth* and *riches* of all the particular members, are the *strength*; *salus populi* (the *people's safety*) its *business*; *counsellors*, by whom all things needful for it to know, are suggested unto it, are the *memory*; *equity* and *laws*, an artificial *reason* and *will*; *concord*, *health*; *sedition*, *sickness*; and *civil war*, *death*. Lastly, the *pacts* and *covenants*, by which the parts of this body politic were at first made, set together, and united, resemble that *fiat*, or the *let us make man*, pronounced by God in the creation.

To describe the nature of this artificial man, I will consider First, the *matter* thereof, and the *artificer*; both which is *Man*.

Secondly, *how*, and by what *covenants* it is made; what are the *rights* and just *power* or *authority* of a *sovereign*; and what it is that *preserveth* and *dissolveth* it.

Thirdly, what is a *Christian Commonwealth*.

Lastly, what is the *Kingdom of Darkness*.

Concerning the first, there is a saying much usurped of late, that *wisdom* is acquired, not by reading of *books*, but of *men*. Consequently whereunto, those persons, that for the most part can give no other proof of being wise, take great delight to show what they think they have read in men, by uncharitable censures of one another behind their backs. But there is another saying not of late understood, by which they might learn truly to read one another, if they would take the pains; and that is, *nosce teipsum*, *read thyself*: which was not meant, as it is now used, to countenance, either the barbarous state of men in power, towards their inferiors; or to encourage men of low degree, to a saucy behaviour towards their betters; but to teach us, that for the similitude of the thoughts and passions of one man, to the thoughts and passions of another, whosoever looketh into himself, and considereth what he doth when he does *think*, *opine*, *reason*, *hope*, *fear*, &c, and upon what grounds; he shall thereby read and know, what are the thoughts and passions of all other men, upon the like occasions. I say the similitude of *passions*, which are the same in all men, *desire*, *fear*, *hope*, &c; not the similitude of the *objects* of the passions, which are the things *desired*, *feared*, *hoped*, &c: for these the constitution individual, and particular education do so vary, and they are so easy to be kept from our knowledge, that the characters of man's heart, blotted and confounded as they are, with dissembling, lying, counterfeiting, and erroneous doctrines, are legible only to him that searcheth hearts. And though by men's actions we do discover their design sometimes; yet to do it without comparing them with our own, and distinguishing all circumstances, by which the case may come to be altered, is to decipher without a key, and be for the most part deceived, by too much trust, or by too much diffidence; as he that reads, is himself a good or evil man.

But let one man read another by his actions never so perfectly, it serves him only with his acquaintance, which are but few. He that is to govern a whole nation, must read in himself, not this or that particular man; but mankind: which though it be hard to do, harder than to learn any language, or science; yet, when I shall have set down my own reading orderly and perspicuously, the pains left another, will be only to consider, if he also find not the same in himself. For this kind of doctrine admitteth no other demonstration.

FIRST PART

Of Man

CHAPTER I

Of Sense

Concerning the thoughts of man, I will consider them first singly, and afterwards in train, or dependence upon one another. Singly, they are every one a *representation* or *appearance*, of some quality, or other accident of a body without us; which is commonly called an *object*. Which object worketh on the eyes, ears, and other parts of a man's body; and by diversity of working, produceth diversity of appearances.

The original of them all, is that which we call SENSE, for there is no conception in a man's mind, which hath not at first, totally or by parts, been begotten upon the organs of sense. The rest are derived from that original.

To know the natural cause of sense, is not very necessary to the business now in hand; and I have elsewhere written of the same at large. Nevertheless, to fill each part of my present method, I will briefly deliver the same in this place.

The cause of sense, is the external body, or object, which presseth the organ proper to each sense, either immediately, as in the taste and touch; or mediately, as in seeing, hearing, and smelling: which pressure, by the mediation of the nerves, and other strings, and membranes of the body, continued inwards to the brain and heart, causeth there a resistance, or counter-pressure, or endeavour of the heart, to deliver itself: which endeavour because *outward*, seemeth to be some matter without. And this *seeming*, or *fancy*, is that which men call *sense*; and consisteth, as to the eye, in a *light*, or *colour figured*; to the ear, in a *sound*; to the nostril, in an *odour*; to the tongue and palate, in a *savour*; and to the rest of the body, in *heat*, *cold*, *hardness*, *softness*, and such other qualities, as we discern by *feeling*. All which qualities called *sensible*, are in the object that causeth them, but so many several motions of the matter, by which it presseth our organs diversely. Neither in us that are pressed, are they any thing else, but divers motions; (for motion produceth nothing but motion.) But their appearance to us is fancy, the same waking, that dreaming. And as pressing, rubbing, or striking the eye, makes us fancy a light; and pressing the ear, produceth a din; so do the bodies also we see, or hear, produce the same by their strong, though unobserved action. For if those colours, and sounds, were in the bodies or objects that cause them, they could not be severed from them, as by glasses, and in echoes by reflection, we see they are; where we know the thing we see, is in one place; the appearance, in another. And though at some certain distance, the real and very object seem invested with the fancy it begets in us; yet still the object is one thing, the image or fancy is another. So that sense in all cases, is nothing else but original fancy, caused (as I have said) by the pressure, that is, by the motion, of external things upon our eyes, and other organs thereunto ordained.

But the philosophy-schools, through all the universities of Christendom, grounded upon certain texts of Aristotle, teach another doctrine; and say, for the cause of *vision*, that the thing seen, sendeth forth on every side a *visible species* (in English) a *visible show*, *apparition*, or *aspect*, or *a being seen*; the receiving whereof into the eye, is *seeing*. And for the cause of *hearing*, that the thing heard, sendeth forth an *audible species*, that is, an *audible aspect*, or *audible being seen*; which entering at the ear, maketh *hearing*. Nay for the cause of *understanding* also, they say the thing understood sendeth forth an *intelligible species*, that is, an *intelligible being seen*; which coming into the understanding, makes us understand. I say not this, as disproving the use of universities: but because I am to speak hereafter of their office in a commonwealth, I must let you see on all occasions by the way, what things would be amended in them; amongst which the frequency of insignificant speech is one.

CHAPTER 2

Of Imagination

That when a thing lies still, unless somewhat else stir it, it will lie still for ever, is a truth that no man doubts of. But that when a thing is in motion, it will eternally be in motion, unless somewhat else stay it, though the reason be the same, (namely, that nothing can change itself,) is not so easily assented to. For men measure, not only other men, but all other things, by themselves: and because they find themselves subject after motion to pain, and lassitude, think every thing else grows weary of motion, and seeks repose of its own accord; little considering, whether it be not some other motion wherein that desire of rest they find in themselves, consisteth. From hence it is, that the schools say, heavy bodies fall downwards, out of an appetite to rest, and to conserve their nature in that place which is most proper for them; ascribing appetite, and knowledge of what is good for their conservation, (which is more than man has) to things inanimate, absurdly.

When a body is once in motion, it moveth (unless something else hinder it) eternally; and whatsoever hindreth it, cannot in an instant, but in time, and by degrees quite extinguish it; and as we see in the water, though the wind cease, the waves give not over rolling for a long time after; so also it happeneth in that motion, which is made in the internal parts of a man, then, when he sees, dreams, &c. For after the object is removed, or the eye shut, we still retain an image of the thing seen, though more obscure than when we see it. And this is it, the Latins call *imagination*, from the image made in seeing; and apply the same, though improperly, to all the other senses. But the Greeks call it *fancy*; which signifies *appearance*, and is as proper to one sense, as to another. IMAGINATION therefore is nothing but *decaying sense*; and is found in men and many other living creatures, as well sleeping, as waking.

The decay of sense in men waking, is not the decay of the motion made in sense; but an obscuring of it, in such manner, as the light of the sun obscureth the light of the stars; which stars do no less exercise their virtue by which they are visible, in the day, than in the night. But because amongst many strokes, which our eyes, ears, and other organs receive from external bodies, the predominant only is sensible; therefore the light of the sun being predominant, we are not affected with the action of the stars. And any object being removed from our eyes, though the impression it made in us remain; yet other objects more present succeeding, and working on us, the imagination of the past is obscured, and made weak; as the voice of a man is in the noise of the day. From whence it followeth, that the longer the time is, after the sight, or sense of any object, the weaker is the imagination. For the continual change of man's body, destroys in time the parts which in sense were moved: so that distance of time, and of place, hath one and the same effect in us. For as at a great distance of place, that which we look at, appears dim, and without distinction of the smaller parts; and as voices grow weak, and inarticulate: so also after great distance of time, our imagination of the past is weak; and we lose (for example) of cities we have seen, many particular streets; and of actions, many particular circumstances. This *decaying sense*, when we would express the thing itself, (I mean *fancy* itself) we call *imagination*, as I said before: but when we would express the decay, and signify that the sense is fading, old, and past, it is called *memory*. So that imagination and memory, are but one thing, which for divers considerations hath divers names.

Much memory, or memory of many things, is called *experience*. Again, imagination being only of those things which have been formerly perceived by sense, either all at once, or by parts at several times; the former, (which is the imagining the whole object, as it was presented to the sense) is *simple* imagination; as when one imagineth a man, or horse, which he hath seen before. The other is *compounded*; as when from the sight of a man at one time, and of a horse at another, we conceive in our mind a Centaur. So when a man compoundeth the image of his own person, with the image of the actions of another man; as when a man imagines himself a Hercules or an Alexander, (which happeneth often to them that are much taken with reading of romances) it is a compound imagination, and properly but a fiction of the mind. There be also other imaginations that rise in men, (though waking) from the great impression made in sense: as from gazing upon the sun, the impression leaves an image of the sun before our eyes a long time after; and from being long and vehemently attent upon geometrical figures, a man shall in the dark (though awake) have the images of lines, and angles before his eyes: which kind of fancy hath no particular name; as being a thing that doth not commonly fall into men's discourse.

The imaginations of them that sleep, are those we call *dreams*. And these also (as all other imaginations) have been before, either totally, or by parcels in the sense. And because in sense, the brain, and nerves, which are the necessary organs of sense, are so benumbed in sleep, as not easily to be moved by the action of external objects, there can happen in sleep, no imagination; and therefore no dream, but what proceeds from the agitation of the inward parts of man's body; which inward parts, for the connexion they have with the brain, and other organs, when they be distempered, do keep the same in motion; whereby the imaginations there formerly made, appear as if a man were waking; saving that the organs of sense being now benumbed, so as there is no new object, which can master and obscure them with a more vigorous impression, a dream must needs be more clear, in this silence of sense, than are our waking thoughts. And hence it cometh to pass, that it is a hard matter, and by many thought impossible to distinguish exactly between sense and dreaming. For my part, when I consider, that in dreams, I do not often, nor constantly think of the same persons, places, objects, and actions that I do waking; nor remember so long a train of coherent thoughts, dreaming, as at other times; and because waking I often observe the absurdity of dreams, but never dream of the absurdities of my waking thoughts; I am well satisfied, that being awake, I know I dream not; though when I dream, I think myself awake.

And seeing dreams are caused by the distemper of some of the inward parts of the body; divers distempers must needs cause different dreams. And hence it is, that lying cold breedeth dreams of fear, and raiseth the thought and image of some fearful object (the motion from the brain to the inner parts, and from the inner parts to the brain being reciprocal:) and that as anger causeth heat in some parts of the body, when we are awake; so when we sleep, the overheating of the same parts causeth anger, and raiseth up in the brain the imagination of an enemy. In the same manner; as natural kindness, when we are awake causeth desire; and desire makes heat in certain other parts of the body; so also, too much heat in those parts, while we sleep, raiseth in the brain an imagination of some kindness shown. In sum, our dreams are the reverse of our waking imaginations; the motion when we are awake, beginning at one end; and when we dream, at another.

The most difficult discerning of a man's dream, from his waking thoughts, is then, when by some accident we observe not that we have slept: which is easy to happen to a man full of fearful thoughts, and whose conscience is much troubled; and that sleepeth, without the circumstances of going to bed, or putting off his clothes, as one that noddeth in a chair. For he that taketh pains, and industriously lays himself to sleep, in case any uncouth and exorbitant fancy come unto him, cannot easily think it other than a dream. We read of Marcus Brutus, (one that had his life given him by Julius Caesar, and was also his favourite, and notwithstanding murdered him) how at Philippi, the night before he gave battle to Augustus Caesar, he saw a fearful apparition, which is commonly related by historians as a vision: but considering the circumstances, one may easily judge to have been but a short dream. For sitting in his tent, pensive and troubled with the horror of his rash act, it was not hard for him, slumbering in the cold, to dream of that which most affrighted him; which fear, as by degrees it made him wake; so also it must needs make the apparition by degrees to vanish: and having no assurance that he slept, he could have no cause to think it a dream, or any thing but a vision. And this is no very rare accident: for even they that be perfectly awake, if they be timorous, and superstitious, possessed with fearful tales, and alone in the dark, are subject to the like fancies; and believe they see spirits and dead men's ghosts walking in churchyards; whereas it is either their fancy only, or else the knavery of such persons as make use of such superstitious fear, to pass disguised in the night, to places they would not be known to haunt.

From this ignorance of how to distinguish dreams, and other strong fancies, from vision and sense, did arise the greatest part of the religion of the Gentiles in time past, that worshipped satyrs, fawns, nymphs, and the like; and nowadays the opinion that rude people have of fairies, ghosts, and goblins, and of the power of witches. For as for witches, I think not that their witchcraft is any real power; but yet that they are justly punished, for the false belief they have, that they can do such mischief, joined with their purpose to do it if they can: their trade being nearer to a new religion, than to a craft or science. And for fairies, and walking ghosts, the opinion of them has I think been on purpose, either taught, or not confuted, to keep in credit the use of exorcism, of crosses, of holy water, and other such inventions of ghostly men. Nevertheless, there is no doubt, but God can make unnatural apparitions: but that he does it so often, as men need to fear such things, more than they fear the stay or change of the course of nature, which he also can stay and change, is no point of Christian faith. But evil men under pretext that God can do any thing, are so bold as to say any thing when it serves their turns, though they think it untrue; it is the part of a wise man, to believe them no further, than right reason makes that which they say, appear credible. If this superstitious fear of spirits were taken away, and with it, prognostics from dreams, false prophecies, and many other things depending thereon, by which crafty ambitious persons abuse the simple people, men would be much more fitted than they are for civil obedience.

And this ought to be the work of the schools: but they rather nourish such doctrine. For (not knowing what imagination, or the senses are), what they receive, they teach: some saying, that imaginations rise of themselves, and have no cause: others that they rise most commonly from the will; and that good thoughts are blown (inspired) into a man, by God; and evil thoughts by the Devil: or that good thoughts are poured (infused) into a man, by God, and evil ones by the Devil. Some say the senses receive the species of things, and deliver them to the common sense; and the common sense delivers them over to the fancy, and the fancy to the memory, and the memory to the judgment, like handing of things from one to another, with many words making nothing understood.

The imagination that is raised in man (or any other creature endued with the faculty of imagining) by words, or other voluntary signs, is that we generally call *understanding*; and is common to man and beast. For a dog by custom will understand the call, or the rating of his master; and so will many other beasts. That understanding which is peculiar to man, is the understanding not only his will, but his conceptions and thoughts, by the sequel and contexture of the names of things into affirmations, negations, and other forms of speech: and of this kind of understanding I shall speak hereafter.

CHAPTER 3

Of the Consequence or Train of Imaginations

By *Consequence*, or train of thoughts, I understand that succession of one thought to another, which is called (to distinguish it from discourse in words) *mental discourse*.

When a man thinketh on any thing whatsoever, his next thought after, is not altogether so casual as it seems to be. Not every thought to every thought succeeds indifferently. But as we have no imagination, whereof we have not formerly had sense, in whole, or in parts; so we have no transition from one imagination to another, whereof we never had the like before in our senses. The reason whereof is this. All fancies are motions within us, relics of those made in the sense: and those motions that immediately succeeded one another in the sense, continue also together after sense: insomuch as the former coming again to take place, and be predominant, the latter followeth, by coherence of the matter moved, in such manner, as water upon a plane table is drawn which way any one part of it is guided by the finger. But because in sense, to one and the same thing perceived, sometimes one thing, sometimes another succeedeth, it comes to pass in time, that in the imagining of any thing, there is no certainty what we shall imagine next; only this is certain, it shall be something that succeeded the same before, at one time or another.

This train of thoughts, or mental discourse, is of two sorts. The first is *unguided*, *without design*, and inconstant; wherein there is no passionate thought, to govern and direct those that follow, to itself, as the end and scope of some desire, or other passion: in which case the thoughts are said to wander, and seem impertinent one to another, as in a dream. Such are commonly the thoughts of men, that are not only without company, but also without care of any thing; though even then their thoughts are as busy as at other times, but without harmony; as the sound which a lute out of tune would yield to any man; or in tune, to one that could not play. And yet in this wild ranging of the mind, a man may oft-times perceive the way of it, and the dependence of one thought upon another. For in a discourse of our present civil war, what could seem more impertinent, than to ask (as one did) what was the value of a Roman penny? Yet the coherence to me was manifest enough. For the thought of the war, introduced the thought of the delivering up the King to his enemies; the thought of that, brought in the thought of the delivering up of Christ; and that again the thought of the 30 pence, which was the price of that treason: and thence easily followed that malicious question; and all this in a moment of time; for thought is quick.

The second is more constant; as being *regulated* by some desire, and design. For the impression made by such things as we desire or fear is strong and permanent, or (if it cease for a time) of quick return: so strong it is sometimes, as to hinder and break our sleep. From desire, ariseth the thought of some means we have seen produce the like of that which we aim at; and from the thought of that, the thought of means to that mean; and so continually, till we come to some beginning within our own power. And because the end, by the greatness of the impression, comes often to mind, in case our thoughts begin to wander, they are quickly again reduced into the way: which observed by one of the seven wise men, made him give men this precept, which is now worn out, *Respice finem*; that is to say, in all your actions, look often upon what you would have, as the thing that directs all your thoughts in the way to attain it.

The train of regulated thoughts is of two kinds; one, when of an effect imagined, we seek the causes or means that produce it; and this is common to man and beast. The other is, when imagining any thing whatsoever, we seek all the possible effects, that can by it be produced; that is to say, we imagine what we can do with it, when we have it. Of which I have not at any time seen any sign, but in man only; for this is a curiosity hardly incident to the nature of any living creature that has no other passion but sensual, such as are hunger, thirst, lust, and anger. In sum, the discourse of the mind, when it is governed by design, is nothing but *seeking*, or the faculty of invention, which the Latins called *sagacitas*, and *sollertia*; a hunting out of the causes of some effect, present or past; or of the effects of some present or past cause. Sometimes a man seeks what he hath lost; and from that place and time, wherein he misses it, his mind runs back, from place to place, and time to time, to find where and when he had it; that is to say, to find some certain, and limited time and place, in which to begin a method of seeking. Again, from thence, his thoughts run over the same places and times, to find what action, or other occasion might make him lose it. This we call *remembrance*, or calling to mind: the Latins call it *reminiscentia*, as it were a *re-conning* of our former actions.

Sometimes a man knows a place determinate, within the compass whereof he is to seek; and then his thoughts run over all the parts thereof, in the same manner, as one would sweep a room, to find a jewel; or as a spaniel ranges the field, till he find a scent; or as a man should run over the alphabet, to start a rhyme.

Sometimes a man desires to know the event of an action; and then he thinketh of some like action past, and the events thereof one after another; supposing like events will follow like actions. As he that foresees what will become of a criminal, re-cons what he has seen follow on the like crime before; having this order of thoughts, the crime, the officer, the prison, the judge, and the gallows. Which kind of thoughts, is called *foresight*, and *prudence*, or *providence*; and sometimes *wisdom*; though such conjecture, through the difficulty of observing all circumstances, be very fallacious. But this is certain; by how much one man has more experience of things past, than another; by so much also he is more prudent, and his expectations the seldomer fail him. The *present* only has a being in nature; things *past* have a being in the memory only, but things *to come* have no being at all; the *future* being but a fiction of the mind, applying the sequels of actions past, to the actions that are present; which with most certainty is done by him that has most experience; but not with certainty enough. And though it be called prudence, when the event answereth our expectation; yet in its own nature, it is but presumption. For the foresight of things to come, which is providence, belongs only to him by whose will they are to come. From him only, and supernaturally, proceeds prophecy. The best prophet naturally is the best guesser; and the best guesser, he that is most versed and studied in the matters he guesses at: for he hath most *signs* to guess by.

A *sign* is the evident antecedent, of the consequent; and contrarily, the consequent of the antecedent, when the like consequences have been observed, before: and the oftener they have been observed, the less uncertain is the sign. And therefore he that has most experience in any kind of business, has most signs, whereby to guess at the future time; and consequently is the most prudent: and so much more prudent than he that is new in that kind of business, as not to be equalled by any advantage of natural and extemporary wit: though perhaps many young men think the contrary.

Nevertheless it is not prudence that distinguisheth man from beast. There be beasts, that at a year old observe more, and pursue that which is for their good, more prudently, than a child can do at ten.

As prudence is a *presumption* of the *future*, contracted from the *experience* of time *past*: so there is a presumption of things past taken from other things (not future but) past also. For he that hath seen by what courses and degrees, a flourishing state hath first come into civil war, and then to ruin; upon the sight of the ruins of any other state, will guess, the like war, and the like courses have been there also. But this conjecture, has the same uncertainty almost with the conjecture of the future; both being grounded only upon experience.

There is no other act of man's mind, that I can remember, naturally planted in him, so as to need no other thing, to the exercise of it, but to be born a man, and live with the use of his five senses. Those other faculties, of which I shall speak by and by, and which seem proper to man only, are acquired, and increased by study and industry; and of most men learned by instruction, and discipline; and proceed all from the invention of words, and speech. For besides sense, and thoughts, and the train of thoughts, the mind of man has no other motion; though by the help of speech, and method, the same faculties may be improved to such a height, as to distinguish men from all other living creatures.

Whatsoever we imagine is *finite*. Therefore there is no idea, or conception of any thing we call *infinite*. No man can have in his mind an image of infinite magnitude; nor conceive infinite swiftness, infinite time, or infinite force, or infinite power. When we say any thing is infinite, we signify only, that we are not able to conceive the ends, and bounds of the things named; having no conception of the thing, but of our own inability. And therefore the name of God is used, not to make us conceive him (for he is incomprehensible; and his greatness, and power are unconceivable;) but that we may honour him. Also because whatsoever (as I said before) we conceive, has been perceived first by sense, either all at once, or by parts; a man can have no thought, representing any thing, not subject to sense. No man therefore can conceive any thing, but he must conceive it in some place; and endued with some determinate magnitude; and which may be divided into parts; nor that any thing is all in this place, and all in another place at the same time; nor that two or more things can be in one and the same place at once: for none of these things ever have, or can be incident to sense; but are absurd speeches, taken upon credit (without any signification at all) from deceived philosophers, and deceived or deceiving Schoolmen.

CHAPTER 4

Of Speech

The invention of *printing*, though ingenious, compared with the invention of *letters*, is no great matter. But who was the first that found the use of letters, is not known. He that first brought them into Greece, men say was Cadmus, the son of Agenor, king of Phoenicia. A profitable invention for continuing the memory of time past, and the conjunction of mankind, dispersed into so many, and distant regions of the earth; and withal difficult, as proceeding from a watchful observation of the divers motions of the tongue, palate, lips, and other organs of speech; whereby to make as many differences of characters, to remember them. But the most noble and profitable invention of all other, was that of speech, consisting of *names* or *appellations*, and their connexion; whereby men register their thoughts; recall them when they are past; and also declare them one to another for mutual utility and conversation; without which, there had been amongst men, neither commonwealth, nor society, nor contract, nor peace, no more than amongst lions, bears, and wolves. The first author of speech was God himself, that instructed Adam how to name such creatures as he presented to his sight; for the Scripture goeth no further in this matter. But this was sufficient to direct him to add more names, as the experience and use of the creatures should give him occasion; and to join them in such manner by degrees, as to make himself understood; and so by succession of time, so much language might be gotten, as he had found use for; though not so copious, as an orator or philosopher has need of. For I do not find any thing in the Scripture, out of which, directly or by consequence can be gathered, that Adam was taught the names of all figures, numbers, measures, colours, sounds, fancies, relations; much less the names of words and speech, as *general*, *special*, *affirmative*, *negative*, *interrogative*, *optative*, *infinitive*, all which are useful; and least of all, of *entity*, *intentionality*, *quiddity*, and other insignificant words of the School.

But all this language gotten, and augmented by Adam and his posterity, was again lost at the Tower of

Babel, when by the hand of God, every man was stricken for his rebellion, with an oblivion of his former language. And being hereby forced to disperse themselves into several parts of the world, it must needs be, that the diversity of tongues that now is, proceeded by degrees from them, in such manner, as need (the mother of all inventions) taught them; and in tract of time grew everywhere more copious.

The general use of speech, is to transfer our mental discourse, into verbal; or the train of our thoughts, into a train of words; and that for two commodities; whereof one is, the registering of the consequences of our thoughts; which being apt to slip out of our memory, and put us to a new labour, may again be recalled, by such words as they were marked by. So that the first use of names, is to serve for *marks*, or *notes* of remembrance. Another is, when many use the same words, to signify (by their connexion and order) one to another, what they conceive, or think of each matter; and also what they desire, fear, or have any other passion for. And for this use they are called *signs*. Special uses of speech are these: first, to register, what by cogitation, we find to be the cause of any thing, present or past; and what we find things present or past may produce, or effect: which in sum, is acquiring of arts. Secondly, to show to others that knowledge which we have attained; which is, to counsel, and teach one another. Thirdly, to make known to others our wills and purposes, that we may have the mutual help of one another. Fourthly, to please and delight ourselves, and others, by playing with our words, for pleasure or ornament, innocently.

To these uses, there are also four correspondent abuses. First, when men register their thoughts wrong, by the inconstancy of the signification of their words; by which they register for their conceptions, that which they never conceived; and so deceive themselves. Secondly, when they use words metaphorically; that is, in other sense than that they are ordained for; and thereby deceive others. Thirdly, when by words they declare that to be their will, which is not. Fourthly, when they use them to grieve one another: for seeing nature hath armed living creatures, some with teeth, some with horns, and some with hands, to grieve an enemy, it is but an abuse of speech, to grieve him with the tongue, unless it be one whom we are obliged to govern; and then it is not to grieve, but to correct and amend.

The manner how speech serveth to the remembrance of the consequence of causes and effects, consisteth in the imposing of *names*, and the *connexion* of them.

Of names, some are *proper*, and singular to one only thing; as *Peter*, *John*, *this man*, *this tree*: and some are *common* to many things; as *man*, *horse*, *tree*; every of which though but one name, is nevertheless the name of divers particular things; in respect of all which together, it is called an *universal*; there being nothing in the world universal but names; for the things named are every one of them individual and singular.

One universal name is imposed on many things, for their similitude in some quality, or other accident: and whereas a proper name bringeth to mind one thing only; universals recall any one of those many.

And of names universal, some are of more, and some of less extent; the larger comprehending the less large: and some again of equal extent, comprehending each other reciprocally. As for example, the name *body* is of larger signification than the word *man*, and comprehendeth it; and the names *man* and *rational*, are of equal extent, comprehending mutually one another. But here we must take notice, that by a name is not always understood, as in grammar, one only word; but sometimes by circumlocution many words together. For all these words, *he that in his actions observeth the laws of his country*, make but one name, equivalent to this one word, *just*.

By this imposition of names, some of larger, some of stricter signification, we turn the reckoning of the consequences of things imagined in the mind, into a reckoning of the consequences of appellations. For example, a man that hath no use of speech at all, (such as is born and remains perfectly deaf and dumb) if he set before his eyes a triangle, and by it two right angles, (such as are the corners of a square figure) he may by meditation compare and find, that the three angles of that triangle, are equal to those two right angles that stand by it. But if another triangle be shown him different in shape from the former, he cannot know without a new labour, whether the three angles of that also be equal to the same. But he that hath the use of words, when he observes, that such equality was consequent, not to the length of the sides, nor to any other particular thing in his triangle; but only to this, that the sides were straight, and the angles three; and that that was all, for which he named it a triangle; will boldly conclude universally, that such equality of angles is in all triangles whatsoever; and register his invention in these general terms, *every triangle hath its three angles equal to two right angles*. And thus the consequence found in one particular, comes to be registered and remembered, as an universal rule; and discharges our mental reckoning, of time and place; and delivers us from all labour of the mind, saving the first; and makes that which was found true *here*, and *now*, to be true in *all times* and *places*.

But the use of words in registering our thoughts, is in nothing so evident as in numbering. A natural fool that could never learn by heart the order of numeral words, as *one*, *two*, and *three*, may observe every stroke of the clock, and nod to it, or say *one*, *one*, *one*; but can never know what hour it strikes. And it seems, there was a time when those names of number were not in use; and men were fain to apply their fingers of one or both hands, to those things they desired to keep account of; and that thence it proceeded, that now our numeral words are but ten, in any nation, and in some but five, and then they begin again. And he that can tell ten, if he recite them out of order, will lose himself, and not know when he has done: much less will he be able to add, and subtract, and perform all other operations of arithmetic. So that without words, there is no possibility of reckoning of numbers; much less of magnitudes, of swiftness, of force, and other things, the reckonings whereof are necessary to the being, or well-being of mankind.

When two names are joined together into a consequence, or affirmation; as thus, *a man is a living creature*; or thus, *if he be a man, he is living creature*, if the latter name *living creature*, signify all that the former name *man* signifieth, then the affirmation, or consequence, is *true*; otherwise *false*. For *true* and *false* are attributes of speech, not of things. And where speech is not, there is neither *truth* nor *falsehood*. *Error* there may be, as when we expect that which shall not be; or suspect what has not been: but in neither case can a man be charged with untruth.

Seeing then that *truth* consisteth in the right ordering of names in our affirmations, a man that seeketh precise truth, had need to remember what every name he uses stands for; and to place it accordingly; or else he will find himself entangled in words, as a bird in lime twigs; the more he struggles, the more belimed. And therefore in geometry, (which is the only science that it hath pleased God hitherto to bestow on mankind) men begin at settling the significations of their words; which settling of significations, they call *definitions*; and place them in the beginning of their reckoning.

By this it appears how necessary it is for any man that aspires to true knowledge, to examine the definitions of former authors; and either to correct them, where they are negligently set down; or to make them himself. For the errors of definitions multiply themselves, according as the reckoning proceeds; and lead men into absurdities, which at last they see, but cannot avoid, without reckoning anew from the beginning; in which lies the foundation of their errors. From whence it happens, that they which trust to books, do as they that cast up many little sums into a greater, without considering whether those little sums were rightly cast up or not; and at last finding the error visible, and not mistrusting their first grounds, know not which way to clear themselves, but spend time in fluttering over their books; as birds that entering by the chimney, and finding themselves enclosed in a chamber, flutter at the false light of a glass window, for want of wit to consider which way they came in. So that in the right definition of names, lies the first use of speech; which is the acquisition of science: and in wrong, or no definitions, lies the first abuse; from which proceed all false and senseless tenets; which make those men that take their instruction from the authority of books, and not from their own meditation, to be as much below the condition of ignorant men, as men endued with true science are above it. For between true science, and erroneous doctrines, ignorance is in the middle. Natural sense and imagination, are not subject to absurdity. Nature itself cannot err: and as men abound in copiousness of language; so they become more wise, or more mad than ordinary. Nor is it possible without letters for any man to become either excellently wise, or (unless his memory be hurt by disease, or ill constitution of organs) excellently foolish. For words are wise men's counters, they do but reckon by them: but they are the money of fools, that value them by the authority of an Aristotle, a Cicero, or a Thomas, or any other doctor whatsoever, if but a man.

Subject to names, is whatsoever can enter into, or be considered in an account; and be added one to another to make a sum; or subtracted one from another and leave a remainder. The Latins called accounts of money *rationes*, and accounting *ratiocinatio*: and that which we in bills or books of account call *items*, they called *nomina*; that is, *names*: and thence it seems to proceed, that they extended the word *ratio*, to the faculty of reckoning in all other things. The Greeks have but one word λόγος, for both *speech* and *reason*; not that they thought there was no speech without reason; but no reasoning without speech: and the act of reasoning they called *syllogism*; which signifieth summing up of the consequences of one saying to another. And because the same things may enter into account for divers accidents; their names are (to show that diversity) diversely wrested, and diversified. This diversity of names may be reduced to four general heads.

First, a thing may enter into account for *matter*, or *body*; as *living*, *sensible*, *rational*, *hot*, *cold*, *moved*, *quiet*; with all which names the word *matter*, or *body*, is understood; all such, being names of matter.

Secondly, it may enter into account, or be considered, for some accident or quality, which we conceive to be in it; as for *being moved*, for *being so long*, for *being hot*, &c; and then, of the name of the thing itself, by a little change or wresting, we make a name for that accident, which we consider; and for *living* put into the account *life*; for *moved*, *motion*; for *hot*, *heat*; for *long*, *length*, and the like: and all such names are the names of the accidents and properties, by which one matter and body is distinguished from another. These are called *names abstract*; because severed (not from matter, but) from the account of matter.

Thirdly, we bring into account the properties of our own bodies, whereby we make such distinction: as when anything is *seen* by us, we reckon not the thing itself; but the *sight*, the *colour*, the *idea* of it in the fancy: and when anything is *heard*, we reckon it not; but the *hearing*, or *sound* only, which is our fancy or conception of it by the ear: and such are names of fancies.

Fourthly, we bring into account, consider, and give names to, *names* themselves, and to *speeches*: for *general*, *universal*, *special*, *equivocal*, are names of names. And *affirmation*, *interrogation*, *commandment*, *narration*, *syllogism*, *sermon*, *oration*, and many other such, are names of speeches. And this is all the variety of names *positive*; which are put to mark somewhat which is in nature, or may be feigned by the mind of man, as bodies that are, or may be conceived to be; or of bodies, the properties that are, or may be feigned to be; or words and speech.

There be also other names, called *negative*; which are notes to signify that a word is not the name of the thing in question; as these words *nothing*, *no man*, *infinite*, *indocible*, *three want four*, and the like; which are nevertheless of use in reckoning, or in correcting of reckoning; and call to mind our past cogitations, though they be not names of any thing; because they make us refuse to admit of names not rightly used.

All other names are but insignificant sounds; and those of two sorts. One, when they are new, and yet their meaning not explained by definition; whereof there have been abundance coined by Schoolmen, and puzzled philosophers.

Another, when men make a name of two names, whose significations are contradictory and inconsistent; as this name, an *incorporeal body*, or (which is all one) an *incorporeal substance*, and a great number more. For whensoever any affirmation is false, the two names of which it is composed, put together and made one, signify nothing at all. For example, if it be a false affirmation to say *a quadrangle is round*, the word *round quadrangle* signifies nothing; but is a mere sound. So likewise, if it be false, to say that virtue can be poured, or blown up and down, the words *inpoured virtue*, *inblown virtue*, are as absurd and insignificant, as a *round quadrangle*. And therefore you shall hardly meet with a senseless and insignificant word, that is not made up of some Latin or Greek names. A Frenchman seldom hears our Saviour called by the name of *parole*, but by the name of *verbe* often; yet *verbe* and *parole* differ no more, but that one is Latin, the other French.

When a man upon the hearing of any speech, hath those thoughts which the words of that speech, and their connexion, were ordained and constituted to signify; then he is said to understand it; *understanding* being nothing else but conception caused by speech. And therefore if speech be peculiar to man (as for aught I know it is) then is understanding peculiar to him also. And therefore of absurd and false affirmations, in case they be universal, there can be no understanding; though many think they understand, then, when they do but repeat the words softly, or con them in their mind.

What kinds of speeches signify the appetites, aversions, and passions of man's mind; and of their use and abuse, I shall speak when I have spoken of the passions.

The names of such things as affect us, that is, which please and displease us, because all men be not alike affected with the same thing, nor the same man at all times, are in the common discourses of men, of *inconstant* signification. For seeing all names are imposed to signify our conceptions; and all our affections are but conceptions; when we conceive the same things differently, we can hardly avoid different naming of them. For though the nature of that we conceive, be the same; yet the diversity of our reception of it, in respect of different constitutions of body, and prejudices of opinion, gives every thing a tincture of our different passions. And therefore in reasoning, a man must take heed of words; which besides the signification of what we imagine of their nature, have a signification also of the nature, disposition, and interest of the speaker; such as are the names of virtues, and vices; for one man calleth *wisdom*, what another called *fear*; and one *cruelty*, what another *justice*; one *prodigality*, what another *magnanimity*; and one *gravity*, what another *stupidity*, &c. And therefore such names can never be true grounds of any ratiocination. No more can metaphors, and tropes of speech: but these are less dangerous, because they profess their inconstancy; which the other do not.

CHAPTER 5

Of Reason and Science

When a man *reasoneth*, he does nothing else but conceive a sum total, from *addition* of parcels; or conceive a remainder, from *substraction* of one sum from another: which (if it be done by words) is conceiving of the consequence from the names of all the parts, to the name of the whole; or from the names of the whole and one part, to the name of the other part. And though in some things, (as in numbers) besides adding and subtracting, men name other operations, as *multiplying* and *dividing*; yet they are the same; for multiplication is but adding together of things equal; and division, but subtracting of one thing, as often as we can. These operations are not incident to numbers only, but to all manner of things that can be added together, and taken one out of another. For as arithmeticians teach to add and subtract in *numbers*; so the geometricians teach the same in *lines*, *figures* (solid and superficial) *angles*, *proportions*, *times*, degrees of *swiftness*, *force*, *power*, and the like; the logicians teach the same in *consequences of words*; adding together two *names*, to make an *affirmation*; and two *affirmations*, to make a *syllogism*; and *many syllogisms* to make a *demonstration*; and from the *sum*, or *conclusion* of a *syllogism*, they subtract one *proposition*, to find the other. Writers of politics, add together *pactions* to find men's *duties*; and lawyers, *laws* and *facts*, to find what is *right* and *wrong* in the actions of private men. In sum, in what matter soever there is place for *addition* and *subtraction*, there also is place for *reason*; and where these have no place, there *reason* has nothing at all to do.

Out of all which we may define, (that is to say determine) what that is, which is meant by this word *reason*, when we reckon it amongst the faculties of the mind. For reason, in this sense, is nothing but *reckoning* (that is, adding and subtracting) of the consequences of general names agreed upon, for the *marking* and *signifying* of our thoughts; I say *marking* them, when we reckon by ourselves; and *signifying*, when we demonstrate, or approve our reckonings to other men.

And as in arithmetic, unpractised men must, and professors themselves may often err, and cast up false; so also in any other subject of reasoning, the ablest, most attentive, and most practised men, may deceive themselves, and infer false conclusions; not but that reason itself is always right reason, as well as arithmetic is a certain and infallible art: but no one man's reason, nor the reason of any one number of men, makes the certainty; no more than an account is therefore well cast up, because a great many men have unanimously approved it. And therefore, as when there is a controversy in an account, the parties must by their own accord, set up for right reason, the reason of some arbitrator, or judge, to whose sentence they will both stand, or their controversy must either come to blows, or be undecided, for want of a right reason constituted by nature; so is it also in all debates of what kind soever: and when men that think themselves wiser than all others, clamour and demand right reason for judge; yet seek no more, but that things should be determined, by no other men's reason but their own, it is as intolerable in the society of men, as it is in play after trump is turned, to use for trump on every occasion, that suit whereof they have most in their hand. For they do nothing else, that will have every of their passions, as it comes to bear sway in them, to be taken for right reason, and that in their own controversies: bewraying their want of right reason, by the claim they lay to it.

The use and end of reason, is not the finding of the sum and truth of one, or a few consequences, remote from the first definitions, and settled significations of names; but to begin at these; and proceed from one consequence to another. For there can be no certainty of the last conclusion, without a certainty of all those affirmations and negations, on which it was grounded, and inferred. As when a master of a family, in taking an account, casteth up the sums of all the bills of expense, into one sum; and not regarding how each bill is summed up, by those that give them in account; nor what it is he pays for; he advantages himself no more, than if he allowed the account in gross, trusting to every of the accountants' skill and honesty: so also in reasoning of all other things, he that takes up conclusions on the trust of authors, and doth not fetch them from the first items in every reckoning (which are the significations of names settled by definitions), loses his labour; and does not know any thing; but only believeth.

When a man reckons without the use of words, which may be done in particular things (as when upon the sight of any one thing, we conjecture what was likely to have preceded, or is likely to follow upon it;) if that which he thought likely to follow, follows not; or that which he thought likely to have preceded it, hath not preceded it, this is called error; to which even the most prudent men are subject. But when we reason in words of general signification, and fall upon a general inference which is false, though it be commonly called *error*, it is indeed an absurdity, or senseless speech. For error is but a deception, in presuming that somewhat is past, or to come; of which, though it were not past, or not to come; yet there was no impossibility discoverable. But when we make a general assertion, unless it be a true one, the possibility of it is inconceivable. And words whereby we conceive nothing but the sound, are those we call *absurd*, *insignificant*, and *nonsense*. And therefore if a man should talk to me of a *round quadrangle*; or *accidents of bread in cheese*; or, *immaterial substances*; or of *a free subject*; *a free will*; or any *free*, but free from being hindered by opposition, I should not say he were in an error, but that his words were without meaning; that is to say, absurd.

I have said before, (in the second chapter) that a man did excel all other animals in this faculty, that when he conceived any thing whatsoever, he was apt to inquire the consequences of it, and what effects he could do with it. And now I add this other degree of the same excellence, that he can by words reduce the consequences he finds to general rules, called *theorems*, or *aphorisms*; that is, he can reason, or reckon, not only in number, but in all other things, whereof one may be added unto, or subtracted from another.

But this privilege, is allayed by another; and that is, by the privilege of absurdity; to which no living creature is subject, but man only. And of men, those are of all most subject to it, that profess philosophy. For it is most true that Cicero saith of them somewhere; that there can be nothing so absurd, but may be found in the books of philosophers. And the reason is manifest. For there is not one of them that begins his ratiocination from the definitions, or explications of the names they are to use; which is a method that hath been used only in geometry; whose conclusions have thereby been made indisputable.

The first cause of absurd conclusions I ascribe to the want of method; in that they begin not their ratiocination from definitions; that is, from settled significations of their words: as if they could cast account, without knowing the value of the numeral words, *one*, *two*, and *three*.

And whereas all bodies enter into account upon divers considerations, (which I have mentioned in the precedent chapter) these considerations being diversely named, divers absurdities proceed from the confusion, and unfit connexion of their names into assertions. And therefore

The second cause of absurd assertions, I ascribe to the giving of names of *bodies*, to *accidents*; or of *accidents* to *bodies*; as they do, that say, *faith is infused*, or *inspired*; when nothing can be *poured*, or *breathed* into anything, but body; and that, *extension* is *body*; that *phantasms* are *spirits*, &c.

The third I ascribe to the giving of the names of the *accidents* of *bodies without us*, to the *accidents* of our *own bodies*; as they do that say the *colour is in the body*; *the sound is in the air*, &c.

The fourth, to the giving of the names of *bodies*, to *names*, or *speeches*; as they do that say, that *there be things universal*; that *a living creature is genus*, or *a general thing*, &c.

The fifth, to the giving of the names of *accidents*, to *names* and *speeches*; as they do that say, *the nature of a thing is its definition*; *a man's command is his will*; and the like.

The sixth, to the use of metaphors, tropes, and other rhetorical figures, instead of words proper. For though it be lawful to say (for example) in common speech, *the way goeth*, *or leadeth hither*, *or thither*; *the proverb says this or that* (whereas ways cannot go, nor proverbs speak) yet in reckoning, and seeking of truth, such speeches are not to be admitted.

The seventh, to names that signify nothing; but are taken up, and learned by rote from the schools, as *hypostatical*, *transubstantiate*, *consubstantiate*, *eternal-now*, and the like canting of Schoolmen.

To him that can avoid these things, it is not easy to fall into any absurdity, unless it be by the length of an account; wherein he may perhaps forget what went before. For all men by nature reason alike, and well, when they have good principles. For who is so stupid, as both to mistake in geometry, and also to persist in it, when another detects his error to him?

By this it appears that reason is not as sense and memory, born with us; nor gotten by experience only, as prudence is; but attained by industry; first in apt imposing of names; and secondly by getting a good and orderly method in proceeding from the elements, which are names, to assertions made by connexion of one of them to another; and so to syllogisms, which are the connexions of one assertion to another, till we come to a knowledge of all the consequences of names appertaining to the subject in hand; and that is it, men call science. And whereas sense and memory are but knowledge of fact, which is a thing past, and irrevocable; *Science* is the knowledge of consequences, and dependence of one fact upon another: by which, out of that we can presently do, we know how to do something else when we will, or the like, another time: because when we see how any thing comes about, upon what causes, and by what manner; when the like causes come into our power, we see how to make it produce the like effects.

Children therefore are not endued with reason at all, till they have attained the use of speech; but are called reasonable creatures, for the possibility apparent of having the use of reason in time to come. And the most part of men, though they have the use of reasoning a little way, as in numbering to some degree; yet it serves them to little use in common life; in which they govern themselves, some better, some worse, according to their differences of experience, quickness of memory, and inclinations to several ends; but specially according to good or evil fortune, and the errors of one another. For as for *science*, or certain rules of their actions, they are so far from it, that they know not what it is. Geometry they have thought conjuring: but for other sciences, they who have not been taught the beginnings, and some progress in them, that they may see how they be acquired and generated, are in this point like children, that having no thought of generation, are made believe by the women, that their brothers and sisters are not born, but found in the garden.

But yet they that have no *science*, are in better, and nobler condition, with their natural prudence; than men, that by mis-reasoning, or by trusting them that reason wrong, fall upon false and absurd general rules. For ignorance of causes, and of rules, does not set men so far out of their way, as relying on false rules, and taking for causes of what they aspire to, those that are not so, but rather causes of the contrary.

To conclude, the light of human minds is perspicuous words, but by exact definitions first snuffed, and purged from ambiguity; *reason* is the *pace*; increase of *science*, the *way*; and the benefit of mankind, the *end*. And on the contrary, metaphors, and senseless and ambiguous words, are like *ignes fatui*; and reasoning upon them, is wandering amongst innumerable absurdities; and their end, contention, and sedition, or contempt.

As much experience s *prudence*; so is much science, *sapience*. For though we usually have one name of wisdom for them both; yet the Latins did always distinguish between *prudentia* and *sapientia*; ascribing the former to experience, the latter to science. But to make their difference appear more clearly, let us suppose one man endued with an excellent natural use, and dexterity in handling his arms; and another to have added to that dexterity, an acquired science, of where he can offend, or be offended by his adversary, in every possible posture, or guard: the ability of the former, would be to the ability of the latter, as prudence to sapience; both useful; but the latter infallible. But they that trusting only to the authority of books, follow the blind blindly, are like him that, trusting to the false rules of a master of fence, ventures presumptuously upon an adversary, that either kills or disgraces him.

The signs of science, are some, certain and infallible; some, uncertain. Certain, when he that pretendeth the science of any thing, can teach the same; that is to say, demonstrate the truth thereof perspicuously to another; uncertain, when only some particular events answer to his pretence, and upon many occasions prove so as he says they must. Signs of prudence are all uncertain; because to observe by experience, and remember all circumstances that may alter the success, is impossible. But in any business, whereof a man has not infallible science to proceed by; to forsake his own natural judgment, and be guided by general sentences read in authors, and subject to many exceptions, is a sign of folly, and generally scorned by the name of pedantry. And even of those men themselves, that in councils of the commonwealth, love to show their reading of politics and history, very few do it in their domestic affairs, where their particular interest is concerned; having prudence enough for their private affairs: but in public they study more the reputation of their own wit, than the success of another's business.

CHAPTER 6

Of the Interior Beginnings of Voluntary Motions; commonly called the Passions. And the Speeches by which they are expressed

There be in animals, two sorts of *motions* peculiar to them: one called *vital*; begun in generation, and continued without interruption through their whole life; such as are the *course* of the *blood*, the *pulse*, the *breathing*, the *concoction*, *nutrition*, *excretion*, &c; to which motions there needs no help of imagination: the other is *animal motion*, otherwise called *voluntary motion*; as to *go*, to *speak*, to *move* any of our limbs, in such manner as is first fancied in our minds. That sense is motion in the organs and interior parts of man's body, caused by the action of the things we see, hear, &c; and that fancy is but the relics of the same motion, remaining after sense has been already said in the first and second chapters. And because *going*, *speaking*, and the like voluntary motions, depend always upon a precedent thought of *whither*, *which way*, and *what*; it is evident, that the imagination is the first internal beginning of all voluntary motion. And although unstudied men, do not conceive any motion at all to be there, where the thing moved is invisible; or the space it is moved in, is (for the shortness of it) insensible; yet that doth not hinder, but that such motions are. For let a space be never so little, that which is moved over a greater space, whereof that little one is part, must first be moved over that. These small beginnings of motion, within the body of man, before they appear in walking, speaking, striking, and other visible actions, are commonly called endeavour.

This endeavour, when it is toward something which causes it, is called appetite, or desire; the latter being the general name; and the other oftentimes restrained to signify the desire of food, namely *hunger* and *thirst*. And when the endeavour is fromward something, it is generally called aversion. These words *appetite* and *aversion* we have from the Latins; and they both of them signify the motions, one of approaching, the other of retiring. So also do the Greek words for the same, which are ὁρμὴ and ἀφορμή. For nature itself does often press upon men those truths, which afterwards, when they look for somewhat beyond nature, they stumble at. For the Schools find in mere appetite to go, or move, no actual motion at all: but because some motion they must acknowledge, they call it metaphorical motion; which is but an absurd speech: for though words may be called metaphorical; bodies, and motions can not.

That which men desire, they are also said to love: and to hate those things, for which they have aversion. So that desire, and love, are the same thing; save that by desire, we always signify the absence of the object; by love, most commonly the presence of the same. So also by aversion, we signify the absence; and by hate, the presence of the object.

Of appetites and aversions, some are born with men; as appetite of food, appetite of excretion, and exoneration, (which may also and more properly be called aversions, from somewhat they feel in their bodies) and some other appetites, not many. The rest, which are appetites of particular things, proceed from experience, and trial of their effects upon themselves, or other men. For of things we know not at all, or believe not to be, we can have no further desire, than to taste and try. But aversion we have for things, not only which we know have hurt us; but also that we do not know whether they will hurt us, or not.

Those things which we neither desire, nor hate, we are said to *contemn*: contempt being nothing else but an immobility, or contumacy of the heart, in resisting the action of certain things; and proceeding from that the heart is already moved otherwise, by other more potent objects; or from want of experience of them.

And because the constitution of a man's body is in continual mutation; it is impossible that all the same things should always cause in him the same appetites, and aversions: much less can all men consent, in the desire of almost any one and the same object.

But whatsoever is the object of any man's appetite or desire; that is it, which he for his part calleth *good*: and the object of his hate, and aversion, *evil*; and of his contempt, *vile* and *inconsiderable*. For these words of good, evil, and contemptible, are ever used with relation to the person that useth them: there being nothing simply and absolutely so; nor any common rule of good and evil, to be taken from the nature of the objects themselves; but from the person of the man (where there is no commonwealth) or, (in a commonwealth) from the person that representeth it; or from an arbitrator or judge, whom men disagreeing shall by consent set up, and make his sentence the rule thereof.

The Latin tongue has two words, whose significations approach to those of good and evil; but are not precisely the same; and those are *pulchrum* and *turpe*. Whereof the former signifies that, which by some apparent signs promiseth good; and the latter, that, which promiseth evil. But in our tongue we have not so general names to express them by. But for *pulchrum*, we say in some things, *fair*; in others, *beautiful*, or *handsome*, or *gallant*, or *honourable*, or *comely*, or *amiable*; and for *turpe*, *foul*, *deformed*, *ugly*, *base*, *nauseous*, and the like, as the subject shall require; all which words, in their proper places, signify nothing else, but the mien or countenance, that promiseth good and evil. So that of good there be three kinds; good in the promise, that is *pulchrum*; good in effect, as the end desired, which is called *jucundum*, *delightful*; and good as the means, which is called *utile*, *profitable*; and as many of evil: for *evil*, in promise, is that they call *turpe*; evil in effect, and end, is *molestum*, *unpleasant*, *troublesome*; and evil in the means, *inutile*, *unprofitable*, *hurtful*.

As, in sense, that which is really within us, is (as I have said before) only motion, caused by the action of external objects, but in appearance; to the sight, light and colour; to the ear, sound; to the nostril, odour, &c: so, when the action of the same object is continued from the eyes, ears, and other organs to the heart, the real effect there is nothing but motion, or endeavour; which consisteth in appetite, or aversion, to or from the object moving. But the appearance, or sense of that motion, is that we either call *delight*, or *trouble of mind*.

This motion, which is called appetite, and for the appearance of it *delight*, and *pleasure*, seemeth to be a corroboration of vital motion, and a help thereunto; and therefore such things as caused delight, were not improperly called *jucunda*, (a *juvando*,) from helping or fortifying; and the contrary, *molesta*, *offensive*, from hindering, and troubling the motion vital.

Pleasure therefore, (or *delight*) is the appearance, or sense of good; and *molestation* or *displeasure*, the appearence, or sense of evil. And consequently all appetite, desire and love, is accompanied with some delight more or less; and all hatred and aversion, with more or less displeasure and offence.

Of pleasures, or delights, some arise from the sense of an object present; and those may be called *pleasures of sense*; (the word *sensual*, as it is used by those only that condemn them, having no place till there be laws.) Of this kind are all onerations and exonerations of the body; as also all that is pleasant, in the *sight*, *hearing*, *smell*, *taste*, or *touch*; others arise from the expectation, that proceeds from foresight of the end, or consequence of things; whether those things in the sense please or displease: and these are *pleasures of the mind* of him that draweth those consequences; and are generally called joy. In the like manner, displeasures, are some in the sense, and called pain; others, in the expectation of consequences, and are called grief.

These simple passions called *appetite*, *desire*, *love*, *aversion*, *hate*, *joy*, and *grief*, have their names for divers considerations diversified. As first, when they one succeed another, they are diversely called from the opinion men have of the likelihood of attaining what they desire. Secondly, from the object loved or hated. Thirdly, from the consideration of many of them together. Fourthly, from the alteration or succession itself.

For *appetite* with an opinion of attaining, is called hope.

The same, without such opinion, despair. *Aversion*, with opinion of hurt from the object, fear.

The same, with hope of avoiding that hurt by resistance, courage.

Sudden *courage*, anger.

Constant *hope*, confidence of ourselves.

Constant *despair*, diffidence of ourselves.

Anger for great hurt done to another, when we conceive the same to be done by injury, indignation.

Desire of good to another, benevolence, good will, charity. If to man generally, good nature.

Desire of riches, covetousness: a name used always in signification of blame; because men contending for them, are displeased with one another's attaining them; though the desire in itself be to be blamed, or allowed, according to the means by which these riches are sought.

Desire of office, or precedence, ambition: a name used also in the worse sense, for the reason before mentioned.

Desire of things that conduce but a little to our ends; and fear of things that are but of little hindrance, pusillanimity.

Contempt of little helps and hindrances, magnanimity.

Magnanimity, in danger of death or wounds, valour, fortitude.

Magnanimity, in the use of riches, liberality.

Pusillanimity, in the same wretchedness, miserableness or parsimony, as it is liked, or disliked.

Love of persons for society, kindness.

Love of persons for pleasing the sense only, natural lust.

Love of the same, acquired from rumination, that is, imagination of pleasure past, luxury.

Love of one singularly, with desire to be singularly beloved, the passion of love. The same, with fear that the love is not mutual, jealousy.

Desire, by doing hurt to another, to make him condemn some fact of his own, revengefulness.

Desire, to know why, and how, curiosity; such as is in no living creature but *man*: so that man is distinguished, not only by his reason, but also by this singular passion from other *animals*; in whom the appetite of food, and other pleasures of sense, by predominance, take away the care of knowing causes; which is a lust of the mind, that by a perseverance of delight in the continual and indefatigable generation of knowledge, exceedeth the short vehemence of any carnal pleasure.

Fear of power invisible, feigned by the mind, or imagined from tales publicly allowed, religion; not allowed, superstition.

And when the power imagined, is truly such as we imagine, true religion.

Fear, without the apprehension of why, or what, panic terror, called so from the fables, that make Pan the author of them; whereas, in truth, there is always in him that so feareth, first, some apprehension of the cause, though the rest run away by example; every one supposing his fellow to know why. And therefore this passion happens to none but in a throng, or multitude of people.

Joy, from apprehension of novelty, admiration; proper to man, because it excites the appetite of knowing the cause.

Joy, arising from imagination of a man's own power and ability, is that exultation of the mind which is called glorying: which if grounded upon the experience of his own former actions, is the same with *confidence*: but if grounded on the flattery of others, or only supposed by himself, for delight in the consequences of it, is called vain-glory: which name is properly given; because a well grounded *confidence* begetteth attempt; whereas the supposing of power does not, and is therefore rightly called *vain*.

Grief, from opinion of want of power, is called dejection of mind.

The *vain-glory* which consisteth in the feigning or supposing of abilities in ourselves, which we know are not, is most incident to young men, and nourished by the histories, or fictions of gallant persons; and is corrected oftentimes by age, and employment.

Sudden glory, is the passion which maketh those *grimaces* called laughter; and is caused either by some sudden act of their own, that pleaseth them; or by the apprehension of some deformed thing in another, by comparison whereof they suddenly applaud themselves. And it is incident most to them, that are conscious of the fewest abilities in themselves; who are forced to keep themselves in their own favour, by observing the imperfections of other men. And therefore much laughter at the defects of others, is a sign of pusillanimity. For of great minds, one of the proper works is, to help and free others from scorn; and compare themselves only with the most able.

On the contrary, *sudden dejection*, is the passion that causeth weeping; and is caused by such accidents, as suddenly take away some vehement hope, or some prop of their power: and they are most subject to it, that rely principally on helps external, such as are women, and children. Therefore some weep for the loss of friends; others for their unkindness; others for the sudden stop made to their thoughts of revenge, by reconciliation. But in all cases, both laughter and weeping, are sudden motions; custom taking them both away. For no man laughs at old jests; or weeps for an old calamity.

Grief, for the discovery of some defect of ability, is shame, or the passion that discovereth itself in blushing; and consisteth in the apprehension of some thing dishonourable; and in young men, is a sign of the love of good reputation, and commendable: in old men it is a sign of the same; but because it comes too late, not commendable. The *contempt* of good reputation is called impudence.

Grief, for the calamity of another, is pity; and ariseth from the imagination that the like calamity may befall himself; and therefore is called also compassion, and in the phrase of this present time a fellow-feeling: and therefore for calamity arriving from great wickedness, the best men have the least pity; and for the same calamity, those hate pity, that think themselves least obnoxious to the same.

Contempt, or little sense of the calamity of others, is that which men call cruelty; proceeding from security of their own fortune. For, that any man should take pleasure in other men's great harms, without other end of his own, I do not conceive it possible.

Grief, for the success of a competitor in wealth, honour, or other good, if it be joined with endeavour to enforce our own abilities to equal or exceed him, is called emulation: but joined with endeavour to supplant, or hinder a competitor, envy.

When in the mind of man, appetites, and aversions, hopes, and fears, concerning one and the same thing, arise alternately; and divers good and evil consequences of the doing, or omitting the thing propounded, come successively into our thoughts; so that sometimes we have an appetite to it; sometimes an aversion from it; sometimes hope to be able to do it; sometimes despair, or fear to attempt it; the whole sum of desires, aversions, hopes and fears, continued till the thing be either done, or thought impossible, is that we call deliberation.

Therefore of things past, there is no *deliberation*; because manifestly impossible to be changed: nor of things known to be impossible, or thought so; because men know, or think such deliberation vain. But of things impossible, which we think possible, we may deliberate, not knowing it is in vain. And it is called *deliberation*; because it is a putting an end to the *liberty* we had of doing, or omitting, according to our own appetite, or aversion.

This alternate succession of appetites, aversions, hopes and fears, is no less in other living creatures than in man: and therefore beasts also deliberate.

Every *deliberation* is then said to *end*, when that whereof they deliberate, is either done, or thought impossible; because till then we retain the liberty of doing, or omitting, according to our appetite, or aversion.

In *deliberation*, the last appetite, or aversion, immediately adhering to the action, or to the omission thereof, is that we call the will; the act (not the faculty) of *willing*. And beasts that have *deliberation*, must necessarily also have *will*. The definition of the *will*, given commonly by the Schools, that it is a *rational appetite*, is not good. For if it were, then could there be no voluntary act against reason. For a *voluntary act* is that, which proceedeth from the *will*, and no other.

But if instead of a rational appetite, we shall say an appetite resulting from a precedent deliberation, then the definition is the same that I have given here. *Will* therefore *is the last appetite in deliberating*. And though we say in common discourse, a man had a will once to do a thing, that nevertheless he forbore to do; yet that is properly but an inclination, which makes no action voluntary; because the action depends not of it, but of the last inclination, or appetite. For if the intervenient appetites, make any action voluntary; then by the same reason all intervenient aversions, should make the same action involuntary; and so one and the same action, should be both voluntary and involuntary.

By this it is manifest, that not only actions that have their beginning from covetousness, ambition, lust, or other appetites to the thing propounded; but also those that have their beginning from aversion, or fear of those consequences that follow the omission, are *voluntary actions*.

The forms of speech by which the passions are expressed, are partly the same, and partly different from those, by which we express our thoughts. And first, generally all passions may be expressed *indicatively*; as *I love*, *I fear*, *I joy*, *I deliberate*, *I will*, *I command*: but some of them have particular expressions by themselves, which nevertheless are not affirmations, unless it be when they serve to make other inferences, besides that of the passion they proceed from. Deliberation is expressed *subjunctively*; which is a speech proper to signify suppositions, with their consequences; as, *if this be done*, *then this will follow*; and differs not from the language of reasoning, save that reasoning is in general words; but deliberation for the most part is of particulars. The language of desire, and aversion, is *imperative*; as *do this*, *forbear that*; which when the party is obliged to do, or forbear, is *command*; otherwise *prayer*; or else *counsel*. The language of vain-glory, of indignation, pity and revengefulness, *optative*: but of the desire to know, there is a peculiar expression, called *interrogative*; as, *what is it*, *when shall it*, *how is it done*, and *why so*? Other language of the passions I find none: for cursing, swearing, reviling, and the like, do not signify as speech; but as the actions of a tongue accustomed.

These forms of speech, I say, are expressions, or voluntary significations of our passions: but certain signs they be not; because they may be used arbitrarily, whether they that use them, have such passions or not. The best signs of passions present, are either in the countenance, motions of the body, actions, and ends, or aims, which we otherwise know the man to have.

And because in deliberation, the appetites, and aversions are raised by foresight of the good and evil consequences, and sequels of the action whereof we deliberate; the good or evil effect thereof dependeth on the foresight of a long chain of consequences, of which very seldom any man is able to see to the end. But for so far as a man seeth, if the good in those consequences, be greater than the evil, the whole chain is that which writers call *apparent*, or *seeming good*. And contrarily, when the evil exceedeth the good, the whole is *apparent*, or *seeming evil*: so that he who hath by experience, or reason, the greatest and surest prospect of consequences, deliberates best himself; and is able when he will, to give the best counsel unto others.

Continual success in obtaining those things which a man from time to time desireth, that is to say, continual prospering, is that men call felicity; I mean the felicity of this life. For there is no such thing as perpetual tranquillity of mind, while we live here; because life itself is but motion, and can never be without desire, nor without fear, no more than without sense. What kind of felicity God hath ordained to them that devoutly honour Him, a man shall no sooner know, than enjoy; being joys, that now are as incomprehensible, as the word of Schoolmen *beatifical vision* is unintelligible.

The form of speech whereby men signify their opinion of the goodness of any thing, is praise. That whereby they signify the power and greatness of any thing, is magnifying. And that whereby they signify the opinion they have of a man's felicity, is by the Greeks called μακαρισμός, for which we have no name in our tongue. And thus much is sufficient for the present purpose, to have been said of the passions.

CHAPTER 7

Of the Ends, or Resolutions of Discourse

Of all *discourse*, governed by desire of knowledge, there is at last an *end*, either by attaining, or by giving over. And in the chain of discourse, wheresoever it be interrupted, there is an end for that time.

If the discourse be merely mental, it consisteth of thoughts that the thing will be, and will not be; or that it has been, and has not been, alternately. So that wheresoever you break off the chain of a man's discourse, you leave him in a presumption of *it will be*, or, *it will not be*; or, *it has been*, or, *has not been*. All which is *opinion*. And that which is alternate appetite, in deliberating concerning good and evil, the same is alternate opinion, in the enquiry of the truth of *past*, and *future*. And as the last appetite in deliberation, is called the *will*; so the last opinion in search of the truth of past and future, is called the judgment, or *resolute* and *final sentence* of him that *discourseth*. And as the whole chain of appetites alternate, in the question of good, or bad, is called *deliberation*, so the whole chain of opinions alternate, in the question of true or false, is called doubt.

No discourse whatsoever, can end in absolute knowledge of fact, past or to come. For, as for the knowledge of fact, it is originally, sense; and ever after, memory. And for the knowledge of consequence, which I have said before is called science, it is not absolute, but conditional. No man can know by discourse, that this, or that, is, has been, or will be; which is to know absolutely: but only, that if this be, that is; if this has been, that has been; if this shall be, that shall be: which is to know conditionally; and that not the consequence of one thing to another; but of one name of a thing, to another name of the same thing.

And therefore, when the discourse is put into speech, and begins with the definitions of words, and proceeds by connexion of the same into general affirmations, and of these again into syllogisms; the end or last sum is called the conclusion; and the thought of the mind by it signified, is that conditional knowledge, or knowledge of the consequence of words, which is commonly called science. But if the first ground of such discourse, be not definitions; or if the definitions be not rightly joined together into syllogisms, then the end or conclusion, is again opinion, namely of the truth of somewhat said, though sometimes in absurd and senseless words, without possibility of being understood. When two, or more men, know of one and the same fact, they are said to be conscious of it one to another; which is as much as to know it together. And because such are fittest witnesses of the facts of one another, or of a third; it was, and ever will be reputed a very evil act, for any man to speak against his *conscience*; or to corrupt or force another so to do: insomuch that the plea of conscience, has been always hearkened unto very diligently in all times. Afterwards, men made use of the same word metaphorically, for the knowledge of their own secret facts, and secret thoughts; and therefore it is rhetorically said, that the conscience is a thousand witnesses. And last of all, men vehemently in love with their own new opinions, (though never so absurd) and obstinately bent to maintain them, gave those their opinions also that reverenced name of conscience, as if they would have it seem unlawful, to change or speak against them; and so pretend to know they are true, when they know at most, but that they think so.

When a man's discourse beginneth not at definitions, it beginneth either at some other contemplation of his own, and then it is still called opinion; or it beginneth at some saying of another, of whose ability to know the truth, and of whose honesty in not deceiving, he doubteth not; and then the discourse is not so much concerning the thing, as the person; and the resolution is called belief, and faith: *faith*, *in* the man; *belief*, both *of* the man, and *of* the truth of what he says. So that in belief are two opinions; one of the saying of the man; the other of his virtue. To *have faith in*, or *trust to*, or *believe a man*, signify the same thing; namely, an opinion of the veracity of the man: but to *believe what is said*, signifieth only an opinion of the truth of the saying. But we are to observe that this phrase, *I believe in*; as also the Latin, *credo in*; and the Greek, πιστεύω εἰς, are never used but in the writings of divines. Instead of them, in other writings are put, *I believe him*; *I trust him*; *I have faith in him*; *I rely on him*: and in Latin, *credo illi: fido illi*: and in Greek, πιστεύω αὐτῷ: and that this singularity of the ecclesiastic use of the word hath raised many disputes about the right object of the Christian faith.

But by *believing in*, as it is in the creed, is meant, not trust in the person; but confession and acknowledgement of the doctrine. For not only Christians, but all manner of men do so believe in God, as to hold all for truth they hear him say, whether they understand it, or not; which is all the faith and trust can possibly be had in any person whatsoever: but they do not all believe the doctrine of the creed.

From whence we may infer, that when we believe any saying whatsoever it be, to be true, from arguments taken, not from the thing itself, or from the principles of natural reason, but from the authority, and good opinion we have, of him that hath said it; then is the speaker, or person we believe in, or trust in, and whose word we take, the object of our faith; and the honour done in believing, is done to him only. And consequently, when we believe that the Scriptures are the word of God, having no immediate revelation from God himself, our belief, faith, and trust is in the church; whose word we take, and acquiesce therein.

And they that believe that which a prophet relates unto them in the name of God, take the word of the prophet, do honour to him, and in him trust, and believe, touching the truth of what he relateth, whether he be a true, or a false prophet. And so it is also with all other history. For if I should not believe all that is written by historians, of the glorious acts of *Alexander*, or *Caesar*; I do not think the ghost of *Alexander*, or *Caesar*, had any just cause to be offended; or any body else, but the historian. If *Livy* say the Gods made once a cow speak, and we believe it not; we distrust not God therein, but *Livy*. So that it is evident, that whatsoever we believe, upon no other reason than what is drawn from authority of men only, and their writings, whether they be sent from God or not, is faith in men only.

CHAPTER 8

Of the Virtues Commonly called Intellectual; and their contrary Defects

Virtue generally, in all sorts of subjects, is somewhat that is valued for eminence; and consisteth in comparison. For if all things were equal in all men, nothing would be prized. And by *virtues* intellectual, are always understood such abilities of the mind, as men praise, value, and desire should be in themselves; and go commonly under the name of a *good wit*; though the same word *wit*, be used also, to distinguish one certain ability from the rest.

These *virtues* are of two sorts; *natural*, and *acquired*.

By natural, I mean not, that which a man hath from his birth: for that is nothing else but sense; wherein men differ so little one from another, and from brute beasts, as it is not to be reckoned amongst virtues. But I mean, that *wit*, which is gotten by use only, and experience; without method, culture, or instruction. This natural wit, consisteth principally in two things; *celerity of imagining* (that is, swift succession of one thought to another) and *steady direction* to some approved end. On the contrary a slow imagination, maketh that defect, or fault of the mind, which is commonly called dullness, *stupidity*, and sometimes by other names that signify slowness of motion, or difficulty to be moved.

And this difference of quickness, is caused by the difference of men's passions; that love and dislike, some one thing, some another: and therefore some men's thoughts run one way, some another; and are held to, and observe differently the things that pass through their imagination. And whereas in this succession of men's thoughts, there is nothing to observe in the things they think on, but either in what they be *like one another*, or in what they be *unlike*, or *what they serve for*, or *how they serve to such a purpose*; those that observe their similitudes, in case they be such as are but rarely observed by others, are said to have a *good wit*; by which, in this occasion, is meant a *good fancy*. But they that observe their differences, and dissimilitudes; which is called *distinguishing*, and *discerning*, and *judging* between thing and thing; in case, such discerning be not easy, are said to have a *good judgment*: and particularly in matter of conversation and business; wherein, times, places, and persons are to be discerned, this virtue is called discretion. The former, that is, fancy, without the help of judgment, is not commended as a virtue: but the latter which is judgment, and discretion, is commended for itself, without the help of fancy. Besides the discretion of times, places, and persons, necessary to a good fancy, there is required also an often application of his thoughts to their end; that is to say, to some use to be made of them. This done; he that hath this virtue, will be easily fitted with similitudes, that will please, not only by illustration of his discourse, and adorning it with new and apt metaphors; but also, by the rarity of their invention. But without steadiness, and direction to some end, a great fancy is one kind of madness; such as they have, that entering into any discourse, are snatched from their purpose, by every thing that comes in their thought, into so many, and so long digressions, and parentheses, that they utterly lose themselves: which kind of folly, I know no particular name for: but the cause of it is, sometimes want of experience; whereby that seemeth to a man new and rare, which doth not so to others: sometimes pusillanimity; by which that seems great to him, which other men think a trifle: and whatsoever is new, or great, and therefore thought fit to be told, withdraws a man by degrees from the intended way of his discourse.

In a good poem, whether it be *epic*, or *dramatic*; as also in *sonnets*, *epigrams*, and other pieces, both judgment and fancy are required: but the fancy must be more eminent; because they please for the extravagancy; but ought not to displease by indiscretion.

In a good history, the judgment must be eminent; because the goodness consisteth, in the method, in the truth, and in the choice of the actions that are most profitable to be known. Fancy has no place, but only in adorning the style.

In orations of praise, and in invectives, the fancy is predominant; because the design is not truth, but to honour or dishonour; which is done by noble, or by vile comparisons. The judgment does but suggest what circumstances make an action laudable, or culpable.

In hortatives and pleadings, as truth or disguise serveth best to the design in hand; so is the judgment or the fancy most required.

In demonstration, in counsel, and all rigorous search of truth, judgment does all, except sometimes the understanding have need to be opened by some apt similitude; and then there is so much use of fancy. But for metaphors, they are in this case utterly excluded. For seeing they openly profess deceit; to admit them into counsel, or reasoning, were manifest folly.

And in any discourse whatsoever, if the defect of discretion be apparent, how extravagant soever the fancy be, the whole discourse will be taken for a sign of want of wit; and so will it never when the discretion is manifest, though the fancy be never so ordinary.

The secret thoughts of a man run over all things, holy, profane, clean, obscene, grave, and light, without shame, or blame; which verbal discourse cannot do, farther than the judgment shall approve of the time, place, and persons. An anatomist or a physician may speak, or write his judgment of unclean things; because it is not to please, but profit: but for another man to write his extravagant, and pleasant fancies of the same, is as if a man, from being tumbled into the dirt, should come and present himself before good company. And 'tis the want of discretion that makes the difference. Again, in professed remissness of mind, and familiar company, a man may play with the sounds, and equivocal significations of words; and that many times with encounters of extraordinary fancy: but in a sermon, or in public, or before persons unknown, or whom we ought to reverence, there is no jingling of words that will not be accounted folly: and the difference is only in the want of discretion. So that where wit is wanting, it is not fancy that is wanting, but discretion. Judgment therefore without fancy is wit, but fancy without judgment, not.

When the thoughts of a man, that has a design in hand, running over a multitude of things, observes how they conduce to that design; or what design they may conduce unto; if his observations be such as are not easy, or usual, this wit of his is called prudence; and dependeth on much experience, and memory of the like things, and their consequences heretofore. In which there is not so much difference of men, as there is in their fancies and judgments; because the experience of men equal in age, is not much unequal, as to the quantity; but lies in different occasions; every one having his private designs. To govern well a family, and a kingdom, are not different degrees of prudence; but different sorts of business; no more than to draw a picture in little, or as great, or greater than the life, are different degrees of art. A plain husbandman is more prudent in affairs of his own house, than a privy-councillor in the affairs of another man.

To prudence, if you add the use of unjust, or dishonest means, such as usually are prompted to men by fear, or want; you have that crooked wisdom, which is called craft; which is a sign of pusillanimity. For magnanimity is contempt of unjust, or dishonest helps. And that which the Latins call *versutia*, (translated into English, *shifting*) and is a putting off of a present danger or incommodity, by engaging into a greater, as when a man robs one to pay another, is but a shorter-sighted craft, called *versutia*, from *versura*, which signifies taking money at usury, for the present payment of interest.

As for *acquired wit*, (I mean acquired by method and instruction) there is none but reason; which is grounded on the right use of speech; and produceth the sciences. But of reason and science, I have already spoken in the fifth and sixth chapters.

The causes of this difference of wits, are in the passions: and the difference of passions, proceedeth partly from the different constitution of the body, and partly from different education. For if the difference proceeded from the temper of the brain, and the organs of sense, either exterior or interior, there would be no less difference of men in their sight, hearing, or other senses, than in their fancies, and discretions. It proceeds therefore from the passions; which are different, not only from the difference of men's complexions; but also from their difference of customs, and education.

The passions that most of all cause the difference of wit, are principally, the more or less desire of power, of riches, of knowledge, and of honour. All which may be reduced to the first, that is, desire of power. For riches, knowledge and honour are but several sorts of power.

And therefore, a man who has no great passion for any of these things; but is as men term it indifferent; though he may be so far a good man, as to be free from giving offence; yet he cannot possibly have either a great fancy, or much judgment. For the thoughts are to the desires, as scouts, and spies, to range abroad, and find the way to the things desired: all steadiness of the mind's motion, and all quickness of the same, proceeding from thence. For as to have no desire, is to be dead: so to have weak passions, is dullness; and to have passions indifferently for every thing, giddiness, and *distraction*; and to have stronger and more vehement passions for any thing, than is ordinarily seen in others, is that which men call madness.

Whereof there be almost as many kinds, as of the passions themselves. Sometimes the extraordinary and extravagant passion, proceedeth from the evil constitution of the organs of the body, or harm done them; and sometimes the hurt, and indisposition of the organs, is caused by the vehemence, or long continuance of the passion. But in both cases the madness is of one and the same nature.

The passion, whose violence, or continuance, maketh madness, is either great *vain-glory*; which is commonly called *pride*, and *self-conceit*; or great *dejection* of mind.

Pride subjecteth a man to anger, the excess whereof is the madness called rage, and fury. And thus it comes to pass that excessive desire of revenge, when it becomes habitual, hurteth the organs, and becomes rage: that excessive love, with jealousy, becomes also rage: excessive opinion of a man's own self, for divine inspiration, for wisdom, learning, form, and the like, becomes distraction, and giddiness: the same, joined with envy, rage: vehement opinion of the truth of any thing, contradicted by others, rage.

Dejection, subjects a man to causeless fears; which is a madness commonly called melancholy, apparent also in divers manners; as in haunting of solitudes, and graves; in superstitious behaviour; and in fearing some one, some another particular thing. In sum, all passions that produce strange and unusual behaviour, are called by the general name of madness. But of the several kinds of madness, he that would take the pains, might enroll a legion. And if the excesses be madness, there is no doubt but the passions themselves, when they tend to evil, are degrees of the same.

(For example,) though the effect of folly, in them that are possessed of an opinion of being inspired, be not visible always in one man, by any very extravagant action, that proceedeth from such passion; yet, when many of them conspire together, the rage of the whole multitude is visible enough. For what argument of madness can there be greater, than to clamour, strike, and throw stones at our best friends? Yet this is somewhat less than such a multitude will do. For they will clamour, fight against, and destroy those, by whom all their lifetime before they have been protected, and secured from injury. And if this be madness in the multitude, it is the same in every particular man. For as in the midst of the sea, though a man perceive no sound of that part of the water next him; yet he is well assured, that part contributes as much to the roaring of the sea, as any other part, of the same quantity: so also, though we perceive no great unquietness in one or two men; yet we may be well assured, that their singular passions, are parts of the seditious roaring of a troubled nation. And if there were nothing else that bewrayed their madness; yet that very arrogating such inspiration to themselves, is argument enough. If some man in Bedlam should entertain you with sober discourse; and you desire in taking leave, to know what he were, that you might another time requite his civility; and he should tell you, he were God the Father, I think you need expect no extravagant action for argument of his madness.

This opinion of inspiration, called commonly, private spirit, begins very often from some lucky finding of an error generally held by others; and not knowing, or not remembering, by what conduct of reason, they came to so singular a truth, (as they think it, though it be many times an untruth they light on) they presently admire themselves; as being in the special grace of God Almighty, who hath revealed the same to them supernaturally, by his Spirit.

Again, that madness is nothing else, but too much appearing passion, may be gathered out of the effects of wine, which are the same with those of the evil disposition of the organs. For the variety of behaviour in men that have drunk too much, is the same with that of madmen: some of them raging, others loving, others laughing, all extravagantly, but according to their several domineering passions: for the effect of the wine, does but remove dissimulation, and take from them the sight of the deformity of their passions. For, (I believe) the most sober men, when they walk alone without care and employment of the mind, would be unwilling the vanity and extravagance of their thoughts at that time should be publicly seen: which is a confession, that passions unguided, are for the most part mere madness.

The opinions of the world, both in ancient and later ages, concerning the cause of madness, have been two. Some deriving them from the passions; some from demons, or spirits, either good or bad, which they thought might enter into a man, possess him, and move his organs in such strange, and uncouth manner, as madmen use to do. The former sort therefore, called such men, madmen: but the latter, called them sometimes *demoniacs*, (that is, possessed with spirits) sometimes *energumeni*, (that is, agitated, or moved with spirits;) and now in Italy they are called, not only *pazzi*, madmen; but also *spiritati*, men possessed.

There was once a great conflux of people in Abdera, a city of the Greeks, at the acting of the tragedy of *Andromeda*, upon an extreme hot day: whereupon, a great many of the spectators falling into fevers, had this accident from the heat, and from the tragedy together, that they did nothing but pronounce iambics, with the names of Perseus and Andromeda; which together with the fever, was cured by the coming on of winter: and this madness was thought to proceed from the passion imprinted by the tragedy. Likewise there reigned a fit of madness in another Grecian city, which seized only the young maidens; and caused many of them to hang themselves. This was by most then thought an act of the Devil. But one that suspected, that contempt of life in them, might proceed from some passion of the mind, and supposing that they did not contemn also their honour, gave counsel to the magistrates, to strip such as so hanged themselves, and let them hang out naked. This, the story says, cured that madness. But on the other side, the same Grecians did often ascribe madness to the operation of Eumenides, or Furies; and sometimes of Ceres, Phoebus, and other gods: so much did men attribute to phantasms, as to think them aërial living bodies; and generally to call them spirits. And as the Romans in this, held the same opinion with the Greeks: so also did the Jews; for they called madmen prophets, or (according as they thought the spirits good or bad) demoniacs; and some of them called both prophets and demoniacs, madmen; and some called the same man both demoniac, and madman. But for the Gentiles, 'tis no wonder; because diseases, and health; vices and virtues; and many natural accidents, were with them termed, and worshipped as demons. So that a man was to understand by demon, as well (sometimes) an ague, as a devil. But for the Jews to have such opinion, is somewhat strange. For neither Moses, nor Abraham pretended to prophesy by possession of a spirit; but from the voice of God; or by a vision or dream: nor is there anything in his Law, moral, or ceremonial, by which they were taught there was any such enthusiasm; or any possession. When God is said, (Numb. 11:25) to take from the spirit that was in Moses, and give to the seventy elders, the Spirit of God (taking it for the substance of God) is not divided. The Scriptures by the Spirit of God in man, mean a man's spirit, inclined to godliness. And where it is said, (Exod. 28:3) *Whom I have filled with the spirit of wisdom to make garments for Aaron*, is not meant a spirit put into them, that can make garments; but the wisdom of their own spirits in that kind of work. In the like sense, the spirit of man, when it produceth unclean actions, is ordinarily called an unclean spirit; and so other spirits, though not always, yet as often as the virtue or vice so styled, is extraordinary, and eminent. Neither did the other prophets of the old Testament pretend enthusiasm; or, that God spake in them; but to them, by voice, vision, or dream; and the *burthen of the Lord*, was not possession, but command. How then could the Jews fall into this opinion of possession? I can imagine no reason, but that which is common to all men; namely, the want of curiosity to search natural causes; and their placing felicity, in the acquisition of the gross pleasures of the senses, and the things that most immediately conduce thereto. For they that see any strange and unusual ability, or defect, in a man's mind; unless they see withal, from what cause it may probably proceed, can hardly think it natural; and if not natural, they must needs think it supernatural; and then what can it be, but that either God, or the Devil is in him? And hence it came to pass, when our Saviour (*Mark* 3. 21) was compassed about with the multitude, those of the house doubted he was mad, and went out to hold him: but the Scribes said he had Beelzebub, and that was it, by which he cast out devils; as if the greater madman had awed the lesser. And that (*John* 10. 20) some said, *He hath a devil, and is mad*; whereas others holding him for a prophet, said, *These are not the words of one that hath a devil.* So in the old Testament he that came to anoint Jehu, (2 *Kings* 9. 11) was a prophet; but some of the company asked Jehu, *what came that madman for*? So that in sum, it is manifest, that whosoever behaved himself in extraordinary manner, was thought by the Jews to be possessed either with a good, or evil spirit; except by the Sadducees, who erred so far on the other hand, as not to believe there were at all any spirits, (which is very near to direct atheism) and thereby perhaps the more provoked others, to term such men demoniacs, rather than madmen.

But why then does our Saviour proceed in the curing of them, as if they were possessed; and not as if they were mad? To which I can give no other kind of answer, but that which is given to those that urge the

Scripture in like manner against the opinion of the motion of the earth. The Scripture was written to shew unto men the kingdom of God, and to prepare their minds to become his obedient subjects; leaving the world, and the philosophy thereof, to the disputation of men, for the exercising of their natural reason. Whether the earth's, or sun's motion make the day, and night; or whether the exorbitant actions of men, proceed from passion, or from the devil, (so we worship him not) it is all one, as to our obedience, and subjection to God Almighty; which is the thing for which the Scripture was written. As for that our Saviour speaketh to the disease, as to a person; it is the usual phrase of all that cure by words only, as Christ did, (and enchanters pretend to do, whether they speak to a devil or not.) For is not Christ also said (Matt. 8:26) to have rebuked the winds? Is not he said also (Luke 4:39) to rebuke a fever? Yet this does not argue that a fever is a devil. And whereas many of the devils are said to confess Christ; it is not necessary to interpret those places otherwise, than that those madmen confessed him. And whereas our Saviour (Matt. 12:43) speaketh of an unclean spirit, that having gone out of a man, wandereth through dry places, seeking rest, and finding none; and returning into the same man, with seven other spirits worse than himself; it is manifestly a parable, alluding to a man, that after a little endeavour to quit his lusts, is vanquished by the strength of them; and becomes seven times worse than he was. So that I see nothing at all in the Scripture, that requireth a belief, that demoniacs were any other thing but madmen.

There is yet another fault in the discourses of some men; which may also be numbered amongst the sorts of madness; namely, that abuse of words, whereof I have spoken before in the fifth chapter, by the name of absurdity. And that is, when men speak such words, as put together, have in them no signification at all; but are fallen upon by some, through misunderstanding of the words they have received, and repeat by rote; by others, from intention to deceive by obscurity. And this is incident to none but those, that converse in questions of matters incomprehensible, as the Schoolmen; or in questions of abstruse philosophy. The common sort of men seldom speak insignificantly, and are therefore, by those other egregious persons counted idiots. But to be assured their words are without any thing correspondent to them in the mind, there would need some examples; which if any man require, let him take a Schoolman in his hands, and see if he can translate any one chapter concerning any difficult point, as the Trinity; the Deity; the nature of Christ; transubstantiation; free-will, &c into any of the modern tongues, so as to make the same intelligible; or into any tolerable Latin, such as they were acquainted withal, that lived when the Latin tongue was vulgar. What is the meaning of these words. *The first cause does not necessarily inflow any thing into the second, by force of the essential subordination of the second causes, by which it may help it to work*? They are the translation of the title of the sixth chapter of *Suarez*' first book, *Of the concourse, motion, and help of God*. When men write whole volumes of such stuff. are they not mad, or intend to make others so? And particularly, in the question of transubstantiation; where after certain words spoken; they that say, the white*ness*, round*ness*, magni*tude*, quali*ty*, corruptibili*ty*, all which are incorporeal, &c. go out of the wafer, into the body of our blessed Saviour, do they not make those *nesses*, *tudes*, and *ties*, to be so many spirits possessing his body? For by spirits, they mean always things, that being incorporeal, are nevertheless moveable from one place to another. So that this kind of absurdity, may rightly be numbered amongst the many sorts of madness; and all the time that guided by clear thoughts of their worldly lust, they forbear disputing or writing thus, but lucid intervals. And thus much of the virtues and defects intellectual.

CHAPTER 9

Of the Several Subjects of Knowledge

There are of knowledge two kinds; whereof one is *knowledge of fact*: the other *knowledge of the consequence of one affirmation to another*. The former is nothing else, but sense and memory, and is *absolute knowledge*; as when we see a fact doing, or remember it done: and this is the knowledge required in a witness. The latter is called *science*; and is *conditional*; as when we know, that, *if* the figure shown be a circle, then any straight line through the centre shall divide it into two equal parts. And this is the knowledge required in a philosopher; that is to say, of him that pretends to reasoning.

The register of *knowledge of fact* is called *history*. Whereof there be two sorts: one called *natural history*; which is the history of such facts, or effects of nature, as have no dependence on man's *will*; such as are the histories of *metals*, *plants*, *animals*, *regions*, and the like.

The other, is *civil history*; which is the history of the voluntary actions of men in commonwealths.

The registers of science, are such *books* as contain the *demonstrations* of consequences of one affirmation, to another; and are commonly called *books of philosophy*; whereof the sorts are many, according to the diversity of the matter; and may be divided in such manner as I have divided them in the following table [see pages 98 and 99].

CHAPTER 10

Of power, worth, dignity, honour, and worthiness

The power *of a man*, (to take it universally) is his present means, to obtain some future apparent good. And is either *original* or *instrumental*.

Natural power, is the eminence of the faculties of body, or mind: as extraordinary strength, form, prudence, arts, eloquence, liberality, nobility. *Instrumental* are those powers, which acquired by these, or by fortune, are means and instruments to acquire more: as riches, reputation, friends, and the secret working of God, which men call good luck. For the nature of power, is in this point, like to fame, increasing as it proceeds; or like the motion of heavy bodies, which the further they go, make still the more haste.

The greatest of human powers, is that which is compounded of the powers of most men, united by consent in one person, natural or civil, that has the use of all their powers depending on his will; such as is the power of a commonwealth: or depending on the wills of each particular; such as is the power of a faction or

SCIENCE, that is, knowledge of consequences which is called also PHILOSOPHY

- Consequences from the accidents of bodies natural; which is called NATURAL PHILOSOPHY
  - Consequences from the accidents common to all bodies natural; which are *quantity* and *motion* . . . .
  - PHYSICS or consequences from *qualities.*
    - Consequences from the qualities of bodies transient, such as sometimes appear, sometimes vanish, *Meteorology*. . . . .
    - Consequences from the qualities of bodies *permanent.*
      - Consequences from the quali of the *stars* . .
      - Consequences the qualities fr *liquid* bodies, t fill the space between the stars; such as the *air*, or substances ethereal
      - Consequences from the quali of *bodies terrestrial.*
- Consequences from the accidents of *politic* bodies: which is called POLITICS and CIVIL PHILOSOPHY
  - 1 Of consequences from the *institution* of COMMONWEALTHS, to the *rights* and *duties* of the *body politic* or *sovereign*
  - 2 Of consequences from the same, to the *duty* and *right* of the *subjects*

sequences from quantity, and motion *indeterminate*; which being the ciples or first foundation of philosophy, is called *Philosophia Prima*. — PHILOSOPHIA PRIMA

sequences
a motion
quantity
mined.

- Consequences from quantity, and motion determined
  - By Figure — *Mathematics* — GEOMETRY
  - By Number — *Mathematics* — ARITHMETIC
- Consequences from motion, and quantity of bodies in *special.*
  - Consequences from motion and quantity of the greater parts of the world, as the *earth* and *stars.* — *Cosmography* — ASTRONOMY, GEOGRAPHY
  - Consequence from the motion of special kinds and figures of body. — *Mechanics* Doctrine of *weight.* — *Science* of ENGINEERS, ARCHITECTURE, NAVIGATION

. . . . METEOROLOGY

sequences from the light of the stars. Out of this ,
he motion of the sun, is made the science of . . . . SCIOGRAPHY

equences from the influences of the stars . . . . ASTROLOGY

equences
the parts
e earth
are *without*

- Consequences from the qualities of *minerals*, as *stones*, *metals*, etc.
- Consequences from the qualities of *vegetables*.

equence
the
ies of
als.

- Consequences from the qualities of *animals in general*.
  - Consequences from *vision* . . . . . OPTICS
  - Consequences from *sounds* . . . . . MUSIC
  - Consequences from the rest of the *senses*.
- Consequences from the qualities of *men in general*.
  - Consequences from the passions of men . . . . . ETHICS
  - Consequences from *speech*.
    - In *magnifying*, *vilifying*, etc. — POETRY
    - In *persuading*, — RHETORIC
    - In *reason*, — LOGIC
    - In *contracting*. — The *Science* of JUST and UNJUST

of divers factions leagued. Therefore to have servants, is power; to have friends, is power: for they are strengths united.

Also riches joined with liberality, is power; because it procureth friends, and servants: without liberality, not so; because in this case they defend not; but expose men to envy, as a prey.

Reputation of power, is power; because it draweth with it the adherence of those that need protection.

So is reputation of love of a man's country, (called popularity) for the same reason.

Also, what quality soever maketh a man belove or feared of many; or the reputation of such quality, is power; because it is a means to have the assistance and service of many.

Good success is power; because it maketh reputation of wisdom, or good fortune; which makes men either fear him, or rely on him.

Affability of men already in power, is increase of power; because it gaineth love.

Reputation of prudence in the conduct of peace or war, is power; because to prudent men, we commit the government of ourselves, more willingly than to others.

Nobility is power, not in all places, but only in those commonwealths, where it has privileges: for in such privileges consisteth their power.

Eloquence is power; because it is seeming prudence.

Form is power; because being a promise of good, it recommendeth men to the favour of women and strangers.

The sciences, are small power; because not eminent; and therefore, not acknowledged in any man; nor are at all, but in a few; and in them, but of a few things. For science is of that nature, as none can understand it to be, but such as in a good measure have attained it.

Arts of public use, as fortification, making of engines, and other instruments of war; because they confer to defence, and victory, are power: and though the true mother of them be science, namely the mathematics; yet, because they are brought into the light, by the hand of the artificer, they be esteemed (the midwife passing with the vulgar for the mother) as his issue.

The *value*, or worth of a man, is as of all other things, his price; that is to say, so much as would be given for the use of his power: and therefore is not absolute; but a thing dependent on the need and judgment of another. An able conductor of soldiers, is of great price in time of war present, or imminent; but in peace not so. A learned and uncorrupt judge, is much worth in time of peace; but not so much in war. And as in other things, so in men, not the seller, but the buyer determines the price. For let a man (as most men do) rate themselves at the highest value they can; yet their true value is no more than it is esteemed by others.

The manifestation of the value we set on one another, is that which is commonly called honouring, and dishonouring. To value a man at a high rate, is to *honour* him; at a low rate, is to *dishonour* him. But high, and low, in this case, is to be understood by comparison to the rate that each man setteth on himself.

The public worth of a man, which is the value set on him by the commonwealth, is that which men commonly call dignity. And this value of him by the commonwealth, is understood, by offices of command, judicature, public employment; or by names and titles, introduced for distinction of such value.

To pray to another, for aid of any kind, is to honour; because a sign we have an opinion he has power to help; and the more difficult the aid is, the more is the honour.

To obey, is to honour, because no man obeys them, whom they think have no power to help or hurt them. And consequently to disobey, is to *dishonour*.

To give great gifts to a man, is to honour him; because 'tis buying of protection, and acknowledging of power. To give little gifts, is to dishonour; because it is but alms, and signifies an opinion of the need of small helps.

To be sedulous in promoting another's good, also to flatter, is to honour; as a sign we seek his protection or aid. To neglect, is to dishonour.

To give way, or place to another, in any commodity, is to honour; being a confession of greater power. To arrogate, is to dishonour.

To show any sign of love, or fear of another, is to honour; for both to love, and to fear, is to value. To contemn, or less to love or fear, than he expects, is to dishonour; for it is undervaluing.

To praise, magnify, or call happy, is to honour; because nothing but goodness, power, and felicity is valued. To revile, mock, or pity, is to dishonour.

To speak to another with consideration, to appear before him with decency and humility, is to honour him; as signs of fear to offend. To speak to him rashly, to do any thing before him obscenely, slovenly, impudently, is to dishonour.

To believe, to trust, to rely on another, is to honour him; sign of opinion of his virtue and power. To distrust, or not believe, is to dishonour.

To hearken to a man's counsel, or discourse of

what kind soever, is to honour; as a sign we think him wise, or eloquent, or witty. To sleep, or go forth, or talk the while, is to dishonour.

To do those things to another, which he takes for signs of honour, or which the law or custom makes so, is to honour; because in approving the honour done by others, he acknowledgeth the power which others acknowledge. To refuse to do them, is to dishonour.

To agree with in opinion, is to honour; as being a sign of approving his judgment, and wisdom. To dissent, is dishonour, and an upbraiding of error; and (if the dissent be in many things) of folly.

To imitate, is to honour; for it is vehemently to approve. To imitate one's enemy, is to dishonour.

To honour those another honours, is to honour him; as a sign of approbation of his judgment. To honour his enemies, is to dishonour him.

To employ in counsel, or in actions of difficulty, is to honour; as a sign of opinion of his wisdom, or other power. To deny employment in the same cases, to those that seek it, is to dishonour.

All these ways of honouring, are natural; and as well within, as without commonwealths. But in commonwealths, where he, or they that have the supreme authority, can make whatsoever they please, to stand for signs of honour, there be other honours.

A sovereign doth honour a subject, with whatsoever title, or office, or employment, or action, that he himself will have taken for a sign of his will to honour him.

The king of Persia honoured Mordecai, when he appointed he should be conducted through the streets in the king's garment, upon one of the king's horses, with a crown on his head, and a prince before him, proclaiming, *thus shall it be done to him that the king will honour*. And yet another king of Persia, or the same another time, to one that demanded for some great service, to wear one of the king's robes, gave him leave so to do; but with this addition, that he should wear it as the king's fool; and then it was dishonour. So that of civil honour, the fountain is in the person of the commonwealth, and dependeth on the will of the sovereign; and is therefore temporary, and called *civil honour*; such as magistracy, offices, titles; and in some places coats and scutcheons painted: and men honour such as have them, as having so many signs of favour in the commonwealth; which favour is power.

Honourable is whatsoever possession, action, or quality, is an argument and sign of power.

And therefore to be honoured, loved, or feared of many, is honourable; as arguments of power. To be honoured of few or none, *dishonourable*.

Dominion and victory is honourable; because acquired by power; and servitude, for need or fear, is dishonourable.

Good fortune (if lasting) honourable; as a sign of the favour of God. Ill fortune, and losses, dishonourable. Riches, are honourable; for they are power. Poverty, dishonourable. Magnanimity, liberality, hope, courage, confidence, are honourable; for they proceed from the conscience of power. Pusillanimity, parsimony, fear, diffidence, are dishonourable.

Timely resolution, or determination of what a man is to do, is honourable; as being the contempt of small difficulties, and dangers. And irresolution, dishonourable; as a sign of too much valuing of little impediments, and little advantages: for when a man has weighed things as long as the time permits, and resolves not, the difference of weight is but little; and therefore if he resolve not, he overvalues little things, which is pusillanimity.

All actions, and speeches, that proceed, or seem to proceed, from much experience, science, discretion, or wit, are honourable; for all these are powers. Actions, or words that proceed from error, ignorance, or folly, dishonourable.

Gravity, as far forth as it seems to proceed from a mind employed on something else, is honourable; because employment is a sign of power. But if it seem to proceed from a purpose to appear grave, it is dishonourable. For the gravity of the former, is like the steadiness of a ship laden with merchandise; but of the latter, like the steadiness of a ship ballasted with sand, and other trash.

To be conspicuous, that is to say, to be known, for wealth, office, great actions, or any eminent good, is honourable; as a sign of the power for which he is conspicuous. On the contrary, obscurity, is dishonourable.

To be descended from conspicuous parents, is honourable; because they the more easily attain the aids, and friends of their ancestors. On the contrary, to be descended from obscure parentage, is dishonourable.

Actions proceeding from equity, joined with loss, are honourable; as signs of magnanimity: for magnanimity is a sign of power. On the contrary, craft, shifting, neglect of equity, is dishonourable.

Covetousness of great riches, and ambition of great honours, are honourable; as signs of power to obtain them. Covetousness, and ambition, of little gains or preferments, is dishonourable.

Nor does it alter the case of honour, whether an

action (so it be great and difficult, and consequently a sign of much power) be just or unjust: for honour consisteth only in the opinion of power. Therefore the ancient heathen did not think they dishonoured, but greatly honoured the Gods, when they introduced them in their poems, committing rapes, thefts, and other great, but unjust, or unclean acts: insomuch as nothing is so much celebrated in Jupiter, as his adulteries; nor in Mercury, as his frauds, and thefts: of whose praises, in a hymn of Homer, the greatest is this, that being born in the morning, he had invented music at noon, and before night, stolen away the cattle of Apollo, from his herdsmen.

Also amongst men, till there were constituted great Commonwealths, it was thought no dishonour to be a pirate, or a highway thief; but rather a lawful trade, not only amongst the Greeks, but also amongst all other nations; as is manifest by the histories of ancient time. And at this day, in this part of the world, private duels are, and always will be honourable, though unlawful, till such time as there shall be honour ordained for them that refuse, and ignominy for them that make the challenge. For duels also are many times effects of courage; and the ground of courage is always strength or skill, which are power; though for the most part they be effects of rash speaking, and of the fear of dishonour, in one or both the combatants; who engaged by rashness, are driven into the lists to avoid disgrace.

Scutcheons, and coats of arms hereditary, where they have any eminent privileges, are honourable; otherwise not: for their power consisteth either in such privileges, or in riches, or some such thing as is equally honoured in other men. This kind of honour, commonly called gentry, hath been derived from the ancient Germans. For there never was any such thing known, where the German customs were unknown. Nor is it now anywhere in use, where the Germans have not inhabited. The ancient Greek commanders, when they went to war, had their shields painted with such devices as they pleased; insomuch as an unpainted buckler was a sign of poverty, and of a common soldier: but they transmitted not the inheritance of them. The Romans transmitted the marks of their families: but they were the images, not the devices of their ancestors. Amongst the people of Asia, Africa, and America, there is not, nor was ever, any such thing. The Germans only had that custom; from whom it has been derived into England, France, Spain, and Italy, when in great numbers they either aided the Romans, or made their own conquests in these western parts of the world.

For Germany, being anciently, as all other countries, in their beginnings, divided amongst an infinite number of little lords, or masters of families, that continually had wars one with another; those masters, or lords, principally to the end they might, when they were covered with arms, be known by their followers; and partly for ornament, both painted their armour, or their scutcheon, or coat, with the picture of some beast, or other thing; and also put some eminent and visible mark upon the crest of their helmets. And this ornament both of the arms, and crest, descended by inheritance to their children; to the eldest pure, and to the rest with some note of diversity, such as the old master, that is to say in Dutch, the *Herealt* thought fit. But when many such families, joined together, made a greater monarchy, this duty of the Herealt, to distinguish scutcheons, was made a private office apart. And the issue of these lords, is the great and ancient gentry; which for the most part bear living creatures, noted for courage, and rapine; or castles, battlements, belts, weapons, bars, palisades, and other notes of war; nothing being then in honour, but virtue military. Afterwards, not only kings, but popular commonwealths, gave divers manners of scutcheons, to such as went forth to the war, or returned from it, for encouragement, or recompense to their service. All which, by an observing reader, may be found in such ancient histories, Greek and Latin, as make mention of the German nation, and manners, in their times.

Titles of *honour*, such as are duke, count, marquis, and baron, are honourable; as signifying the value set upon them by the sovereign power of the commonwealth: which titles, were in old time titles of office, and command, derived some from the Romans, some from the Germans and French. Dukes, in Latin *duces*, being generals in war: counts, *comites*, such as bear the general company out of friendship, and were left to govern and defend places conquered, and pacified: marquises, *marchiones*, were counts that governed the marches, or bounds of the empire. Which titles of duke, count, and marquis, came into the empire, about the time of Constantine the Great, from the customs of the German *militia*. But baron, seems to have been a title of the Gauls, and signifies a great man; such as were the king's, or prince's men, whom they employed in war about their persons; and seems to be derived from *vir*, to *ber*, and *bar*, that signified the same in the language of the Gauls, that *vir* in Latin; and thence to *bero*, and *baro*: so that such men were called *berones*, and after *barones*; and (in Spanish) *varones*. But he that would know more particularly the original of titles of honour, may find it, as I have done this, in Mr Selden's most excellent treatise of that subject. In process of time these offices of honour, by occasion of trouble, and for reasons of good and peaceable government, were turned into mere titles; serving for the most part, to distinguish the precedence, place, and order of subjects in the commonwealth: and men were made dukes, counts, marquises, and barons of places, wherein they had neither possession, nor command: and other titles also, were devised to the same end.

Worthiness, is a thing different from the worth, or value of a man; and also from his merit, or desert, and consisteth in a particular power, or ability for that, whereof he is said to be worthy: which particular ability, is usually named fitness, or *aptitude*.

For he is worthiest to be a commander, to be a judge, or to have any other charge, that is best fitted, with the qualities required to the well discharging of it; and worthiest of riches, that has the qualities most requisite for the well using of them: any of which qualities being absent, one may nevertheless be a worthy man, and valuable for something else. Again, a man may be worthy of riches, office, and employment, that nevertheless, can plead no right to have it before another; and therefore cannot be said to merit or deserve it. For merit, presupposeth a right, and that the thing deserved is due by promise: of which I shall say more hereafter, when I shall speak of contracts.

CHAPTER II

Of the difference of manners

By manners, I mean not here, decency of behaviour; as how one should salute another, or how a man should wash his mouth, or pick his teeth before company, and such other points of the *small morals*; but those qualities of mankind, that concern their living together in peace, and unity. To which end we are to consider, that the felicity of this life, consisteth not in the repose of a mind satisfied. For there is no such *finis ultimus* (utmost aim) nor *summum bonum*, (greatest good) as is spoken of in the books of the old moral philosophers. Nor can a man any more live, whose desires are at an end, than he, whose senses and imaginations are at a stand. Felicity is a continual progress of the desire, from one object to another; the attaining of the former, being still but the way to the latter. The cause whereof is, that the object of man's desire, is not to enjoy once only, and for one instant of time; but to assure for ever, the way of his future desire. And therefore the voluntary actions, and inclinations of all men, tend, not only to the procuring, but also to the assuring of a contented life; and differ only in the way: which ariseth partly from the diversity of passions, in diverse men; and partly from the difference of the knowledge, or opinion each one has of the causes, which produce the effect desired.

So that in the first place, I put for a general inclination of all mankind, a perpetual and restless desire of power after power, that ceaseth only in death. And the cause of this, is not always that a man hopes for a more intensive delight, than he has already attained to; or that he cannot be content with a moderate power: but because he cannot assure the power and means to live well, which he hath present, without the acquisition of more. And from hence it is, that kings, whose power is greatest, turn their endeavours to the assuring it at home by laws, or abroad by wars: and when that is done, there succeedeth a new desire; in some, of fame from new conquest; in others, of ease and sensual pleasure; in others, of admiration, or being flattered for excellence in some art, or other ability of the mind.

Competition of riches, honour, command, or other power, inclineth to contention, enmity, and war: because the way of one competitor, to the attaining of his desire, is to kill, subdue, supplant, or repel the other. Particularly, competition of praise, inclineth to a reverence of antiquity. For men contend with the living, not with the dead; to these ascribing more than due, that they may obscure the glory of the other.

Desire of ease, and sensual delight, disposeth men to obey a common power: because by such desires, a man doth abandon the protection that might be hoped for from his own industry, and labour. Fear of death, and wounds, disposeth to the same; and for the same reason. On the contrary, needy men, and hardy, not contented with their present condition; as also, all men that are ambitious of military command, are inclined to continue the causes of war; and to stir up trouble and sedition: for there is no honour military but by war; nor any such hope to mend an ill game, as by causing a new shuffle.

Desire of knowledge, and arts of peace, inclineth

men to obey a common power: for such desire, containeth a desire of leisure; and consequently protection from some other power than their own.

Desire of praise, disposeth to laudable actions, such as please them whose judgment they value; for of those men whom we contemn, we contemn also the praises. Desire of fame after death does the same. And though after death, there be no sense of the praise given us on earth, as being joys, that are either swallowed up in the unspeakable joys of Heaven, or extinguished in the extreme torments of hell: yet is not such fame vain; because men have a present delight therein, from the foresight of it, and of the benefit that may redound thereby to their posterity: which though they now see not, yet they imagine; and any thing that is pleasure to the sense, the same also is pleasure in the imagination.

To have received from one, to whom we think ourselves equal, greater benefits than there is hope to requite, disposeth to counterfeit love; but really secret hatred; and puts a man into the estate of a desperate debtor, that in declining the sight of his creditor, tacitly wishes him there, where he might never see him more. For benefits oblige; and obligation is thraldom; and unrequitable obligation, perpetual thraldom; which is to one's equal, hateful. But to have received benefits from one, whom we acknowledge for superior, inclines to love; because the obligation is no new depression: and cheerful acceptation (which men call *gratitude*) is such an honour done to the obliger, as is taken generally for retribution. Also to receive benefits, though from an equal, or inferior, as long as there is hope of requital, disposeth to love: for in the intention of the receiver, the obligation is of aid, and service mutual; from whence proceedeth an emulation of who shall exceed in benefiting; the most noble and profitable contention possible; wherein the victor is pleased with his victory, and the other revenged by confessing it.

To have done more hurt to a man, than he can, or is willing to expiate, inclineth the doer to hate the sufferer. For he must expect revenge, or forgiveness; both which are hateful.

Fear of oppression, disposeth a man to anticipate or to seek aid by society: for there is no other way by which a man can secure his life and liberty.

Men that distrust their own subtlety, are in tumult and sedition, better disposed for victory, than they that suppose themselves wise, or crafty. For these love to consult, the other (fearing to be circumvented) to strike first. And in sedition, men being always in the precincts of battle, to hold together, and use all advantages of force, is a better stratagem, than any that can proceed from subtlety of wit.

Vain-glorious men, such as without being conscious to themselves of great sufficiency, delight in supposing themselves gallant men, are inclined only to ostentation; but not to attempt: because when danger or difficulty appears, they look for nothing but to have their insufficiency discovered.

Vain-glorious men, such as estimate their sufficiency by the flattery of other men, or the fortune of some precedent action, without assured ground of hope from the true knowledge of themselves, are inclined to rash engaging; and in the approach of danger, or difficulty, to retire if they can: because not seeing the way of safety, they will rather hazard their honour, which may be salved with an excuse; than their lives, for which no salve is sufficient.

Men that have a strong opinion of their own wisdom in matter of government, are disposed to ambition. Because without public employment in council or magistracy, the honour of their wisdom is lost. And therefore eloquent speakers are inclined to ambition; for eloquence seemeth wisdom, both to themselves and others.

Pusillanimity disposeth men to irresolution, and consequently to lose the occasions, and fittest opportunities of action. For after men have been in deliberation till the time of action approach, if it be not then manifest what is best to be done, 'tis a sign, the difference of motives, the one way and the other, are not great: therefore not to resolve then, is to lose the occasion by weighing of trifles; which is pusillanimity.

Frugality, (though in poor men a virtue) maketh a man unapt to achieve such actions, as require the strength of many men at once: for it weakeneth their endeavour, which is be nourished and kept in vigour by reward.

Eloquence, with flattery, disposeth men to confide in them that have it; because the former is seeming wisdom, the latter seeming kindness. Add to them military reputation, and it disposeth men to adhere, and subject themselves to those men that have them. The two former, having given them caution against danger from him; the latter gives them caution against danger from others.

Want of science, that is, ignorance of causes, disposeth, or rather constraineth a man to rely on the advice, and authority of others. For all men whom the truth concerns, if they rely not on their own, must rely on the opinion of some other, whom they think wiser than themselves, and see not why he should deceive them.

Ignorance of the signification of words; which is, want of understanding, disposeth men to take on trust, not only the truth they know not; but also the errors; and which is more, the nonsense of them they trust: for neither error, nor nonsense, can without a perfect understanding of words, be detected.

From the same it proceedeth, that men give different names, to one and the same thing, from the difference of their own passions: as they that approve a private opinion, call it opinion; but they that mislike it, heresy: and yet heresy signifies no more than private opinion; but has only a greater tincture of choler.

From the same also it proceedeth, that men cannot distinguish, without study and great understanding, between one action of many men, and many actions of one multitude; as for example, between one action of all the senators of Rome in killing Catiline, and the many actions of a number of senators in killing Caesar; and therefore are disposed to take for the action of the people, that which is a multitude of actions done by a multitude of men, led perhaps by the persuasion of one.

Ignorance of the causes, and original constitution of right, equity, law, and justice, disposeth a man to make custom and example the rule of his actions; in such manner, as to think that unjust which it hath been the custom to punish; and that just, of the impunity and approbation whereof they can produce an example, or (as the lawyers which only use this false measure of justice barbarously call it) a precedent; like little children, that have no other rule of good and evil manners, but the correction they receive from their parents, and masters; save that children are constant to their rule, whereas, men are not so; because grown strong, and stubborn, they appeal from custom to reason, and from reason to custom, as it serves their turn; receding from custom when their interest requires it, and setting themselves against reason, as oft as reason is against them: which is the cause, that the doctrine of right and wrong, is perpetually disputed, both by the pen and the sword: whereas the doctrine of lines, and figures, is not so; because men care not, in that subject what be truth, as a thing that crosses no man's ambition, profit or lust. For I doubt not, but if it had been a thing contrary to any man's right of dominion, or to the interest of men that have dominion, *that the three angles of a triangle, should be equal to two angles of a square*; that doctrine should have been, if not disputed, yet by the burning of all books of geometry, suppressed, as far as he whom it concerned was able.

Ignorance of remote causes, disposeth men to attribute all events, to the causes immediate, and instrumental: for these are all the causes they perceive. And hence it comes to pass, that in all places, men that are grieved with payments to the public, discharge their anger upon the publicans, that is to say, farmers, collectors, and other officers of the public revenue; and adhere to such as find fault with the public government; and thereby, when they have engaged themselves beyond hope of justification, fall also upon the supreme authority, for fear of punishment, or shame of receiving pardon.

Ignorance of natural causes disposeth a man to credulity, so as to believe many times impossibilities:

for such know nothing to the contrary, but that they may be true; being unable to detect the impossibility. And credulity, because men like to be hearkened unto in company, disposeth them to lying: so that ignorance itself without malice, is able to make a man both to believe lies, and tell them; and sometimes also to invent them.

Anxiety for the future time, disposeth men to inquire into the causes of things: because the knowledge of them, maketh men the better able to order the present to their best advantage.

Curiosity, or love of the knowledge of causes, draws a man from the consideration of the effect, to seek the cause; and again, the cause of that cause; till of necessity he must come to this thought at last, that there is some cause, whereof there is no former cause, but is eternal; which is it men call God. So that it is impossible to make any profound inquiry into natural causes, without being inclined thereby to believe there is one God eternal; though they cannot have any idea of him in their mind, answerable to his nature. For as a man that is born blind, hearing men talk of warming themselves by the fire, and being brought to warm himself by the same, may easily conceive, and assure himself, there is somewhat there, which men call *fire*, and is the cause of the heat he feels; but cannot imagine what it is like; nor have an idea of it in his mind, such as they have that see it; so also, by the visible things in this world, and their admirable order, a man may conceive there is a cause of them, which men call God; and yet not have an idea, or image of him in his mind.

And they that make little or no inquiry into the natural causes of things, yet from the fear that proceeds from the ignorance itself, of what it is that hath the power to do them much good or harm, are inclined to suppose, and feign unto themselves, several kinds of powers invisible; and to stand in awe of their own imaginations; and in time of distress to invoke them; as also in the time of expected good success, to give them thanks; making the creatures of their own fancy, their gods. By which means it hath come to pass, that from the innumerable variety of fancy, men have created in the world innumerable sorts of gods. And this fear of things invisible, is the natural seed of that, which every one in himself calleth religion; and in them that worship, or fear that power otherwise than they do, superstition.

And this seed of religion, having been observed by many; some of those that have observed it, have been inclined thereby to nourish, dress, and form it into laws; and to add to it of their own invention, any opinion of the causes of future events, by which they thought they should be best able to govern others, and make unto themselves the greatest use of their powers.

CHAPTER 12

Of Religion

Seeing there are no signs, nor fruit of *religion*, but in man only; there is no cause to doubt, but that the seed of *religion*, is also only in man; and consisteth in some peculiar quality, or at least in some eminent degree thereof, not to be found in any other living creatures.

And first, it is peculiar to the nature of man, to be inquisitive into the causes of the events they see, some more, some less; but all men so much, as to be curious in the search of the causes of their own good and evil fortune.

Secondly, upon the sight of any thing that hath a beginning, to think also it had a cause, which determined the same to begin, then when it did, rather than sooner or later.

Thirdly, whereas there is no other felicity of beasts, but the enjoying of their quotidian food, ease, and lusts; as having little or no foresight of the time to come, for want of observation, and memory of the order, consequence, and dependence of the things they see; man observeth how one event hath been produced by another; and remembereth in them antecedence and consequence; and when he cannot assure himself of the true causes of things, (for the causes of good and evil fortune for the most part are invisible) he suppose causes of them, either such as his own fancy suggesteth; or trusteth to the authority of other men, such as he thinks to be his friends, and wiser than himself.

The two first, make anxiety. For being assured that there be causes of all things that have arrived hitherto, or shall arrive hereafter; it is impossible for a man, who continually endeavoureth to secure himself against the evil he fears, and procure the good he desireth, not to be in a perpetual solicitude of the time to come; so that every man, especially those that are over provident, are in a state like to that of Prometheus. For as Prometheus, (which interpreted, is, *the prudent man*) was bound to the hill Caucasus, a place of large prospect, where, an eagle feeding on his liver, devoured in the day, as much as was repaired in the night: so that man, which looks too far before him, in the care of future time, hath his heart all the day long, gnawed on by fear of death, poverty, or other calamity; and has no repose, nor pause of his anxiety, but in sleep.

This perpetual fear, always accompanying mankind in the ignorance of causes, as it were in the dark, must needs have for object something. And therefore when there is nothing to be seen, there is nothing to accuse, either of their good, or evil fortune, but some *power*, or agent *invisible*: in which sense perhaps it was, that some of the old poets said, that the gods were at first created by human fear: which spoken of the gods, (that is to say, of the many gods of the Gentiles) is very true. But the acknowledging of one God, eternal, infinite, and omnipotent, may more easily be derived, from the desire men have to know the causes of natural bodies, and their several virtues and operations, than from the fear of what was to befall them in time to come. For he that from any effect he seeth come to pass, should reason to the next and immediate cause thereof, and from thence to the cause of that cause, and plunge himself profoundly in the pursuit of causes; shall at last come to this, that there must be (as even the heathen philosophers confessed) one first mover; that is, a first, and an eternal cause of all things; which is that which men mean by the name of God: and all this without thought of their fortune; the solicitude whereof, both inclines to fear, and hinders them from the search of the causes of other things; and thereby gives occasion of feigning of as many gods, as there be men that feign them.

And for the matter, or substance of the invisible agents, so fancied; they could not by natural cogitation, fall upon any other conceit, but that it was the same with that of the soul of man; and that the soul of man, was of the same substance, with that which appeareth in a dream, to one that sleepeth; or in a looking-glass, to one that is awake; which, men not knowing that such apparitions are nothing else but creatures of the fancy, think to be real, and external substances; and therefore call them ghosts; as the Latins called them *imagines*, and *umbrae*; and thought them spirits, that is, thin aërial bodies; and those invisible agents, which they feared, to be like them; save that they appear and vanish when they please. But the opinion that such spirits were incorporeal, or immaterial, could never enter into the mind of any man by nature; because, though men may put together words of contradictory signification, as *spirit*, and *incorporeal*; yet they can never have the imagination of any thing answering to them: and therefore, men that by their own meditation, arrive to the acknowledgement of one infinite, omnipotent, and eternal God, choose rather to confess he is incomprehensible, and above their understanding, than to define his nature by *spirit incorporeal*, and then confess their definition to be unintelligible: or if they give him such a title, it is not *dogmatically*, with intention to make the divine nature understood; but *piously*, to honour him with attributes, of significations as remote as they can from the grossness of bodies visible.

Then, for the way by which they think these invisible agents wrought their effects; that is to say, what immediate causes they used, in bringing things to pass, men that know not what it is that we call *causing*, (that is, almost all men) have no other rule to guess by, but by observing, and remembering what they have seen to precede the like effect at some other time or times before, without seeing between the antecedent and subsequent event, any dependence or connexion at all: and therefore from the like things past, they expect the like things to come; and hope for good or evil luck, superstitiously, from things that have no part at all in the causing of it: as the Athenians did for their war at Lepanto, demand another Phormio; the Pompeian faction for their war in Africa, another Scipio; and others have done in divers other occasions since. In like manner they attribute their fortune to a stander by, to a lucky or unlucky place, to words spoken, especially if the name of God be amongst them; as charming and conjuring (the liturgy of witches) insomuch as to believe, they have power to turn a stone into bread, bread into a man, or any thing, into any thing.

Thirdly, for the worship which naturally men exhibit to powers invisible, it can be no other, but such expressions of their reverence, as they would use towards men; gifts, petitions, thanks, submission of body, considerate addresses, sober behaviour, premediated words, swearing (that is, assuring one another of their promises) by invoking them. Beyond that reason suggesteth nothing; but leaves them either to rest there; or for further ceremonies, to rely on those they believe to be wiser than themselves.

Lastly, concerning how these invisible powers declare to men the things which shall hereafter come to pass, especially concerning their good or evil fortune in general, or good or ill success in any particular undertaking, men are naturally at a stand; save that using to conjecture of the time to come, by the time past, they are very apt, not only to take casual things, after one or two encounters, for prognostics of the like encounter ever after, but also to believe the like prognostics from other men, of whom they have once conceived a good opinion.

And in these four things, opinion of ghosts, ignorance of second causes, devotion towards what men fear, and taking of things casual for prognostics, consisteth the natural seed of *religion*; which by reason of the different fancies, judgments, and passions of several men, hath grown up into ceremonies so different, that those which are used by one man, are for the most part ridiculous to another.

For these seeds have received culture from two sorts of men. One sort have been they, that have nourished, and ordered them, according to their own invention. The other have done it, by God's commandment, and direction: but both sorts have done it, with a purpose to make those men that relied on them, the more apt to obedience, laws, peace, charity, and civil society. So that the religion of the former sort, is a part of human politics; and teacheth part of the duty which earthly kings require of their subjects. And the religion of the latter sort is divine politics; and containeth precepts to those that have yielded themselves subjects in the kingdom of God. Of the former sort, were all the founders of commonwealths, and the law-givers of the Gentiles: of the latter sort, were Abraham, Moses, and our blessed Saviour; by whom have been derived unto us the laws of the kingdom of God.

And for that part of religion, which consisteth in opinions concerning the nature of powers invisible, there is almost nothing that has a name, that has not been esteemed amongst the Gentiles, in one place or another, a god, or devil; or by their poets feigned to be inanimated, inhabited, or possessed by some spirit or other.

The unformed matter of the world, was a god, by the name of Chaos.

The heaven, the ocean, the planets, the fire, the earth, the winds, were so many gods.

Men, women, a bird, a crocodile, a calf, a dog, a snake, an onion, a leek, were deified. Besides, that they filled almost all places, with spirits called *demons*: the plains, with Pan, and Panises, or Satyrs; the woods, with Fauns, and Nymphs; the sea, with Tritons, and other Nymphs; every river and fountain, with a ghost of his name, and with Nymphs; every house with its *Lares*, or familiars; every man, with his *Genius*; hell, with ghosts, and spiritual officers, as Charon, Cerberus, and the Furies; and in the night time, all places with *larvae*, *lemures*, ghosts of men deceased, and a whole kingdom of fairies, and bugbears. They have also ascribed divinity, and built temples, to mere accidents, and qualities; such as are time, night, day, peace, concord, love, contention, virtue, honour, health, rust, fever, and the like; which when they prayed for, or against, they prayed to, as if there were ghosts of those names hanging over their heads, and letting fall or withholding that good or evil, for or against which they prayed. They invoked also their own wit, by the name of Muses; their own ignorance, by the name of Fortune; their own lusts by the name of Cupid; their own rage, by the name of Furies; their own privy members, by the name of Priapus; and attributed their pollutions, to Incubi, and Succubae: insomuch as there was nothing, which a poet could introduce as a person in his poem, which they did not make either a *god*, or a *devil*.

The same authors of the religion of the Gentiles, observing the second ground for religion, which is men's ignorance of causes; and thereby their aptness to attribute their fortune to causes, on which there was no dependence at all apparent, took occasion to obtrude on their ignorance, instead of second causes, a kind of second and ministerial gods; ascribing the cause of fecundity, to Venus; the cause of arts, to Apollo; of subtlety and craft, to Mercury, of tempests and storms, to Aeolus; and of other effects, to other gods; insomuch as there was amongst the heathen almost as great variety of gods, as of business.

And to the worship, which naturally men conceived fit to be used towards their gods, namely, oblations, prayers, thanks, and the rest formerly named; the same legislators of the Gentiles have added their images, both in picture, and sculpture; that the more ignorant sort, (that is to say, the most part or generality of the people) thinking the gods for whose representation they were made, were really included, and as it were housed within them, might so much the more stand in fear of them: and endowed them with lands, and houses, and officers, and revenues, set apart from all other human uses; that is, consecrated, and made holy to those their idols; as caverns, groves, woods, mountains, and whole islands; and have attributed to them, not only the shapes, some of men, some of beasts, some of monsters; but also the faculties and passions of men and beasts; as sense, speech, sex, lust, generation, (and this not only by mixing one with another, to propagate the kind of gods; but also by mixing with men and women, to beget mongrel gods, and but inmates of heaven, as Bacchus, Hercules, and others) besides anger, revenge, and other passions of living creatures, and the actions proceeding from them, as fraud, theft, adultery, sodomy, and any vice that may be taken for an effect of power, or a cause of pleasure; and all such vices, as amongst men are taken to be against law, rather than against honour.

Lastly, to the prognostics of time to come; which are naturally, but conjectures upon experience of time past; and supernaturally, divine revelation; the same authors of the religion of the Gentiles, partly upon pretended experience, partly upon pretended revelation, have added innumerable other superstitious ways of divination; and made men believe they should find their fortunes, sometimes in the ambiguous or senseless answers of the priests at Delphi, Delos, Ammon, and other famous oracles; which answers, were made ambiguous by design, to own the event both ways; or absurd, by the intoxicating vapour of the place, which is very frequent in sulphurous caverns: sometimes in the leaves of the Sybils; of whose prophecies (like those perhaps of Nostradamus, for the fragments now extant seem to be the invention of later times) there were some books in reputation in the time of the Roman republic: sometimes in the insignificant speeches of madmen, supposed to be possessed with a divine spirit, which possession they called enthusiasm; and these kinds of foretelling events, were accounted theomancy, or prophecy: sometimes in the aspect of the stars at their nativity; which was called horoscopy, and esteemed a part of judiciary astrology: sometimes in their own hopes and fears, called thumomancy, or presage: sometimes in the prediction of witches, that pretended conference with the dead; which is called necromancy, conjuring, and witchcraft; and is but juggling and confederate knavery: sometimes in the casual flight, or feeding of birds; called augury: sometimes in the entrails of a sacrificed beast; which was *aruspicina*: sometimes in dreams: sometimes in croaking of ravens, or chattering of birds: sometimes in the lineaments of the face; which was called metoposcopy; or by palmistry in the lines of the hand; in casual words, called *omina*: sometimes in monsters, or unusual accidents; as eclipses, comets, rare meteors, earthquakes, inundations, uncouth births, and the like, which they called *portenta*, and *ostenta*, because they thought them to portend, or foreshow, some great calamity to come; sometimes, in mere lottery, as cross and pile; counting holes in a sieve; dipping of verses in Homer, and Virgil; and innumerable other such vain conceits. So easy are men to be drawn to believe any thing, from such men as have gotten credit with them; and can with gentleness, and dexterity, take hold of their fear, and ignorance.

And therefore the first founders, and legislators of commonwealths among the Gentiles, whose ends were only to keep the people in obedience, and peace, have in all places taken care: first, to imprint in their minds a belief, that those precepts which they gave concerning religion, might not be thought to proceed from their own device, but from the dictates of some god, or other spirit; or else that they themselves were of a higher nature than mere mortals, that their laws might the more easily be received: so Numa Pompilius pretended to receive the ceremonies he instituted amongst the Romans, from the nymph Egeria: and the first king and founder of the kingdom of Peru, pretended himself and his wife to be the children of the Sun; and Mahomet, to set up his new religion, pretended to have conferences with the Holy Ghost, in form of a dove. Secondly, they have had a care, to make it believed, that the same things were displeasing to the gods, which were forbidden by the laws. Thirdly, to prescribe ceremonies, supplications, sacrifices, and festivals, by which they were to believe, the anger of the gods might be appeased; and that ill success in war, great contagions of sickness, earthquakes, and each man's private misery, came from the anger of the gods; and their anger from the neglect of their worship, or the forgetting, or mistaking some point of the ceremonies required. And though amongst the ancient Romans, men were not forbidden to deny, that which in the poets is written of the pains and pleasures after this life; which divers of great authority, and gravity in that state have in their harangues openly derided; yet that belief was always more cherished, than the contrary.

And by these, and such other institutions, they obtained in order to their end, (which was the peace of the commonwealth) that the common people in their misfortunes, laying the fault on neglect, or error in their ceremonies, or on their own disobedience to the laws, were the less apt to mutiny against their governors. And being entertained with the pomp and pastime of festivals, and public games, made in honour of the gods, needed nothing else but bread, to keep them from discontent, murmuring, and commotion against the state. And therefore the Romans, that had conquered the greatest part of the then known world, made no scruple of tolerating any religion whatsoever in the city of Rome itself; unless it had something in it, that could not consist with their civil government; nor do we read, that any religion was there forbidden, but that of the Jews; who (being the peculiar kingdom of God) thought it unlawful to acknowledge subjection to any mortal king or state whatsoever. And thus you see how the religion of the Gentiles was a part of their policy.

But where God himself, by supernatural revelation, planted religion; there he also made to himself a peculiar kingdom; and gave laws, not only of behaviour towards himself; but also towards one another; and thereby in the kingdom of God, the policy, and laws civil, are a part of religion; and therefore the distinction of temporal and spiritual domination, hath there no place. It is true, that God is king of all the earth: yet may he be king of a peculiar, and chosen nation. For there is no more incongruity therein, than that he that hath the general command of the whole army, should have withal a peculiar regiment, or company of his own. God is king of all the earth by his power: but of his chosen people, he is king by covenant. But to speak more largely of the kingdom of God, both by nature, and covenant, I have in the following discourse assigned another place.

From the propagation of religion, it is not hard to understand the cause of the resolution of the same into its first seeds, or principles; which are only an opinion of a deity, and of powers invisible, and supernatural; that can never be so abolished out of human nature, but that new religions may again be made to spring out of them, by the culture of such men, as for such purpose are in reputation.

For seeing all formed religion, is founded at first, upon the faith which a multitude hath in some one person, whom they believe not only to be a wise man, and to labour to procure their happiness, but also to be a holy man, to whom God himself vouchsafeth to declare his will supernaturally; it followeth necessarily, when they that have the government of religion, shall come to have either the wisdom of those men, their sincerity, or their love suspected; or when they shall be unable to show any probable token of divine revelation; that the religion which they desire to uphold, must be suspected likewise; and (without the fear of the civil sword) contradicted and rejected.

That which taketh away the reputation of wisdom, in him that formeth a religion, or addeth to it when it is already formed, is the enjoining of a belief of contradictories: for both parts of a contradiction cannot possibly be true: and therefore to enjoin the belief of them, is an argument of ignorance; which detects the author in that; and discredits him in all things else he shall propound as from revelation supernatural: which revelation a man may indeed have of many things above, but of nothing against natural reason.

That which taketh away the reputation of sincerity, is the doing or saying of such things, as appear to be signs, that what they require other men to believe, is not believed by themselves; all which doings or sayings are therefore called scandalous, because they be stumbling blocks, that make men to fall in the way of religion: as injustice, cruelty, profaneness, avarice, and luxury. For who can believe, that he that doth ordinarily such actions, as proceed from any of these roots, believeth there is any such invisible power to be feared, as he affrighteth other men withal, for lesser faults?

That which taketh away the reputation of love, is the being detected of private ends: as when the belief they require of others, conduceth or seemeth to conduce to the acquiring of dominion, riches, dignity, or secure pleasure, to themselves only, or specially. For that which men reap benefit by to themselves, they are thought to do for their own sakes, and not for love of others.

Lastly, the testimony that men can render of divine calling, can be no other, than the operation of miracles; or true prophecy (which also is a miracle) or extraordinary felicity. And therefore, to those points of religion, which have been received from them that did such miracles; those that are added by such, as approve not their calling by some miracle, obtain no greater belief, than what the custom, and laws of the places, in which they be educated, have wrought into them. For as in natural things, men of judgment require natural signs and arguments; so in supernatural things they require signs supernatural, (which are miracles) before they consent inwardly, and from their hearts.

All which causes of the weakening of men's faith, do manifestly appear in the examples following. First, we have the example of the children of Israel; who when Moses, that had approved his calling to them by miracles, and by the happy conduct of them out of Egypt, was absent but forty days, revolted from the worship of the true God, recommended to them by him; and setting up (Exod. 32:1, 2) a golden calf for their god, relapsed into the idolatry of the Egyptians; from whom they had been so lately delivered. And again, after Moses, Aaron, Joshua, and that generation which had seen the great works of God in Israel, (Judges 2:11) were dead; another generation arose, and served Baal. So that miracles failing, faith also failed.

Again, when the sons of Samuel, (I Sam. 8: 3) being

constituted by their father judges in Bersabee, received bribes, and judged unjustly, the people of Israel refused any more to have God to be their king, in other manner than he was king of other people; and therefore cried out to Samuel, to choose them a king after the manner of the nations. So that justice failing, faith also failed; insomuch, as they deposed their God, from reigning over them.

And whereas in the planting of Christian religion, the oracles ceased in all parts of the Roman empire, and the number of Christians increased wonderfully every day, and in every place, by the preaching of the Apostles, and Evangelists; a great part of that success, may reasonably be attributed to the contempt into which the priests of the Gentiles of that time, had brought themselves, by their uncleanness, avarice, and juggling between princes. Also the religion of the church of Rome was partly for the same cause abolished in England, and many other parts of Christendom; insomuch, as the failing of virtue in the pastors, maketh faith fail in the people: and partly from bringing of the philosophy, and doctrine of Aristotle into religion, by the Schoolmen; from whence there arose so many contradictions, and absurdities, as brought the clergy into a reputation both of ignorance, and of fraudulent intention; and inclined people to revolt from them, either against the will of their own princes, as in France and Holland; or with their will, as in England.

Lastly, amongst the points by the church of Rome declared necessary for salvation, there be so many, manifestly to the advantage of the Pope, and of his spiritual subjects, residing in the territories of other Christian princes, that were it not for the mutual emulation of those princes, they might without war, or trouble, exclude all foreign authority, as easily as it has been excluded in England. For who is there that does not see, to whose benefit it conduceth, to have it believed, that a king hath not his authority from Christ, unless a bishop crown him? That a king, if he be a priest, cannot marry? That whether a prince be born in lawful marriage, or not, must be judged by authority from Rome? That subjects may be freed from their allegiance, if by the court of Rome, the king be judged an heretic? That a king (as Childeric of France) may be deposed by a pope (as Pope Zachary) for no cause; and his kingdom given to one of his subjects? That the clergy, and regulars, in what country soever, shall be exempt from the jurisdiction of their king, in cases criminal? Or who does not see, to whose profit redound the fees of private masses, and vales of purgatory; with other signs of private interest, enough to mortify the most lively faith, if (as I said) the civil magistrate, and custom did not more sustain it, than any opinion they have of the sanctity, wisdom, or probity of their teachers? So that I may attribute all the changes of religion in the world, to one and the same cause; and that is, unpleasing priests; and those not only amongst Catholics, but even in that church that hath presumed most of reformation.

CHAPTER 13

Of the natural condition of mankind as concerning their felicity, and misery

Nature hath made men so equal, in the faculties of the body and mind as that though there be found one man sometimes manifestly stronger in body, or of quicker mind than another; yet when all is reckoned together, the difference between man and man, is not so considerable, as that one man can thereupon claim to himself any benefit, to which another may not pretend, as well as he. For as to the strength of body, the weakest has strength enough to kill the strongest, either by secret machination, or by confederacy with others, that are in the same danger with himself.

And as to the faculties of the mind, (setting aside the arts grounded upon words, and especially that skill of proceeding upon general and infallible rules, called science; which very few have, and but in few things; as being not a native faculty, born with us; nor attained (as prudence) while we look after somewhat else) I find yet a greater equality amongst men, than that of strength. For prudence, is but experience; which equal time equally bestows on all men, in those things they equally apply themselves unto. That which may perhaps make such equality incredible, is but a vain conceit of one's own wisdom, which almost all men think they have in a greater degree, than the vulgar; that is, than all men but themselves, and a few others, whom by fame, or for concurring with themselves, they approve. For such is the nature of men, that howsoever they may acknowledge many others to be more witty, or more eloquent, or more learned; yet they will hardly believe there be many so wise as themselves; for they see their own wit at hand, and other men's at a distance. But this proveth rather that men are in that point equal, than unequal. For there is not ordinarily a greater sign of the equal distribution of any thing, than that every man is contented with his share.

From this equality of ability, ariseth equality of hope in the attaining of our ends. And therefore if any two men desire the same thing, which nevertheless they cannot both enjoy, they become enemies; and in the way to their end, (which is principally their own conservation, and sometimes their delectation only) endeavour to destroy, or subdue one another. And from hence it comes to pass, that where an invader hath no more to fear, than another man's single power; if one plant, sow, build, or possess a convenient seat, others may probably be expected to come prepared with forces united, to dispossess and deprive him, not only of the fruit of his labour, but also of his life, or liberty. And the invader again is in the like danger of another.

And from this diffidence of one another, there is no way for any man to secure himself, so reasonable, as anticipation; that is, by force, or wiles, to master the persons of all men he can, so long, till he see no other power great enough to endanger him: and this is no more than his own conservation requireth, and is generally allowed. Also because there be some, that take pleasure in contemplating their own power in the acts of conquest, which they pursue farther than their security requires; if others, that otherwise would be glad to be at ease within modest bounds, should not by invasion increase their power, they would not be able, long time, by standing only on their defence, to subsist. And by consequence, such augmentation of dominion over men, being necessary to a man's conservation, it ought to be allowed him.

Again, men have no pleasure, (but on the contrary a great deal of grief) in keeping company, where there is no power able to over-awe them all. For every man looketh that his companion should value him, at the same rate he sets upon himself: and upon all signs of contempt, or undervaluing, naturally endeavours, as far as he dares (which amongst them that have no common power to keep them in quiet, is far enough to make them destroy each other) to extort a greater value from his contemners, by damage; and from others, by the example.

So that in the nature of man, we find three principal causes of quarrel. First, competition; secondly, diffidence; thirdly, glory.

The first, maketh men invade for gain; the second, for safety; and the third, for reputation. The first use violence, to make themselves masters of other men's persons, wives, children, and cattle; the second, to defend them; the third, for trifles, as a word, a smile, a different opinion, and any other sign of undervalue, either direct in their persons, or by reflection in their kindred, their friends, their nation, their profession, or their name.

Hereby it is manifest, that during the time men live without a common power to keep them all in awe, they are in that condition which is called war; and such a war, as is of every man, against every man. For war, consisteth not in battle only, or the act of fighting; but in a tract of time, wherein the will to contend by battle is sufficiently known: and therefore the notion of *time*, is to be considered in the nature of war; as it is in the nature of weather. For as the nature of foul weather, lieth not in a shower or two of rain; but in an inclination thereto of many days together: so the nature of war, consisteth not in actual fighting; but in the known disposition thereto, during all the time there is no assurance to the contrary. All other time is peace.

Whatsoever therefore is consequent to a time of war, where every man is enemy to every man; the same is consequent to the time, wherein men live without other security, than what their own strength, and their own invention shall furnish them withal. In such condition, there is no place for industry; because the fruit thereof is uncertain: and consequently no culture of the earth; no navigation, nor use of the commodities that may be imported by sea; no commodious building; no instruments of moving, and removing such things as require much force; no knowledge of the face of the earth; no account of time; no arts; no letters; no society; and which is worst of all, continual fear, and danger of violent death; and the life of man, solitary, poor, nasty, brutish, and short.

It may seem strange to some man, that has not well weighed these things; that nature should thus dissociate, and render men apt to invade, and destroy one another: and he may therefore, not trusting to this inference, made from the passions, desire perhaps to have the same confirmed by experience. Let him therefore consider with himself, when taking a journey, he arms himself, and seeks to go well accompanied; when going to sleep, he locks his doors; when even in his house he locks his chests; and this when he knows there be laws, and public officers, armed, to revenge all injuries shall be done him; what opinion he has of his fellow-subjects, when he rides armed; of his fellow citizens, when he locks his doors; and of his children, and servants, when he locks his chests. Does he not there as much accuse mankind by his actions, as I do by my words? But neither of us accuse man's nature in it. The desires, and other passions of man, are in themselves no sin. No more are the actions, that proceed from those passions, till they know a law that forbids them: which till laws be made they cannot know: nor can any law be made, till they have agreed upon the person that shall make it.

It may peradventure be thought, there was never such a time, nor condition of war as this; and I believe it was never generally so, over all the world: but there are many places, where they live so now. For the savage people in many places of America, except the government of small families, the concord whereof dependeth on natural lust, have no government at all; and live at this day in that brutish manner, as I said before. Howsoever, it may be perceived what manner of life there would be, where there were no common power to fear; by the manner of life, which men that have formerly lived under a peaceful government, use to degenerate into, in a civil war.

But though there had never been any time, wherein particular men were in a condition of war one against another; yet in all times kings, and persons of sovereign authority, because of their independency, are in continual jealousies, and in the state and posture of gladiators; having their weapons pointing, and their eyes fixed on one another; that is, their forts, garrisons, and guns upon the frontiers of their kingdoms; and continual spies upon their neighbours; which is a posture of war. But because they uphold thereby the industry of their subjects; there does not follow from it that misery, which accompanies the liberty of particular men.

To this war of every man against every man, this also is consequent; that nothing can be unjust. The notions of right and wrong, justice and injustice have there no place. Where there is no common power, there is no law: where no law, no injustice. Force, and fraud, are in war the two cardinal virtues. Justice, and injustice are none of the faculties neither of the body, nor mind. If they were, they might be in a man that were alone in the world, as well as his senses, and passions. They are qualities, that relate to men in society, not in solitude. It is consequent also to the same condition, that there be no propriety, no dominion, no *mine* and *thine* distinct; but only that to be every man's, that he can get; and for so long, as he can keep it. And thus much for the ill condition, which man by mere nature is actually placed in; though with a possibility to come out of it, consisting partly in the passions, partly in his reason.

The passions that incline men to peace, are fear of death; desire of such things as are necessary to commodious living; and a hope by their industry to obtain them. And reason suggesteth convenient articles of peace, upon which men may be drawn to agreement. These articles, are they, which otherwise are called the Laws of Nature: whereof I shall speak more particularly, in the two following chapters.

CHAPTER 14

Of the First and Second Natural Laws, and of Contracts

The right of nature, which writers commonly call *jus naturale*, is the liberty each man hath, to use his own power, as he will himself, for the preservation of his own nature; that is to say, of his own life; and consequently, of doing any thing, which in his own judgment, and reason, he shall conceive to be the aptest means thereunto.

By liberty, is understood, according to the proper signification of the word, the absence of external impediments: which impediments may oft take away part of a man's power to do what he would; but cannot hinder him from using the power left him, according as his judgment, and reason shall dictate to him.

A law of nature (*lex naturalis*) is a precept, or general rule, found out by reason, by which a man is forbidden to do that which is destructive of his life, or taketh away the means of preserving the same; and to omit that, by which he thinketh it may be best preserved. For though they that speak of this subject, use to confound *jus* and *lex*, *right* and *law*; yet they ought to be distinguished; because right consisteth in liberty to do, or to forbear: whereas law determineth, and bindeth to one of them: so that law and right, differ as much, as obligation and liberty; which in one and the same matter are inconsistent.

And because the condition of man, (as hath been declared in the precedent chapter) is a condition of war of every one against every one; in which case every one is governed by his own reason; and there is nothing he can make use of, that may not be a help unto him, in preserving his life against his enemies; it followeth, that in such a condition, every man has a right to every thing; even to one another's body. And therefore, as long as this natural right of every man to every thing endureth, there can be no security to any man, (how strong or wise soever he be) of living out the time, which nature ordinarily alloweth men to live. And consequently it is a precept, or general rule of reason, *that every man, ought to endeavour peace, as far as he has hope of obtaining it; and when he cannot obtain it, that he may seek, and use, all helps and advantages of war.* The first branch of which rule, containeth the first, and fundamental law of nature; which is, *to seek peace, and follow it.* The second, the sum of the right of nature; which is, *by all means we can, to defend ourselves.*

From this fundamental law of nature, by which men are commanded to endeavour peace, is derived this second law; *that a man be willing, when others are so too, as far-forth as for peace and defence of himself he shall think it necessary, to lay down this right to all things; and be contented with so much liberty against other men, as he would allow other men against himself.* For as long as every man holdeth this right, of doing any thing he liketh; so long are all men in the condition of war. But if other men will not lay down their right, as well as he; then there is no reason for any one, to divest himself of his: for that were to expose himself to prey, (which no man is bound to) rather than to dispose himself to peace. This is that law of the Gospel; *whatsoever you require that others should do to you, that do ye to them.* And that law of all men, *quod tibi fieri non vis, alteri ne feceris.*

To *lay down* a man's *right* to any thing, is to *divest* himself of the *liberty*, of hindering another of the benefit of his own right to the same. For he that renounceth, or passeth away his right, giveth not to any other man a right which he had not before; because there is nothing to which every man had not right by nature: but only standeth out of his way, that he may enjoy his own original right, without hindrance from him; not without hindrance from another. So that the effect which redoundeth to one man, by another man's defect of right, is but so much diminution of impediments to the use of his own right original.

Right is laid aside, either by simply renouncing it; or by transferring it to another. By *simply* renouncing; when he cares not to whom the benefit thereof redoundeth. By transferring; when he intendeth the benefit thereof to some certain person, or persons. And when a man hath in either manner abandoned, or granted away his right; then he is said to be obliged, or bound, not to hinder those, to whom such right is granted, or abandoned, from the benefit of it: and that he *ought*, and it is his duty, not to make void that voluntary act of his own: and that such hindrance is injustice, and injury, as being *sine jure*; the right being before renounced, or transferred. So that *injury*, or *injustice*, in the controversies of the world, is somewhat like to that, which in the disputations of scholars is called *absurdity*. For as it is there called an absurdity, to contradict what one maintained in the beginning:

so in the world, it is called injustice, and injury, voluntarily to undo that, which from the beginning he had voluntarily done. The way by which a man either simply renounceth, or transferreth his right, is a declaration, or signification, by some voluntary and sufficient sign or signs, that he doth so renounce, or transfer; or hath so renounced, or transferred the same, to him that accepteth it. And these signs are either words only, or actions only; or (as it happeneth most often) both words and actions. And the same are the bonds, by which men are bound, and obliged: bonds, that have their strength, not from their own nature, (for nothing is more easily broken than a man's word) but from fear of some evil consequence upon the rupture.

Whensoever a man transferreth his right, or renounceth it; it is either in consideration of some right reciprocally transferred to himself; or for some other good he hopeth for thereby. For it is a voluntary act: and of the voluntary acts of every man, the object is some *good to himself*. And therefore there be some rights, which no man can be understood by any words, or other signs, to have abandoned, or transferred. As first a man cannot lay down the right of resisting them that assault him by force, to take away his life; because he cannot be understood to aim thereby, at any good to himself. The same may be said of wounds, and chains, and imprisonment; both because there is no benefit consequent to such patience; as there is to the patience of suffering another to be wounded, or imprisoned: as also because a man cannot tell, when he seeth men proceed against him by violence, whether they intend his death or not. And lastly the motive and end for which this renouncing, and transferring of right is introduced, is nothing else but the security of a man's person, in his life, and in the means of so preserving life, as not to be weary of it. And therefore if a man by words, or other signs, seem to despoil himself of the end, for which those signs were intended, he is not to be understood as if he meant it, or that it was his will; but that he was ignorant of how such words and actions were to be interpreted.

The mutual transferring of right, is that which men call contract.

There is difference, between transferring of right to the thing; and transferring, or tradition, that is, delivery of the thing itself. For the thing may be delivered together with the translation of the right; as in buying and selling with ready-money; or exchange of goods, or lands: and it may be delivered some time after.

Again, one of the contractors, may deliver the thing contracted for on his part, and leave the other to perform his part at some determinate time after, and in the mean time be trusted; and then the contract on his part, is called pact, or covenant: or both parts may contract now, to perform hereafter: in which cases, he that is to perform in time to come, being trusted, his performance is called *keeping of promise*, or faith; and the failing of performance (if it be voluntary) *violation of faith*.

When the transferring of right, is not mutual; but one of the parties transferreth, in hope to gain thereby friendship, or service from another, or from his friends; or in hope to gain the reputation of charity, or magnanimity; or to deliver his mind from the pain of compassion; or in hope of reward in heaven; this is not contract, but gift, free-gift, grace: which words signify one and the same thing.

Signs of contract, are either *express*, or *by inference*. Express, are words spoken with understanding of what they signify: and such words are either of the time *present*, or *past*; as, *I give*, *I grant*, *I have given*, *I have granted*, *I will that this be yours*: or of the future; as, *I will give*, I will grant: which words of the future are called promise.

Signs by inference, are sometimes the consequence of words; sometimes the consequence of silence; sometimes the consequence of actions; sometimes the consequence of forbearing an action: and generally a sign by inference, of any contract, is whatsoever sufficiently argues the will of the contractor.

Words alone, if they be of the time to come, and contain a bare promise, are an insufficient sign of a free-gift, and therefore not obligatory. For if they be of the time to come, as, *tomorrow I will give*, they are a sign I have not given yet, and consequently that my right is not transferred, but remaineth till I transfer it by some other act. But if the words be of the time present, or past, as, *I h*ave given, or *do give to be delivered tomorrow*, then is my morrow's right given away today; and that by the virtue of the words, though there were no other argument of my will. And there is a great difference in the signification of these words, *volo hoc tuum esse cras*, and *cras dabo*; that is, between *I will that this be thine tomorrow*, and, *I will give it thee tomorrow*: for the word *I will*, in the former manner of speech, signifies an act of the will present; but in the latter, it signifies a promise of an act of the will to come: and therefore the former words, being of the present, transfer a future right; the latter, that be of the future, transfer nothing. But if there be other signs of the will to transfer a right, besides words; then, though the gift be free, yet may the right be understood to pass by words of the future: as if a man propound a prize to him that comes first to the end of a race, the gift is free; and though the words be of the future, yet the right passeth: for if he would not have his words so be understood, he should not have let them run.

In contracts, the right passeth, not only where the words are of the time present, or past; but also where they are of the future: because all contract is mutual translation, or change of right; and therefore he that promiseth only, because he hath already received the benefit for which he promiseth, is to be understood as if he intended the right should pass: for unless he had been content to have his words so understood, the other would not have performed his part first. And for that cause, in buying and selling, and other acts of contract, a promise is equivalent to a covenant; and therefore obligatory.

He that performeth first in the case of a contract, is said to merit that which he is to receive by the performance of the other; and he hath it as *due*. Also when a prize is propounded to many, which is to be given to him only that winneth; or money is thrown amongst many, to be enjoyed by them that catch it; though this be a free gift; yet so to win, or so to catch, is to *merit*, and to have it as due. For the right is transferred in the propounding of the prize, and in throwing down the money; though it be not determined to whom, but by the event of the contention. But there is between these two sorts of merit, this difference, that in contract, I merit by virtue of my own power, and the contractor's need; but in this case of free gift, I am enabled to merit only by the benignity of the giver: in contract, I merit at the contractor's hand that he should depart with his right; in this case of gift, I merit not that the giver should part with his right; but that when he has parted with it, it should be mine, rather than another's. And this I think to be the meaning of that distinction of the Schools, between *meritum congrui*, and *meritum condigni*. For God Almighty, having promised Paradise to those men (hoodwinked with carnal desires) that can walk through this world according to the precepts, and limits prescribed by him; they say, he that shall so walk, shall merit Paradise *ex congruo*. But because no man can demand a right to it, by his own righteousness, or any other power in himself, but by the free grace of God only; they say, no man can merit Paradise *ex condigno*. This I say, I think is the meaning of that distinction; but because disputers do not agree upon the signification of their own terms of art, longer than it serves their turn; I will not affirm any thing of their meaning: only this I say; when a gift is given indefinitely, as a prize to be contended for, he that winneth meriteth, and may claim the prize as due.

If a covenant be made, wherein neither of the parties perform presently, but trust one another; in the condition of mere nature, (which is a condition of war of every man against every man) upon any reasonable suspicion, it is void: but if there be a common power set over them both, with right and force sufficient to compel performance, it is not void. For he that performeth first, has no assurance the other will perform after; because the bonds of words are too weak to bridle men's ambition, avarice, anger, and other passions, without the fear of some coercive power; which in the condition of mere nature, where all men are equal, and judges of the justness of their own fears, cannot possibly be supposed. And therefore he which performeth first, does but betray himself to his enemy; contrary to the right (he can never abandon) of defending his life, and means of living.

But in a civil estate, where there is a power set up to constrain those that would otherwise violate their faith, that fear is no more reasonable; and for that cause, he which by the covenant is to perform first, is obliged so to do.

The cause of fear, which maketh such a covenant invalid, must be always something arising after the covenant made; as some new fact, or other sign of the will not to perform: else it cannot make the covenant void. For that which could not hinder a man from promising, ought not to be admitted as a hindrance of performing.

He that transferreth any right, transferreth the means of enjoying it, as far as lieth in his power. As he that selleth land, is understood to transfer the herbage, and whatsoever grows upon it; nor can he that sells a mill turn away the stream that drives it. And they that give to a man the right of government in sovereignty, are understood to give him the right of levying money to maintain soldiers; and of appointing magistrates for the administration of justice.

To make covenants with brute beasts, is impossible; because not understanding our speech, they understand not, nor accept of any translation of right; nor can translate any right to another: and without mutual acceptation, there is no covenant.

To make covenant with God, is impossible, but by mediation of such as God speaketh to, either by revelation supernatural, or by his lieutenants that govern under him, and in his name: for otherwise we know not whether our covenants be accepted, or not. And therefore they that vow anything contrary to any law of nature, vow in vain; as being a thing unjust to pay such vow. And if it be a thing commanded by the law of nature, it is not the vow, but the law that binds them.

The matter, or subject of a covenant, is always something that falleth under deliberation; (for to covenant, is an act of the will; that is to say an act, and the last act, of deliberation) and is therefore always understood to be something to come; and which is judged possible for him that covenanteth, to perform.

And therefore, to promise that which is known to be impossible, is no covenant. But if that prove impossible afterwards, which before was thought possible, the covenant is valid, and bindeth, (though not to the thing itself) yet to the value; or, if that also be impossible, to the unfeigned endeavour of performing as much as is possible: for to more no man can be obliged.

Men are freed of their covenants two ways; by performing; or by being forgiven. For performance, is the natural end of obligation; and forgiveness, the restitution of liberty; as being a retransferring of that right, in which the obligation consisted.

Covenants entered into by fear, in the condition of mere nature, are obligatory. For example, if I covenant to pay a ransom or service for my life, to an enemy; I am bound by it. For it is a contract, wherein one receiveth the benefit of life; the other is to receive money or service for it; and consequently, where no other law (as in the condition of mere nature) forbiddeth the performance, the covenant is valid. Therefore prisoners of war, if trusted with the payment of their ransom, are obliged to pay it: and if a weaker prince make a disadvantageous peace with a stronger, for fear; he is bound to keep it; unless (as hath been said before) there ariseth some new, and just cause of fear, to renew the war. And even in commonwealths, if I be forced to redeem myself from a thief by promising him money, I am bound to pay it, till the civil law discharge me. For whatsoever I may lawfully do without obligation, the same I may lawfully covenant to do through fear: and what I lawfully covenant, I cannot lawfully break.

A former covenant, makes void a later. For a man that hath passed away his right to one man today, hath it not to pass tomorrow to another: and therefore the later promise passeth no right, but is null.

A covenant not to defend myself from force, by force, is always void. For (as I have showed before) no man can transfer, or lay down his right to save himself from death, wounds, and imprisonment, (the avoiding whereof is the only end of laying down any right) and therefore the promise of not resisting force, in no covenant transferreth any right; nor is obliging. For though a man may covenant thus, *unless I do so, or so, kill me*; he cannot covenant thus, *unless I do so, or so*, I will not resist you, when you come to kill me. For man by nature chooseth the lesser evil, which is danger of death in resisting; rather than the greater, which is certain and present death in not resisting. And this is granted to be true by all men, in that they lead criminals to execution, and prison, with armed men, notwithstanding that such criminals have consented to the law, by which they are condemned.

A covenant to accuse oneself, without assurance of pardon, is likewise invalid. For in the condition of nature, where every man is judge, there is no place for accusation: and in the civil state, the accusation is followed with punishment; which being force, a man is not obliged not to resist. The same is also true, of the accusation of those, by whose condemnation a man falls into misery; as of a father, wife, or benefactor. For the testimony of such an accuser, if it be not willingly given, is presumed to be corrupted by nature: and therefore not to be received: and where a man's testimony is not to be credited, he is not bound to give it. Also accusations upon torture, are not to be reputed as testimonies. For torture is to be used but as means of conjecture, and light, in the further examination and search of truth: and what is in that case confessed, tendeth to the ease of him that is tortured; not to the informing of the torturers: and therefore ought not to have the credit of a sufficient testimony: for whether he deliver himself by true, or false accusation, he does it by the right of preserving his own life.

The force of words, being (as I have formerly noted) too weak to hold men to the performance of their covenants; there are in man's nature, but two imaginable helps to strengthen it. And those are either a fear of the consequence of breaking their word; or a glory, or pride in appearing not to need to break it. This latter is a generosity too rarely found to be presumed on, especially in the pursuers of wealth, command, or sensual pleasure; which are the greatest part of mankind. The passion to be reckoned upon, is fear; whereof there be two very general objects: one, the power of spirits invisible; the other, the power of those men they shall therein offend. Of these two, though the former be the greater power, yet the fear of the latter is commonly the greater fear. The fear of the former is in every man, his own religion: which hath place in the nature of man before civil society. The latter hath not so; at least not place enough, to keep men to their promises; because in the condition of mere nature, the inequality of power is not discerned, but by the event of battle. So that before the time of civil society, or in the interruption thereof by war, there is nothing can strengthen a covenant of peace agreed on, against the temptations of avarice, ambition, lust, or other strong desire, but the fear of that invisible power, which they every one worship as God; and fear as a revenger of their perfidy. All therefore that can be done between two men not subject to civil power, is to put one another to swear by the God he feareth: which *swearing, or oath*, is a *form of speech, added to a promise; by which he that promiseth, signifieth, that unless he perform, he renounceth the mercy of his God, or calleth to him for vengeance on himself.* Such was the heathen form, *Let Jupiter kill me else, as I kill this beast*. So is our form, *I shall do thus, and thus, so help me God*. And this, with the rites and ceremonies, which every one useth in his own religion, that the fear of breaking faith might be the greater.

By this it appears, that an oath taken according to any other form, or rite, than his that sweareth, is in vain; and no oath: and that there is no swearing by any thing which the swearer thinks not God. For though men have sometimes used to swear by their kings, for fear, or flattery; yet they would have it thereby understood, they attributed to them divine honour. And that swearing unnecessarily by God, is but profaning of his name: and swearing by other things, as men do in common discourse, is not swearing, but an impious custom, gotten by too much vehemence of talking.

It appears also, that the oath adds nothing to the obligation. For a covenant, if lawful, binds in the sight of God, without the oath, as much as with it: if unlawful, bindeth not at all; though it be confirmed with an oath.

CHAPTER 15

Of other Laws of Nature

From that law of nature, by which we are obliged to transfer to another, such rights, as being retained, hinder the peace of mankind, there followeth a third; which is this, *that men perform their covenants made*: without which, covenants are in vain, and but empty words; and the right of all men to all things remaining, we are still in the condition of war.

And in this law of nature, consisteth the fountain and original of justice. For where no covenant hath preceded, there hath no right been transferred, and every man has right to every thing; and consequently, no action can be unjust. But when a covenant is made, then to break it is *unjust*: and the definition of injustice, is no other than *the not performance of covenant*. And whatsoever is not unjust, is *just*.

But because covenants of mutual trust, where there is a fear of not performance on either part, (as hath been said in the former chapter) are invalid; though the original of justice be the making of covenants; yet injustice actually there can be none, till the cause of such fear be taken away; which while men are in the natural condition of war, cannot be done. Therefore before the names of just and unjust can have place, there must be some coercive power, to compel men equally to the performance of their covenants, by the terror of some punishment, greater than the benefit they expect by the breach of their covenant; and to make good that propriety, which by mutual contract men acquire, in recompense of the universal right they abandon: and such power there is none before the erection of a commonwealth. And this is also to be gathered out of the ordinary definition of justice in the Schools: for they say, that *justice is the constant will of giving to every man his own*. And therefore where there is no *own*, that is, no propriety, there is no injustice; and where there is no coercive power erected, that is, where there is no commonwealth, there is no propriety; all men having right to all things: therefore where there is no commonwealth, there nothing is unjust. So that the nature of justice, consisteth in keeping of valid covenants: but the validity of covenants begins not but with the constitution of a civil power, sufficient to compel men to keep them: and then it is also that propriety begins.

The fool hath said in his heart, there is no such thing as justice; and sometimes also with his tongue; seriously alleging, that every man's conservation, and contentment, being committed to his own care, there could be no reason, why every man might not do what he thought conduced thereunto: and therefore also to make, or not make; keep, or not keep covenants, was not against reason, when it conduced to one's benefit. He does not therein deny, that there be covenants; and that they are sometimes broken, sometimes kept; and that such breach of them may be called injustice, and the observance of them justice: but he questioneth, whether injustice, taking away the fear of God, (for the same fool hath said in his heart there is no God) may not sometimes stand with that reason, which dictateth to every man his own good; and particularly then, when it conduceth to such a benefit, as shall put a man in a condition, to neglect not only the dispraise, and revilings, but also the power of other men. The kingdom of God is gotten by violence: but what if it could be gotten by unjust violence? Were it against reason so to get it, when it is impossible to receive hurt by it? And if it be not against reason, it is not against justice: or else justice is not to be approved for good. From such reasoning as this, successful wickedness hath obtained the name of virtue: and some that in all other things have disallowed the violation of faith; yet have allowed it, when it is for the getting of a kingdom. And the heathen that believed, that Saturn was deposed by his son Jupiter, believed nevertheless the same Jupiter to be the avenger of injustice: somewhat like to a piece of law in Coke's *Commentaries on Littleton*; where he says, if the right heir of the crown be attainted of treason; yet the crown shall descend to him, and *eo instante* the attainder be void: from which instances a man will be very prone to infer; that when the heir apparent of a kingdom, shall kill him that is in possession, though his father; you may call it injustice, or by what other name you will; yet it can never be against reason, seeing all the voluntary actions of men tend to the benefit of themselves; and those actions are most reasonable, that conduce most to their ends. This specious reasoning is nevertheless false.

For the question is not of promises mutual, where

there is no security of performance on either side; as when there is no civil power erected over the parties promising; for such promises are no covenants: but either where one of the parties has performed already; or where there is a power to make him perform; there is the question whether it be against reason, that is, against the benefit of the other to perform, or not. And I say it is not against reason. For the manifestation whereof, we are to consider; first, that when a man doth a thing, which notwithstanding any thing can be foreseen, and reckoned on, tendeth to his own destruction, howsoever some accident which he could not expect, arriving may turn it to his benefit; yet such events do not make it reasonably or wisely done. Secondly, that in a condition of war, wherein every man to every man, for want of a common power to keep them all in awe, is an enemy, there is no man can hope by his own strength, or wit, to defend himself from destruction, without the help of confederates; where every one expects the same defence by the confederation, that any one else does: and therefore he which declares he thinks it reason to deceive those that help him, can in reason expect no other means of safety, than what can be had from his own single power. He therefore that breaketh his covenant, and consequently declareth that he thinks he may with reason do so, cannot be received into any society, that unite themselves for peace and defence, but by the error of them that receive him; nor when he is received, be retained in it, without seeing the danger of their error; which errors a man cannot reasonably reckon upon as the means of his security: and therefore if he be left, or cast out of society, he perisheth; and if he live in society, it is by the errors of other men, which he could not foresee, nor reckon upon; and consequently against the reason of his preservation; and so, as all men that contribute not to his destruction, forbear him only out of ignorance of what is good for themselves.

As for the instance of gaining the secure and perpetual felicity of heaven, by any way; it is frivolous: there being but one way imaginable; and that is not breaking, but keeping of covenant.

And for the other instance of attaining sovereignty by rebellion; it is manifest, that though the event follow, yet because it cannot reasonably be expected, but rather the contrary; and because by gaining it so, others are taught to gain the same in like manner, the attempt thereof is against reason. Justice therefore, that is to say, keeping of covenant, is a rule of reason, by which we are forbidden to do any thing destructive to our life; and consequently a law of nature.

There be some that proceed further; and will not have the law of nature, to be those rules which conduce to the preservation of man's life on earth; but to the attaining of an eternal felicity after death; to which they think the breach of covenant may conduce; and consequently be just and reasonable; (such are they that think it a work of merit to kill, or depose, or rebel against, the sovereign power constituted over them by their own consent.) But because there is no natural knowledge of man's estate after death; much less of the reward that is then to be given to breach of faith; but only a belief grounded upon other men's saying that they know it supernaturally, or that they know those, that knew them, that knew others, that knew it supernaturally; breach of faith cannot be called a precept of reason, or nature.

Others, that allow for a law of nature, the keeping of faith, do nevertheless make exception of certain persons; as heretics, and such as use not to perform their covenant to others: and this also is against reason. For if any fault of a man, be sufficient to discharge our covenant made; the same ought in reason to have been sufficient to have hindered the making of it.

The names of just, and unjust, when they are attributed to men, signify one thing; and when they are attributed to actions, another. When they are attributed to men, they signify conformity, or inconformity of manners, to reason. But when they are attributed to actions, they signify the conformity, or inconformity to reason, not of manners, or manner of life, but of particular actions. A just man therefore, is he that taketh all the care he can, that his actions may be all just: and an unjust man, is he that neglecteth it. And such men are more often in our language styled by the names of righteous, and unrighteous; than just, and unjust; though the meaning be the same. Therefore a righteous man does not lose that title, by one, or a few unjust actions, that proceed from sudden passion, or mistake of things, or persons: nor does an unrighteous man lose his character, for such actions as he does, or forbears to do, for fear: because his will is not framed by the justice, but by the apparent benefit of what he is to do. That which gives to human actions the relish of justice, is a certain nobleness or gallantness of courage, (rarely found) by which a man scorns to be beholding for the contentment of his life, to fraud, or breach of promise. This justice of the manners, is that which is meant, where justice is called a virtue; and injustice a vice.

But the justice of actions denominates men, not

just, but *guiltless*: and the injustice of the same, (which is also called injury) gives them but the name of *guilty*.

Again, the injustice of manners, is the disposition, or aptitude to do injury; and is injustice before it proceed to act; and without supposing any individual person injured. But the injustice of an action, (that is to say injury) supposeth an individual person injured; namely him, to whom the covenant was made: and therefore many times the injury is received by one man, when the damage redoundeth to another. As when the master commandeth his servant to give money to a stranger; if it be not done, the injury is done to the master, whom he had before covenanted to obey; but the damage redoundeth to the stranger, to whom he had no obligation; and therefore could not injure him. And so also in commonwealths, private men may remit to one another their debts; but not robberies or other violences, whereby they are endamaged; because the detaining of debt, is an injury to themselves; but robbery and violence, are injuries to the person of the commonwealth.

Whatsoever is done to a man, conformable to his own will signified to the doer, is no injury to him. For if he that doeth it, hath not passed away his original right to do what he please, by some antecedent covenant, there is no breach of covenant; and therefore no injury done him. And if he have; then his will to have it done being signified, is a release of that covenant: and so again there is no injury done him.

Justice of actions, is by writers divided into *commutative*, and *distributive*: and the former they say consisteth in proportion arithmetical; the latter in proportion geometrical. Commutative therefore, they place in the equality of value of the things contracted for; and distributive, in the distribution of equal benefit, to men of equal merit. As if it were injustice to sell dearer than we buy; or to give more to a man than he merits. The value of all things contracted for, is measured by the appetite of the contractors: and therefore the just value, is that which they be contented to give. And merit (besides that which is by covenant, where the performance on one part, meriteth the performance of the other part, and falls under justice commutative, not distributive) is not due by justice; but is rewarded of grace only. And therefore this distinction, in the sense wherein it useth to be expounded, is not right. To speak properly, commutative justice, is the justice of a contractor; that is, a performance of covenant, in buying, and selling; hiring, and letting to hire; lending, and borrowing; exchanging, bartering, and other acts of contract.

And distributive justice, the justice of an arbitrator; that is to say, the act of defining what is just. Wherein, (being trusted by them that make him arbitrator,) if he perform his trust, he is said to distribute to every man his own: and this is indeed just distribution, and may be called (though improperly) distributive justice; but more properly equity; which also is a law of nature, as shall be shown in due place.

As justice dependeth on antecedent covenant; so does gratitude depend on antecedent grace; that is to say, antecedent free gift: and is the fourth law of nature; which may be conceived in this form, *that a man which receiveth benefit from another of mere grace, endeavour that he which giveth it, have no reasonable cause to repent him of his good will.* For no man giveth, but with intention of good to himself, because gift is voluntary; and of all voluntary acts, the object is to every man his own good; of which if men see they shall be frustrated, there will be no beginning of benevolence, or trust; nor consequently of mutual help; nor of reconciliation of one man to another; and therefore they are to remain still in the condition of *war*; which is contrary to the first and fundamental law of nature, which commandeth men to *seek peace*. The breach of this law, is called *ingratitude*; and hath the same relation to grace, that injustice hath to obligation by covenant.

A fifth law of nature, is complaisance; that is to say, *that every man strive to accommodate himself to the rest*. For the understanding whereof, we may consider, that there is in men's aptness to society, a diversity of nature, rising from their diversity of affections; not unlike to that we see in stones brought together for building of an edifice. For as that stone which by the asperity, and irregularity of figure, takes more room from others, than itself fills; and for the hardness, cannot be easily made plain, and thereby hindereth the building, is by the builders cast away as unprofitable, and troublesome: so also, a man that by asperity of nature, will strive to retain those things which to himself are superfluous, and to others necessary; and for the stubbornness of his passions, cannot be corrected, is to be left, or cast out of society, as cumbersome thereunto. For seeing every man, not only by right, but also by necessity of nature, is supposed to endeavour all he can, to obtain that which is necessary for his conservation; he that shall oppose himself against it, for things superfluous, is guilty of the war that thereupon is to follow; and therefore doth that, which is contrary to the fundamental law of nature, which commandeth *to seek peace*. The observers of this law, may be called sociable, (the Latins call them *commodi*) the contrary, *stubborn, insociable, froward, intractable.*

A sixth law of nature, is this, *that upon caution of the future time*, a man ought to pardon the offences past of them that repenting, desire it. For pardon, is nothing but granting of peace; which though granted to them that persevere in their hostility, be not peace, but fear; yet not granted to them that give caution of the future time, is sign of an aversion to peace; and therefore contrary to the law of nature.

A seventh is, *that in revenges*, (that is, retribution of evil for evil) *men look not at the greatness of the evil past, but the greatness of the good to follow*. Whereby we are forbidden to inflict punishment with any other design, than for correction of the offender, or direction of others. For this law is consequent to the next before it, that commandeth pardon, upon security of the future time. Besides, revenge without respect to the example, and profit to come, is a triumph, or glorying in the hurt of another, tending to no end; (for the end is always somewhat to come) and glorying to no end, is vain-glory, and contrary to reason; and to hurt without reason, tendeth to the introduction of war; which is against the law of nature; and is commonly styled by the name of *cruelty*.

And because all signs of hatred, or contempt, provoke to fight; insomuch as most men choose rather to hazard their life, than not to be revenged; we may in the eighth place, for a law of nature, set down this precept, *that no man by deed, word, countenance, or gesture, declare hatred, or contempt of another*. The breach of which law, is commonly called *contumely*.

The question who is the better man, has no place in the condition of mere nature; where, (as has been shown before) all men are equal. The inequality that now is, has been introduced by the laws civil. I know that Aristotle in the first book of his *Politics*, for a foundation of his doctrine, maketh men by nature, some more worthy to command, meaning the wiser sort (such as he thought himself to be for his philosophy) others to serve, (meaning those that had strong bodies, but were not philosophers as he) as if master and servant were not introduced by consent of men, but by difference of wit: which is not only against reason; but also against experience. For there are very few so foolish, that had not rather govern themselves, than be governed by others: nor when the wise in their own conceit, contend by force, with them who distrust their own wisdom, do they always, or often, or almost at any time, get the victory. If nature therefore have made men equal, that equality is to be acknowledged: or if nature have made men unequal; yet because men that think themselves equal, will not enter into conditions of peace, but upon equal terms, such equality must be admitted. And therefore for the ninth law of nature, I put this, *that every man acknowledge another for his equal by nature*. The breach of this precept is *pride*.

On this law, dependeth another, *that at the entrance into conditions of peace, no man require to reserve to himself any right, which he is not content should be reserved to every one of the rest*. As it is necessary for all men that seek peace, to lay down certain rights of nature; that is to say, not to have liberty to do all they list: so is it necessary for man's life, to retain some; as right to govern their own bodies; enjoy air, water, motion, ways to go from place to place; and all things else, without which a man cannot live, or not live well. If in this case, at the making of peace, men require for themselves, that which they would not have to be granted to others, they do contrary to the precedent law, that commandeth the acknowledgment of natural equality, and therefore also against the law of nature. The observers of this law, are those we call *modest*, and the breakers *arrogant* men. The Greeks call the violation of this law πλεονεξία; that is, a desire of more than their share.

Also if *a man be trusted to judge between man and man*, it is a precept of the law of nature, *that he deal equally between them*. For without that, the controversies of men cannot be determined but by war. He therefore that is partial in judgment, doth what in him lies, to deter men from the use of judges, and arbitrators; and consequently, (against the fundamental law of nature) is the cause of war.

The observance of this law, from the equal distribution to each man, of that which in reason belongeth to him, is called equity, and (as I have said before) distributive justice: the violation, *acception of persons*, προσωποληψία.

And from this followeth another law, *that such things as cannot be divided, be enjoyed in common, if it can be*; *and if the quantity of the thing permit, without stint*; *otherwise proportionably to the number of them that have right*. For otherwise the distribution is unequal, and contrary to equity.

But some things there be, that can neither be divided, nor enjoyed in common. Then, the law of nature, which prescribeth equity, requireth, *that the entire right*; *or else (making the use alternate) the first possession, be determined by lot.* For equal distribution, is of the law of nature; and other means of equal distribution cannot be imagined.

Of *lots* there be two sorts, *arbitrary*, and *natural*. Arbitrary, is that which is agreed on by the competitors: natural, is either *primogeniture*, (which the Greek calls κληρονομία, which signifies, *given by lot*) or *first seizure*.

And therefore those things which cannot be enjoyed in common, nor divided, ought to be adjudged to the first possessor; and in some cases to the first born, as acquired by lot.

It is also a law of nature, *that all men that mediate peace, be allowed safe conduct*. For the law that commandeth peace, as the *end*, commandeth intercession, as the *means*; and to intercession the means is safe conduct.

And because, though men be never so willing to observe these laws, there may nevertheless arise questions concerning a man's action; first, whether it were done, or not done; secondly (if done) whether against the law, or not against the law; the former whereof, is called a question *of fact*; the latter a question *of right*, therefore unless the parties to the question, covenant mutually to stand to the sentence of another, they are as far from peace as ever.

This other, to whose sentence they submit is called an arbitrator. And therefore it is of the law of nature, *that they that are at controversy, submit their right to the judgment of an arbitrator*.

And seeing every man is presumed to do all things in order to his own benefit, no man is a fit arbitrator in his own cause: and if he were never so fit; yet equity allowing to each party equal benefit, if one be admitted to be judge, the other is to be admitted also; and so the controversy, that is, the cause of war, remains, against the law of nature.

For the same reason no man in any cause ought to be received for arbitrator, to whom greater profit, or honour, or pleasure apparently ariseth out of the victory of one party, than of the other: for he hath taken (though an unavoidable bribe, yet) a bribe; and no man can be obliged to trust him. And thus also the controversy, and the condition of war remaineth, contrary to the law of nature.

And in a controversy *of fact*, the judge being to give no more credit to one, than to the other, (if there be no other arguments) must give credit to a third; or to a third and fourth; or more: for else the question is undecided, and left to force, contrary to the law of nature.

These are the laws of nature, dictating peace, for a means of the conservation of men in multitudes; and which only concern the doctrine of civil society. There be other things tending to the destruction of particular men; as drunkenness, and all other parts of intemperance; which may therefore also be reckoned amongst those things which the law of nature hath forbidden; but are not necessary to be mentioned, nor are pertinent enough to this place.

And though this may seem too subtle a deduction of the laws of nature, to be taken notice of by all men; whereof the most part are too busy in getting food, and the rest too negligent to understand; yet to leave all men inexcusable, they have been contracted into one easy sum, intelligible even to the meanest capacity; and that is, *Do not that to another, which thou wouldest not have done to thyself*; which sheweth him, that he has no more to do in learning the laws of nature, but, when weighing the actions of other men with his own, they seem too heavy, to put them into the other part of the balance, and his own into their place, that his own passions, and self-love, may add nothing to the weight; and then there is none of these laws of nature that will not appear unto him very reasonable.

The laws of nature oblige *in foro interno*; that is to say, they bind to a desire they should take place: but *in foro externo*; that is, to the putting them in act, not always. For he that should be modest, and tractable, and perform all he promises, in such time, and place, where no man else should do so, should but make himself a prey to others, and procure his own certain ruin, contrary to the ground of all laws of nature, which tend to nature's preservation. And again, he that having sufficient security, that others shall observe the same laws towards him, observes them not himself, seeketh not peace, but war; and consequently the destruction of his nature by violence.

And whatsoever laws bind *in foro interno*, may be broken, not only by a fact contrary to the law, but also by a fact according to it, in case a man think it contrary. For though his action in this case, be according to the law; yet his purpose was against the law; which where the obligation is *in foro interno*, is a breach.

The laws of nature are immutable and eternal; for injustice, ingratitude, arrogance, pride, iniquity, acception of persons, and the rest, can never be made lawful. For it can never be that war shall preserve life, and peace destroy it.

The same laws, because they oblige only to a desire, and endeavour, I mean an unfeigned and constant endeavour, are easy to be observed. For in that they require nothing but endeavour; he that endeavoureth their performance, fulfilleth them; and he that fulfilleth the law, is just.

And the science of them, is the true and only moral philosophy. For moral philosophy is nothing else but the science of what is *good*, and *evil*, in the conversation, and society of mankind. *Good*, and *evil*, are names that signify our appetites, and aversions; which in different tempers, customs, and doctrines of men, are different: and divers men differ not only in their judgment, on the senses of what is pleasant and unpleasant to the taste, smell, hearing, touch, and sight; but also of what is conformable, or disagreeable to reason, in the actions of common life. Nay, the same man, in divers times, differs from himself; and one time praiseth, that is, calleth good, what another time he dispraiseth, and calleth evil: from whence arise disputes, controversies, and at last war. And therefore so long as a man is in the condition of mere nature, (which is a condition of war) as private appetite is the measure of good, and evil: and consequently all men agree on this, that peace is good, and therefore also the way, or means of peace, which (as I have shewed before) are *justice*, *gratitude*, *modesty*, *equity*, *mercy*, and the rest of the laws of nature, are good; that is to say; *moral virtues*; and their contrary *vices*, evil. Now the science of virtue and vice, is moral philosophy; and therefore the true doctrine of the laws of nature, is the true moral philosophy. But the writers of moral philosophy, though they acknowledge the same virtues and vices; yet not seeing wherein consisted their goodness; nor that they come to be praised, as the means of peaceable, sociable, and comfortable living, place them in a mediocrity of passions: as if not the cause, but the degree of daring, made fortitude; or not the cause, but the quantity of a gift, made liberality.

These dictates of reason, men used to call by the name of laws; but improperly: for they are but conclusions, or theorems concerning what conduceth to the conservation and defence of themselves; whereas law, properly is the word of him that by right hath command over others. But yet if we consider the same theorems, as delivered in the world of God, that by right commandeth all things; then are they properly called laws.

CHAPTER 16

Of Persons, Authors, and Things Personated

A person, is he, *whose words or actions are considered, either as his own, or as representing the words or actions of another man, or of any other thing to whom they are attributed, whether truly or by fiction.*

When they are considered as his own, then is he called a *natural person*: and when they are considered as representing the words and actions of another, then is he a *feigned* or *artificial person.*

The word person is Latin: instead whereof the Greeks have πρόσωπον, which signifies the *face*, as *persona* in Latin signifies the *disguise*, or *outward appearance* of a man, counterfeited on the stage; and sometimes more particularly that part of it, which disguiseth the face, as a mask or vizard: and from the stage, hath been translated to any representer of speech and action, as well in tribunals, as theatres. So that a *person*, is the same that an *actor* is, both on the stage and in common conversation; and to *personate*, is to *act*, or *represent* himself, or another; and he that acteth another, is said to bear his person, or act in his name; (in which sense Cicero useth it where he says, *Unus sustineo tres personas; mei, adversarii, et judicis*, I bear three persons; my own, my adversary's, and the judge's) and is called in divers occasions, diversely; as a *representer*, or *representative*, a *lieutenant*, a *vicar*, an *attorney*, a *deputy*, a *procurator*, an *actor*, and the like.

Of persons artificial, some have their words and actions *owned* by those whom they represent. And then the person is the *actor*; and he that owneth his words and actions, is the author: in which case the actor acteth by authority. For that which in speaking of goods and possessions, is called an *owner*, and in Latin *dominus*, in Greek κύριος; speaking of actions, is called author. And as the right of possession, is called dominion; so the right of doing any action, is called authority and sometimes warrant. So that by authority, is always understood a right of doing any act: and *done by authority*, done by commission, or licence from him whose right it is.

From hence it followeth, that when the actor maketh a covenant by authority, he bindeth thereby the author, no less than if he had made it himself; and no less subjecteth him to all the consequences of the same. And therefore all that hath been said formerly, (chapter 14) of the nature of covenants between man and man in their natural capacity, is true also when they are made by their actors, representers, or procurators, that have authority from them, so far forth as is in their commission, but no further.

And therefore he that maketh a covenant with the

actor, or representer, not knowing the authority he hath, doth it at his own peril. For no man is obliged by a covenant, whereof he is not author; nor consequently by a covenant made against, or beside the authority he gave.

When the actor doth any thing against the law of nature by command of the author, if he be obliged by former covenant to obey him, not he, but the author breaketh the law of nature: for though the action be against the law of nature; yet it is not his: but contrarily, to refuse to do it, is against the law of nature, that forbiddeth breach of covenant.

And he that maketh a covenant with the author, by mediation of the actor, not knowing what authority he hath, but only takes his word; in case such authority be not made manifest unto him upon demand, is no longer obliged: for the covenant made with the author, is not valid, without his counter-assurance. But if he that so covenanteth, knew beforehand he was to expect no other assurance, than the actor's word; then is the covenant valid; because the actor in this case maketh himself the author. And therefore, as when the authority is evident, the covenant obligeth the author, not the actor; so when the authority is feigned, it obligeth the actor only; there being no author but himself.

There are few things, that are incapable of being represented by fiction. Inanimate things, as a church, an hospital, a bridge, may be personated by a rector, master, or overseer. But things inanimate, cannot be authors, nor therefore give authority to their actors: yet the actors may have authority to procure their maintenance, given them by those that are owners, or governors of those things. And therefore, such things cannot be personated, before there be some state of civil government.

Likewise children, fools, and madmen that have no use of reason, may be personated by guardians, or curators; but can be no authors (during that time) of any action done by them, longer than (when they shall recover the use of reason) they shall judge the same reasonable. Yet during the folly, he that hath right of governing them, may give authority to the guardian. But this again has no place but in a state civil, because before such estate, there is no dominion of persons.

An idol, or mere figment of the brain, may be personated; as were the gods of the heathen; which by such officers as the state appointed, were personated, and held possessions, and other goods, and rights, which men from time to time dedicated, and consecrated unto them. But idols cannot be authors: for an idol is nothing. The authority proceeded from the state: and therefore before introduction of civil government, the gods of the heathen could not be personated.

The true God may be personated. As he was: first, by Moses; who governed the Israelites (that were not his, but God's people) not in his own name, with *hoc dicit Moses*; but in God's name, with *hoc dicit Dominus*. Secondly, by the Son of man, his own Son, our blessed Saviour Jesus Christ, that came to reduce the Jews, and induce all nations into the kingdom of his father; not as of himself, but as sent from his father. And thirdly, by the Holy Ghost, or Comforter, speaking and working in the Apostles: which Holy Ghost, was a Comforter that came not of himself; but was sent, and proceeded from them both on the day of Pentecost.

A multitude of men, are made *one* person, when

they are by one man, or one person, represented; so that it be done with the consent of every one of that multitude in particular. For it is the *unity* of the representer, not the *unity* of the represented, that maketh the person *one*. And it is the representer that beareth the person, and but one person: and *unity*, cannot otherwise be understood in multitude.

And because the multitude naturally is not *one*, but *many*; they cannot be understood for one; but many authors, of every thing their representative saith or doth in their names; every man giving their common representer, authority from himself in particular; and owning all the actions the representer doth, in case they give him authority without stint: otherwise, when they limit him in what, and how far he shall represent them, none of them owneth more, than they gave him commission to act.

And if the representative consist of many men, the voice of the greater number, must be considered as the voice of them all. For if the lesser number pronounce (for example) in the affirmative, and the greater in the negative, there will be negatives more than enough to destroy the affirmatives; and thereby the excess of negatives, standing uncontradicted, are the only voice the representative hath.

And a representative of even number, especially when the number is not great, whereby the contradictory voices are oftentimes equal, is therefore oftentimes mute, and incapable of action. Yet in some cases contradictory voices equal in number, may determine a question; as in condemning, or absolving, equality of votes, even in that they condemn not, do absolve; but not on the contrary condemn, in that they absolve not. For when a cause is heard; not to condemn, is to absolve: but on the contrary, to say that not absolving is condemning, is not true. The like it is in a deliberation of executing presently, or deferring till another time: for when the voices are equal, the not decreeing execution, is a decree of dilation.

Or if the number be odd, as three or more, (men or assemblies) whereof every one has by a negative voice, authority to take away the effect of all the affirmative voices of the rest, this number is no representative; because by the diversity of opinions, and interests of men, it becomes oftentimes, and in cases of the greatest consequence, a mute person, and unapt, as for many things else, so for the government of a multitude, especially in time of war.

Of authors there be two sorts. The first simply so called; which I have before defined to be him, that owneth the action of another simply. The second is he, that owneth an action, or covenant of another conditionally; that is to say, he undertaketh to do it, if the other doth it not, at or before a certain time. And these authors conditional, are generally called sureties, in Latin, *fidejussores*, and *sponsores*; and particularly for debt, *praedes*; and for appearance before a judge, or magistrate, *vades*.

SECOND PART

Of Commonwealth

CHAPTER 17

Of the Causes, Generation, and Definition of a Commonwealth

The final cause, end, or design of men, (who naturally love liberty, and dominion over others) in the introduction of that restraint upon themselves, (in which we see them live in commonwealths) is the foresight of their own preservation, and of a more contented life thereby; that is to say, of getting themselves out from that miserable condition of war, which is necessarily consequent (as hath been shown, chapter 13) to the natural passions of men, when there is no visible power to keep them in awe, and tie them by fear of punishment to the performance of their covenants, and observation of those laws of nature set down in the fourteenth and fifteenth chapters.

For the laws of nature (as *justice*, *equity*, *modesty*, *mercy*, and (in sum) *doing to others, as we would be done to*) of themselves, without the terror of some power, to cause them to be observed, are contrary to our natural passions, that carry us to partiality, pride, revenge, and the like. And covenants, without the sword, are but words, and of no strength to secure a man at all. Therefore notwithstanding the laws of nature (which every one hath then kept, when he has the will to keep them, when he can do it safely) if there be no power erected, or not great enough for our security; every man will, and may lawfully rely on his own strength and art, for caution against all other men. And in all places, where men have lived by small families, to rob and spoil one another has been a trade, and so far from being reputed against the law of nature, that the greater spoils they gained, the greater was their honour; and men observed no other laws therein, but the laws of honour; that is, to abstain from cruelty, leaving to men their lives, and instruments of husbandry. And as small families did then; so now do cities and kingdoms which are but greater families (for their own security) enlarge their dominions, upon all pretences of danger, and fear of invasion, or assistance that may be given to invaders, and endeavour as much as they can, to subdue or weaken their neighbours, by open force and secret arts, for want of other caution, justly; and are remembered for it in after ages with honour.

Nor is it the joining together of a small number of men, that gives them this security; because in small numbers, small additions on the one side or the other, make the advantage of strength so great, as is sufficient to carry the victory; and therefore gives encouragement to an invasion. The multitude sufficient to confide in for our security, is not determined by any certain number, but by comparison with the enemy we fear; and is then sufficient, when the odds of the enemy is not of so visible and conspicuous moment, to determine the event of war, as to move him to attempt.

And be there never so great a multitude; yet if their actions be directed according to their particular judgments, and particular appetites, they can expect thereby no defence, nor protection, neither against a common enemy, nor against the injuries of one another. For being distracted in opinions concerning the best use and application of their strength, they do not help, but hinder one another; and reduce their strength by mutual opposition to nothing: whereby they are easily, not only subdued by a very few that agree together; but also when there is no common enemy, they make war upon each other, for their particular interests. For if we could suppose a great multitude of men to consent in the observation of justice, and other laws of nature, without a common power to keep them all in awe; we might as well suppose all mankind to do the same; and then there neither would be, nor need to be any civil government, or commonwealth at all; because there would be peace without subjection.

Nor is it enough for the security, which men desire should last all the time of their life, that they be governed, and directed by one judgment, for a limited time; as in one battle, or one war. For though they obtain a victory by their unanimous endeavour against a foreign enemy; yet afterwards, when either they have no common enemy, or he that by one part is held for an enemy, is by another part held for a friend, they must needs by the difference of their interests dissolve, and fall again into a war amongst themselves.

It is true, that certain living creatures, as bees and ants, live sociably one with another, (which are therefore by Aristotle numbered amongst political creatures) and yet have no other direction, than their particular judgments and appetites; nor speech, whereby one of them can signify to another, what he thinks expedient for the common benefit: and therefore some man may perhaps desire to know, why mankind cannot do the same. To which I answer, First, that men are continually in competition for honour and dignity, which these creatures are not; and consequently amongst men there ariseth on that ground, envy and hatred, and finally war; but amongst these not so.

Secondly, that amongst these creatures, the common good differeth not from the private; and being by nature inclined to their private, they procure thereby the common benefit. But man, whose joy consisteth in comparing himself with other men, can relish nothing but what is eminent.

Thirdly, that these creatures, having not (as man) the use of reason, do not see, nor think they see any fault, in the administration of their common business: whereas amongst men, there are very many, that think themselves wiser, and abler to govern the public, better than the rest; and these strive to reform and innovate, one this way, another that way; and thereby bring it into distraction and civil war.

Fourthly, that these creatures, though they have some use of voice, in making known to one another their desires, and other affections; yet they want that art of words, by which some men can represent to others, that which is good, in the likeness of evil; and evil, in the likeness of good; and augment, or diminish the apparent greatness of good and evil; discontenting men, and troubling their peace at their pleasure.

Fifthly, irrational creatures cannot distinguish between injury, and damage; and therefore as long as they be at ease, they are not offended with their fellows: whereas man is then most troublesome, when he is most at ease: for then it is that he loves to shew his wisdom, and control the actions of them that govern the commonwealth.

Lastly, the agreement of these creatures is natural;

that of men, is by covenant only, which is artificial: and therefore it is no wonder if there be somewhat else required (besides covenant) to make their agreement constant and lasting; which is a common power, to keep them in awe, and to direct their actions to the common benefit.

The only way to erect such a common power, as may be able to defend them from the invasion of foreigners, and the injuries of one another, and thereby to secure them in such sort, as that by their own industry, and by the fruits of the earth, they may nourish themselves and live contentedly; is, to confer all their power and strength upon one man, or upon one assembly of men, that may reduce all their wills, by plurality of voices, unto one will: which is as much as to say, to appoint one man, or assembly of men, to bear their person; and every one to own, and acknowledge himself to be author of whatsoever he that so beareth their person, shall act, or cause to be acted, in those things which concern the common peace and safety; and therein to submit their wills, every one to his will, and their judgments, to his judgment. This is more than consent, or concord; it is a real unity of them all, in one and the same person, made by covenant of every man with every man, in such manner, as if every man should say to every man, I authorize and give up my right of governing myself, to this man, or to this assembly of men, on this condition, that thou give up thy right to him, and authorize all his actions in like manner. This done, the multitude so united in one person, is called a commonwealth, in Latin *civitas*. This is the generation of that great Leviathan, or rather (to speak more reverently) of that Mortal God, to which we owe under the

Immortal God, our peace and defence. For by this authority, given him by every particular man in the commonwealth, he hath the use of so much power and strength conferred on him, that by terror thereof, he is enabled to conform the wills of them all, to peace at home, and mutual aid against their enemies abroad. And in him consisteth the essence of the commonwealth; which (to define it,) is *one person, of whose acts a great multitude, by mutual covenants one with another, have made themselves every one the author, to the end he may use the strength and means of them all, as he shall think expedient, for their peace and common defence.*

And he that carrieth this person, is called sovereign, and said to have sovereign power; and every one besides, his subject.

The attaining to this sovereign power, is by two ways. One, by natural force; as when a man maketh his children to submit themselves and their children to his government, as being able to destroy them if they refuse; or by war subdueth his enemies to his will, giving them their lives on that condition. The other, is when men agree amongst themselves, to submit to some man, or assembly of men, voluntarily, on confidence to be protected by him against all others. This latter, may be called a political commonwealth, or commonwealth by institution; and the former, a commonwealth by acquisition. And first, I shall speak of a commonwealth by institution.

CHAPTER 18

Of the Rights of Sovereigns by Institution

A commonwealth is said to be instituted, when a multitude of men do agree, and covenant, every one with every one, that to whatsoever man, or assembly of men, shall be given by the major part, the right to present the person of them all (that is to say, to be their representative) every one, as well he that voted for it, as he that voted against it, shall authorise all the actions and judgments, of that man, or assembly of men, in the same manner, as if they were his own, to the end, to live peaceably amongst themselves, and be protected against other men.

From this institution of a commonwealth are derived all the rights, and faculties of him, or them, on whom the sovereign power is conferred by the consent of the people assembled.

First, because they covenant, it is to be understood, they are not obliged by former covenant to any thing repugnant hereunto. And consequently they that have already instituted a commonwealth, being thereby bound by covenant, to own the actions and judgments of one, cannot lawfully make a new covenant, amongst themselves, to be obedient to any other, in any thing whatsoever, without his permission. And therefore, they that are subjects to a monarch, cannot without his leave cast off monarchy, and return to the confusion of a disunited multitude; nor transfer their person from him that beareth it, to another man, or other assembly of men: for they are bound, every man to every man, to own, and be reputed author of all, that he that already is their sovereign, shall do, and judge fit to be done: so that any one man dissenting, all the rest should break their covenant made to that man, which is injustice: and they have also every man given the sovereignty to him that beareth their person; and therefore if they depose him, they take from him that which is his own, and so again it is injustice. Besides, if he that attempteth to depose his sovereign, be killed, or punished by him for such attempt, he is author of his own punishment, as being by the institution, author of all his sovereign shall do: and because it is injustice for a man to do any thing, for which he may be punished by his own authority, he is also upon that title, unjust. And whereas some men have pretended for their disobedience to their sovereign, a new covenant, made, not with men, but with God; this also is unjust: for there is no covenant with God, but by mediation of somebody that representeth God's person; which none doth but God's lieutenant, who hath the sovereignty under God. But this pretence of covenant with God, is so evident a lie, even in the pretenders' own consciences, that it is not only an act of an unjust, but also of a vile, and unmanly disposition.

Secondly, because the right of bearing the person of them all, is given to him they make sovereign, by covenant only of one to another, and not of him to any of them; there can happen no breach of covenant on the part of the sovereign; and consequently none of his subjects, by any pretence of forfeiture, can be freed from his subjection. That he which is made sovereign maketh no covenant with his subjects beforehand, is manifest; because either he must make it with the whole multitude, as one party to the covenant; or he must make a several covenant with every man. With the whole, as one party, it is impossible; because as yet they are not one person: and if he make so many several covenants as there be men, those covenants after he hath the sovereignty are void; because what act soever can be pretended by any one of them for breach thereof, is the act both of himself, and of all the rest, because done in the person, and by the right of every one of them in particular. Besides, if any one or more of them, pretend a breach of the covenant made by the sovereign at his institution; and others, or one other of his subjects, or himself alone, pretend there was no such breach, there is in this case, no judge to decide the controversy; it returns therefore to the sword again; and every man recovereth the right of protecting himself by his own strength, contrary to the design they had in the institution. It is therefore in vain to grant sovereignty by way of precedent covenant. The opinion that any monarch receiveth his power by covenant, that is to say on condition, proceedeth from want of understanding this easy truth, that covenants being but words, and breath, have no force to oblige, contain, constrain, or protect any man, but what it has from the public sword; that is, from the untied hands of that man, or assembly of men that hath the sovereignty, and whose actions are avouched by them all, and performed by the strength of them all, in him united. But when an assembly of men is made sovereign; then no man imagineth any such covenant to have passed in the institution; for no man is so dull as to say, for example, the people of Rome, made a covenant with the Romans, to hold the sovereignty on such or such conditions; which not performed, the Romans might lawfully depose the

Roman people. That men see not the reason to be alike in a monarchy, and in a popular government, proceedeth from the ambition of some, that are kinder to the government of an assembly, whereof they may hope to participate, than of monarchy, which they despair to enjoy.

Thirdly, because the major part hath by consenting voices declared a sovereign; he that dissented must now consent with the rest; that is, be contented to avow all the actions he shall do, or else justly be destroyed by the rest. For if he voluntarily entered into the congregation of them that were assembled, he sufficiently declared thereby his will (and therefore tacitly covenanted) to stand to what the major part should ordain: and therefore if he refuse to stand thereto, or make protestation against any of their decrees, he does contrary to his covenant, and therefore unjustly. And whether he be of the congregation, or not; and whether his consent be asked, or not, he must either submit to their decrees, or be left in the condition of war he was in before; wherein he might without injustice be destroyed by any man whatsoever.

Fourthly, because every subject is by this institution author of all the actions, and judgments of the sovereign instituted; it follows, that whatsoever he doth, it can be no injury to any of his subjects; nor ought he to be by any of them accused of injustice. For he that doth anything by authority from another, doth therein no injury to him by whose authority he acteth: but by this institution of a commonwealth, every particular man is author of all the sovereign doth: and consequently he that complaineth of injury from his sovereign, complaineth of that whereof he himself is author; and therefore ought not to accuse any man but himself; no nor himself of injury; because to do injury to one's self, is impossible. It is true that they that have sovereign power, may commit iniquity; but not injustice, or injury in the proper signification.

Fifthly, and consequently to that which was said last, no man that hath sovereign power can justly be put to death, or otherwise in any manner by his subjects punished. For seeing every subject is author of the actions of his sovereign; he punisheth another, for the actions committed by himself.

And because the end of this institution, is the peace and defence of them all; and whosoever has right to the end, has right to the means; it belongeth of right, to whatsoever man, or assembly that hath the sovereignty, to be judge both of the means of peace and defence; and also of the hindrances, and disturbances of the same; and to do whatsoever he shall think necessary to be done, both beforehand, for the preserving of peace and security, by prevention of discord at home, and hostility from abroad; and, when peace and security are lost, for the recovery of the same. And therefore,

Sixthly, it is annexed to the sovereignty, to be judge of what opinions and doctrines are averse, and what conducing to peace; and consequently, on what occasions, how far, and what, men are to be trusted withal, in speaking to multitudes of people; and who shall examine the doctrines of all books before they be published. For the actions of men proceed from their opinions; and in the well-governing of opinions, consisteth the well-governing of men's actions, in order to their peace, and concord. And though in matter of doctrine, nothing ought to be regarded but the truth; yet this is not repugnant to regulating the same by peace. For doctrine repugnant to peace, can no more be true, than peace and concord can be against the law of nature. It is true, that in a commonwealth, where by the negligence or unskilfulness of governors, and teachers, false doctrines are by time generally received; the contrary truths may be generally offensive: Yet the most sudden, and rough bustling in of a new truth, that can be, does never break the peace, but only sometimes awake the war. For those men that are so remissly governed, that they dare take up arms to defend, or introduce an opinion, are still in war; and their condition not peace, but only a cessation of arms for fear of one another; and they live as it were, in the precincts of battle continually. It belongth therefore to him that hath the sovereign power, to be judge, or constitute all judges of opinions and doctrines, as a thing necessary to peace; thereby to prevent discord and civil war.

Seventhly, is annexed to the sovereignty, the whole power of prescribing the rules, whereby every man may know, what goods he may enjoy, and what actions he may do, without being molested by any of his fellow-subjects: and this is it men call *propriety*. For before constitution of sovereign power (as hath already been shown) all men had right to all things; which necessarily causeth war: and therefore this propriety, being necessary to peace, and depending on sovereign power, is the act of that power, in order to the public peace. These rules of propriety (or *meum* and *tuum*) and of *good, evil, lawful, and unlawful* in the actions of subjects, are the civil laws, that is to say, the laws of each commonwealth in particular; though the name of civil law be now restrained to the ancient civil laws of the city of Rome; which being the head of a great part of the world, her laws at that time were in these parts the civil law.

Eighthly, is annexed to the sovereignty, the right of judicature; that is to say, of hearing and deciding all controversies, which may arise concerning law, either civil, or natural, or concerning fact. For without the decision of controversies, there is no protection of one subject, against the injuries of another; the laws concerning *meum* and *tuum* are in vain; and to every man remaineth, from the natural and necessary appetite of his own conservation, the right of protecting himself by his private strength, which is the condition of war, and contrary to the end for which every commonwealth is instituted.

Ninthly, is annexed to the sovereignty, the right of making war, and peace with other nations, and commonwealths; that is to say, of judging when it is for the public good, and how great forces are to be assembled, armed, and paid for that end; and to levy money upon the subjects, to defray the expenses thereof. For the power by which the people are to be defended, consisteth in their armies; and the strength of an army, in the union of their strength under one command; which command the sovereign instituted, therefore hath, because the command of the *militia*, without other institution, maketh him that hath it sovereign. And therefore whosoever is made general of an army, he that hath the sovereign power is always generalissimo.

Tenthly, is annexed to the sovereignty, the choosing of all counsellors, ministers, magistrates, and officers, both in peace, and war. For seeing the sovereign is charged with the end, which is the common peace and defence; he is understood to have power to use such means, as he shall think most fit for his discharge.

Eleventhly, to the sovereign is committed the power of rewarding with riches, or honour; and of punishing with corporal, or pecuniary punishment, or with ignominy every subject according to the law he hath formerly made; or if there be no law made, according as he shall judge most to conduce to the encouraging of men to serve the commonwealth, or deterring of them from doing disservice to the same.

Lastly, considering what value men are naturally apt to set upon themselves; what respect they look for from others; and how little they value other men; from whence continually arise amongst them, emulation, quarrels, factions, and at last war, to the destroying of one another, and diminution of their strength against a common enemy; it is necessary that there be laws of honour, and a public rate of the worth of such men as have deserved, or are able to deserve well of the commonwealth; and that there be force in the hands of some or other, to put those laws in execution. But it hath already been shown, that not only the whole militia, or forces of the commonwealth, but also the judicature of all controversies, is annexed to the sovereignty. To the sovereign therefore it belongeth also to give titles of honour; and to appoint what order of place, and dignity, each man shall hold; and what signs of respect, in public or private meetings, they shall give to one another.

These are the rights, which make the essence of sovereignty, and which are the marks, whereby a man may discern in what man, or assembly of men, the sovereign power is placed, and resideth. For these are incommunicable, and inseparable. The power to coin money; to dispose of the estate and persons of infant heirs; to have preemption in markets; and all other statute prerogatives, may be transferred by the sovereign; any yet the power to protect his subjects be retained. But if he transfer the militia, he retains the judicature in vain, for want of execution of the laws: or if he grant away the power of raising money, the militia is in vain: or if he give away the government of doctrines, men will be frighted into rebellion with the fear of spirits. And so if we consider any one of the said rights, we shall presently see, that the holding of all the rest, will produce no effect, in the conservation of peace and justice, the end for which all commonwealths are instituted. And this division is it, whereof it is said, *a kingdom divided in itself cannot stand*. For unless this division precede, division into opposite armies can never happen. If there had not first been an opinion received of the greatest part of England, that these powers were divided between the King, and the Lords and the House of Commons, the people had never been divided and fallen into this civil war; first between those that disagreed in politics; and after between the dissenters about the liberty of religion; which have so instructed men in this point of sovereign right, that there be few now (in England) that do not see, that these rights are inseparable, and will be so generally acknowledged at the next return of peace; and so continue, till their miseries are forgotten; and no longer, except the vulgar be better taught than they have hitherto been.

And because they are essential and inseparable rights, it follows necessarily, that in whatsoever words any of them seem to be granted away, yet if the sovereign power itself be not in direct terms renounced, and the name of sovereign no more given by the grantees to him that grants them, the grant is void: for when he has granted all he can, if we grant back the sovereignty, all is restored, as inseparably annexed thereunto.

This great authority being indivisible, and inseparably annexed to the sovereignty, there is little ground for the opinion of them, that say of sovereign kings, though they be *singulis majores*, of greater power than every one of their subjects, yet they be *universis minores*, of less power than them all together. For if by *all together*, they mean not the collective body as one person, then *all together*, and *every one*, signify the same; and the speech is absurd. But if by *all together*, they understand them as one person (which person the sovereign bears) then the power of all together, is the same with the sovereign's power; and so again the speech is absurd: which absurdity they see well enough, when the sovereignty is in an assembly of the people; but in a monarch they see it not; and yet the power of sovereignty is the same in whomsoever it be placed.

And as the power, so also the honour of the sovereign, ought to be greater, than that of any, or all the subjects. For in the sovereignty is the fountain of honour. The dignities of lord, earl, duke, and prince are his creatures. As in the presence of the master, the servants are equal, and without any honour at all; so are the subjects, in the presence of the sovereign. And though they shine some more, some less, when they are out of his sight; yet in his presence, they shine no more than the stars in the presence of the sun.

But a man may here object, that the condition of

subjects is very miserable, as being obnoxious to the lusts, and other irregular passions of him or them that have so unlimited a power in their hands. And commonly they that live under a monarch, think it the fault of monarchy; and they that live under the government of democracy, or other sovereign assembly, attribute all the inconvenience to that form of commonwealth; whereas the power in all forms, if they be perfect enough to protect them, is the same; not considering that the state of man can never be without some incommodity or other; and that the greatest, that in any form of government can possibly happen to the people in general, is scarce sensible, in respect of the miseries, and horrible calamities, that accompany a civil war; or that dissolute condition of masterless men, without subjection to laws, and a coercive power to tie their hands from rapine and revenge: nor considering that the greatest pressure of sovereign governors, proceedeth not from any delight or profit they can expect in the damage, or weakening of their subjects, in whose vigour consisteth their own strength and glory; but in the restiveness of themselves, that unwillingly contributing to their own defence, make it necessary for their governors to draw from them what they can in time of peace, that they may have means on any emergent occasion, or sudden need, to resist, or take advantage on their enemies. For all men are by nature provided of notable multiplying glasses (that is, their passions and self-love) through which, every little payment appeareth a great grievance; but are destitute of those prospective glasses, (namely moral and civil science) to see afar off the miseries that hang over them, and cannot without such payments be avoided.

CHAPTER 19

Of the several Kinds of Commonwealth by Institution, and of Succession to the Sovereign Power

The difference of Commonwealths, consisteth in the difference of the sovereign, or the person representative of all and every one of the multitude. And because the sovereignty is either in one man, or in an assembly of more than one; and into that assembly either every man hath right to enter, or not every one, but certain men distinguished from the rest; it is manifest, there can be but three kinds of Commonwealth. For the representative must needs be one man, or more: and if more, then it is the assembly of all, or but of a part. When the representative is one man, then is the Commonwealth a monarchy: when an assembly of all that will come together, then it is a democracy, or popular Commonwealth: when an assembly of a part only, then it is called an Aristocracy. Other kind of Commonwealth there can be none: for either one, or more, or all, must have the sovereign power (which I have shown to be indivisible) entire.

There be other names of government, in the histories, and books of policy; as *tyranny*, and *oligarchy*: but they are not the names of other forms of government, but of the same forms misliked. For they that are discontented under *monarchy*, call it *tyranny*; and they that are displeased with *aristocracy*, call it *oligarchy*: so also, they which find themselves grieved under a *democracy*, call it *anarchy*, (which signifies want of government) and yet I think no man believes, that want of government, is any new kind of government: nor by the same reason ought they to believe, that the government is of one kind, when they like it, and another, when they mislike it, or are oppressed by the governors.

It is manifest, that men who are in absolute liberty, may, if they please, give authority to one man, to represent them every one; as well as give such authority to any assembly of men whatsoever; and consequently may subject themselves, if they think good, to a monarch, as absolutely as to any other representative. Therefore, where there is already erected a sovereign power, there can be no other representative of the same people, but only to certain particular ends, by the sovereign limited. For that were to erect two sovereigns; and every man to have his person represented by two actors, that by opposing one another, must needs divide that power, which (if men will live in peace) is indivisible; and thereby reduce the multitude into the condition of war, contrary to the end for which all sovereignty is instituted. And therefore as it is absurd, to think that a sovereign assembly, inviting the people of their dominion, to send up their deputies, with power to make known their advice, or desires, should therefore hold such deputies, rather than themselves, for the absolute representatives of the people: so it is absurd also, to think the same in a monarchy. And I know not how this so manifest a truth, should of late be so little observed; that in a monarchy, he that had the sovereignty from a descent of six hundred years, was alone called sovereign, had the title of Majesty from every one of his subjects, and was unquestionably taken by them for their king, was notwithstanding never considered as their representative; that name without contradiction passing for the title of those men, which at his command were sent up by the people to carry their petitions, and give him (if he permitted it) their advice. Which may serve as an admonition, for those that are the true, and absolute representative of a people, to instruct men in the nature of that office, and to take heed how they admit of any other general representation upon any occasion whatsoever, if they mean to discharge the trust committed to them.

The difference between these three kinds of Commonwealth, consisteth not in the difference of power; but in the difference of convenience, or aptitude to produce the peace and security of the people; for which end they were instituted. And to compare monarchy with the other two, we may observe; first, that whosoever beareth the person of the people, or is one of that assembly that bears it, beareth also his own natural person. And though he be careful in his politic person to procure the common interest; yet he is more, or no less careful to procure the private good of himself, his family, kindred, and friends; and for the most part, if the public interest chance to cross the private, he prefers the private: for the passions of men, are commonly more potent than their reason. From whence it follows, that where the public and private interest are most closely united, there is the public most advanced. Now in monarchy, the private interest is the same with the public. The riches, power, and honour of a monarch arise only from the riches, strength, and reputation of his subjects. For no king can be rich, nor glorious, nor secure, whose subjects are either poor, or contemptible, or too weak through want, or dissension, to maintain a war against their enemies: whereas in a democracy, or aristocracy, the public prosperity confers not so much to the private fortune of one that is corrupt, or ambitious, as doth many times a perfidious advice, a treacherous action, or a civil war.

Secondly, that a monarch receiveth counsel of whom, when, and where he pleaseth; and consequently may hear the opinion of men versed in the matter about which he deliberates, of what rank or quality soever, and as long before the time of action, and with as much secrecy, as he will. But when a sovereign assembly has need of counsel, none are admitted but such as have a right thereto from the beginning; which for the most part are of those who have been versed more in the acquisition of wealth than of knowledge; and are to give their advice in long discourses, which may, and do commonly excite men to action, but not govern them in it. For the *understanding* is by the flame of the passions, never enlightened, but dazzled. Nor is there any place, or time, wherein an assembly can receive counsel with secrecy, because of their own multitude.

Thirdly, that the resolutions of a monarch, are subject to no other inconstancy, than that of human nature; but in assemblies, besides that of nature, there ariseth an inconstancy from the number. For the absence of a few, that would have the resolution once taken, continue firm, (which may happen by security, negligence, or private impediments) or the diligent appearance of a few of the contrary opinion, undoes today, all that was concluded yesterday.

Fourthly, that a monarch cannot disagree with himself, out of envy or interest; but an assembly may; and that to such a height, as may produce a civil war.

Fifthly, that in monarchy there is this inconvenience; that any subject, by the power of one man, for the enriching of a favourite or flatterer, may be deprived of all he possesseth; which I confess is a great and inevitable inconvenience. But the same may as well happen, where the sovereign power is in an assembly: for their power is the same; and they are as subject to evil counsel, and to be seduced by orators, as a monarch by flatterers; and becoming one another's flatterers, serve one another's covetousness and ambition by turns.

And whereas the favourites of monarchs are few, and they have none else to advance but their own kindred; the favourites of an assembly are many; and the kindred much more numerous, than of any monarch. Besides, there is no favourite of a monarch, which cannot as well succour his friends, as hurt his enemies: but orators, that is to say, favourites of sovereign assemblies, though they have great power to hurt, have little to save. For to accuse, requires less eloquence (such is man's nature) than to excuse; and condemnation than absolution more resembles justice.

Sixthly, that it is an inconvenience in monarchy, that the sovereignty may descend upon an infant, or one that cannot discern between good and evil: and consisteth in this, that the use of his power must be in the hand of another man, or of some assembly of men, which are to govern by his right, and in his name; as curators, and protectors of his person and authority. But to say there is inconvenience, in putting the use of the sovereign power into the hand of a man, or an assembly of men, is to say that all government is more inconvenient, than confusion, and civil war. And therefore all the danger that can be pretended, must arise from the contention of those, that for an office of so great honour, and profit, may become competitors. To make it appear, that this inconvenience, proceedeth not from that form of government we call monarchy, we are to consider, that the precedent monarch, hath appointed who shall have the tuition of his infant successor, either expressly by testament, or tacitly, by not controlling the custom in that case received: and then such inconvenience (if it happen) is to be attributed, not to the monarchy, but to the ambition and injustice of the subjects; which in all kinds of government, where the people are not well instructed in their duty, and the rights of sovereignty, is the same. Or else the precedent monarch hath not at all taken order for such tuition; and then the law of nature hath provided this sufficient rule, that the tuition shall be in him, that hath by nature most interest in the preservation of the authority of the infant, and to whom least benefit can accrue by his death, or diminution. For seeing every man by nature seeketh his own benefit, and promotion; to put an infant into the power of those, that can promote themselves by his destruction, or damage, is not tuition, but treachery. So that sufficient provision being taken, against all just quarrel, about the government under a child, if any contention arise to the disturbance of the public peace, it is not to be attributed to the form of monarchy, but to the ambition of subjects, and ignorance of their duty. On the other side, there is no great Commonwealth, the sovereignty whereof is in a great assembly, which is not, as to consultations of peace, and war, and making of laws, in the same condition, as if the government were in a child. For as a child wants the judgment to dissent from counsel given him, and is thereby necessitated to take the advice of them, or him, to whom he is committed: so an assembly wanteth the liberty, to dissent from the counsel of the major part, be it good or bad. And as a child has need of a tutor, or protector, to preserve his person, and authority: so also (in great Commonwealths) the sovereign assembly, in all great dangers and troubles, have need of *custodes libertatis*; that is of dictators, or protectors of their authority; which are as much as temporary monarchs; to whom for a time, they may commit the entire exercise of their power; and have (at the end of that time) been oftener deprived thereof, than infant kings, by their protectors, regents, or any other tutors.

Though the kinds of sovereignty be, as I have now shown, but three; that is to say, monarchy, where one man has it; or democracy, where the general assembly of subjects hath it; or aristocracy, where it is in an assembly of certain persons nominated, or otherwise distinguished from the rest: yet he that shall consider the particular Commonwealths that have been, and are in the world, will not perhaps easily reduce them to three, and may thereby be inclined to think there be other forms, arising from these mingled together. As for example, elective kingdoms; where kings have the sovereign power put into their hands for a time; or kingdoms, wherein the king hath a power limited: which governments, are nevertheless by most writers called monarchy. Likewise if a popular, or aristocratical Commonwealth, subdue an enemy's country, and govern the same, by a president, procurator, or other magistrate; this may seem perhaps at first sight, to be a democratical, or aristocratical government. But it is not so. For elective kings, are not sovereigns, but ministers of the sovereign; nor limited kings sovereigns, but ministers of them that have the sovereign power: nor are those provinces which are in subjection to a democracy, or aristocracy of another Commonwealth, democratically or aristocratically governed, but monarchically.

And first, concerning an elective king, whose power is limited to his life, as it is in many places of Christendom at this day; or to certain years or months, as the dictator's power amongst the Romans; if he have right to appoint his successor, he is no more elective but hereditary. But if he have no power to elect his successor, then there is some other man, or assembly known, which after his decease may elect anew, or else the Commonwealth dieth, and dissolveth with him, and returneth to the condition of war. If it be known who have the power to give the sovereignty after his death, it is known also that the sovereignty was in them before: for none have right to give that which they have not right to possess, and keep to themselves, if they think good. But if there be none that can give the sovereignty, after the decease of him that was first elected; then has he power, nay he is obliged by the law of nature, to provide, by establishing his successor, to keep those that had trusted him with the government, from relapsing into the miserable condition of civil war. And consequently he was, when elected, a sovereign absolute.

Secondly, that king whose power is limited, is not superior to him or them that have the power to limit it; and he that is not superior, is not supreme; that is to say not sovereign. The sovereignty therefore was always in that assembly which had the right to limit him; and by consequence the government not monarchy, but either democracy or aristocracy; as of old time in Sparta, where the kings had a privilege to lead their armies, but the sovereignty was in the Ephori.

Thirdly, whereas heretofore the Roman people governed the land of Judea (for example) by a president; yet was not Judea therefore a democracy; because they were not governed by any assembly, into the which any of them had right to enter; nor an aristocracy; because they were not governed by any assembly, into which any man could enter by their election: but they were governed by one person, which though as to the people of Rome was an assembly of the people, or democracy; yet as to the people of Judea, which had no right at all of participating in the government, was a monarch. For though where the people are governed by an assembly, chosen by themselves out of their own number, the government is called a democracy, or aristocracy; yet when they are governed by an assembly, not of their own choosing, 'tis a monarchy; not of *one* man, over another man; but of one people, over another people.

Of all these forms of government, the matter being mortal, so that not only monarchs, but also whole assemblies die, it is necessary for the conservation of the peace of men, that as there was order taken for an artificial man, so there be order also taken, for an artificial eternity of life; without which, men that are governed by an assembly, should return into the condition of war in every age; and they that are governed by one man, as soon as their governor dieth. This artificial eternity, is that which men call the right of *succession*.

There is no perfect form of government, where the disposing of the succession is not in the present sovereign. For if it be in any other particular man, or private assembly, it is in a person subject, and may be assumed by the sovereign at his pleasure; and consequently the right is in himself. And if it be in no particular man, but left to a new choice; then is the Commonwealth dissolved; and the right is in him that can get it; contrary to the intention of them that did institute the Commonwealth, for their perpetual, and not temporary security.

In a democracy, the whole assembly cannot fail, unless the multitude that are to be governed fail. And therefore questions of the right of succession, have in that form of government no place at all.

In an aristocracy, when any of the assembly dieth, the election of another into his room belongeth to the assembly, as the sovereign, to whom belongeth the choosing of all counsellors, and officers. For that which the representative doth, as actor, every one of the subjects doth, as author. And though the sovereign assembly may give power to others, to elect new men, for supply of their court; yet it is still by their authority that the election is made; and by the same it may (when the public shall require it) be recalled.

The greatest difficulty about the right of succession, is in monarchy: and the difficulty ariseth from this, that at first sight, it is not manifest who is to appoint the successor; nor many times, who it is whom he hath appointed. For in both these cases, there is required a more exact ratiocination, than every man is accustomed to use. As to the question, who shall appoint the successor, of a monarch that hath the sovereign authority; that is to say, who shall determine of the right of inheritance, (for elective kings and princes have not the sovereign power in propriety, but in use only) we are to consider, that either he that is in possession, has right to dispose of the succession, or else that right is again in the dissolved multitude. For the death of him that hath the sovereign power in propriety, leaves the multitude without any sovereign at all; that is, without any representative in whom they should be united, and be capable of doing any one action at all: and therefore they are incapable of election of any new monarch; every man having equal right to submit himself to such as he thinks best able to protect him; or if he can, protect himself by his own sword; which is a return to confusion, and to the condition of a war of every man against every man, contrary to the end for which monarchy had its first institution. Therefore it is manifest, that by the institution of monarchy, the disposing of the successor, is always left to the judgment and will of the present possessor.

And for the question (which may arise sometimes) who it is that the monarch in possession, hath designed to the succession and inheritance of his power; it is determined by his express words, and testament; or by other tacit signs sufficient.

By express words, or testament, when it is declared by him in his lifetime, *viva voce*, or by writing; as the first emperors of Rome declared who should be their heirs. For the word heir does not of itself imply the children, or nearest kindred of a man; but whomsoever a man shall any way declare, he would have to succeed him in his estate. If therefore a monarch declare expressly, that such a man shall be his heir, either by word or writing, then is that man immediately after the decease of his predecessor, invested in the right of being monarch.

But where testament, and express words are wanting, other natural signs of the will are to be followed: whereof the one is custom. And therefore where the custom is, that the next of kindred absolutely succeedeth, there also the next of kindred hath right to the succession; for that, if the will of him that was in possession had been otherwise, he might easily have declared the same in his life-time. And likewise where the custom is, that the next of the male kindred succeedeth, there also the right of succession is in the next of the kindred male, for the same reason. And so it is if the custom were to advance the female. For whatsoever custom a man may by a word control, and does not, it is a natural sign he would have that custom stand.

But where neither custom, nor testament hath preceded, there it is to be understood, first, that a monarch's will is, that the government remain monarchical; because he hath approved that government in himself. Secondly, that a child of his own, male or female, be preferred before any other; because men are presumed to be more inclined by nature, to advance their own children, than the children of other men; and of their own, rather a male than a female; because men, are naturally fitter than women, for actions of labour and danger. Thirdly, where his own issue faileth, rather a brother than a stranger; and so still the nearer in blood, rather than the more remote; because it is always presumed that the nearer of kin, is the nearer in affection; and 'tis evident that a man receives always, by reflection, the most honour from the greatness of his nearest kindred.

But if it be lawful for a monarch to dispose of the succession by words of contract, or testament, men may perhaps object a great inconvenience: for he may sell, or give his right of governing to a stranger; which, because strangers (that is, men not used to live under the same government, nor speaking the same language) do commonly undervalue one another, may turn to the oppression of his subjects; which is indeed a great inconvenience: but it proceedeth not necessarily from the subjection to a stranger's government, but from the unskilfulness of the governors, ignorant of the true rules of politics. And therefore the Romans when they had subdued many nations, to make their government digestible, were wont to take away that grievance, as much as they thought necessary, by giving sometimes to whole nations, and sometimes to principal men of every nation they conquered, not only the privileges, but also the name of Romans; and took many of them into the senate, and offices of charge, even in the Roman city. And this was it our most wise king James aimed at, in endeavouring the union of his two realms of England and Scotland. Which if he could have obtained, had in all likelihood prevented the civil wars, which make both those kingdoms, at this present, miserable. It is not therefore any injury to the people, for a monarch to dispose of the succession by will; though by the fault of many princes, it hath been sometimes found inconvenient. Of the lawfulness of it, this also is an argument, that whatsoever inconvenience can arrive by giving a kingdom to a stranger, may arrive also by so marrying with strangers, as the right of succession may descend upon them: yet this by all men is accounted lawful.

CHAPTER 20

Of Dominion Paternal, and Despotical

A commonwealth *by acquisition*, is that, where the sovereign power is acquired by force; and it is acquired by force, when men singly, or many together by plurality of voices, for fear of death or bonds, do authorise all the actions of that man, or assembly, that hath their lives and liberty in his power.

And this kind of dominion, or sovereignty, differeth from sovereignty by institution, only in this, that men who choose their sovereign, do it for fear of one another, and not of him whom they institute: but in this case, they subject themselves to him they are afraid of. In both cases they do it for fear: which is to be noted by them, that hold all such covenants, as proceed from fear of death or violence, void: which if it were true, no man, in any kind of Commonwealth, could be obliged to obedience. It is true, that in a Commonwealth once instituted, or acquired, promises proceeding from fear of death, or violence, are no covenants, nor obliging, when the thing promised is contrary to the laws; but the reason is not, because it was made upon fear, but because he that promiseth, hath no right in the thing promised. Also, when he may lawfully perform, and doth not, it is not the invalidity of the covenant, that absolveth him, but the sentence of the sovereign. Otherwise, whensoever a man lawfully promiseth, he unlawfully breaketh: but when the sovereign, who is the actor, acquitteth him, then he is acquitted by him that extorted the promise, as by the author of such absolution.

But the rights and consequences of sovereignty, are the same in both. His power cannot, without his consent, be transferred to another: he cannot forfeit it: he cannot be accused by any of his subjects, of injury: he cannot be punished by them: he is judge of what is necessary for peace; and judge of doctrines: he is sole legislator; and supreme judge of controversies; and of the times, and occasions of war, and peace: to him it belongeth to choose magistrates, counsellors, commanders, and all other officers and ministers; and to determine of rewards and punishments, honour and order. The reasons whereof, are the same which are alleged in the precedent chapter, for the same rights, and consequences of sovereignty by institution.

Dominion is acquired two ways; by generation, and by conquest. The right of dominion by generation, is that, which the parent hath over his children; and is called Paternal. And is not so derived from the generation, as if therefore the parent had dominion over his child because he begat him; but from the child's consent, either express, or by other sufficient arguments declared. For as to the generation, God hath ordained to man a helper; and there be always two that are equally parents: the dominion therefore over the child, should belong equally to both; and he be equally subject to both, which is impossible; for no man can obey two masters. And whereas some have attributed the dominion to the man only, as being of the more excellent sex; they misreckon in it. For there is not always that difference of strength, or prudence between the man and the woman, as that the right can be determined without war. In Commonwealths, this controversy is decided by the civil law: and for the most part, (but not always) the sentence is in favour of the father; because for the most part Commonwealths have been erected by the fathers, not by the mothers of families. But the question lieth now in the state of mere nature; where there are supposed no laws of matrimony; no laws for the education of children; but the law of nature, and the natural inclination of the sexes, one to another, and to their children. In this condition of mere nature, either the parents between themselves dispose of the dominion over the child by contract; or do not dispose thereof at all. If they dispose thereof, the right passeth according to the contract. We find in history that the Amazons contracted with the men of the neighbouring countries, to whom they had recourse for issue, that the issue male should be sent back, but the female remain with themselves: so that the dominion of the females was in the mother.

If there be no contract, the dominion is in the mother. For in the condition of mere nature, where there are no matrimonial laws, it cannot be known who is the father, unless it be declared by the mother: and therefore the right of dominion over the child dependeth on her will, and is consequently hers. Again, seeing the infant is first in the power of the mother, so as she may either nourish, or expose it; if she nourish it, it oweth its life to the mother; and is therefore obliged to obey her, rather than any other; and by consequence the dominion over it is hers. But if she expose it, and another find, and nourish it, the dominion is in him that nourisheth it. For it ought to obey him by whom it is preserved; because preservation of life being the end, for which one man becomes subject to another, every man is supposed to promise obedience to him, in whose power it is to save, or destroy him.

If the mother be the father's subject, the child is in the father's power: and if the father be the mother's subject, (as when a sovereign queen marrieth one of her subjects) the child is subject to the mother; because the father also is her subject.

If a man and woman, monarchs of two several kingdoms, have a child, and contract concerning who shall have the dominion of him, the right of the dominion passeth by the contract. If they contract not, the dominion followeth the dominion of the place of his residence. For the sovereign of each country hath dominion over all that reside therein.

He that hath the dominion over the child, hath dominion also over the children of the child; and over their children's children. For he that hath dominion over the person of a man, hath dominion over all that is his; without which, dominion were but a title, without the effect.

The right of succession to paternal dominion, proceedeth in the same manner, as doth the right of succession of monarchy; of which I have already sufficiently spoken in the precedent chapter.

Dominion acquired by conquest, or victory in war, is that which some writers call despotical, from δεσπότης, which signifieth a *lord*, or *master*; and is the dominion of the master over his servant. And this dominion is then acquired to the victor, when the vanquished, to avoid the present stroke of death, covenanteth either in express words, or by other sufficient signs of the will, that so long as his life, and the liberty of his body is allowed him, the victor shall have the use thereof, at his pleasure. And after such covenant made, the vanquished is a servant, and not before: for by the word *servant* (whether it be derived from *servire*, to serve, or from *servare*, to save, which I leave to grammarians to dispute) is not meant a captive, which is kept in prison, or bonds, till the owner of him that took him, or bought him of one that did, shall consider what to do with him: (for such men, (commonly called slaves) have no obligation at all; but may break their bonds, or the prison; and kill, or carry away captive their master, justly): but one, that being taken, hath corporal liberty allowed him; and upon promise not to run away, nor to do violence to his master, is trusted by him.

It is not therefore the victory, that giveth the right of dominion over the vanquished, but his own covenant. Nor is he obliged because he is conquered; that is to say, beaten, and taken, or put to flight; but because he cometh in, and submitteth to the victor; nor is the victor obliged by an enemy's rendering himself, (without promise of life) to spare him for this his yielding to discretion; which obliges not the victor longer, than in his own discretion he shall think fit.

And that which men do, when they demand (as it is now called) *quarter*, (which the Greeks called ζωγρία, *taking alive*) is to evade the present fury of the victor, by submission, and to compound for their life, with ransom, or service: and therefore he that hath quarter, hath not his life given, but deferred till farther deliberation; for it is not a yielding on condition of life, but to discretion. And then only is his life in security, and his service due, when the victor hath trusted him with his corporal liberty. For slaves that work in prisons, or fetters, do it not of duty, but to avoid the cruelty of their task-masters.

The master of the servant, is master also of all he hath; and may exact the use thereof; that is to say, of his goods, of his labour, of his servants, and of his children, as often as he shall think fit. For he holdeth his life of his master, by the covenant of obedience; that is, of owning and authorising whatsoever the master shall do. And in case the master, if he refuse, kill him, or cast him into bonds, or otherwise punish him for his disobedience, he is himself the author of the same; and cannot accuse him of injury.

In sum, the rights and consequences of both *paternal* and *despotical* dominion, are the very same with those of a sovereign by institution; and for the same reasons: which reasons are set down in the precedent chapter. So that for a man that is monarch of divers nations, whereof he hath, in one the sovereignty by institution of the people assembled, and in another by conquest, that is by the submission of each particular, to avoid death or bonds; to demand of one nation more than of the other, from the title of conquest, as being a conquered nation, is an act of ignorance of the rights of sovereignty; for the sovereign is absolute over both alike; or else there is no sovereignty at all; and so every man may lawfully protect himself, if he can, with his own sword, which is the condition of war.

By this it appears, that a great family if it be not part

of some Commonwealth, is of itself, as to the rights of sovereignty, a little monarchy, whether that family consist of a man and his children; or of a man and his servants; or of a man and his children and servants together: wherein the father or master is the sovereign. But yet a family is not properly a Commonwealth; unless it be of that power by its own number, or by other opportunities, as not to be subdued without the hazard of war. For where a number of men are manifestly too weak to defend themselves united, every one may use his own reason in time of danger, to save his own life, either by flight, or by submission to the enemy, as he shall think best; in the same manner as a very small company of soldiers, surprised by an army, may cast down their arms, and demand quarter, or run away, rather than be put to the sword. And thus much shall suffice, concerning what I find by speculation and deduction, of sovereign rights, from the nature, need, and designs of men, in erecting of Commonwealths, and putting themselves under monarchs, or assemblies, entrusted with power enough for their protection.

Let us now consider what the Scripture teacheth in the same point. To Moses, the children of Israel say thus: *Speak thou to us, and we will hear thee; but let not God speak to us, lest we die.* (Exod. 20:19) This is absolute obedience to Moses. Concerning the right of kings, God himself by the mouth of Samuel, saith, (I Sam. 11:12, &c.) *This shall be the right of the king you will have to reign over you. He shall take your sons, and set them to drive his chariots, and to be his horsemen, and to run before his chariots; and gather in his harvest; and to make his engines of war, and instruments of his chariots; and shall take your daughters to make perfumes, to be his cooks, and bakers. He shall take your fields, your vineyards, and your olive-yards, and give them to his servants. He shall take the tithe of your corn and wine, and give it to the men of his chamber, and to his other servants. He shall take your man-servants, and your maid-servants, and the choice of your youth, and employ them in his business. He shall take the tithe of your flocks; and you shall be his servants.* This is absolute power, and summed up in the last words, *you shall be his servants.* Again, when the people heard what power their king was to have, yet they consented thereto, and say thus, (*verse* 19) *we will be as all other nations, and our king shall judge our causes, and go before us, to conduct our wars.* Here is confirmed the right that sovereigns have, both to the *militia*, and to all *judicature*; in which is contained as absolute power, as one man can possibly transfer to another. Again, the prayer of king Solomon to God, was this (1 Kings 3:9): *Give to thy servant understanding, to judge thy people, and to discern between good and evil.* It belongeth therefore to the sovereign to be *judge*, and to prescribe the rules of *discerning good* and *evil*: which rules are laws; and therefore in him is the legislative power. Saul sought the life of David; yet when it was in his power to slay Saul, and his servants would have done it, David forbad them, saying, (1 *Sam.* 24. 9) *God forbid I should do such an act against my Lord, the anointed of God.* For obedience of servants St Paul saith: (Col. 3:22) *Servants obey your masters in all things*; and, (Col. 3:20) *children obey your parents in all things.* There is simple obedience in those that are subject to paternal, or despotical dominion. Again, (Matt. 23:2, 3) *The Scribes and Pharisees sit in Moses' chair, and therefore all that they shall bid you observe, that observe and do.* There again is simple obedience. And

St Paul, (Titus 3:2) *Warn them that they subject themselves to princes, and to those that are in authority, and obey them.* This obedience is also simple. Lastly, our Saviour himself acknowledges, that men ought to pay such taxes as are by kings imposed, where he says, *give to Caesar that which is Caesar's*; and paid such taxes himself. And that the king's word is sufficient to take any thing from any subject, when there is need; and that the king is judge of that need: for he himself, as king of the Jews, commanded his disciples to take the ass, and ass's colt to carry him into Jerusalem, saying, (Matt. 21:2, 3) *Go into the village over against you, and you shall find a she ass tied, and her colt with her; untie them, and bring them to me. And if any man ask you, what you mean by it, say the Lord hath need of them: and they will let them go.* They will not ask whether his necessity be a sufficient title; nor whether he be judge of that necessity; but acquiesce in the will of the Lord.

To these places may be added also that of Genesis, (3:5) *Ye shall be as gods, knowing good and evil.* And verse 11. *Who told thee that thou wast naked? Hast thou eaten of the tree, of which I commanded thee thou shouldest not eat?* For the cognizance or judicature of *good* and *evil*, being forbidden by the name of the fruit of the tree of knowledge, as a trial of Adam's obedience; the devil to inflame the ambition of the woman, to whom that fruit already seemed beautiful, told her that by tasting it, they should be as gods, knowing *good* and *evil*. Whereupon having both eaten, they did indeed take upon them God's office, which is judicature of good and evil; but acquired no new ability to distinguish between them aright. And whereas it is said, that having eaten, they saw they were naked; no man hath so interpreted that place, as if they had been formerly blind, and saw not their own skins: the meaning is plain, that it was then they first judged their nakedness (wherein it was God's will to create them) to be uncomely; and by being ashamed, did tacitly censure God himself. And thereupon God saith, *Hast thou eaten, etc., &c.* as if he should say, doest thou that owest me obedience, take upon thee to judge of my commandments? Whereby it is clearly, (though allegorically) signified, that the commands of them that have the right to command, are not by their subjects to be censured, nor disputed.

So that it appeareth plainly, to my understanding, both from reason and Scripture, that the sovereign power, whether placed in one man, as in monarchy, or in one assembly of men, as in popular and aristocratical commonwealths, is as great, as possibly men can be imagined to make it. And though of so unlimited a power, men may fancy many evil consequences, yet the consequences of the want of it, which is perpetual war of every man against his neighbour, are much worse. The condition of man in this life shall never be without inconveniences; but there happeneth in no commonwealth any great inconvenience, but what proceeds from the subject's disobedience, and breach of those covenants, from which the commonwealth hath its being. And whosoever thinking sovereign power too great, will seek to make it less, must subject himself o the power that can limit it; that is to say, to a greater.

The greatest objection is, that of the practice; when men ask, where and when, such power has by subjects been acknowledged. But one may ask them again, when or where has there been a kingdom long free from sedition and civil war. In those nations, whose commonwealths have been long-lived, and not been destroyed but by foreign war, the subjects never did dispute of the sovereign power. But howsoever, an argument from the practice of men, that have not sifted to the bottom, and with exact reason weighed the causes and nature of commonwealths, and suffer daily those miseries, that proceed from the ignorance thereof, is invalid. For though in all places of the world, men should lay the foundation of their houses on the sand, it could not thence be inferred, that so it ought to be. The skill of making, and maintaining commonwealths, consisteth in certain rules, as doth arithmetic and geometry; not (as tennis-play) on practice only: which rules, neither poor men have the leisure, nor men that have had the leisure, have hitherto had the curiosity or the method to find out.

CHAPTER 21

Of the Liberty of Subjects

Liberty, or freedom, signifieth (properly) the absence of opposition; (by opposition, I mean external impediments of motion) and may be applied no less to irrational, and inanimate creatures, than to rational. For whatsoever is so tied, or environed, as it cannot move, but within a certain space, which space is determined by the opposition of some external body, we say it hath not liberty to go further. And so of all living creatures, whilst they are imprisoned, or restrained, with walls, or chains; and of the water whilst it is kept in by banks, or vessels, that otherwise would spread itself into a larger space, we use to say, they are not at liberty, to move in such manner, as without those external impediments they would. But when the impediment of motion, is in the constitution of the thing itself, we use not to say, it wants the liberty, but the power to move; as when a stone lieth still, or a man is fastened to his bed by sickness.

And according to this proper, and generally received meaning of the word, a freeman, *is he, that in those things, which by his strength and wit he is able to do, is not hindered to do what he has a will to.* But when the words *free*, and *liberty*, are applied to any thing but *bodies*, they are abused; for that which is not subject to motion, is not subject to impediment: and therefore, when 'tis said (for example) the way is free, no liberty of the way is signified, but of those that walk in it without stop. And when we say a gift is free, there is not meant any liberty of the gift, but of the giver, that was not bound by any law, or covenant to give it. So when we *speak freely*, it is not the liberty of voice, or pronunciation, but of the man, whom no law hath obliged to speak otherwise than he did. Lastly, from the use of the word *free-will*, no liberty can be inferred of the will, desire, or inclination, but the liberty of the man; which consisteth in this, that he finds no stop, in doing what he has the will, desire, or inclination to do.

Fear and *liberty* are consistent; as when a man throweth his goods into the sea for *fear* the ship should sink, he doth it nevertheless very willingly, and may refuse to do it if he will: it is therefore the action, of one that was *free*: so a man sometimes pays his debt, only for *fear* of imprisonment, which because nobody hindered him from detaining, was the action of a man at *liberty*. And generally all actions which men do in commonwealths, for *fear* of the law, are actions, which the doers had *liberty* to omit.

Liberty, and *necessity* are consistent: as in the water, that hath not only *liberty*, but a *necessity* of descending by the channel; so likewise in the actions which men voluntarily do: which, because they proceed from their will, proceed from *liberty*; and yet, because every act of man's will, and every desire and inclination proceedeth from some cause, and that from another cause, in a continual chain, (whose first link is in the hand of God the first of all causes) they proceed from *necessity*. So that to him that could see the connexion of those causes, the *necessity* of all men's voluntary actions, would appear manifest. And therefore God, that seeth and disposeth all things, seeth also that the *liberty* of man in doing what he will, is accompanied with the *necessity* of doing that which God will, and no more, nor less. For though men may do many things, which God does not command, nor is therefore author of them; yet they can have no passion, nor appetite to any thing, of which appetite God's will is not the cause. And did not his will assure the *necessity* of man's will, and consequently of all that on man's will dependeth, the *liberty* of men would be a contradiction, and impediment to the omnipotence and *liberty* of God. And this shall suffice (as to the matter in hand) of that natural *liberty*, which only is properly called *liberty*.

But as men, for the attaining of peace, and conservation of themselves thereby, have made an artificial man, which we call a commonwealth; so also have they made artificial chains, called *civil laws*, which they themselves, by mutual covenants, have fastened at one end, to the sovereign power; and at the other end to their own ears. These bonds, in their own nature but weak, may nevertheless be made to hold, by the danger, though not by the difficulty, of breaking them.

In relation to these bonds only it is, that I am to speak now, of the *liberty of subjects*. For seeing there is no commonwealth in the world, wherein there be rules enough set down, for the regulating of all the actions, and words of men; (as being a thing impossible) it followeth necessarily, that in all kinds of actions, by the laws praetermitted, men have the liberty, of doing what their own reasons shall suggest, for the most profitable to themselves. For if we take liberty in the proper sense, for corporal liberty; that is to say, freedom from chains, and prison, it were very absurd for men to clamour as they do, for the liberty they so manifestly enjoy. Again, if we take liberty, for an exemption from laws, it is no less absurd, for men to demand as they do, that liberty, by which all other men may be masters of their lives. And yet as absurd as it is, this is it they demand; not knowing that the laws are of no power to protect them, without a sword in the hands of a man, or men, to cause those laws to be put in execution. The liberty of a subject, lieth therefore only in those things, which in regulating their actions, the sovereign hath praetermitted: such as is the liberty to buy, and sell, and otherwise contract with one another; to choose their own abode, their own diet, their own trade of life, and institute their children as they themselves think fit; and the like.

Nevertheless we are not to understand, that by such liberty, the sovereign power of life and death is either abolished, or limited. For it has been already shown, that nothing the sovereign representative can do to a subject, on what pretence soever, can properly be called injustice, or injury; because every subject is author of every act the sovereign doth; so that he never wanteth right to any thing, otherwise than as he himself is the subject of God, and bound thereby to observe the laws of nature. And therefore it may, and doth often happen in commonwealths, that a subject may be put to death, by the command of the sovereign power; and yet neither do the other wrong: as when Jeptha caused his daughter to be sacrificed: in which, and the like cases, he that so dieth, had liberty to do the action, for which he is nevertheless, without injury put to death. And the same holdeth also in a sovereign prince, that putteth to death an innocent subject. For though the action be against the law of nature, as being contrary to equity, (as was the killing of Uriah, by David) yet it was not an injury to Uriah, but to God. Not to Uriah, because the right to do what he pleased, was given him by Uriah himself: and yet to God, because David was God's subject; and prohibited all iniquity by the law of nature. Which distinction, David himself, when he repented the fact, evidently confirmed, saying, *To thee only have I sinned.* In the same manner, the people of Athens, when they banished the most potent of their commonwealth for ten years, thought they committed no injustice; and yet they never questioned what crime he had done; but what hurt he would do: nay they commanded the banishment of they knew not whom; and every citizen bringing his oystershell into the market place, written with the name of him he desired should be banished, without actually accusing him, sometimes banished an Aristides, for his reputation of justice; and sometimes a scurrilous jester, as Hyperbolus, to make a jest of it. And yet a man cannot say, the sovereign people of Athens wanted right to banish them; or an Athenian the liberty to jest, or to be just.

The liberty, whereof there is so frequent, and honourable mention, in the histories and philosophy of the ancient Greeks, and Romans, and in the writings and discourse of those that from them have received all their learning in the politics, is not the liberty of particular men; but the liberty of the commonwealth: which is the same with that, which every man then should have, if there were no civil laws, nor commonwealth at all. And the effects of it also be the same. For as amongst masterless men, there is perpetual war, of every man against his neighbour; no inheritance, to transmit to the son, nor to expect from the father; no propriety of goods, or lands; no security; but a full and absolute liberty in every particular man: so in states and commonwealths not dependent on one another, every commonwealth (not every man) has an absolute liberty, to do what it shall judge (that is to say, what that man, or assembly that representeth it, shall judge) most conducing to their benefit. But withal, they live in the condition of a perpetual war, and upon the confines of battle, with their frontiers armed, and cannons planted against their neighbours round about. The Athenians and Romans were free; that is, free commonwealths: not that any particular men had the liberty to resist their own representative but that their representative had the liberty to resist, or invade other people. There is written on the turrets of the city of Lucca in great characters at this day, the word LIBERTAS; yet no man can thence infer, that a particular man has more liberty, or immunity from the service of the commonwealth there, than in Constantinople. Whether a commonwealth be monarchical or popular, the freedom is still the same.

But it is an easy thing, for men to be deceived, by the specious name of liberty; and for want of judgment to distinguish, mistake that for their private inheritance, and birth-right, which is the right of the public only. And when the same error is confirmed by the authority of men in reputation for their writings on this subject, it is no wonder if it produce sedition, and change of government. In these western parts of the world, we are made to receive our opinions concerning the institution, and rights of commonwealths, from Aristotle, Cicero, and other men, Greeks and Romans, that living under popular states, derived those rights, not from the principles of nature, but transcribed them into their books, out of the practice of their own commonwealths, which were popular; as the grammarians describe the rules of language, out of the practice of the time; or the rules of poetry, out of the poems of Homer and Virgil. And because the Athenians were taught, (to keep them from desire of changing their government) that they were freemen, and all that lived under monarchy were slaves; therefore Aristotle puts it down in his *Politics*, (lib. 6, ch. 2.) *In democracy, Liberty is to be supposed: for it is commonly held, that no man is Free in any other government*. And as Aristotle; so Cicero, and other writers have grounded their civil doctrine, on the opinions of the Romans, who were taught to hate monarchy, at first, by them that having deposed their sovereign, shared amongst them the sovereignty of Rome; and afterwards by their successors. And by reading of these Greek and Latin authors, men from their childhood have gotten a habit (under a false show of liberty) of favouring tumults, and of licentious controlling the actions of their sovereigns; and again of controlling those controllers; with the effusion of so much blood, as I think I may truly say, there was never any thing so dearly bought, as these western parts have bought the learning of the Greek and Latin tongues.

To come now to the particulars of the true liberty of a subject; that is to say, what are the things, which though commanded by the sovereign, he may nevertheless, without injustice, refuse to do; we are to consider, what rights we pass away, when we make a commonwealth; or (which is all one) what liberty we deny ourselves, by owning all the actions (without exception) of the man, or assembly we make our sovereign. For in the act of our *submission*, consisteth both our *obligation*, and our *liberty*; which must therefore be inferred by arguments taken from thence; there being no obligation on any man, which ariseth not from some act of his own; for all men equally, are by nature free. And because such arguments, must either be drawn from the express words, *I authorise all his actions*, or from the intention of him that submitteth himself to his power, (which intention is to be understood by the end for which he so submitteth) the obligation, and liberty of the subject, is to be derived, either from those words, (or others equivalent) or else from the end of the institution of sovereignty; namely, the peace of the subjects within themselves, and their defence against a common enemy.

First therefore, seeing sovereignty by institution, is by covenant of every one to every one; and sovereignty by acquisition, by covenants of the vanquished to the victor, or child to the parent; it is manifest, that every subject has liberty in all those things, the right whereof cannot by covenant be transferred. I have shewn before in the 14th chapter, that covenants, not to defend a man's own body, are void. Therefore, if the sovereign command a man (though justly condemned, to kill, wound, or maim himself; or not to resist those that assault him; or to abstain from the use of food, air, medicine, or any other thing, without which he cannot live; yet hath that man the liberty to disobey.

If a man be interrogated by the sovereign, or his authority, concerning a crime done by himself, he is not bound (without assurance of pardon) to confess it; because no man (as I have shown in the same chapter) can be obliged by covenant to accuse himself.

Again, the consent of a subject to sovereign power, is contained in these words, *I authorise, or take upon me, all his actions*; in which there is no restriction at all, of his own former natural liberty: for by allowing him to *kill me*, I am not bound to kill myself when he commands me. It is one thing to say, *kill me, or my fellow, if you please*; another thing to say, *I will kill myself, or my fellow*. It followeth therefore, that no man is bound by the words themselves, either to kill himself, or any other man; and consequently, that the obligation a man may sometimes have, upon the command of the sovereign to execute any dangerous or dishonourable office, dependeth not on the words of our submission; but on the intention, which is to be understood by the end thereof. When therefore our refusal to obey, frustrates the end for which the sovereignty was ordained; then there is no liberty to refuse; otherwise there is.

Upon this ground, a man that is commanded as a

soldier to fight against the enemy, though his sovereign have right enough to punish his refusal with death, may nevertheless in many cases refuse, without injustice; as when he substituteth a sufficient soldier in his place: for in this case he deserteth not the service of the commonwealth. And there is allowance to be made for natural timorousness; not only to women, (of whom no such dangerous duty is expected) but also to men of feminine courage. When armies fight, there is on one side, or both, a running away; yet when they do it not out of treachery, but fear, they are not esteemed to do it unjustly, but dishonourably. For the same reason, to avoid battle is not injustice, but cowardice. But he that enrolleth himself a soldier, or taketh imprest money, taketh away the excuse of a timorous nature; and is obliged, not only to go to the battle, but also not to run from it, without his captain's leave. And when the defence of the commonwealth requireth at once the help of all that are able to bear arms, every one is obliged; because otherwise the institution of the commonwealth, which they have not the purpose, or courage to preserve, was in vain.

To resist the sword of the commonwealth, in defence of another man, guilty or innocent, no man hath liberty; because such liberty takes away from the sovereign, the means of protecting us; and is therefore destructive of the very essence of government. But in case a great many men together, have already resisted the sovereign power unjustly, or committed some capital crime, for which every one of them expecteth death, whether have they not the liberty then to join together, and assist, and defend one another?

Certainly they have: for they but defend their lives,

which the guilty man may as well do, as the innocent. There was indeed injustice in the first breach of their duty; their bearing of arms subsequent to it, though it be to maintain what they have done, is no new unjust act. And if it be only to defend their persons, it is not unjust at all. But the offer of pardon taketh from them, to whom it is offered, the plea of self-defence, and maketh their perseverance in assisting, or defending the rest, unlawful.

As for other liberties, they depend on the silence of the law. In cases where the sovereign has prescribed no rule, there the subject hath the liberty to do, or forbear, according to his own discretion. And therefore such liberty is in some places more, and in some less; and in some times more, in other times less, according as they that have the sovereignty shall think most convenient. As for example, there was a time, when in England a man might enter into his own land, (and dispossess such as wrongfully possessed it) by force. But in aftertimes, that liberty of forcible entry, was taken away by a statute made (by the king) in parliament. And in some places of the world, men have the liberty of many wives: in other places, such liberty is not allowed.

If a subject have a controversy with his sovereign, of debt, or of right of possession of lands or goods, or concerning any service required at his hands, or concerning any penalty, corporal or pecuniary, grounded on a precedent law; he hath the same liberty to sue for his right, as if it were against a subject; and before such judges, as are appointed by the sovereign. For seeing the sovereign demandeth by force of a former law, and not by virtue of his power; he declareth thereby, that he requireth no more, than shall appear to be due by that law. The suit therefore is not contrary to the will of the sovereign; and consequently the subject hath the liberty to demand the hearing of his cause; and sentence, according to that law. But if he demand, or take any thing by pretence of his power, there lieth, in that case, no action of law; for all that is done by him in virtue of his power, is done by the authority of every subject, and consequently he that brings an action against the sovereign, brings it against himself.

If a monarch, or sovereign assembly, grant a liberty to all, or any of his subjects, which grant standing, he is disabled to provide for their safety, the grant is void; unless he directly renounce, or transfer the sovereignty to another. For in that he might openly, (if it had been his will) and in plain terms, have renounced, or transferred it, and did not; it is to be understood it was not his will; but that the grant proceeded from ignorance of the repugnancy between such a liberty and the sovereign power: and therefore the sovereignty is still retained; and consequently all those powers, which are necessary to the exercising thereof; such as are the power of war, and peace, of judicature, of appointing officers, and councillors, of levying money, and the rest named in the eighteenth chapter.

The obligation of subjects to the sovereign, is understood to last as long, and no longer, than the power lasteth, by which he is able to protect them. For the right men have by nature to protect themselves, when none else can protect them, can by no covenant be relinquished. The sovereignty is the soul of the commonwealth; which once departed from the body, the members do no more receive their motion from it. The end of obedience is protection; which, wheresoever a man seeth it, either in his own, or in another's sword, nature applieth his obedience to it, and his endeavour to maintain it. And though sovereignty, in the intention of them that make it, be immortal; yet is it in its own nature, not only subject to violent death, by foreign war; but also through the ignorance and passions of men, it hath in it, from the very institution, many seeds of a natural mortality, by intestine discord.

If a subject be taken prisoner in war; or his person, or his means of life be within the guards of the enemy, and hath his life and corporal liberty given him, on condition to be subject to the victor, he hath liberty to accept the condition; and having accepted it, is the subject of him that took him; because he had no other way to preserve himself. The case is the same, if he be detained on the same terms, in a foreign country. But if a man be held in prison, or bonds, or is not trusted with the liberty of his body; he cannot be understood to be bound by covenant to subjection; and therefore may, if he can, make his escape by any means whatsoever.

If a monarch shall relinquish the sovereignty, both for himself, and his heirs; his subjects return to the absolute liberty of nature; because, though nature may declare who are his sons, and who are the nearest of his kin; yet it dependeth on his own will, (as hath been said in the precedent chapter) who shall be his heir. If therefore he will have no heir, there is no sovereignty, nor subjection. The case is the same, if he die without known kindred, and without declaration of his heir. For then there can no heir be known, and consequently no subjection be due.

If the sovereign banish his subject; during the banishment, he is not subject. But he that is sent on a message, or hath leave to travel, is still subject; but it is, by contract between sovereigns, not by virtue of the covenant of subjection. For whosoever entereth into another's dominion, is subject to all the laws thereof, unless he have a privilege by the amity of the sovereigns, or by special licence.

If a monarch subdued by war, render himself subject to the victor; his subjects are delivered from their former obligation, and become obliged to the victor. But if he be held prisoner, or have not the liberty of his own body; he is not understood to have given away the right of sovereignty; and therefore his subjects are obliged to yield obedience to the magistrates formerly placed, governing not in their own name, but in his. For, his right remaining, the question is only of the administration; that is to say, of the magistrates and officers; which, if he have not means to name, he is supposed to approve those, which he himself had formerly appointed.

CHAPTER 22

Of Systems Subject, Political and Private

Having spoken of the generation, form, and power of a commonwealth, I am in order to speak next of the parts thereof. And first of systems, which resemble the similar parts, or muscles of a body natural. By systems; I understand any numbers of men joined in one interest, or one business. Of which, some are *regular*, and some *irregular*. *Regular* are those, where one man, or assembly of men, is constituted representative of the whole number. All other are *irregular*.

Of regular, some are *absolute*, and *independent*, subject to none but their own representative: such are only commonwealths; of which I have spoken already in the five last precedent chapters. Others are dependent; that is to say, subordinate to some sovereign power, to which every one, as also their representative is *subject*.

Of systems subordinate, some are *political*, and some *private*. *Political* (otherwise called *bodies politic*, and *persons in law*) are those which are made by authority from the sovereign power of the commonwealth. *Private*, are those which are constituted by subjects amongst themselves, or by authority from a stranger. For no authority derived from foreign power, within the dominion of another, is public there, but private.

And of private systems, some are *lawful*; some *unlawful*. *Lawful*, are those which are allowed by the commonwealth: all other are *unlawful*. *Irregular* systems, are those which having no representative, consist only in concourse of people; which if not forbidden by the commonwealth, nor made on evil design, (such as are conflux of people to markets, or shows, or any other harmless end) are lawful. But when the intention is evil, or (if the number be considerable) unknown, they are unlawful.

In bodies politic, the power of the representative is always limited: and that which prescribeth the limits thereof, is the power sovereign. For power unlimited, is absolute sovereignty. And the sovereign in every commonwealth, is the absolute representative of all the subjects; and therefore no other can be representative of any part of them, but so far forth, as he shall give leave. And to give leave to a body politic of subjects, to have an absolute representative to all intents and purposes, were to abandon the government of so much of the commonwealth, and to divide the dominion, contrary to their peace and defence; which the sovereign cannot be understood to do, by any grant, that does not plainly and directly discharge them of their subjection. For consequences of words, are not the signs of his will, when other consequences are signs of the contrary; but rather signs of error, and misreckoning; to which all mankind is too prone.

The bounds of that power, which is given to the representative of a body politic, are to be taken notice of, from two things. One is their writ, or letters from the sovereign: the other is the law of the commonwealth.

For though in the institution or acquisition of a commonwealth, which is independent, there needs no writing, because the power of the representative has there no other bounds, but such as are set out by the unwritten law of nature; yet in subordinate bodies, there are such diversities of limitation necessary, concerning their businesses, times, and places, as can neither be remembered without letters, nor taken notice of, unless such letters be patent, that they may be read to them, and withal sealed, or testified, with the seals or other permanent signs of the authority sovereign.

And because such limitation is not always easy, or perhaps possible to be described in writing; the ordinary laws, common to all subjects, must determine what the representative may lawfully do, in all cases, where the letters themselves are silent. And therefore, in a body politic, if the representative be one man, whatsoever he does in the person of the body, which is not warranted in his letters, nor by the laws, is his own act, and not the act of the body, nor of any other member thereof besides himself: because further than his letters or the laws limit, he representeth no man's person, but his own. But what he does according to these, is the act of every one: for of the act of the sovereign every one is author, because he is their representative unlimited; and the act of him that recedes not from the letters of the sovereign, is the act of the sovereign, and therefore every member of the body is author of it.

But if the representative be an assembly; whatsoever that assembly shall decree, not warranted by their letters, or the laws, is the act of the assembly, or body politic, and the act of every one by whose vote the decree was made; but not the act of any man that being present voted to the contrary; nor of any man absent, unless he voted it by procuration. It is the act of the assembly, because voted by the major part; and if it be a crime, the assembly may be punished, as far forth as it is capable, as by dissolution, or forfeiture of their letters, (which is to such artificial, and fictitious bodies, capital) or (if the assembly have a common stock, wherein none of the innocent members have propriety) by pecuniary mulct. For from corporal penalties nature hath exempted all bodies politic. But they that gave not their vote, are therefore innocent, because the assembly cannot represent any man in things unwarranted by their letters, and consequently are not involved in their votes.

If the person of the body politic being in one man, borrow money of a stranger, that is, of one that is not of the same body, (for no letters need limit borrowing, seeing it is left to men's own inclinations to limit lending), the debt is the representative's. For if he should have authority from his letters, to make the members pay what he borroweth, he should have by consequence the sovereignty of them; and therefore the grant were either void, as proceeding from error, commonly incident to human nature, and an insufficient sign of the will of the granter; or if it be avowed by him, then is the representer sovereign, and falleth not under the present question, which is only of bodies subordinate. No member therefore is obliged to pay the debt so borrowed, but the representative himself: because he that lendeth it, being a stranger to the letters, and to the qualification of the body, understandeth those only for his debtors, that are engaged: and seeing the representer can engage himself, and none else, has him only for debtor; who must therefore pay him, out of the common stock (if there be any) or, (if there be none) out of his own estate.

If he come into debt by contract, or mulct, the case is the same.

But when the representative is an assembly, and the debt to a stranger; all they, and only they are responsible for the debt, that gave their votes to the borrowing of it, or to the contract that made it due, or to the fact for which the mulct was imposed; because every one of those in voting did engage himself for the payment: for he that is author of the borrowing, is obliged to the payment, even of the whole debt, though when paid by any one, he be discharged.

But if the debt be to one of the assembly, the assembly only is obliged to the payment, out of their common stock (if they have any): for having liberty of vote, if he vote the money shall be borrowed, he votes it shall be paid; if he vote it shall not be borrowed, or be absent, yet because in lending, he voteth the borrowing, he contradicteth his former vote, and is obliged by the latter, and becomes both borrower and lender, and consequently cannot demand payment from any particular man, but from the common treasure only; which failing he hath no remedy, nor complaint, but against himself, that being privy to the acts of the assembly, and to their means to pay, and not being enforced, did nevertheless through his own folly lend his money.

It is manifest by this, that in bodies politic subordinate, and subject to a sovereign power, it is sometimes not only lawful, but expedient, for a particular man to make open protestation against the decrees of the representative assembly, and cause their dissent to be registered, or to take witness of it; because otherwise they may be obliged to pay debts contracted, and be responsible for crimes committed by other men. But in a sovereign assembly, that liberty is taken away, both because he that protesteth there, denies their sovereignty; and also because whatsoever is commanded by the sovereign power, is as to the subject (though not so always in the sight of God) justified by the command; for of such command every subject is the author.

The variety of bodies politic, is almost infinite: for they are not only distinguished by the several affairs, for which they are constituted, wherein there is an unspeakable diversity; but also by the times, places, and numbers, subject to many limitations. And as to their affairs, some are ordained for government; as first, the government of a province may be committed to an assembly of men, wherein all resolutions shall depend on the votes of the major part; and then this assembly is a body politic, and their power limited by commission. This word province signifies a charge, or care of business, which he whose business it is, committeth to another man, to be administered for, and under him; and therefore when in one commonwealth there be divers countries, that have their laws distinct one from another, or are far distant in place, the administration of the government being committed to divers persons, those countries where the sovereign is not resident, but governs by commission, are called provinces. But of the government of a province, by an assembly residing in the province itself, there be few examples. The Romans who had the sovereignty of many provinces; yet governed them always by presidents, and praetors; and not by assemblies, as they governed the city of Rome, and territories adjacent. In like manner, when there were colonies sent from England, to plant Virginia, and Sommer-islands]; though the governments of them here, were committed to assemblies in London, yet did those assemblies never commit the government under them to any assembly there, but did to each plantation send one governor. For though every man, where he can be present by nature, desires to participate of government; yet where they cannot be present, they are by nature also inclined, to commit the government of their common interest rather to a monarchical, than a popular form of government: which is also evident in those men that have great private estates; who when they are unwilling to take the pains of administering the business that belongs to them, choose rather to trust one servant, than an assembly either of their friends or servants. But howsoever it be in fact, yet we may suppose the government of a province, or colony committed to an assembly: and when it is, that which in this place I have to say, is this; that whatsoever debt is by that assembly contracted; or whatsoever unlawful act is decreed, is the act only of those that assented, and not of any that dissented, or were absent, for the reasons before alleged. Also that an assembly residing out of the bounds of that colony whereof they have the government, cannot execute any power over the persons, or goods of any of the colony, to seize on them for debt, or other duty, in any place without the colony itself, as having no jurisdiction, nor authority elsewhere, but are left to the remedy which the law of the place alloweth them. And though the assembly have right, to impose a mulct upon any of their members, that shall break the laws they make; yet out of the colony itself, they have no right to execute the same. And that which is said here, of the rights of an assembly, for the government of a province, or a colony, is applicable also to an assembly for the government of a town, an university, or a college, or a church, or for any other government over the persons of men.

And generally, in all bodies politic, if any particular member conceive himself injured by the body itself, the cognizance of his cause belongeth to the sovereign, and those the sovereign hath ordained for judges in such causes, or shall ordain for that particular cause; and not to the body itself. For the whole body is in this case his fellow-subject, which in a sovereign assembly, is otherwise: for there, if the sovereign be not judge, though in his own cause, there can be no judge at all.

In a body politic, for the well ordering of foreign

traffic, the most commodious representative is an assembly of all the members; that is to say, such a one, as every one that adventureth his money, may be present at all the deliberations, and resolutions of the body, if they will themselves. For proof whereof, we are to consider the end, for which men that are merchants, and may buy and sell, export and import their merchandise, according to their own discretions, do nevertheless bind themselves up in one corporation. It is true, there be few merchants, that with the merchandise they buy at home, can freight a ship, to export it; or with that they buy abroad, to bring it home; and have therefore need to join together in one society; where every man may either participate of the gain, according to the proportion of his adventure; or take his own, and sell what he transports, or imports, at such prices as he thinks fit. But this is no body politic, there being no common representative to oblige them to any other law, than that which is common to all other subjects. The end of their incorporating, is to make their gain the greater; which is done two ways; by sole buying, and sole selling, both at home, and abroad. So that to grant to a company of merchants to be a corporation, or body politic, is to grant them a double monopoly, whereof one is to be sole buyers; another to be sole sellers. For when there is a company incorporate for any particular foreign country, they only export the commodities vendible in that country; which is sole buying at home, and sole selling abroad. For at home there is but one buyer, and abroad but one that selleth: both which is gainful to the merchant, because thereby they buy at home at lower, and sell abroad at higher rates: and abroad there is but one buyer of foreign merchandise, and but one that sells them at home; both which again are gainful to the adventurers.

Of this double monopoly one part is disadvantageous to the people at home, the other to foreigners. For at home by their sole exportation they set what price they please on the husbandry, and handy-works of the people; and by the sole importation, what price they please on all foreign commodities the people have need of; both which are ill for the people. On the contrary, by the sole selling of the native commodities abroad, and sole buying the foreign commodities upon the place, they raise the price of those, and abate the price of these, to the disadvantage of the foreigner: for where but one selleth, the merchandise is the dearer; and where but one buyeth, the cheaper. Such corporations therefore are no other than monopolies; though they would be very profitable for a commonwealth, if being bound up into one body in foreign markets they were at liberty at home, every man to buy and sell at what price he could.

The end then of these bodies of merchants, being not a common benefit to the whole body, (which have in this case no common stock, but what is deducted out of the particular adventures, for building, buying, victualling and manning of ships) but the particular gain of every adventurer, it is reason that every one be acquainted with the employment of his own; that is, that every one be of the assembly, that shall have the power to order the same; and be acquainted with their accounts. And therefore the representative of such a body must be an assembly, where every member of the body may be present at the consultations, if he will.

If a body politic of merchants, contract a debt to a

stranger by the act of their representative assembly, every member is liable by himself for the whole. For a stranger can take no notice of their private laws, but considereth them as so many particular men, obliged every one to the whole payment, till payment made by one dischargeth all the rest: but if the debt be to one of the company, the creditor is debtor for the whole to himself, and cannot therefore demand his debt, but only from the common stock, if there be any.

If the commonwealth impose a tax upon the body, it is understood to be laid upon every member proportionably to his particular adventure in the company. For there is in this case no other common stock, but what is made of their particular adventures.

If a mulct be laid upon the body for some unlawful act, they only are liable by whose votes the act was decreed, or by whose assistance it was executed; for in none of the rest is there any other crime but being of the body; which if a crime, (because the body was ordained by the authority of the commonwealth) is not his.

If one of the members be indebted to the body, he may be sued by the body; but his goods cannot be taken, nor his person imprisoned by the authority of the body; but only by authority of the commonwealth: for if they can do it by their own authority, they can by their own authority give judgment that the debt is due; which is as much as to be judge in their own cause.

These bodies made for the government of men, or of traffic, be either perpetual, or for a time prescribed by writing. But there be bodies also whose times are limited, and that only by the nature of their business. For example, if a sovereign monarch, or a sovereign assembly, shall think fit to give command to the towns, and other several parts of their territory, to send to him their deputies, to inform him of the condition, and necessities of the subjects, or to advise with him for the making of good laws, or for any other cause, as with one person representing the whole country, such deputies, having a place and time of meeting assigned them, are there, and at that time, a body politic, representing every subject of that dominion; but it is only for such matters as shall be propounded unto them by that man, or assembly, that by the sovereign authority sent for them; and when it shall be declared that nothing more shall be propounded, nor debated by them, the body is dissolved. For if they were the absolute representatives of the people, then were it the sovereign assembly; and so there would be two sovereign assemblies, or two sovereigns, over the same people; which cannot consist with their peace. And therefore where there is once a sovereignty, there can be no absolute representation of the people, but by it. And for the limits of how far such a body shall represent the whole people, they are set forth in the writing by which they were sent for. For the people cannot choose their deputies to other intent, than is in the writing directed to them from their sovereign expressed.

Private bodies regular, and lawful, are those that are constituted without letters, or other written authority, saving the laws common to all other subjects. And because they be united in one person representative, they are held for regular; such as are all families, in which the father or master ordereth the whole family. For he obligeth his children and servants, as far as the law permitteth, though not further, because none of them are bound to obedience in those actions, which the law hath forbidden to be done. In all other actions, during the time they are under domestic government, they are subject to their fathers, and masters, as to their immediate sovereigns. For the father, and master, being before the institution of commonwealth, absolute sovereigns in their own families, they lose afterward no more of their authority, than the law of the commonwealth taketh from them.

Private bodies regular, but unlawful, are those that unite themselves into one person representative, without any public authority at all; such as are the corporations of beggars, thieves, and gipsies, the better to order their trade of begging and stealing; and the corporations of men, that by authority from any foreign person, unite themselves in another's dominion, for the easier propagation of doctrines, and for making a party, against the power of the commonwealth.

Irregular systems, in their nature but leagues, or sometimes mere concourse of people, without union to any particular design, by obligation of one to another, but proceeding only from a similitude of wills and inclinations, become lawful or unlawful, according to the lawfulness or unlawfulness of every particular man's design therein: and his design is to be understood by the occasion.

The leagues of subjects, (because leagues are commonly made for mutual defence) are in a commonwealth (which is no more than a league of all the subjects together) for the most part unnecessary, and savour of unlawful design; and are for that cause unlawful, and go commonly by the name of factions, or conspiracies. For a league being a connexion of men by covenants, if there be no power given to any one man or assembly (as in the condition of mere nature) to compel them to performance, is so long only valid, as there ariseth no just cause of distrust: and therefore leagues between commonwealths, over whom there is no human power established, to keep them all in awe, are not only lawful, but also profitable for the time they last. But leagues of the subjects of one and the same commonwealth, where every one may obtain his right by means of the sovereign power, are unnecessary to the maintaining of peace and justice, and (in case the design of them be evil or unknown to the commonwealth) unlawful. For all uniting of strength by private men, is, if for evil intent, unjust; if for intent unknown, dangerous to the public, and unjustly concealed.

If the sovereign power be in a great assembly, and a number of men, part of the assembly, without authority, consult apart, to contrive the guidance of the rest; this is a faction, or conspiracy unlawful, as being a fraudulent seducing of the assembly for their particular interest. But if he, whose private interest is to be debated and judged in the assembly, make as many friends as he can; in him it is no injustice; because in this case he is no part of the assembly. And though he hire such friends with money, (unless there be an express law against it) yet it is not injustice. For sometimes, (as men's manners are) justice cannot be had without money; and every man may think his own cause just, till it be heard, and judged.

In all commonwealths, if private men entertain more servants, than the government of his estate, and lawful employment he has for them requires, it is faction, and unlawful. For having the protection of the commonwealth, he needeth not the defence of private force. And whereas in nations not thoroughly civilized, several numerous families have lived in continual hostility, and invaded one another with private force; yet it is evident enough, that they have done unjustly; or else they had no commonwealth.

And as factions for kindred, so also factions for government of religion, as of Papists, Protestants, &c. or of state, as patricians and plebeians of old time in Rome, and of aristocraticals and democraticals of old time in Greece, are unjust, as being contrary to the peace and safety of the people, and a taking of the sword out of the hand of the sovereign.

Concourse of people is an irregular system, the lawfulness or unlawfulness whereof dependeth on the occasion, and on the number of them that are assembled. If the occasion be lawful, and manifest, the concourse is lawful; as the usual meeting of men at church, or at a public show, in usual numbers: for if the numbers be extraordinarily great, the occasion is not evident; and consequently he that cannot render a particular and good account of his being amongst them, is to be judged conscious of an unlawful, and tumultuous design. It may be lawful for a thousand men, to join to a petition to be delivered to a judge, or magistrate; yet if a thousand men come to present it, it is a tumultuous assembly; because there needs but one or two for that purpose. But in such cases as these, it is not a set number that makes the assembly unlawful, but such a number, as the present officers are not able to suppress, and bring to justice.

When an unusual number of men, assemble against a man whom they accuse; the assembly is an unlawful tumult; because they may deliver their accusation to the magistrate by a few, or by one man. Such was the case of St Paul at Ephesus; where Demetrius and a great number of other men, brought two of Paul's companions before the magistrate, saying with one voice, *Great is Diana of the Ephesians*; which was their way of demanding justice against them for teaching the people such doctrine, as was against their religion, and trade. The occasion here, considering the laws of that people, was just; yet was their assembly judged unlawful, and the magistrate reprehended them for it in these words (Acts 19:40), *If Demetrius and the other workmen can accuse any man, of any thing, there be pleas, and deputies, let them accuse one another. And if you have any other thing to demand, your case may be judged in an assembly lawfully called.*

For we are in danger to be accused for this day's sedition, because there is no cause by which any man can render any reason of this concourse of people. Where he calleth an assembly, whereof men can give no just account, a sedition, and such as they could not answer for. And this is all I shall say concerning *systems*, and assemblies of people, which may be compared (as I said) to the similar parts of man's body; such as be lawful, to the muscles; such as are unlawful, to wens, biles, and apostems, engendered by the unnatural conflux of evil humours.

CHAPTER 23

Of the Public Ministers of Sovereign Power

In the last chapter I have spoken of the similar parts of a commonwealth: in this I shall speak of the parts organical, which are public ministers.

A public minister, is he, that by the sovereign, (whether a monarch or an assembly) is employed in any affairs, with authority to represent in that employment, the person of the commonwealth. And whereas every man, or assembly that hath sovereignty, representeth two persons, or (as the more common phrase is) has two capacities, one natural, and another politic (as a monarch hath the person not only of the commonwealth, but also of a man; and a sovereign assembly hath the person not only of the commonwealth, but also of the assembly); they that be servants to them in their natural capacity, are not public ministers; but those only that serve them in the administration of the public business. And therefore neither ushers, nor sergeants, nor other officers that wait on the assembly, for no other purpose but for the commodity of the men assembled, in an aristocracy, or democracy; nor stewards, chamberlains, cofferers, or any other officers of the household of a monarch, are public ministers in a monarchy.

Of public ministers, some have charge committed to them of a general administration, either of the whole dominion, or of a part thereof. Of the whole, as to a protector or regent may be committed by the predecessor of an infant king, during his minority, the whole administration of his kingdom. In which case, every subject is so far obliged to obedience, as the ordinances he shall make, and the commands he shall give be in the king's name, and not inconsistent with his sovereign power. Of a part, or province; as when either a monarch, or a sovereign assembly, shall give the general charge thereof to a governor, lieutenant, praefect, or viceroy: and in this case also, every one of that province is obliged to all he shall do in the name of the sovereign, and that is not incompatible with the sovereign's right. For such protectors, viceroys, and governors, have no other right but what depends on the sovereign's will; and no commission that can be given them, can be interpreted for a declaration of the will to transfer the sovereignty, without express and perspicuous words to that purpose. And this kind of public ministers resembleth the nerves and tendons that move the several limbs of a body natural.

Others have special administration; that is to say, charges of some special business, either at home, or abroad: as at home, first, for the economy of a commonwealth, they that have authority concerning the *treasure*, as tributes, impositions, rents, fines, or whatsoever public revenue, to collect, receive, issue, or take the accounts thereof, are public ministers: ministers, because they serve the person representative, and can do nothing against his command, nor without his authority: public, because they serve him in his political capacity.

Secondly, they that have authority concerning the *militia*; to have the custody of arms, forts, ports; to levy, pay, or conduct soliders; or to provide for any necessary thing for the use of war, either by land or sea, are public ministers. But a soldier without command, though he fight for the commonwealth, does not therefore represent the person of it; because there is none to represent it to. For every one that hath command, represents it to them only whom he commandeth.

They also that have authority to teach, or to enable others to teach the people their duty to the sovereign power, and instruct them in the knowledge of what is just and unjust, thereby to render them more apt to live in godliness, and in peace amongst themselves, and resist the public enemy, are public ministers: ministers, in that they do it not by their own authority, but by another's; and public, because they do it (or should do it) by no authority but that of the sovereign. The monarch, or the sovereign assembly only hath immediate authority from God, to teach and instruct the people; and no man but the sovereign, receiveth his power *Dei gratia* simply; that is to say, from the favour of none but God: all other, receive theirs from the favour and providence of God and their sovereigns; as in a monarchy *Dei gratia et regis*; or *Dei providentia et voluntate regis*.

They also to whom jurisdiction is given, are public ministers. For in their seats of justice they represent the person of the sovereign; and their sentence, is his sentence; for (as hath been before declared) all judicature is essentially annexed to the sovereignty; and therefore all other judges are but ministers of him or them that have the sovereign power. And as controversies are of two sorts, namely of *fact* and of *law*; so are judgments, some of fact, some of law: and consequently in the same controversy, there may be two judges, one of fact, another of law.

And in both these controversies, there may arise a controversy between the party judged, and the judge; which because they be both subjects to the sovereign, ought in equity to be judged by men agreed on by consent of both; for no man can be judge in his own cause. But the sovereign is already agreed on for judge by them both, and is therefore either to hear the cause, and determine it himself, or appoint for judge such as they shall both agree on. And this agreement is then understood to be made between them divers ways; as first, if the defendant be allowed to except against such of his judges, whose interest maketh him suspect them, (for as to the complainant he hath already chosen his own judge) those which he excepteth not against, are judges he himself agrees on. Secondly, if he appeal to any other judge, he can appeal no further; for his appeal is his choice. Thirdly, if he appeal to the sovereign himself, and he by himself, or by delegates which the parties shall agree on, give sentence; that sentence is final, for the defendant is judged by his own judges, that is to say, by himself.

These properties of just and rational judicature considered, I cannot forbear to observe the excellent constitution of the courts of justice, established both for Common, and also for Public Pleas in England. By Common Pleas, I mean those, where both the complainant and defendant are subjects: and by public, (which are also called Pleas of the Crown) those, where the complainant is the sovereign. For whereas there were two orders of men, whereof one was Lords, the other Commons; the Lords had this privilege, to have for judges if the plea were public in all capital crimes, none but Lords, and of them, as many as would be present; which being ever acknowledged as a privilege of favour, their judges were none but such as they had themselves desired. And in all controversies, every subject (as also in civil controversies the Lords) had for judges, men of the country where the matter in controversy lay; against which he might make his exceptions, till at last twelve men without exception being agreed on, they were judged by those twelve. So that having his own judges, there could be nothing alleged by the party, why the sentence should not be final. These public persons, with authority from the sovereign power, either to instruct or judge the people, are such members of the commonwealth, as may fitly be compared to the organs of voice in a body natural.

Public ministers are also all those, that have authority from the sovereign, to procure the execution of judgments given; to publish the sovereign's commands; to suppress tumults; to apprehend, and imprison malefactors; and other acts tending to the conservation of the peace. For every act they do by such authority, is the act of the commonwealth, and their service answerable to that of the hands, in a body natural.

Public ministers abroad, are those that represent the person of their own sovereign, to foreign states. Such are ambassadors, messengers, agents, and heralds, sent by public authority, and on public business.

But such as are sent by authority only of some private party of a troubled state, though they be received, are neither public nor private ministers of the commonwealth; because none of their actions have the commonwealth for author. Likewise, an ambassador sent from a prince, to congratulate, condole, or to assist at a solemnity; though the authority be public; yet because the business is private, and belonging to him in his natural capacity; is a private person. Also if a man be sent into another country, secretly to explore their counsels, and strength; though both the authority, and the business be public; yet because there is none to take notice of any person in him, but his own; he is but a private minister; but yet a minister of the commonwealth; and may be compared to an eye in the body natural. And those that are appointed to receive the petitions or other informations of the people, and are as it were the public ear, are public ministers, and represent their sovereign in that office.

Neither a councillor (nor a council of state, if we consider it with no authority of judicature or command, but only of giving advice to the sovereign when it is required, or of offering it when it is not required) is a public person. For the advice is addressed to the sovereign only, whose person cannot in his own presence, be represented to him, by another. But a body of councillors, are never without some other authority, either of judicature, or of immediate administration: as in a monarchy, they represent the monarch, in delivering his commands to the public ministers: in a democracy, the council, or senate propounds the result of their deliberations to the people, as a council; but when they appoint judges, or hear causes, or give audience to ambassadors, it is in the quality of a minister of the people: and in an aristocracy the council of state is the sovereign assembly itself; and gives counsel to none but themselves.

CHAPTER 24

Of the Nutrition, and Procreation, of a Commonwealth

The nutrition of a commonwealth consisteth, in the *plenty*, and *distribution of materials* conducing to life: in *concoction*, or *preparation*; and (when concocted) in the *conveyance* of it, by convenient conduits, to the public use.

As for the plenty of matter, it is a thing limited by nature, to those commodities, which from (the two breasts of our common mother) land and sea, God usually either freely giveth, or for labour selleth to mankind.

For the matter of this nutriment, consisting in animals, vegetals, and minerals, God hath freely laid them before us, in or near to the face of the earth; so as there needeth no more but the labour and industry of receiving them. Insomuch as plenty dependeth (next to God's favour) merely on the labour and industry of men.

This matter, commonly called commodities, is partly *native*, and partly *foreign: native*, that which is to be had within the territory of the commonwealth: *foreign*, that which is imported from without.

And because there is no territory under the dominion of one commonwealth, (except it be of very vast extent) that produceth all things needful for the maintenance, and motion of the whole body; and few that produce not some thing more than necessary; the superfluous commodities to be had within, become no more superfluous, but supply these wants at home, by importation of that which may be had abroad, either by exchange, or by just war, or by labour: for a man's labour also, is a commodity exchangeable for benefit, as well as any other thing: and there have been commonwealths that having no more territory, than hath served them for habitation, have nevertheless, not only maintained, but also increased their power, partly by the labour of trading from one place to another, and partly by selling the manufactures, whereof the materials were brought in from other places.

The distribution of the materials of this nourishment, is the constitution of *mine*, and *thine*, and *his*; that is to say, in one word *propriety*; and belongeth in all kinds of commonwealth to the sovereign power. For where there is no commonwealth, there is (as hath been already shown) a perpetual war of every man against his neighbour; and therefore every thing is his that getteth it, and keepeth it by force; which is neither *propriety*, nor *community*; but *uncertainty*. Which is so evident, that even Cicero, (a passionate defender of liberty) in a public pleading, attributeth all propriety to the law civil, *Let the civil law*, saith he, *be once abandoned, or but negligently guarded, (not to say oppressed) and there is nothing, that any man can be sure to receive from his ancestor, or leave to his children*. And again; *Take away the civil law, and no man knows what is his own, and what another man's*. Seeing therefore the introduction of *propriety* is an effect of commonwealth; which can do nothing but by the person that represents it, it is the act only of the sovereign; and consisteth in the laws, which none can make that have not the sovereign power. And this they well knew of old, who called that νόμος (that is to say, *distribution*) which we call law; and defined justice, by *distributing* to every man *his own*.

In this distribution, the first law, is for division of the land itself: wherein the sovereign assigneth to every man a portion, according as he, and not according as any subject, or any number of them, shall judge agreeable to equity, and the common good. The children of Israel, were a commonwealth in the wilderness; but wanted the commodities of the earth, till they were masters of the Land of Promise; which afterward was divided amongst them, not by their own discretion, but by the discretion of Eleazar the Priest, and Joshua their General: who when there were twelve tribes, making them thirteen by subdivision of the tribe of Joseph; made nevertheless but twelve portions of the land; and ordained for the tribe of Levi no land; but assigned them the tenth part of the whole fruits; which division was therefore arbitrary. And though a people coming into possession of a land by war, do not always exterminate the ancient inhabitants, (as did the Jews) but leave to many, or most, or all of them their estates; yet it is manifest they hold them afterwards, as of the victors' distribution; as the people of England held all theirs of William the Conqueror.

From whence we may collect, that the propriety which a subject hath in his lands, consisteth in a right to exclude all other subjects from the use of them; and not to exclude their sovereign, be it an assembly, or a monarch. For seeing the sovereign, that is to say, the commonwealth (whose person he representeth) is understood to do nothing but in order to the common peace and security, this distribution of lands, is to be understood as done in order to the same: and consequently, whatsoever distribution another shall make in prejudice thereof, is contrary to the will of every subject, that committed his peace and safety to his discretion and conscience; and therefore by the will of every one of them, is to be reputed void. It is true, that a sovereign monarch, or the greater part of a sovereign assembly, may ordain the doing of many things in pursuit of their passions, contrary to their own consciences, which is a breach of trust, and of the law of nature; but this is not enough to authorise any subject, either to make war upon, or so much as to accuse of injustice, or any way to speak evil of their sovereign; because they have authorized all his actions, and in bestowing the sovereign power, made them their own. But in what cases the commands of sovereigns are contrary to equity, and the law of nature, is to be considered hereafter in another place.

In the distribution of land, the commonwealth itself may be conceived to have a portion, and possess and improve that same by their representative; and that such portion may be made sufficient, to sustain the whole expense to the common peace and defence necessarily required: which were very true, if there could be any representative conceived free from human passions, and infirmities. But the nature of men being as it is, the setting forth of public land, or of any certain revenue for the commonwealth, is in vain; and tendeth to the dissolution of government, and to the condition of mere nature, and war, as soon as ever the sovereign power falleth into the hands of a monarch, or of an assembly, that are either too negligent of money, or too hazardous in engaging the public stock into a long or costly war. Commonwealths can endure no diet: for seeing their expense is not limited by their own appetite, but by external accidents, and the appetites of their neighbours, the public riches cannot be limited by other limits, than those which the emergent occasions shall require. And whereas in England, there were by the Conqueror, divers lands reserved to his own use, (besides forests, and chases, either for his recreation, or preservation of woods) and divers services reserved on the land he gave his subjects; yet it seems they were not reserved for his maintenance in his public, but in his natural capacity: for he and his successors did for all that, lay arbitrary taxes on all subjects' land, when they judged it necessary. Or if those public lands, and services, were ordained as a sufficient maintenance of the commonwealth, it was contrary to the scope of the institution; being (as it appears by those ensuing taxes) insufficient, and (as it appears by the late small revenue of the crown) subject to alienation, and diminution. It is therefore in vain, to assign a portion to the commonwealth; which may sell, or give it away; and does sell, and give it away, when 'tis done by their representative.

As the distribution of lands at home; so also to assign in what places, and for what commodities, the subject shall traffic abroad, belongeth to the sovereign. For if it did belong to private persons to use their own discretion therein, some of them would be drawn for gain, both to furnish the enemy with means to hurt the commonwealth, and hurt it themselves, by importing such things, as pleasing men's appetites, be nevertheless noxious, or at least unprofitable to them. And therefore it belongeth to the commonwealth (that is, to the sovereign only) to approve, or disapprove both of the places and matter of foreign traffic.

Further, seeing it is not enough to the sustentation of a commonwealth, that every man have a propriety in a portion of land, or in some few commodities, or a natural property in some useful art, and that there is no art in the world, but is necessary either for the being, or well-being almost of every particular man; it is necessary, that men distribute that which they can spare, and transfer their propriety therein, mutually one to another, by exchange, and mutual contract. And therefore it belongeth to the commonwealth, (that is to say, to the sovereign) to appoint in what manner, all kinds of contract between subjects, (as buying, selling, exchanging, borrowing, lending, letting, and taking to hire) are to be made; and by what words and signs they shall be understood for valid. And for the matter, and distribution of the nourishment, to the several members of the commonwealth, thus much (considering the model of the whole work) is sufficient.

By concoction, I understand the reducing of all commodities, which are not presently consumed, but reserved for nourishment in time to come, to something of equal value, and withal so portable, as not to hinder the motion of men from place to place; to the end a man may have in what place soever, such nourishment as the place affordeth. And this is nothing else but gold, and silver, and money. For gold and silver, being (as it happens) almost in all countries of the world highly valued, is a commodious measure of the value of all things else between nations; and money (of what matter soever coined by the sovereign of a commonwealth) is a sufficient measure of the value of all things else, between the subjects of that commonwealth. By the means of which measures, all commodities, movable and immovable, are made to accompany a man to all places of his resort, within and without the place of his ordinary residence; and the same passeth from man to man, within the commonwealth; and goes round about, nourishing (as it passeth) every part thereof; in so much as this concoction, is as it were the sanguification of the commonwealth: for natural blood is in like manner made of the fruits of the earth; and circulating, nourisheth by the way every member of the body of man.

And because silver and gold have their value from the matter itself; they have first this privilege, that the value of them cannot be altered by the power of one, nor of a few commonwealths; as being a common measure of the commodities of all places. But base money may easily be enhanced or abased. Secondly, they have the privilege to make commonwealths move, and stretch out their arms, when need is, into foreign countries; and supply, not only private subjects that travel, but also whole armies with provision. But that coin, which is not considerable for the matter, but for the stamp of the place, being unable to endure change of air, hath its effect at home only; where also it is subject to the change of laws, and thereby to have the value diminished, to the prejudice many times of those that have it.

The conduits, and ways by which it is conveyed to the public use, are of two sorts; one, that conveyeth it to the public coffers; the other, that issueth the same out again for public payments. Of the first sort, are collectors, receivers, and treasures; of the second are the treasurers again, and the officers appointed for payment of several public or private ministers. And in this also, the artificial man maintains his resemblance with the natural; whose veins receiving the blood from the several parts of the body, carry it to the heart; where being made vital, the heart by the arteries sends it out again, to enliven, and enable for motion all the members of the same.

The procreation, or children of a Commonwealth, are those we call *plantations*, or *colonies*; which are numbers of men sent out from the Commonwealth, under a conductor, or governor, to inhabit a foreign country, either formerly void of inhabitants, or made void then by war. And when a colony is settled, they are either a Commonwealth of themselves, discharged of their subjection to their sovereign that sent them, (as hath been done by many Commonwealths, of ancient time) in which case the Commonwealth from which they went, was called their metropolis, or mother, and requires no more of them, than fathers require of the children, whom they emancipate, and make free from their domestic government, which is honour, and friendship; or else they remain united to their metropolis, as were the colonies of the people of Rome; and then they are no Commonwealths themselves, but provinces, and parts of the Commonwealth that sent them. So that the right of colonies (saving honour, and league with their metropolis) dependeth wholly on their licence, or letters, by which their sovereign authorised them to plant.

CHAPTER 25

Of Counsel

How fallacious it is to judge of the nature of things, by the ordinary and inconstant use of words, appeareth in nothing more, than in the confusion of counsels, and commands, arising from the imperative manner of speaking in them both, and in many other occasions besides. For the words *do this*, are the words not only of him that commandeth; but also of him that giveth counsel; and of him that exhorteth; and yet there are but few, that see not that these are very different things; or that cannot distinguish between them, when they perceive who it is that speaketh, and to whom the speech is directed, and upon what occasion. But finding those phrases in men's writings, and being not able, or not willing to enter into a consideration of the circumstances, they mistake sometimes the precepts of counsellors, for the precepts of them that command; and sometimes the contrary; according as it best agreeth with the conclusions they would infer, or the actions they approve. To avoid which mistakes, and render to those terms of commanding, counselling, and exhorting, their proper and distinct significations, I define them thus.

Command is, where a man saith, *do this*, or *do not this*, without expecting other reason than the will of him that says it. From this it followeth manifestly, that he that commandeth, pretendeth thereby his own benefit: for the reason of his command is his own will only, and the proper object of every man's will, is some good to himself.

Counsel, is where a man saith, *do*, or *do not this*, and deduceth his reasons from the benefit that arriveth by it to him to whom he saith it. And from this it is evident, that he that giveth counsel, pretendeth only (whatsoever he intendeth) the good of him, to whom he giveth it.

Therefore between counsel and command, one great difference is, that command is directed to a man's own benefit; and counsel to the benefit of another man. And from this ariseth another difference, that a man may be obliged to do what he is commanded; as when he hath covenanted to obey: but he cannot be obliged to do as he is counselled, because the hurt of not following it, is his own; or if he should covenant to follow it, then is the counsel turned into the nature of a command. A third difference between them is, that no man can pretend a right to be of another man's counsel; because he is not to pretend benefit by it to himself: but to demand right to counsel another, argues a will to know his designs, or to gain some other good to himself; which (as I said before) is of every man's will the proper object.

This also is incident to the nature of counsel; that whatsoever it be, he that asketh it, cannot in equity accuse, or punish it: for to ask counsel of another, is to permit him to give such counsel as he shall think best; and consequently, he that giveth counsel to his sovereign, (whether a monarch, or an assembly) when he asketh it, cannot in equity be punished for it, whether the same be conformable to the opinion of the most, or not, so it be to the proposition in debate.

For if the sense of the assembly can be taken notice of, before the debate be ended, they should neither ask, nor take any further counsel; for the sense of the assembly, is the resolution of the debate, and end of all deliberation. And generally he that demandeth counsel, is author of it; and therefore cannot punish it; and what the sovereign cannot, no man else can. But if one subject giveth counsel to another, to do anything contrary to the laws, whether that counsel proceed from evil intention, or from ignorance only, it is punishable by the Commonwealth; because ignorance of the law, is no good excuse, where every man is bound to take notice of the laws to which he is subject.

Exhortation and dehortation is counsel, accompanied with signs in him that giveth it, of vehement desire to have it followed: or to say it more briefly, *counsel vehemently pressed.* For he that exhorteth, doth not deduce the consequences of what he adviseth to be done, and tie himself therein to the rigour of true reasoning; but encourages him he counselleth, to action: as he that dehorteth, deterreth him from it. And, therefore, they have in their speeches, a regard to the common passions, and opinions of men, in deducing their reasons; and make use of similitudes, metaphors, examples, and other tools of oratory, to persuade their hearers of the utility, honour, or justice of following their advice.

From whence may be inferred, first, that exhortation and dehortation is directed to the good of him that giveth the counsel, not of him that asketh it, which is contrary to the duty of a counsellor; who (by the definition of counsel) ought to regard, not his own benefit, but his whom he adviseth. And that he directeth his counsel to his own benefit, is manifest enough, by the long and vehement urging, or by the artificial giving thereof; which being not required of him, and consequently proceeding from his own occasions, is directed principally to his own benefit, and but accidentally to the good of him that is counselled, or not at all.

Secondly, that the use of exhortation and dehortation lieth only where a man is to speak to a multitude; because when the speech is addressed to one, he may interrupt him, and examine his reasons more rigorously, than can be done in a multitude; which are too many to enter into dispute and dialogue with him that speaketh indifferently to them all at once.

Thirdly, that they that exhort and dehort, where they are required to give counsel, are corrupt counsellors, and as it were bribed by their own interest. For though the counsel they give be never so good; yet he that gives it, is no more a good counsellor, than he that giveth a just sentence for a reward, is a just judge. But where a man may lawfully command, as a father in his family, or a leader in an army, his exhortations and dehortations, are not only lawful, but also necessary, and laudable: but then they are no more counsels, but commands; which when they are for execution of sour labour, sometimes necessity, and always humanity requireth to be sweetened in the delivery, by encouragement, and in the tune and phrase of counsel, rather than in harsher language of command.

Examples of the difference between command and counsel, we may take from the forms of speech that express them in Holy Scripture. *Have no other Gods but me*; *make to thyself no graven image*; *take not God's name in vain*; *sanctify the sabbath*; *honour thy parents*; *kill not*; *steal not*, etc. are commands; because the reason for which we are to obey them, is drawn from the will of God our king, whom we are obliged to obey. But these words, *Sell all thou hast*; *give it to the poor*; *and follow me*, are counsel; because the reason for which we are to do so, is drawn from our own benefit; which is this, that we shall have *treasure in Heaven*. These words, *Go into the village over against you*, *and you shall find an ass tied*, *and her colt*; *loose her*, *and bring her to me*, are a command: for the reason of their fact is drawn from the will of their Master: but these words, *Repent and be baptized in the name of Jesus*, are counsel; because the reason why we should so do, tendeth not to any benefit of God Almighty, who shall still be king in what manner soever we rebel; but of ourselves, who have no other means of avoiding the punishment hanging over us for our sins past.

As the difference of counsel from command, hath been now deduced from the nature of counsel, consisting in a deducing of the benefit or hurt that may arise to him that is to be counselled, by the necessary or probable consequences of the action he propoundeth; so may also the differences between *apt*, and *inept* counsellors be derived from the same. For experience, being but memory of the consequences of like actions formerly observed, and counsel but the speech whereby that experience is made known to another; the virtues and defects of counsel, are the same with the virtues and defects intellectual: and to the person of a Commonwealth, his counsellors serve him in the place of memory, and mental discourse. But with this resemblance of the Commonwealth, to a natural man, there is one dissimilitude joined, of great importance; which is, that a natural man receiveth his experience, from the natural objects of sense, which work upon him without passion, or interest of their own; whereas they that give counsel to the representative person of a Commonwealth, may have, and have often their particular ends, and passions, that render their counsels always suspected, and many times unfaithful. And therefore we may set down for the first condition of a good counsellor, *that his ends and interests, be not inconsistent with the ends and interests of him he counselleth*.

Secondly, because the office of a counsellor, when an action comes into deliberation, is to make manifest the consequences of it, in such manner, as he that is counselled may be truly and evidently informed; he ought to propound his advice, in such form of speech, as may make the truth most evidently appear; that is to say, with as firm ratiocination, as significant and proper language, and as briefly, as the evidence will permit. And therefore *rash and unevident inferences*, (such as are fetched only from examples, or authority of books, and are not arguments of what is good or evil but witnesses of fact, or of opinion) *obscure, confused, and ambiguous expression, also all metaphorical speeches, tending to the stirring up of passion*, (because such reasoning, and such expressions, are useful only to deceive, or to lead him we counsel towards other ends than his own) *are repugnant to the office of a counsellor*.

Thirdly, because the ability of counselling proceedeth from experience, and long study; and no man is presumed to have experience in all those things that to the administration of a great Commonwealth are necessary to be known, *no man is presumed to be a good counsellor, but in such business, as he hath not only been much versed in, but hath also much meditated on, and considered.* For seeing the business of a Commonwealth is this, to preserve the people in peace at home, and defend them against foreign invasion, we shall find, it requires great knowledge of the disposition of mankind, of the rights of government, and of the nature of equity, law, justice, and honour, not to be attained without study; and of the strength, commodities, places, both of their own country, and their neighbours; as also of the inclinations and designs of all nations that may any way annoy them. And this is not attained to, without much experience. Of which things, not only the whole sum, but every one of the particulars requires the age, and observation of a man in years, and of more than ordinary study. The wit required for counsel, as I have said before (chapter 8) is judgment. And the differences of men in that point come from different education, of some to one kind of study, or business, and of others to another. When for the doing of any thing, there be infallible rules, (as in engines, and edifices, the rules of geometry) all the experience of the world cannot equal his counsel, that has learnt, or found out the rule. And when there is no such rule, he that hath most experience in that particular kind of business, has therein the best judgment, and is the best counsellor.

Fourthly, to be able to give counsel to a Commonwealth, in a business that hath reference to another Commonwealth, *it is necessary to be acquainted with the intelligences, and letters* that come from thence, *and with all the records of treaties, and other transactions of state* between them; which none can do, but such as the representative shall think fit. By which we may see, that they who are not called to counsel, can have no good counsel in such cases to obtrude.

Fifthly, supposing the number of counsellors equal, a man is better counselled by hearing them apart, than in an assembly; and that for many causes. First, in hearing them apart, you have the advice of every man; but in an assembly many of them deliver their advice with *aye*, or *no*, or with their hands, or feet, not moved by their own sense, but by the eloquence of another, or for fear of displeasing some that have spoken, or the whole assembly, by contradiction; or for fear of appearing duller in apprehension, than those that have applauded the contrary opinion. Secondly, in an assembly of many, there cannot choose but be some whose interests are contrary to that of the public; and these their interests make passionate, and passion eloquent, and eloquence draws others into the same advice. For the passions of men, which asunder are moderate, as the heat of one brand; in an assembly are like many brands, that inflame one another (especially when they blow one another with orations) to the setting of the Commonwealth on fire, under pretence of counselling it. Thirdly, in hearing every man apart, one may examine (when there is need) the truth or probability of his reasons, and of the grounds of the advice he gives, by frequent interruptions and objections; which cannot be done in an assembly, where (in every difficult question) a man is rather astonied, and dazzled with the variety of discourse upon it, than informed of the course he ought to take. Besides, there cannot be an assembly of many, called together for advice, wherein there be not some, that have the ambition to be thought eloquent, and also learned in the politics; and give not their advice with care of the business propounded, but of the applause of their motley orations made of the divers coloured threads, or shreds of authors; which is an impertinence at least, that takes away the time of serious consultation, and in the secret way of counselling apart, is easily avoided. Fourthly, in deliberations that ought to be kept secret, (whereof there be many occasions in public business) the counsels of many, and especially in assemblies, are dangerous; and therefore great assemblies are necessitated to commit such affairs to lesser numbers, and of such persons as are most versed in them, and in whose fidelity they have most confidence.

To conclude, who is there that so far approves the taking of counsel from a great assembly of counsellors, that wisheth for, or would accept of their pains, when there is a question of marrying his children, disposing of his lands, governing his household, or managing his private estate, especially if there be amongst them such as wish not his prosperity? A man that doth his business by the help of many and prudent counsellors, with every one consulting apart in his proper element, does it best, as he that useth able seconds at tennis play, placed in their proper stations. He does next best, that useth his own judgment only; as he that has no second at all. But he that is carried up and down to his business in a framed counsel, which cannot move but by the plurality of consenting opinions, the execution whereof is commonly (out of envy, or interest) retarded by the part dissenting, does it worst of all, and is like one that is carried to the ball, though by good players, yet in a wheel-barrow, or other frame, heavy of itself, and retarded also by the inconcurrent judgments, and endeavours of them that drive it; and so much the more, as they be more that set their hands to it; and most of all, when there is one or more amongst them, that desire to have him lose. And though it be true, that many eyes see more than one; yet it is not to be understood of many counsellors; but then only, when the final resolution is in one man. Otherwise, because many eyes see the same thing in divers lines, and are apt to look asquint towards their private benefit; they that desire not to miss their mark, though they look about with two eyes, yet they never aim but with one; and therefore no great popular Commonwealth was ever kept up, but either by a foreign enemy that united them; or by the reputation of some eminent man amongst them; or by the secret counsel of a few; or by the mutual fear of equal factions; and not by the open consultations of the assembly. And as for very little Commonwealths, be they popular or monarchical, there is no human wisdom can uphold them, longer than the jealousy lasteth of their potent neighbours.

CHAPTER 26

Of Civil Laws

By civil laws, I understand the laws, that men are therefore bound to observe, because they are members, not of this or that Commonwealth in particular, but of a Commonwealth. For the knowledge of particular laws belongeth to them, that profess the study of the laws of their several countries; but the knowledge of civil law in general, to any man. The ancient law of Rome was called their *civil law*, from the word *civitas*s, which signifies a Commonwealth: and those countries, which having been under the Roman empire, and governed by that law, retain still such part thereof as they think fit, and call that part the civil law, to distinguish it from the rest of their own civil laws. But that is not it I intend to speak of here; my design being not to show what is law here, and there; but what is law; as Plato, Aristotle, Cicero, and divers others have done, without taking upon them the profession of the study of the law.

And first it is manifest, that law in general, is not counsel, but command; nor a command of any man to any man; but only of him, whose command is addressed to one formerly obliged to obey him.

And as for civil law, it addeth only the name of the person commanding, which is *persona civitatis*, the person of the Commonwealth.

Which considered, I define civil law in this manner. Civil law, *is to every subject, those rules, which the Commonwealth hath commanded him, by word, writing, or other sufficient sign of the will, to make use of, for the distinction of right and wrong; that is to say, of what is contrary, and what is not contrary to the rule.*

In which definition, there is nothing that is not at first sight evident. For every man seeth, that some laws are addressed to all the subjects in general; some to particular provinces; some to particular vocations; and some to particular men; and are therefore laws, to every of those to whom the command is directed; and to none else. As also, that laws are the rules of just, and unjust; nothing being reputed unjust, that is not contrary to some law. Likewise, that none can make laws but the Commonwealth; because our subjection is to the Commonwealth only: and that commands are to be signified by sufficient signs; because a man knows not otherwise how to obey them. And therefore, whatsoever can from this definition by necessary consequence be deduced, ought to be acknowledged for truth. Now I deduce from it this that followeth.

The legislator in all Commonwealths, is only the sovereign, be he one man, as in a monarchy, or one assembly of men, as in a democracy or aristocracy. For the legislator, is he that maketh the law. And the Commonwealth only, prescribes, and commandeth the observation of those rules, which we call law: therefore the Commonwealth is the legislator. But the Commonwealth is no person, nor has capacity to do any thing, but by the representative, (that is, the sovereign) and therefore the sovereign is the sole legislator. For the same reason, none can abrogate a law made, but the sovereign; because a law is not abrogated, but by another law, that forbiddeth it to be put in execution.

The sovereign of a Commonwealth, be it an

assembly, or one man, is not subject to the civil laws. For having power to make, and repeal laws, he may when he pleaseth, free himself from that subjection, by repealing those laws that trouble him, and making of new; and consequently he was free before. For he is free, that can be free when he will: nor is it possible for any person to be bound to himself; because he that can bind, can release; and therefore he that is bound to himself only, is not bound.

When long use obtaineth the authority of a law, it is not the length of time that maketh the authority, but the will of the sovereign signified by his silence, (for silence is sometimes an argument of consent) and it is no longer law, than the sovereign shall be silent therein. And therefore if the sovereign shall have a question of right grounded, not upon his present will, but upon the laws formerly made; the length of time shall bring no prejudice to his right; but the question shall be judged by equity. For many unjust actions, and unjust sentences, go uncontrolled a longer time, than any man can remember. And our lawyers account no customs law, but such as are reasonable, and that evil customs are to be abolished: but the judgment of what is reasonable, and of what is to be abolished, belongeth to him that maketh the law, which is the sovereign assembly, or monarch.

The law of nature, and the civil law, contain each other, and are of equal extent. For the laws of nature, which consist in equity, justice, gratitude, and other moral virtues on these depending, in the condition of mere nature (as I have said before in the end of the fifteenth chapter) are not properly laws, but qualities that dispose men to peace, and obedience. When a Commonwealth is once settled, then are they actually laws, and not before; as being then the commands of the Commonwealth; and therefore also civil laws: for it is the sovereign power that obliges men to obey them. For in the differences of private men, to declare, what is equity, what is justice, and what is moral virtue, and to make them binding, there is need of the ordinances of sovereign power, and punishments to be ordained for such as shall break them; which ordinances are therefore part of the civil law. The law of nature therefore is a part of the civil law in all Commonwealths of the world. Reciprocally also, the civil law is a part of the dictates of nature. For justice, that is to say, performance of covenant, and giving to every man his own, is a dictate of the law of nature. But every subject in a Commonwealth, hath covenanted to obey the civil law; (either one with another, as when they assemble to make a common representative, or with the representative itself one by one, when subdued by the sword they promise obedience, that they may receive life) and therefore obedience to the civil law is part also of the law of nature. Civil and natural law are not different kinds, but different parts of law; whereof one part being written, is called civil, the other unwritten, natural. But the right of nature, that is, the natural liberty of man, may by the civil law be abridged, and restrained: nay, the end of making laws, is no other, but such restraint; without the which there cannot possibly be any peace. And law was brought into the world for nothing else, but to limit the natural liberty of particular men, in such manner, as they might not hurt, but assist one another, and join together against a common enemy.

If the sovereign of one Commonwealth, subdue a

people that have lived under other written laws, and afterwards govern them by the same laws, by which they were governed before; yet those laws are the civil laws of the victor, and not of the vanquished Commonwealth. For the legislator is he, not by whose authority the laws were first made, but by whose authority they now continue to be laws. And therefore where there be divers provinces, within the dominion of a Commonwealth, and in those provinces diversity of laws, which commonly are called the customs of each several province, we are not to understand that such customs have their force, only from length of time; but that they were anciently laws written, or otherwise made known, for the constitutions, and statutes of their sovereigns; and are now laws, not by virtue of the prescription of time, but by the constitutions of their present sovereigns. But if an unwritten law, in all the provinces of a dominion, shall be generally observed, and no iniquity appear in the use thereof; that law can be no other but a law of nature, equally obliging all mankind.

Seeing then all laws, written and unwritten, have their authority, and force, from the will of the Commonwealth; that is to say, from the will of the representative; which in a monarchy is the monarch, and in other Commonwealths the sovereign assembly; a man may wonder from whence proceed such opinions, as are found in the books of lawyers of eminence in several Commonwealths, directly or by consequence making the legislative power depend on private men, or subordinate judges. As for example, *that the common law, hath no controller but the parliament*; which is true only where a parliament has the sovereign power, and cannot be assembled, nor dissolved, but by their own discretion. For if there be a right in any else to dissolve them, there is a right also to control them, and consequently to control their controllings. And if there be no such right, then the controller of laws is not *parliamentum*, but *rex in parliamento*. And where a parliament is sovereign, if it should assemble never so many, or so wise men, from the countries subject to them, for whatsoever cause; yet there is no man will believe, that such an assembly hath thereby acquired to themselves a legislative power. *Item*, that the two arms of a Commonwealth, are *force and justice*; *the first whereof is in the king*; *the other deposited in the hands of the parliament*. As if a Commonwealth could consist, where the force were in any hand, which justice had not the authority to command and govern.

That law can never be against reason, our lawyers are agreed; and that not the letter, (that is every construction of it) but that which is according to the intention of the legislator, is the law. And it is true: but the doubt is, of whose reason it is, that shall be received for law. It is not meant of any private reason; for then there would be as much contradiction in the laws, as there is in the Schools; nor yet, (as Sir Edward Coke makes it) an *artificial perfection of reason, gotten by long study, observation, and experience*, (as his was.) For it is possible long study may increase and confirm erroneous sentences: and where men build on false grounds, the more they build, the greater is the ruin: and of those that study and observe with equal time and diligence, the reasons and resolutions are, and must remain discordant: and therefore it is not that *juris prudentia*, or wisdom of subordinate judges; but the reason of this our artificial man the Commonwealth, and his command, that maketh law: and the

Commonwealth being in their representative but one person, there cannot easily arise any contradiction in the laws; and when there doth, the same reason is able, by interpretation, or alteration, to take it away. In all courts of justice, the sovereign (which is the person of the Commonwealth) is he that judgeth: the subordinate judge, ought to have regard to the reason, which moved his sovereign to make such law, that his sentence may be according thereunto; which then is his sovereign's sentence; otherwise it is his own, and an unjust one.

From this, that the law is a command, and a command consisteth in declaration, or manifestation of the will of him that commandeth, by voice, writing, or some other sufficient argument of the same, we may understand, that the command of the Commonwealth, is law only to those, that have means to take notice of it. Over natural fools, children, or madmen there is no law, no more than over brute beasts; nor are they capable of the title of just, or unjust; because they had never power to make any covenant, or to understand the consequences thereof; and consequently never took upon them to authorize the actions of any sovereign, as they must do that make to themselves a Commonwealth. And as those from whom nature or accident hath taken away the notice of all laws in general; so also every man, from whom any accident, not proceeding from his own default, hath taken away the means to take notice of any particular law, is excused, if he observe it not; and to speak properly, that law is no law to him. It is therefore necessary, to consider in this place, what arguments and signs be sufficient for the knowledge of what is the law; that is to say, what is the will of the sovereign, as well in monarchies, as in other forms of government.

And first, if it be a law that obliges all the subjects without exception, and is not written, nor otherwise published in such places as they may take notice thereof, it is a law of nature. For whatsoever men are to take knowledge of for law, not upon other men's words, but every one from his own reason, must be such as is agreeable to the reason of all men; which no law can be, but the law of nature. The laws of nature therefore need not any publishing, nor proclamation; as being contained in this one sentence, approved by all the world, *Do not that to another, which thou thinkest unreasonable to be done by another to thyself.*

Secondly, if it be a law that obliges only some condition of men, or one particular man, and be not written, nor published by word, then also it is a law of nature; and known by the same arguments, and signs, that distinguish those in such a condition, from other subjects. For whatsoever law is not written, or some way published by him that makes it law, can be known no way, but by the reason of him that is to obey it; and is therefore also a law not only civil, but natural. For example, if the sovereign employ a public minister, without written instructions what to do; he is obliged to take for instructions the dictates of reason; as if he make a judge, the judge is to take notice, that his sentence ought to be according to the reason of his sovereign, which being always understood to be equity, he is bound to it by the law of nature: or if an ambassador, he is (in all things not contained in his written instructions) to take for instruction that which reason dictates to be most conducing to his sovereign's interests; and so of all other ministers of the sovereignty, public and private. All which instructions of natural reason may be comprehended under one name of *fidelity*; which is a branch of natural justice.

The law of nature excepted, it belongeth to the essence of all other laws, to be made known, to every man that shall be obliged to obey them, either by word, or writing, or some other act, known to proceed from the sovereign authority. For the will of another, cannot be understood, but by his own word, or act, or by conjecture taken from his scope and purpose; which in the person of the Commonwealth, is to be supposed always consonant to equity and reason. And in ancient time, before letters were in common use, the laws were many times put into verse; that the rude people taking pleasure in singing, or reciting them, might the more easily retain them in memory. And for the same reason Solomon (Prov. 7:3) adviseth a man, to bind the ten commandments upon his ten fingers. And for the law which Moses gave to the people of Israel at the renewing of the covenant (Deut. 11:19), he biddeth them to teach it their children, by discoursing of it both at home, and upon the way; at going to bed, and at rising from bed; and to write it upon the posts and doors of their houses; and (Deut. 31:12) to assemble the people, man, woman, and child, to hear it read.

Nor is it enough the law be written, and published; but also that there be manifest signs, that it proceedeth from the will of the sovereign. For private men, when they have, or think they have force enough to secure their unjust designs, and convoy them safely to their ambitious ends, may publish for laws what they please, without or against the legislative authority.

There is therefore requisite, not only a declaration of the law, but also sufficient signs of the author, and authority. The author, or legislator is supposed in every Commonwealth to be evident, because he is the sovereign, who having been constituted by the consent of every one, is supposed by every one to be sufficiently known. And though the ignorance, and security of men be such, for the most part, as that when the memory of the first constitution of their Commonwealth is worn out, they do not consider, by whose power they used to be defended against their enemies, and to have their industry protected, and to be righted when injury is done them; yet because no man that considers, can make question of it, no excuse can be derived from the ignorance of where the sovereignty is placed. And it is a dictate of natural reason, and consequently an evident law of nature, that no man ought to weaken that power, the protection whereof he hath himself demanded, or wittingly received against others. Therefore of who is sovereign, no man, but by his own fault, (whatsoever evil men suggest) can make any doubt. The difficulty consisteth in the evidence of the authority derived from him; the removing whereof, dependeth on the knowledge of the public registers, public counsels, public ministers, and public seals; by which all laws are sufficiently verified; verified, I say, not authorized: for the verification, is but the testimony and record, not the authority of the law; which consisteth in the command of the sovereign only.

If therefore a man have a question of injury, depending on the law of nature; that is to say, on common equity; the sentence of the judge, that by commission hath authority to take cognizance of such causes, is a sufficient verification of the law of nature in that individual case. For though the advice of one that professeth the study of the law, be useful for the avoiding of contention; yet it is but advice: 'tis the judge must tell men what is law, upon the hearing of the controversy.

But when the question is of injury, or crime, upon a written law; every man by recourse to the registers, by himself or others, may (if he will) be sufficiently informed, before he do such injury, or commit the crime, whether it be an injury, or not: nay he ought to do so: for when a man doubts whether the act he goeth about, be just or unjust: and may inform himself, if he will; the doing is unlawful. In like manner, he that supposeth himself injured, in a case determined by the written law, which he may by himself or others see and consider; if he complain before he consults with the law, he does unjustly, and bewrayeth a disposition rather to vex other men, than to demand his own right.

If the question be of obedience to a public officer; to have seen his commission, with the public seal, and heard it read; or to have had the means to be informed of it, if a man would, is a sufficient verification of his authority. For every man is obliged to do his best endeavour, to inform himself of all written laws, that may concern his own future actions.

The legislator known; and the laws, either by writing, or by the light of nature, sufficiently published; there wanteth yet another very material circumstance to make them obligatory. For it is not the letter, but the intendment, or meaning; that is to say, the authentic interpretation of the law (which is the sense of the legislator) in which the nature of the law consisteth;

and therefore the interpretation of all laws dependeth on the authority sovereign; and the interpreters can be none but those which the sovereign (to whom only the subject oweth obedience) shall appoint. For else, by the craft of an interpreter, the law may be made to bear a sense contrary to that of the sovereign; by which means the interpreter becomes the legislator.

All laws, written and unwritten, have need of interpretation. The unwritten law of nature, though it be easy to such as without partiality and passion, make use of their natural reason, and therefore leaves the violators thereof without excuse; yet considering there be very few, perhaps none, that in some cases are not blinded by self-love, or some other passion, it is now become of all laws the most obscure; and has consequently the greatest need of able interpreters. The written laws, if they be short, are easily misinterpreted, from the divers significations of a word, or two: if long, they be more obscure by the divers significations of many words: insomuch as no written law, delivered in few or many words, can be well understood, without a perfect understanding of the final causes, for which the law was made; the knowledge of which final causes is in the legislator. To him therefore there cannot be any knot in the law, insoluble; either by finding out the ends, to undo it by; or else by making what ends he will, (as Alexander did with his sword in the Gordian knot) by the legislative power; which no other interpreter can do.

The interpretation of the laws of nature, in a Commonwealth, dependeth not on the books of moral philosophy. The authority of writers, without the authority of the Commonwealth, maketh not their opinions law, be they never so true. That which I have written in this treatise, concerning the moral virtues, and of their necessity, for the procuring and maintaining peace, though it be evident truth, is not therefore presently law; but because in all Commonwealths in the world, it is part of the civil law. For though it be naturally reasonable; yet it is by the sovereign power that it is law: otherwise, it were a great error, to call the laws of nature unwritten law; whereof we see so many volumes published by divers authors, and in them so many contradictions of one another, and of themselves.

The interpretation of the law of nature, is the sentence of the judge constituted by the sovereign authority, to hear and determine such controversies, as depend thereon; and consisteth in the application of the law to the present case. For in the act of judicature, the judge doth no more but consider, whether the demand of the party, be consonant to natural reason, and equity; and the sentence he giveth, is therefore the interpretation of the law of nature; which interpretation is authentic; not because it is his private sentence; but because he giveth it by authority of the sovereign, whereby it becomes the sovereign's sentence; which is law for that time, to the parties pleading.

But because there is no judge subordinate, nor sovereign, but may err in a judgment of equity; if afterward in another like case he find it more consonant to equity to give a contrary sentence, he is obliged to do it. No man's error becomes his own law; nor obliges him to persist in it. Neither (for the same reason) becomes it a law to other judges, though sworn to follow it. For though a wrong sentence given by authority of the sovereign, if he know and allow it, in such laws as are mutable, be a constitution of a new law, in cases in which every little circumstance is the same; yet in laws immutable, such as are the laws of nature, they are no laws to the same, or other judges, in the like cases for ever after. Princes succeed one another; and one judge passeth, another cometh; nay, heaven and earth shall pass; but not one tittle of the law of nature shall pass; for it is the eternal law of God. Therefore all the sentences of precedent judges that have ever been, cannot altogether make a law contrary to natural equity: nor any examples of former judges, can warrant an unreasonable sentence, or discharge the present judge of the trouble of studying what is equity (in the case he is to judge) from the principles of his own natural reason. For example sake, 'tis against the law of nature, *to punish the innocent*; and innocent is he that acquitteth himself judicially, and is acknowledged for innocent by the judge. Put the case now, that a man is accused of a capital crime, and seeing the power and malice of some enemy, and the frequent corruption and partiality of judges, runneth away for fear of the event, and afterwards is taken, and brought to a legal trial, and maketh it sufficiently appear, he was not guilty of the crime, and being thereof acquitted, is nevertheless condemned to lose his goods; this is a manifest condemnation of the innocent. I say therefore, that there is no place in the world, where this can be an interpretation of a law of nature, or be made a law by the sentences of precedent judges, that had done the same. For he that judged it first, judged unjustly; and no injustice can be a pattern of judgment to succeeding judges. A written law may forbid innocent men to fly, and they may be punished for flying: but that flying for fear of injury, should be taken for a presumption of guilt, after a man is already absolved of the crime judicially, is contrary to the nature of a presumption, which hath no place after judgment given. Yet this is set down by a great lawyer for the common law of England. *If a man* (saith he) *that is innocent, be accused of felony, and for fear flyeth for the same; albeit he judicially acquitteth himself of the felony; yet if it be found that he fled for the felony, he shall notwithstanding his innocency, forfeit all his goods, chattels, debts, and duties. For as to the forfeiture of them, the law will admit no proof against the presumption in law, grounded upon his flight.* Here you see, *an innocent man, judicially acquitted, notwithstanding his innocency,* (when no written law forbad him to fly) after his acquittal, *upon a presumption in law,* condemned to lose all the goods he hath. If the law ground upon his flight a presumption of the fact, (which was capital) the sentence ought to have been capital: if the presumption were not of the fact, for what then ought he to lose his goods? This therefore is no law of England; nor is the condemnation grounded upon a presumption of law, but upon the presumption of the judges. It is also against law, to say that no proof shall be admitted against a presumption of law. For all judges, sovereign and subordinate, if they refuse to hear proof, refuse to do justice: for though the sentence be just, yet the judges that condemn without hearing the proofs offered, are unjust judges; and their presumption is but prejudice; which no man ought to bring with him to the seat of justice, whatsoever precedent judgments, or examples he shall pretend to follow. There be other things of this nature, wherein men's judgments have been perverted, by trusting to precedents: but this is enough to show, that though the sentence of the judge be a law to the party pleading, yet it is no law to any judge, that shall succeed him in that office.

In like manner, when question is of the meaning of written laws, he is not the interpreter of them, that writeth a commentary upon them. For commentaries are commonly more subject to cavil, than the text; and therefore need other commentaries; and so there will be no end of such interpretation. And therefore unless there be an interpreter authorised by the sovereign, from which the subordinate judges are not to recede, the interpreter can be no other than the ordinary judges, in the same manner, as they are in cases of the unwritten law; and their sentences are to be taken by them that plead, for laws in that particular case; but not to bind other judges in like cases to give like judgments. For a judge may err in the interpretation even of written laws; but no error of a subordinate judge can change the law, which is the general sentence of the sovereign.

In written laws, men use to make a difference between the letter, and the sentence of the law: and when by the letter, is meant whatsoever can be gathered from the bare words, 'tis well distinguished. For the significations of almost all words, are either in themselves, or in the metaphorical use of them, ambiguous, and may be drawn in argument, to make many senses; but there is only one sense of the law. But if by the letter, be meant the literal sense, then the letter, and the sentence or intention of the law, is all one. For the literal sense is that, which the legislator intended, should by the letter of the law be signified. Now the intention of the legislator is always supposed to be equity: for it were a great contumely for a judge to think otherwise of the sovereign. He ought therefore, if the words of the law do not fully authorise a reasonable sentence, to supply it with the law of nature; or if the case be difficult, to respite judgment till he have received more ample authority. For example, a written law ordaineth, that he which is thrust out of his house by force, shall be restored by force: it happens that a man by negligence leaves his house empty, and returning is kept out by force, in which case there is no special law ordained. It is evident, that this case is contained in the same law: for else there is no remedy for him at all; which is to be supposed against the intention of the legislator. Again, the word of the law, commandeth to judge according to the evidence: a man is accused falsely of a fact, which the judge himself saw done by another; and not by him that is accused. In this case neither shall the letter of the law be followed to the condemnation of the innocent, nor shall the judge give sentence against the evidence of the witnesses; because the letter of the law is to the contrary: but procure of the sovereign that another be made judge, and himself witness. So that the incommodity that follows the bare words of a written law, may lead him to the intention of the law, whereby to interpret the same the better; though no incommodity can warrant a sentence against the law. For every judge of right and wrong, is not judge of what is commodious, or incommodious to the Commonwealth.

The abilities required in a good interpreter of the law, that is to say, in a good judge, are not the same with those of an advocate; namely the study of the laws. For a judge, as he ought to take notice of the fact, from none but the witnesses; so also he ought to take notice of the law from nothing but the statutes, and constitutions of the sovereign, alleged in the pleading, or declared to him by some that have authority from the sovereign power to declare them; and need not take care beforehand, what he shall judge; for it shall be given him what he shall say concerning the fact, by witnesses; and what he shall say in point of law, from those that shall in their pleadings show it, and by authority interpret it upon the place. The Lords of Parliament in England were judges, and most difficult causes have been heard and determined by them; yet few of them were much versed in the study of the laws, and fewer had made profession of them: and though they consulted with lawyers, that were appointed to be present there for that purpose; yet they alone had the authority of giving sentence. In like manner, in the ordinary trials of right, twelve men of the common people, are the judges, and give sentence, not only of the fact, but of the right; and pronounce simply for the complainant, or for the defendant; that is to say, are judges, not only of the fact, but also of the right: and in a question of crime, not only determine whether done, or not done; but also whether it be *murder*, *homicide*, *felony*, *assault*, and the like, which are determinations of law: but because they are not supposed to know the law of themselves, there is one that hath authority to inform them of it, in the particular case they are to judge of. But yet if they judge not according to that he tells them, they are not subject thereby to any penalty; unless it be made appear, that they did it against their consciences, or had been corrupted by reward.

The things that make a good judge, or good interpreter of the laws, are, first, *a right understanding* of that principal law of nature called *equity*; which depending not on the reading of other men's writings, but on the goodness of a man's own natural reason and meditation, is presumed to be in those most, that have had most leisure, and had the most inclination to meditate thereon. Secondly, *contempt of unnecessary riches, and preferments*. Thirdly, *to be able in judgment to divest himself of all fear, anger, hatred, love, and compassion*. Fourthly, and lastly, *patience to hear; diligent attention in hearing; and memory to retain, digest, and apply what he hath heard.*

The difference and division of the laws, has been made in divers manners, according to the different methods, of those men that have written of them. For it is a thing that dependeth not on nature, but on the scope of the writer; and is subservient to every man's proper method. In the *Institutions* of Justinian, we find seven sorts of civil laws. The *edicts, constitutions,* and *epistles of the prince*, that is, of the emperor; because the whole power of the people was in him. Like these, are the proclamations of the kings of England.

The decrees of the whole people of Rome (comprehending the senate) when they were put to the question by the *senate*. These were laws, at first, by the virtue of the sovereign power residing in the people; and such of them as by the emperors were not abrogated, remained laws by the authority imperial. For all laws that bind, are understood to be laws by his authority that has power to repeal them. Somewhat like to these laws, are the Acts of Parliament in England.

The decrees of the common people (excluding the senate) when they were put to the question by the *tribune* of the people. For such of them as were not abrogated by the emperors, remained laws by the authority imperial. Like to these, were the orders of the House of Commons in England.

Senatus consulta, the *orders of the senate*; because when the people of Rome grew so numerous, as it was inconvenient to assemble them; it was thought fit by the emperor, that men should consult the senate, instead of the people; and these have some resemblance with the Acts of Council.

The edicts of praetors, and (in some cases) of *aediles*: such as are the chief justices in the courts of England.

Responsa prudentium; which were the sentences and opinion of those lawyers, to whom the emperor gave authority to interpret the law, and to give answer to such as in matter of law demanded their advice; which answers, the judges in giving judgment were obliged by the constitutions of the emperor to observe: and should be like the reports of cases judged, if other judges be by the law of England bound to observe them. For the judges of the common law of England, are not properly judges, but *juris consulti*; of whom the judges, who are either the lords, or twelve men of the country, are in point of law to ask advice.

Also, *unwritten customs*, (which in their own nature are an imitation of law) by the tacit consent of the emperor, in case they be not contrary to the law of nature, are very laws.

Another division of laws, is into *natural* and *positive*. *Natural* are those which have been laws from all eternity; and are called not only *natural*, but also *moral* laws; consisting in the moral virtues, as justice, equity, and all habits of the mind that conduce to peace, and charity; of which I have already spoken in the fourteenth and fifteenth chapters.

Positive, are those which have not been from

eternity; but have been made laws by the will of those that have had the sovereign power over others; and are either written, or made known to men by some other argument of the will of their legislator.

Again, of positive laws some are *human*, some *divine*; and of human positive laws, some are *distributive*, some *penal*. *Distributive* are those that determine the rights of the subjects, declaring to every man what it is, by which he acquireth and holdeth a propriety in lands, or goods, and a right or liberty of action: and these speak to all the subjects. *Penal* are those which declare, what penalty shall be inflicted on those that violate the law; and speak to the ministers and officers ordained for execution. For though every one ought to be informed of the punishments ordained beforehand for their transgression; nevertheless the command is not addressed to the delinquent, (who cannot be supposed will faithfully punish himself) but to public ministers appointed to see the penalty executed. And these penal laws are for the most part written together with the laws distributive; and are sometimes called judgments. For all laws are general judgments, or sentences of the legislator; as also every particular judgment, is a law to him, whose case is judged.

Divine positive laws (for natural laws being eternal, and universal, are all divine) are those, which being the commandments of God, (not from all eternity, nor universally addressed to all men, but only to a certain people, or to certain persons) are declared for such, by those whom God hath authorised to declare them. But this authority of man to declare what be these positive laws of God, how can it be known? God may command a man by a supernatural way, to deliver laws to other men. But because it is of the essence of law, that he who is to be obliged, be assured of the authority of him that declareth it, which we cannot naturally take notice to be from God, *how can a man without supernatural revelation be assured of the revelation received by the declarer*? And *how can he be bound to obey them*?

For the first question, how a man can be assured of the revelation of another, without a revelation particularly to himself, it is evidently impossible. For though a man may be induced to believe such revelation, from the miracles they see him do, or from seeing the extraordinary sanctity of his life, or from seeing the extraordinary wisdom, or extraordinary felicity of his actions, all which are marks of God's extraordinary favour; yet they are not assured evidences of special revelation. Miracles are marvellous works: but that which is marvellous to one, may not be so to another. Sanctity may be feigned; and the visible felicities of this world, are most often the work of God by natural and ordinary causes. And therefore no man can infallibly know by natural reason, that another has had a supernatural revelation of God's will, but only a belief; every one (as the signs thereof shall appear greater, or lesser) a firmer or a weaker belief.

But for the second, how can he be bound to obey them; it is not so hard. For if the law declared, be not against the law of nature (which is undoubtedly God's law) and he undertake to obey it, he is bound by his own act; bound I say to obey it, but not bound to believe it: for men's belief, and interior cogitations, are not subject to the commands, but only to the operation of God, ordinary or extraordinary. Faith of supernatural law, is not a fulfilling, but only an assenting to the same; and not a duty that we exhibit to God, but a gift which God freely giveth to whom he pleaseth; as also unbelief is not a breach of any of his laws; but a rejection of them all, except the laws natural. But this that I say, will be made yet clearer, by the examples and testimonies concerning this point in holy Scripture. The covenant God made with Abraham (in a supernatural manner) was thus (Gen. 17. 10) *This is the covenant which thou shalt observe between me and thee and thy seed after thee*. Abraham's seed had not this revelation, nor were yet in being; yet they are a party to the covenant, and bound to obey what Abraham should declare to them for God's law; which they could not be, but in virtue of the obedience they owed to their parents; who (if they be subject to no other earthly power, as here in the case of Abraham) have sovereign power over their children, and servants. Again, where God saith to Abraham, *In thee shall all nations of the earth be blessed: for I know thou wilt command thy children, and thy house after thee to keep the way of the Lord, and to observe righteousness and judgment*, it is manifest, the obedience of his family, who had no revelation, depended on their former obligation to obey their sovereign. At Mount Sinai Moses only went up to God; the people were forbidden to approach on pain of death; yet they were bound to obey all that Moses declared to them for God's law. Upon what ground, but on this submission of their own, *Speak thou to us, and we will hear thee; but let not God speak to us, lest we die*? By which two places it sufficiently appeareth, that in a Commonwealth, a subject that has no certain and assured revelation particular to himself concerning the will of God, is to obey for such, the command of the Commonwealth: for if men were at liberty to take for God's commandments, their own dreams and fancies, or the dreams and fancies of private men; scarce two men would agree upon what are God's commandments; and yet in respect of them, every man would despise the commandments of the Commonwealth. I conclude therefore, that in all things not contrary to the moral law, (that is to say, to the law of nature) all subjects are bound to obey that for divine law, which is declared to be so, by the laws of the Commonwealth. Which also is evident to any man's reason; for whatsoever is not against the law of nature, may be made law in the name of them that have the sovereign power; and there is no reason men should be the less obliged by it, when it is propounded in the name of God. Besides, there is no place in the world where men are permitted to pretend other commandments of God, than are declared for such by the Commonwealth. Christian states punish those that revolt from Christian religion, and all other states, those that set up any religion by them forbidden. For in whatsoever is not regulated by the Commonwealth, 'tis equity (which is the law of nature, and therefore an eternal law of God) that every man equally enjoy his liberty.

There is also another distinction of laws, into *fundamental*, and *not fundamental*: but I could never see in any author, what a fundamental law signifieth. Nevertheless one may very reasonably distinguish laws in that manner.

For a fundamental law in every Commonwealth is that, which being taken away, the Commonwealth faileth, and is utterly dissolved; as a building whose foundation is destroyed. And therefore a fundamental law is that, by which subjects are bound to uphold whatsoever power is given to the sovereign, whether a monarch, or a sovereign assembly, without which the Commonwealth cannot stand; such as is the power of war and peace, of judicature, of election of officers, and of doing whatsoever he shall think necessary for the public good. Not fundamental is that, the abrogating whereof, draweth not with it the dissolution of the commonwealth; such as are the laws concerning controversies between subject and subject. Thus much of the division of laws.

I find the words *lex civilis*, and *jus civile*, that is to say *law* and *right civil*, promiscuously used for the same thing, even in the most learned authors; which nevertheless ought not to be so. For *right* is *liberty*, namely that liberty which the civil law leaves us: but *civil law* is an *obligation*; and takes from us the liberty which the law of nature gave us. Nature gave a right to every man to secure himself by his own strength, and to invade a suspected neighbour, by way of prevention: but the civil law takes away that liberty, in all cases where the protection of the law may be safely stayed for. Insomuch as *lex* and *jus*, are as different as *obligation* and *liberty*.

Likewise *laws* and *charters* are taken promiscuously for the same thing. Yet charters are donations of the sovereign; and not laws, but exemptions from law. The phrase of a law is, *jubeo*, *injungo*, *I command* and *enjoin*: the phrase of a charter is, *dedi*, *concessi*, *I have given*, *I have granted*: but what is given or granted, to a man, is not forced upon him, by a law. A law may be made to bind all the subjects of a commonwealth: a liberty or charter is only to one man, or some one part of the people. For to say all the people of a commonwealth, have liberty in any case whatsoever, is to say, that in such case, there hath been no law made; or else having been made, is now abrogated.

CHAPTER 27

Of Crimes, Excuses, and Extenuations

A sin, is not only a transgression of a law, but also any contempt of the legislator. For such contempt is a breach of all his laws at once. And therefore may consist, not only in the *commission* of a fact, or in speaking of words by the laws forbidden, or in the *comission* of what the law commandeth, but also in the *intention*, or purpose to transgress. For the purpose to break the law, is some degree of contempt of him, to whom it belongeth to see it executed. To be delighted in the imagination only, of being possessed of another man's goods, servants, or wife, without any intention to take them from him by force or fraud, is no breach of the law, that saith, *Thou shalt not covet*: nor is the pleasure a man may have in imagining, or dreaming of the death of him, from whose life he expecteth nothing but damage and displeasure, a sin; but the resolving to put some act in execution, that tendeth thereto. For to be pleased in the fiction of that, which would please a man if it were real, is a passion so adherent to the nature both of man, and every other living creature, as to make it a sin, were to make sin of being a man. The consideration of this, has made me think them too severe, both to themselves and others, that maintain, that the first motions of the mind, (though checked with the fear of God) be sins. But I confess it is safer to err on that hand, than on the other.

A crime is a sin, consisting in the committing (by deed, or word) of that which the law forbiddeth, or the omission of what it hath commanded. So that every crime is a sin; but not every sin a crime. To intend to steal, or kill, is a sin, though it never appear in word, or fact: for God that seeth the thoughts of man, can lay it to his charge: but till it appear by something done, or said, by which the intention may be argued by a human judge, it hath not the name of crime: which distinction the Greeks observed, in the word ἁμάρτημα and ἔγκλημα or αἰτία; whereof the former, (which is translated *sin*) signifieth any swerving from the law whatsoever; but the two latter, (which are translated *crime*) signify that sin only, whereof one man may accuse another. But of intentions, which never appear by any outward act, there is no place for human accusation. In like manner the Latins by *peccatum*, which is *sin*, signify all manner of deviation from the law; but by *crimen*, (which word they derive from *cerno*, which signifies to *perceive*) they mean only such sins, as may be made appear before a judge; and therefore are not mere intentions.

From this relation of sin to the law, and of crime to the civil law, may be inferred, first, that where law ceaseth, sin ceaseth. But because the law of nature is eternal, violation of covenants, ingratitude, arrogance, and all facts contrary to any moral virtue, can never cease to be sin. Secondly, that the civil law ceasing, crimes cease: for there being no other law remaining, but that of nature, there is no place for accusation;

every man being his own judge, and accused only by his own conscience, and cleared by the uprightness of his own intention. When therefore his intention is right, his fact is no sin: if otherwise, his fact is sin; but not crime. Thirdly, that when the sovereign power ceaseth, crime also ceaseth: for where there is no such power, there is no protection to be had from the law; and therefore every one may protect himself by his own power: for no man in the institution of sovereign power can be supposed to give away the right of preserving his own body; for the safety whereof all sovereignty was ordained. But this is to be understood only of those, that have not themselves contributed to the taking away of the power that protected them: for that was a crime from the beginning.

The source of every crime, is some defect of the understanding; or some error in reasoning; or some sudden force of the passions. Defect in the understanding, is *ignorance*; in reasoning, *erroneous opinion*. Again, ignorance is of three sorts; of the *law*, and of the *sovereign*, and of the *penalty*. Ignorance of the law of nature excuseth no man; because every man that hath attained to the use of reason, is supposed to know, he ought not to do to another, what he would not have done to himself. Therefore into what place soever a man shall come, if he do any thing contrary to that law, it is a crime. If a man come from the Indies hither, and persuade men here to receive a new religion, or teach them anything that tendeth to disobedience of the laws of this country, though he be never so well persuaded of the truth of what he teacheth, he commits a crime, and may be justly punished for the same, not only because his doctrine is false, but also because he does that which he would not approve in another, namely, that coming from hence, he should endeavour to alter the religion there. But ignorance of the civil law, shall excuse a man in a strange country, till it be declared to him; because, till then no civil law is binding.

In the like manner, if the civil law of a man's own country, be not so sufficiently declared, as he may know it if he will, nor the action against the law of nature, the ignorance is a good excuse: in other cases ignorance of the civil law, excuseth not.

Ignorance of the sovereign power, in the place of a man's ordinary residence, excuseth him not; because he ought to take notice of the power, by which he hath been protected there.

Ignorance of the penalty, where the law is declared, excuseth no man: for in breaking the law, which without a fear of penalty to follow, were not a law, but vain words, he undergoeth the penalty, though he know not what it is; because, whosoever voluntarily doth any action, accepteth all the known consequences of it; but punishment is a known consequence of the violation of the laws, in every commonwealth; which punishment, if it be determined already by the law, he is subject to that; if not, then he is subject to arbitrary punishment. For it is reason, that he which does injury, without other limitation than that of his own will, should suffer punishment without other limitation, than that of his will whose law is thereby violated.

But when a penalty, is either annexed to the crime in the law itself, or hath been usually inflicted in the like cases; there the delinquent is excused from a greater penalty. For the punishment foreknown, if it be not great enough to deter men from the action, is an invitement to it: because when men compare the benefit of their injustice, with the harm of their punishment, by necessity of nature they choose that which appeareth best for themselves: and therefore when they are punished more than the law had formerly determined, or more than others were punished for the same crime; it is the law that tempted, and deceiveth them.

No law made after a fact done, can make it a crime: because if the fact be against the law of nature, the law was before the fact; and a positive law cannot be taken notice of, before it be made; and therefore cannot be obligatory. But when the law that forbiddeth a fact, is made before the fact be done; yet he that doth the fact, is liable to the penalty ordained after, in case no lesser penalty were made known before, neither by writing, nor by example, for the reason immediately before alleged.

From defect in reasoning, (that is to say, from error) men are prone to violate the laws, three ways. First, by presumption of false principles: as when men, from having observed how in all places, and in all ages, unjust actions have been authorised by the force and victories of those who have committed them; and that potent men, breaking through the cobweb laws of their country, the weaker sort, and those that have failed in their enterprises, have been esteemed the only criminals; have thereupon taken for principles, and grounds of their reasoning, *that justice is but a vain word: that whatsoever a man can get by his own industry, and hazard, is his own: that the practice of all nations cannot be unjust: that examples of former times are good arguments of doing the like again*; and many more of that kind: which being granted, no act in itself can be a crime, but must be made so (not by the law, but) by the success of them that commit it; and the same fact be virtuous, or vicious, as fortune pleaseth; so that what Marius makes a crime, Sylla shall make meritorious, and Caesar (the same laws standing) turn again into a crime, to the perpetual disturbance of the peace of the commonwealth.

Secondly, by false teachers, that either misinterpret the law of nature, making it thereby repugnant to the law civil; or by teaching for laws, such doctrines of their own, or traditions of former times, as are inconsistent with the duty of a subject.

Thirdly, by erroneous inferences from true principles; which happens commonly to men that are hasty, and precipitate in concluding, and resolving what to do; such as are they, that have both a great opinion of their own understanding, and believe that things of this nature require not time and study, but only common experience, and a good natural wit; whereof no man thinks himself unprovided: whereas the knowledge of right and wrong, which is no less difficult, there is no man will pretend to, without great and long study. And of those defects in reasoning, there is none that can excuse (though some of them may extenuate) a crime, in any man, that pretendeth to the administration of his own private business; much less in them that undertake a public charge; because they pretend to the reason, upon the want whereof they would ground their excuse.

Of the passions that most frequently are the causes of crime, one is vainglory, or a foolish overrating of their own worth; as if difference of worth, were an effect of their wit, or riches, or blood, or some other natural quality, not depending on the will of those that have the sovereign authority. From whence proceedeth a presumption that the punishments ordained by the laws, and extended generally to all subjects, ought not to be inflicted on them, with the same rigour they are inflicted on poor, obscure, and simple men, comprehended under the name of the *vulgar*.

Therefore it happeneth commonly, that such as value themselves by the greatness of their wealth, adventure on crimes, upon hope of escaping punishment, by corrupting public justice, or obtaining pardon by money, or other rewards.

And that such as have multitude of potent kindred; and popular men, that have gained reputation amongst the multitude, take courage to violate the laws, from a hope of oppressing the power, to whom it belongeth to put them in execution.

And that such as have a great, and false opinion of their own wisdom, take upon them to reprehend the actions, and call in question the authority of them that govern, and so to unsettle the laws with their public discourse, as that nothing shall be a crime, but what their own designs require should be so. It happeneth also to the same men, to be prone to all such crimes, as consist in craft, and in deceiving of their neighbours; because they think their designs are too subtle to be perceived. These I say are effects of a false presumption of their own wisdom. For of them that are the first movers in the disturbance of commonwealth, (which can never happen without a civil war) very few are left alive long enough, to see their new designs established: so that the benefit of their crimes, redoundeth to posterity, and such as would least have wished it: which argues they were not so wise, as they thought they were. And those that deceive upon hope of not being observed, do commonly deceive themselves, (the darkness in which they believe they lie hidden, being nothing else but their own blindness) and are no wiser than children, that think all hid, by hiding their own eyes.

And generally all vain-glorious men, (unless they be withal timorous), are subject to anger; as being more prone than others to interpret for contempt, the ordinary liberty of conversation: and there are few crimes that may not be produced by anger.

As for the passions, of hate, lust, ambition, and covetousness, what crimes they are apt to produce, is so obvious to every man's experience and understanding, as there needeth nothing to be said of them, saving that they are infirmities, so annexed to the nature, both of man, and all other living creatures, as that their effects cannot be hindered, but by extraordinary use of reason, or a constant severity in punishing them. For in those things men hate, they find a continual, and unavoidable molestation; whereby either a man's patience must be everlasting, or he must be eased by removing the power of that which molesteth him: the former is difficult; the latter is many times impossible, without some violation of the law. Ambition, and covetousness are passions also that are perpetually incumbent, and pressing; whereas reason is not perpetually present, to resist them: and therefore whensoever the hope of impunity appears, their effects proceed. And for lust, what it wants in the lasting, it hath in the vehemence, which sufficeth to weigh down the apprehension of all easy, or uncertain punishments.

Of all passions, that which inclineth men least to break the laws, is fear. Nay, (excepting some generous natures) it is the only thing, (when there is appearance of profit, or pleasure by breaking the laws), that makes men keep them. And yet in many cases a crime may be committed through fear.

For not every fear justifies the action it produceth, but the fear only of corporeal hurt, which we call *bodily fear*, and from which a man cannot see how to be delivered, but by the action. A man is assaulted, fears present death, from which he sees not how to escape, but by wounding him that assaulteth him: if he wound him to death, this is no crime; because no man is supposed at the making of a commonwealth, to have abandoned the defence of his life, or limbs, where the law cannot arrive in time enough to his assistance. But to kill a man, because from his actions, or his threatenings, I may argue he will kill me when he can, (seeing I have time, and means to demand protection, from the sovereign power) is a crime. Again, a man receives words of disgrace or some little injuries (for which they that made the laws, had assigned no punishment, nor thought it worthy of a man that hath the use of reason, to take notice of) and is afraid, unless he revenge it, he shall fall into contempt, and consequently be obnoxious to the like injuries from others; and to avoid this, breaks the law, and protects himself for the future, by the terror of his private revenge. This is a crime: for the hurt is not corporeal, but phantastical, and (though in this corner of the world, made sensible by a custom not many years since begun, amongst young and vain men) so light, as a gallant man, and one that is assured of his own courage, cannot take notice of. Also a man may stand in fear of spirits, either through his own superstition, or through too much credit given to other men, that tell him of strange dreams and visions; and thereby be made believe they will hurt him, for doing or omitting divers things, which nevertheless, to do or omit, is contrary to the laws; and that which is so done or omitted, is not to be excused by this fear; but is a crime. For (as I have shown before in the second chapter) dreams be naturally but the fancies remaining in sleep, after the impressions our senses had formerly received waking; and when men are by any accident unassured they have slept, seem to be real visions; and therefore he that presumes to break the law upon his own, or another's dream, or pretended vision, or upon other fancy of the power of invisible spirits, than is permitted by the commonwealth, leaveth the law of nature, which is a certain offence, and followeth the imagery of his own, or another private man's brain, which he can never know whether it signifieth any thing, or nothing, nor whether he that tells his dream, say true, or lie; which if every private man should have leave to do, (as they must by the law of nature, if any one have it) there could no law be made to hold, and so all commonwealth would be dissolved.

From these different sources of crimes, it appears already, that all crimes are not (as the Stoics of old time maintained) of the same alloy. There is place, not only for excuse, by which that which seemed a crime, is proved to be none at all; but also for extenuation, by which the crime that seemed great, is made less. For though all crimes do equally deserve the name of injustice, as all deviation from a straight line is equally crookedness, which the Stoics rightly observed: yet it does not follow that all crimes are equally unjust, no more than that all crooked lines are equally crooked; which the Stoics not observing, held it as great a crime, to kill a hen, against the law, as to kill one's father.

That which totally excuseth a fact, and takes away from it the nature of a crime, can be none but that which at the same time, taketh away the obligation of the law. For the fact committed once against the law, if he that committed it be obliged to the law, can be no other than a crime.

The want of means to know the law, totally excuseth: for the law whereof a man has no means to inform himself, is not obligatory. But the want of diligence to inquire, shall not be considered as a want of means; nor shall any man, that pretendeth to reason enough for the government of his own affairs, be supposed to want means to know the laws of nature; because they are known by the reason he pretends to: only children and madmen are excused from offences against the law natural.

Where a man is captive, or in the power of the enemy, (and he is then in the power of the enemy, when his person, or his means of living, is so) if it be without his own fault, the obligation of the law ceaseth; because he must obey the enemy, or die; and consequently such obedience is no crime: for no man is obliged (when the protection of the law faileth) not to protect himself, by the best means he can.

If a man by the terror of present death, be compelled to do a fact against the law, he is totally excused; because no law can oblige a man to abandon his own preservation. And supposing such a law were obligatory; yet a man would reason thus, *If I do it not, I die presently*; *if I do it*, *I die afterwards*; *therefore by doing it, there is time of life gained*; nature therefore compels him to the fact.

When a man is destitute of food, or other thing necessary for his life, and cannot preserve himself any other way, but by some fact against the law; as if in a great famine he take the food by force, or stealth, which he cannot obtain for money, nor charity; or in defence of his life, snatch away another man's sword; he is totally excused, for the reason next before alleged.

Again, facts done against the law, by the authority of another, are by that authority excused against the author; because no man ought to accuse his own fact in another, that is but his instrument: but it is not excused against a third person thereby injured; because in the violation of the law, both the author, and actor are criminals. From hence it followeth that when that man, or assembly, that hath the sovereign power, commandeth a man to do that which is contrary to a former law, the doing of it is totally excused: for he ought not to condemn it himself, because he is the author; and what cannot justly be condemned by the sovereign, cannot justly be punished by any other. Besides, when the sovereign commandeth any thing to be done against his own former law, the command, as to that particular fact, is an abrogation of the law.

If that man, or assembly, that hath the sovereign power, disclaim any right essential to the sovereignty, whereby there accrueth to the subject, any liberty inconsistent with the sovereign power, that is to say, with the very being of a commonwealth, if the subject shall refuse to obey the command in any thing, contrary to the liberty granted, this is nevertheless a sin, and contrary to the duty of the subject: for he ought to take notice of what is inconsistent with the sovereignty, because it was erected by his own consent, and for his own defence; and that such liberty as is inconsistent with it, was granted through ignorance of the evil consequence thereof. But if he not only disobey, but also resist a public minister in the execution of it, then it is a crime; because he might have been righted, (without any breach of the peace) upon complaint.

The degrees of crime are taken on divers scales, and measured, first, by the malignity of the source, or cause; secondly, by the contagion of the example; thirdly, by the mischief of the effect; and fourthly, by the concurrence of times, places, and persons.

The same fact done against the law, if it proceed from presumption of strength, riches, or friends to resist those that are to execute the law, is a greater crime, than if it proceed from hope of not being discovered, or of escape by flight: for presumption of impunity by force, is a root from whence springeth, at all times, and upon all temptations, a contempt of all laws; whereas in the latter case, the apprehension of danger, that makes a man fly, renders him more obedient for the future. A crime which we know to be so, is greater than the same crime proceeding from a false persuasion that it is lawful; for he that committeth it against his own conscience, presumeth on his force, or other power, which encourages him to commit the same again: but he that doth it by error, after the error is shewn him, is conformable to the law.

He, whose error proceeds from the authority of a teacher, or an interpreter of the law publicly authorised, is not so faulty, as he whose error proceedeth from a peremptory pursuit of his own principles and reasoning: for what is taught by one that teacheth by public authority, the commonwealth teacheth, and hath a resemblance of law, till the same authority controlleth it; and in all crimes that contain not in them a denial of the sovereign power, nor are against an evident law or authorised doctrine, excuseth totally: whereas he that groundeth his actions on his private judgment, ought according to the rectitude or error thereof, to stand or fall.

The same fact, if it have been constantly punished in other men, is a greater crime, than if there have been many precedent examples of impunity. For those examples, are so many hopes of impunity, given by the sovereign himself: and because he which furnishes a man with such a hope, and presumption of mercy, as encourageth him to offend, hath his part in the offence; he cannot reasonably charge the offender with the whole.

A crime arising from a sudden passion, is not so great, as when the same ariseth from long meditation: for in the former case there is a place for extenuation, in the common infirmity of human nature: but he that doth it with premeditation, has used circumspection, and cast his eye on the law, on the punishment, and on the consequence thereof to human society; all which, in committing the crime, he hath contemned and postposed to his own appetite. But there is no suddenness of passion sufficient for a total excuse: for all the time between the first knowing of the law, and the commission of the fact, shall be taken for a time of deliberation; because he ought by meditation of the law, to rectify the irregularity of his passions continually.

Where the law is publicly, and with assiduity, before all the people read, and interpreted; a fact done against it, is a greater crime, than where men are left without such instruction, to enquire of it with difficulty, uncertainty, and interruption of their callings, and be informed by private men: for in this case, part of the fault is discharged upon common infirmity; but, in the former, there is apparent negligence, which is not without some contempt of the sovereign power.

Those facts which the law expressly condemneth, but the law-maker by other manifest signs of his will tacitly approveth, are less crimes, than the same facts, condemned both by the law, and law-maker. For seeing the will of the law-maker is a law, there appear in this case two contradictory laws; which would totally excuse, if men were bound to take notice of the sovereign's approbation, by other arguments, than are expressed by his command. But because there are punishments consequent, not only to the transgression of his law, but also to the observing of it, he is in part a cause of the transgression, and therefore cannot reasonably impute the whole crime to the delinquent. For example, the law condemneth duels; the punishment is made capital: on the contrary part, he that refuseth duel, is subject to contempt and scorn, without remedy; and sometimes by the sovereign himself thought unworthy to have any charge, or preferment in war: if thereupon he accept duel, considering all men lawfully endeavour to obtain the good opinion of them that have the sovereign power, he ought not in reason to be rigorously punished; seeing part of the fault may be discharged on the punisher: which I say, not as wishing liberty of private revenges, or any other kind of disobedience; but a care in governors, not to countenance any thing obliquely, which directly they forbid. The examples of princes, to those that see them, are, and ever have been, more potent to govern their actions, than the laws themselves. And though it be our duty to do, not what they do, but what they say; yet will that duty never be performed, till it please God to give man an extraordinary, and supernatural grace to follow that precept.

Again, if we compare crimes by the mischief of their effects, first, the same fact, when it redounds to the damage of many, is greater, than when it redounds to the hurt of few. And therefore, when a fact hurteth, not only in the present, but also, (by example) in the future, it is a greater crime, than if it hurt only in the present: for the former, is a fertile crime, and multiplies to the hurt of many; the latter is barren. To maintain doctrines contrary to the religion established in the commonwealth, is a greater fault in an authorised preacher, than in a private person: so also is it, to live profanely, incontinently, or do any irreligious act whatsoever. Likewise in a professor of the law, to maintain any point, or do any act, that tendeth to the weakening of the sovereign power, is a greater crime, than in another man: also in a man that hath such reputation for wisdom, as that his counsels are followed, or his actions imitated by many, his fact against the law, is a greater crime, than the same fact in another: for such men not only commit crime, but teach it for law to all other men. And generally all crimes are the greater, by the scandal they give; that is to say, by becoming stumbling-blocks to the weak, that look not so much upon the way they go in, as upon the light that other man carry before them.

Also facts of hostility against the present state of the commonwealth, are greater crimes, than the same acts done to private men: for the damage extends itself to all: such are the betraying of the strengths, or revealing of the secrets of the commonwealth to an enemy; also all attempts upon the representative of the commonwealth, be it a monarch, or an assembly; and all endeavours by word, or deed, to diminish the authority of the same, either in the present time, or in succession: which crimes the Latins understand by *crimina laesae majestatis*, and consist in design, or act, contrary to a fundamental law.

Likewise those crimes, which render judgments of no effect, are greater crimes, than injuries done to one, or a few persons; as to receive money to give false judgment, or testimony, is a greater crime, than otherwise to deceive a man of the like or a greater sum; because not only he has wrong, that falls by such judgments; but all judgments are rendered useless, and occasion ministered to force, and private revenges.

Also robbery, and depeculation of the public treasure, or revenues, is a greater crime, than the robbing or defrauding of a private man; because to rob the public, is to rob many at once.

Also the counterfeit usurpation of public ministry, the counterfeiting of public seals, or public coin, than counterfeiting of a private man's person, or his seal; because the fraud thereof, extendeth to the damage of many.

Of facts against the law, done to private men, the greater crime, is that, where the damage in the common opinion of men, is most sensible. And therefore to kill against the law, is a greater crime, than any other injury, life preserved.

And to kill with torment, greater, than simply to kill.

And mutilation of a limb, greater, than the spoiling a man of his goods.

And the spoiling a man of his goods, by terror of death or wounds, than by clandestine surreption.

And by clandestine surreption, than by consent fraudulently obtained.

And the violation of chastity by force, greater than by flattery.

And of a woman married, than of a woman not married.

For all these things are commonly so valued; though some men are more, and some less sensible of the same offence. But the law regardeth not the particular, but the general inclination of mankind.

And therefore the offence men take, from contumely, in words or gesture, when they produce no other harm, than the present grief of him that is reproached, hath been neglected in the laws of the Greeks, Romans, and other both ancient and modern commonwealths; supposing the true cause of such grief to consist, not in the contumely, (which takes no hold upon men conscious of their own virtue) but in the pusillanimity of him that is offended by it.

Also a crime against a private man, is much aggravated by the person, time, and place. For to kill one's parent, is a greater crime, than to kill another: for the parent ought to have the honour of a sovereign, (though he surrendered his power to the civil law) because he had it originally by nature. And to rob a poor man, is a greater crime, than to rob a rich man; because it is to the poor a more sensible damage.

And a crime committed in the time or place appointed for devotion, is greater, than if committed at another time or place: for it proceeds from a greater contempt of the law.

Many other cases of aggravation, and extenuation might be added: but by these I have set down, it is obvious to every man, to take the altitude of any other crime proposed.

Lastly, because in almost all crimes there is an injury done, not only to some private men, but also to the commonwealth; the same crime, when the accusation is in the name of the commonwealth, is called a public crime: and when in the name of a private man, a private crime; and the pleas according thereunto called public, *judicia publica*, Pleas of the Crown; or Private Pleas. As in an accusation of murder, if the accuser be a private man, the plea is a Private Plea; if the accuser be the sovereign, the plea is a Public Plea.

CHAPTER 28

Of Punishments, and Rewards

A punishment, *is an evil inflicted by public authority, on him that hath done, or omitted, that which is judged by the same authority to be a transgression of the law; to the end that the will of men may thereby the better be disposed to obedience.*

Before I infer any thing from this definition, there is a question to be answered, of much importance; which is, by what door the right, or authority of punishing in any case, came in. For by that which has been said before, no man is supposed bound by covenant, not to resist violence; and consequently it cannot be intended, that he gave any right to another to lay violent hands upon his person. In the making of a commonwealth, every man giveth away the right of defending another; but not of defending himself. Also he obligeth himself, to assist him that hath the sovereignty, in the punishing of another; but of himself not. But to covenant to assist the sovereign, in doing hurt to another, unless he that so covenanteth have a right to do it himself, is not to give him a right to punish. It is manifest therefore that the right which the commonwealth (that is, he or they that represent it) hath to punish, is not grounded on any concession, or gift of the subjects. But I have also showed formerly, that before the institution of commonwealth, every man had a right to every thing, and to do whatsoever he thought necessary to his own preservation; subduing, hurting, or killing any man in order thereunto. And this is the foundation of that right of punishing, which is exercised in every commonwealth. For the subjects did not give the sovereign that right; but only in laying down theirs, strengthened him to use his own, as he should think fit, for the preservation of them all: so that it was not given, but left to him, and to him only; and (excepting the limits set him by natural law) as entire, as in the condition of mere nature, and of war of every one against his neighbour.

From the definition of punishment, I infer, first, that neither private revenges, nor injuries of private men, can properly be styled punishments; because they proceed not from public authority.

Secondly, that to be neglected, and unpreferred by the public favour, is not a punishment; because no new evil is thereby on any man inflicted; he is only left in the estate he was in before.

Thirdly, that the evil inflicted by public authority, without precedent public condemnation, is not to be styled by the name of punishment; but of an hostile act; because the fact for which a man is punished, ought first to be judged by public authority, to be a transgression of the law.

Fourthly, that the evil inflicted by usurped power, and judges without authority from the sovereign, is not punishment; but an act of hostility; because the acts of power usurped, have not for author, the person condemned; and therefore are not acts of public authority.

Fifthly, that all evil which is inflicted without intention, or possibility of disposing the delinquent, or (by his example) other men, to obey the laws, is not punishment; but an act of hostility: because without such an end, no hurt done is contained under that name.

Sixthly, whereas to certain actions, there be annexed by nature, divers hurtful consequences; as when a man in assaulting another, is himself slain, or wounded; or when he falleth into sickness by the doing of some unlawful act; such hurt, though in respect of God, who is the author of nature, it may be said to be inflicted, and therefore a punishment divine; yet it is not contained in the name of punishment in respect of men, because it is not inflicted by the authority of man.

Seventhly, if the harm inflicted be less than the benefit, or contentment that naturally followeth the crime committed, that harm is not within the definition; and is rather the price, or redemption, than the punishment of a crime: because it is of the nature of punishment, to have for end, the disposing of men to obey the law; which end (if it be less than the benefit of the transgression) it attaineth not, but worketh a contrary effect.

Eighthly, if a punishment be determined and prescribed in the law itself, and after the crime committed, there be a greater punishment inflicted, the excess is not punishment, but an act of hostility. For seeing the aim of punishment is not a revenge, but terror; and the terror of a great punishment unknown, is taken away by the declaration of a less, the unexpected addition is no part of the punishment. But where there is no punishment at all determined by the law, there whatsoever is inflicted, hath the nature of punishment. For he that goes about the violation of a law, wherein no penalty is determined, expecteth an indeterminate, that is to say, an arbitrary punishment.

Ninthly, harm inflicted for a fact done before there was a law that forbade it, is not punishment, but an act of hostility: for before the law, there is no transgression of the law: but punishment supposeth a fact judged, to have been a transgression of the law; therefore harm inflicted before the law made, is not punishment, but an act of hostility.

Tenthly, hurt inflicted on the representative of the commonwealth, is not punishment, but an act of hostility: because it is of the nature of punishment, to be inflicted by public authority, which is the authority only of the representative itself.

Lastly, harm inflicted upon one that is a declared enemy, falls not under the name of punishment: because seeing they were either never subject to the law, and therefore cannot transgress it; or having been subject to it, and professing to be no longer so, by consequence deny they can transgress it, all the harms that can be done them, must be taken as acts of hostility. But in declared hostility, all infliction of evil is lawful. From whence it followeth, that if a subject shall by fact or word, wittingly and deliberately deny the authority of the representative of the commonwealth, (whatsoever penalty hath been formerly ordained for treason) he may lawfully be made to suffer whatsoever the representative will: for in denying subjection, he denies such punishment as by the law hath been ordained; and therefore suffers as an enemy of the commonwealth; that is, according to the will of the representative. For the punishments set down in the law, are to subjects, not to enemies; such as are they, that having been by their own acts subjects deliberately revolting, deny the sovereign power.

The first, and most general distribution of punishments, is into *divine*, and *human*. Of the former I shall have occasion to speak, in a more convenient place hereafter.

Human, are those punishments that be inflicted by the commandment of man; and are either *corporal*, or *pecuniary*, or *ignominy*, or *imprisonment*, or *exile*, or mixed of these.

Corporal punishment is that, which is inflicted on the body directly, and according to the intention of him that inflicteth it: such as are stripes, or wounds, or deprivation of such pleasures of the body, as were before lawfully enjoyed.

And of these, some be *capital*, some *less than capital*. Capital is the infliction of death; and that either simply, or with torment. Less than capital, are stripes, wounds, chains, and any other corporal pain, not in its own nature mortal. For if upon the infliction of a punishment death follow not in the intention of the inflictor, the punishment is not to be esteemed capital, though the harm prove mortal by an accident not to be foreseen; in which case death is not inflicted, but hastened.

Pecuniary punishment, is that which consisteth not only in the deprivation of a sum of money, but also of lands, or any other goods which are usually bought and sold for money. And in case the law, that ordaineth such a punishment, be made with design to gather money, from such as shall transgress the same, it is not properly a punishment, but the price of privilege, and exemption from the law, which doth not absolutely forbid the fact, but only to those that are not able to pay the money: except where the law is natural, or part of religion; for in that case it is not an exemption from the law, but a transgression of it. As where a law exacteth a pecuniary mulct, of them that take the name of God in vain, the payment of the mulct, is not the price of a dispensation to swear, but the punishment of the transgression of a law indispensable. In like manner if the law impose a sum of money to be paid, to him that has been injured; this is but a satisfaction for the hurt done him; and extinguisheth the accusation of the party injured, not the crime of the offender.

Ignominy, is the infliction of such evil, as is made dishonourable; or the deprivation of such good as is made honourable by the commonwealth. For there be some things honourable by nature; as the effects of courage, magnanimity, strength, wisdom, and other abilities of body and mind: others made honourable by the commonwealth; as badges, titles, offices, or any other singular mark of the sovereign's favour. The former, (though they may fail by nature, or accident) cannot be taken away by a law; and therefore the loss of them is not punishment. But the latter, may be taken away by the public authority that made them honourable, and are properly punishments: such are degrading men condemned, of their badges, titles, and offices; or declaring them incapable of the like in time to come.

Imprisonment, is when a man is by public authority deprived of liberty; and may happen from two divers ends; whereof one is the safe custody of a man accused; the other is the inflicting of pain on a man condemned. The former is not punishment; because no man is supposed to be punished, before he be judicially heard, and declared guilty. And therefore whatsoever hurt a man is made to suffer by bonds, or restraint, before his cause be heard, over and above that which is necessary to assure his custody, is against the law of nature. But the latter is punishment, because evil, and inflicted by public authority, for somewhat that has by the same authority been judged a transgression of the law. Under this word imprisonment, I comprehend all restraint of motion, caused by an external obstacle, be it a house, which is called by the general name of a prison; or an island, as when men are said to be confined to it; or a place where men are set to work, as in old time men have been condemned to quarries, and in these times to galleys; or be it a chain, or any other such impediment.

Exile (banishment) is when a man is for a crime, condemned to depart out of the dominion of the commonwealth, or out of a certain part thereof: and during a prefixed time, or for ever, not to return into it: and seemeth not in its own nature, without other circumstances, to be a punishment; but rather an escape, or a public commandment to avoid punishment by flight. And Cicero says, there was never any such punishment ordained in the city of Rome; but calls it a refuge of men in danger. For if a man banished, be nevertheless permitted to enjoy his goods, and the revenue of his lands, the mere change of air is no punishment; nor does it tend to that benefit of the commonwealth, for which all punishments are ordained, (that is to say, to the forming of men's wills to the observation of the law) but many times to the damage of the commonwealth. For a banished man, is a lawful enemy of the commonwealth that banished him; as being no more a member of the same. But if he be withal deprived of his lands, or goods, then the punishment lieth not in the exile, but is to be reckoned amongst punishments pecuniary.

All punishments of innocent subjects, be they great or little, are against the law of nature; for punishment is only for transgression of the law, and therefore there can be no punishment of the innocent. It is therefore a violation, first, of that law of nature, which forbiddeth all men, in their revenges, to look at any thing but some future good: for there can arrive no good to the commonwealth, by punishing the innocent. Secondly, of that, which forbiddeth ingratitude: for seeing all sovereign power, is originally given by the consent of every one of the subjects, to the end they should as long as they are obedient, be protected thereby; the punishment of the innocent, is a rendering of evil for good. And thirdly, of the law that commandeth equity; that is to say, an equal distribution of justice; which in punishing the innocent is not oberved.

But the infliction of what evil soever, on an innocent man, that is not a subject, if it be for the benefit of the commonwealth, and without violation of any former covenant, is no breach of the law of nature. For all men that are not subjects are either enemies, or else thay have ceased from being so by some precedent covenants. But against enemies, whom the commonwealth judgeth capable to do them hurt, it is lawful by the original right of nature to make war; wherein the sword judgeth not, nor doth the victor make distinction of nocent, and innocent, as to the time past; nor has other respect of mercy, than as it conduceth to the good of his own people. And upon this ground it is, that also in subjects, who deliberately deny the authority of the commonwealth established, the vengeance is lawfully extended, not only to the fathers, but also to the third and fourth generation not yet in being, and consequently innocent of the fact, for which they are afflicted: because the nature of this offence, consisteth in the renouncing of subjection; which is a relapse into the condition of war, commonly called rebellion; and they that so offend, suffer not as subjects, but as enemies. For *rebellion*, is but war renewed.

Reward, is either of *gift*, or by *contract*. When by contract, it is called *salary*, and *wages*; which is benefit due for service performed, or promised. When of gift, it is benefit proceeding from the *grace* of them that bestow it, to encourage, or enable men to do them service. And therefore when the sovereign of a commonwealth appointeth a salary to any public office, he that receiveth it, is bound in justice to perform his office; otherwise, he is bound only in honour, to acknowledgment, and an endeavour of requital. For though men have no lawful remedy, when they be commanded to quit their private business, to serve the public, without reward or salary; yet they are not bound thereto, by the law of nature, nor by the institution of the commonwealth, unless the service cannot otherwise be done; because it is supposed the sovereign may make use of all their means, insomuch as the most common soldier, may demand the wages of his warfare, as a debt.

The benefits which a sovereign bestoweth on a subject, for fear of some power and ability he hath to do hurt to the commonwealth, are not properly rewards; for they are not salaries; because there is in this case no contract supposed, every man being obliged already not to do the commonwealth disservice: nor are they graces; because they be extorted by fear, which ought not to be incident to the sovereign power: but are rather sacrifices, which the sovereign (considered in his natural person, and not in the person of the commonwealth) makes, for the appeasing the discontent of him he thinks more potent than himself; and encourage not to obedience, but on the contrary, to the continuance, and increasing of further extortion.

And whereas some salaries are certain, and proceed from the public treasure; and others uncertain, and casual, proceeding from the execution of the office for which the salary is ordained; the latter is in some cases hurtful to the commonwealth; as in the case of judicature. For where the benefit of the judges, and ministers of a court of justice, ariseth from the multitude of causes that are brought to their cognizance, there must needs follow two inconveniences: one, is the nourishing of suits; for the more suits, the greater benefit: and another that depends on that, which is contention about jurisdiction; each court drawing to itself, as many causes as it can. But in offices of execution there are not those inconveniences; because their employment cannot be increased by any endeavour of their own. And thus much shall suffice for the nature of punishment and reward; which are, as it were, the nerves and tendons, that move the limbs and joints of a commonwealth.

Hitherto I have set forth the nature of man, (whose pride and other passions have compelled him to submit himself to government) together with the great power of his governor, whom I compared to

Leviathan, taking that comparison out of the two last verses of the one-and-fortieth of *Job*; where God having set forth the great power of *Leviathan*, calleth him King of the Proud. *There is nothing*, saith he, *on earth, to be compared with him. He is made so as not to be afraid. He seeth every high thing below him*; *and is king of all the children of pride*. But because he is mortal, and subject to decay, as all other earthly creatures are; and because there is that in heaven, (though not on earth) that he should stand in fear of, and whose laws he ought to obey; I shall in the next following chapters speak of his diseases, and the causes of his mortality, and of what laws of nature he is bound to obey.

CHAPTER 29

Of those things that Weaken, or tend to the Dissolution of a Commonwealth

Though nothing can be immortal, which mortals make; yet, if men had the use of reason they pretend to, their commonwealths might be secured, at least from perishing by internal diseases. For by the nature of their institution, they are designed to live, as long as mankind, or as the laws of nature, or as justice itself, which gives them life. Therefore when they come to be dissolved, not by external violence, but intestine disorder, the fault is not in men, as they are the *matter*; but as they are the *makers*, and orderers of them. For men, as they become at last weary of irregular jostling, and hewing one another, and desire with all their hearts, to conform themselves into one firm and lasting edifice; so for want, both of the art of making fit laws, to square their actions by, and also of humility and patience, to suffer the rude and cumbersome points of their present greatness to be taken off, they cannot without the help of a very able architect, be compiled into any other than a crazy building, such as hardly lasting out their own time, must assuredly fall upon the heads of their posterity.

Amongst the *infirmities* therefore of a commonwealth, I will reckon in the first place, those that arise from an imperfect institution, and resemble the diseases of a natural body, which proceed from a defectuous procreation.

Of which, this is one, *that a man to obtain a kingdom, is sometimes content with less power, than to the peace and defence of the commonwealth is necessarily required.* From whence it cometh to pass, that when the exercise of the power laid by, is for the public safety to be resumed, it hath the resemblance of an unjust act; which disposeth great numbers of men (when occasion is presented) to rebel; in the same manner as the bodies of children, gotten by diseased parents, are subject either to untimely death, or to purge the ill quality, derived from their vicious conception, by breaking out into biles and scabs. And when kings deny themselves some such necessary power, it is not always (though sometimes) out of ignorance of what is necessary to the office they undertake; but many times out of a hope to recover the same again at their pleasure: wherein they reason not well; because such as will hold them to their promises, shall be maintained against them by foreign commonwealths; who in order to the good of their own subjects let slip few occasions to *weaken* the estate of their neighbours. So was Thomas Becket, Archbishop of Canterbury, supported against Henry II, by the Pope; the subjection of ecclesiastics to the commonwealth, having been dispensed with by William the Conqueror at his reception, when he took an oath, not to infringe the liberty of the church. And so were the barons, whose power was by William Rufus (to have their help in transferring the succession from his elder brother, to himself) increased to a degree, inconsistent with the sovereign power, maintained in their rebellion against King John, by the French.

Nor does this happen in monarchy only. For whereas the style of the ancient Roman commonwealth was, *The Senate and People of Rome*; neither senate, nor people pretended to the whole power; which first caused the seditions of Tiberius Gracchus, Caius Gracchus, Lucius Saturninus, and others; and afterwards the wars between the senate and the people, under Marius and Sylla; and again under Pompey and Caesar, to the extinction of their democracy, and the setting up of monarchy.

The people of Athens bound themselves but from one only action; which was, that no man on pain of death should propound the renewing of the war for the island of Salamis; and yet thereby, if Solon had not caused to be given out he was mad, and afterwards in gesture and habit of a madman, and in verse, propounded it to the people that flocked about him, they had had an enemy perpetually in readiness, even at the gates of their city; such damage, or shifts, are all commonwealths forced to, that have their power never so little limited.

In the second place, I observe the *diseases* of a

commonwealth, that proceed from the poison of seditious doctrines, whereof one is, *That every private man is judge of good and evil actions*. This is true in the condition of mere nature, where there are no civil laws; and also under civil government, in such cases as are not determined by the law. But otherwise, it is manifest, that the measure of good and evil actions, is the civil law; and the judge the legislator, who is always the representative of the commonwealth. From this false doctrine, men are disposed to debate with themselves, and dispute the commands of the commonwealth; and afterwards to obey or disobey them, as in their private judgments they shall think fit. Whereby the commonwealth is distracted and *weakened*.

Another doctrine repugnant to civil society, is, that *whatsoever a man does against his conscience, is sin*; and it dependeth on the presumption of making himself judge of good and evil. For a man's conscience and his judgment is the same thing; and as the judgment, so also the conscience may be erroneous. Therefore, though he that is subject to no civil law, sinneth in all he does against his conscience, because he has no other rule to follow but his own reason; yet it is not so with him that lives in a commonwealth; because the law is the public conscience, by which he hath already undertaken to be guided. Otherwise in such diversity, as there is of private consciences, which are but private opinions, the commonwealth must needs be distracted, and no man dare to obey the sovereign power, further than it shall seem good in his own eyes.

It hath been also commonly taught, *that faith and sanctity, are not to be attained by study and reason, but by supernatural inspiration, or infusion*. Which granted,

I see not why any man should render a reason of his faith; or why every Christian should not be also a prophet; or why any man should take the law of his country, rather than his own inspiration, for the rule of his action. And thus we fall again in the fault of taking upon us to judge of good and evil; or to make judges of it, such private men as pretend to be supernaturally inspired, to the dissolution of all civil government. Faith comes by hearing, and hearing by those accidents, which guide us into the presence of them that speak to us; which accidents are all contrived by God Almighty; and yet are not supernatural, but only, for the great number of them that concur to every effect, unobservable. Faith, and sanctity, are indeed not very frequent; but yet they are not miracles, but brought to pass by education, discipline, correction, and other natural ways, by which God worketh them in his elect, at such times as he thinketh fit. And these three opinions, pernicious to peace and government, have in this part of the world, proceeded chiefly from the tongues and pens of unlearned divines; who joining the words of Holy Scripture together, otherwise than is agreeable to reason, do what they can, to make men think, that sanctity and natural reason, cannot stand together.

A fourth opinion, repugnant to the nature of a commonwealth, is this, *that he that hath the sovereign power is subject to the civil laws*. It is true, that sovereigns are all subject to the laws of nature; because such laws be divine, and cannot by any man, or commonwealth be abrogated. But to those laws which the sovereign himself, that is, which the commonwealth maketh, he is not subject. For to be subject to laws, is to be subject to the commonwealth, that is to the sovereign representative, that is to himself; which is not subjection, but freedom from the laws. Which error, because it setteth the laws above the sovereign, setteth also a judge above him, and a power to punish him; which is to make a new sovereign; and again for the same reason a third, to punish the second; and so continually without end, to the confusion and dissolution of the commonwealth.

A fifth doctrine, that tendeth to the dissolution of a commonwealth, is, *that every private man has an absolute propriety in his goods; such, as excludeth the right of the sovereign.* Every man has indeed a propriety that excludes the right of every other subject: and he has it only from the sovereign power; without the protection whereof, every other man should have equal right to the same. But if the right of the sovereign also be excluded, he cannot perform the office they have put him into; which is to defend them both from foreign enemies and from the injuries of one another; and consequently there is no longer a commonwealth.

And if the propriety of subjects exclude not the right of the sovereign representative to their goods, much less to their offices of judicature, or execution, in which they represent the sovereign himself.

There is a sixth doctrine, plainly and directly against the essence of a commonwealth; and 'tis this, *that the sovereign power may be divided.* For what is it to divide the power of a commonwealth, but to dissolve it? For powers divided mutually destroy each other. And for these doctrines, men are chiefly beholding to some of those, that making profession of the laws, endeavour to make them depend upon their own learning, and not upon the legislative power.

And as false doctrine, so also oftentimes the example of different government in a neighbouring nation, disposeth men to alteration of the form already settled. So the people of the Jews were stirred up to reject God, and to call upon the prophet Samuel for a king after the manner of the nations: so also the lesser cities of Greece, were continually disturbed with seditions of the aristocratical and democratical factions; one part of almost every commonwealth, desiring to imitate the Lacedemonians; the other, the Athenians. And I doubt not, but many men have been contented to see the late troubles in England, out of an imitation of the Low Countries; supposing there needed no more to grow rich, than to change, as they had done, the form of their government. For the constitution of man's nature, is of itself subject to desire novelty: when therefore they are provoked to the same, by the neighbourhood also of those that have been enriched by it, it is almost impossible for them, not to be content with those that solicit them to change; and love the first beginnings, (though they be grieved with the continuance) of disorder; like hot bloods, that having gotten the itch, tear themselves with their own nails, till they can endure the smart no longer.

And as to rebellion in particular against monarchy; one of the most frequent causes of it, is the reading of the books of policy, and histories of the ancient Greeks and Romans; from which young men, and all others that are unprovided of the antidote of solid reason, receiving a strong and delightful impression of the great exploits of war, achieved by the conductors of their armies, receive withal a pleasing idea, of all they have done besides; and imagine their great prosperity, not to have proceeded from the emulation of particular men, but from the virtue of their popular form of government: not considering the frequent seditions, and civil wars, produced by the imperfection of their policy. From the reading, I say, of such books, men have undertaken to kill their kings, because the Greek and Latin writers, in their books, and discourses of policy make it lawful, and laudable, for any man so to do; provided, before he do it, he call him tyrant. For they say not *regicide*, that is, killing a king, but *tyrannicide*, that is, killing of a tyrant is lawful. From the same books, they that live under a monarch conceive an opinion, that the subjects in a popular commonwealth enjoy liberty; but that in a monarchy they are all slaves. I say, they that live under a monarchy conceive such an opinion; not they that live under a popular government: for they find no such matter. In sum, I cannot imagine, how any thing can be more prejudicial to a monarchy, than the allowing of such books to be publicly read, without present applying such correctives of discreet masters, as are fit to take away their venom: which venom I will not doubt to compare to the biting of a mad dog, which is a disease the physicians call *hydrophobia*, or *fear of water*. For as he that is so bitten, has a continual torment of thirst, and yet abhorreth water; and is in such an estate, as if the poison endeavoured to convert him into a dog: so when a monarchy is once bitten to the quick, by those democratical writers, that continually snarl at that estate; it wanteth nothing more than a strong monarch, which nevertheless out of a certain *tyrannophobia*, or fear of being strongly governed, when they have him, they abhor.

As there have been doctors, that hold there be three

souls in a man; so there be also that think there may be more souls, (that is, more sovereigns) than one, in a commonwealth; and set up a *supremacy* against the *sovereignty*; *canons* against *laws*; and a *ghostly authority* against the *civil*; working on men's minds, with words and distinctions that of themselves signify nothing, but bewray (by their obscurity) that there walketh (as some think invisibly) another kingdom, as it were a kingdom of fairies, in the dark. Now seeing it is manifest, that the civil power and the power of the commonwealth is the same thing; and that supremacy, and the power of making canons, and granting faculties, implieth a commonwealth; it followeth, that where one is sovereign, another supreme; where one can make laws, and another make canons; there must needs be two commonwealths, of one and the same subjects; which is a kingdom divided in itself, and cannot stand. For notwithstanding the insignificant distinction of *temporal*, and *ghostly*, they are still two kingdoms, and every subject is subject to two masters. For seeing the *ghostly* power challengeth the right to declare what is sin, it challengeth by consequence to declare what is law, (sin being nothing but the transgression of the law) and again, the civil power challenging to declare what is law, every subject must obey two masters, who both will have their commands be observed as law; which is impossible. Or, if it be but one kingdom, either the *civil*, which is the power of the commonwealth, must be subordinate to the *ghostly*, and then there is no sovereignty but the *ghostly*; or the *ghostly* must be subordinate to the *temporal*, and then there is no *supremacy* but the *temporal*. When therefore these two powers oppose one another, the commonwealth cannot but be in great danger of civil war and dissolution. For the *civil* authority being more visible, and standing in the clearer light of natural reason, cannot choose but draw to it in all times a very considerable part of the people: and the *spiritual*, though it stand in the darkness of School distinctions, and hard words; yet because the fear of darkness, and ghosts, is greater than other fears, cannot want a party sufficient to trouble, and sometimes to destroy a commonwealth. And this is a disease which not unfitly may be compared to the epilepsy, or falling sickness (which the Jews took to be one kind of possession by spirits) in the body natural. For as in this disease, there is an unnatural spirit, or wind in the head that obstructeth the roots of the nerves, and moving them violently, taketh away the motion which naturally they should have from the power of the soul in the brain, thereby causeth violent and irregular motions (which men call convulsions) in the parts; insomuch as he that is seized therewith, falleth down sometimes into the water, and sometimes into the fire, as a man deprived of his senses; so also in the body politic, when the spiritual power moveth the members of a commonwealth, by the terror of punishments and hope of rewards (which are the nerves of it) otherwise than by the civil power (which is the soul of the commonwealth) they ought to be moved; and by strange and hard words suffocates their understanding, it must needs thereby distract the people, and either overwhelm the commonwealth with oppression, or cast it into the fire of a civil war.

Sometimes also in the merely civil government, there be more than one soul; as when the power of levying money, (which is the nutritive faculty) has depended on a general assembly; the power of conduct and command, (which is the motive faculty) on one man; and the power of making laws, (which is the rational faculty), on the accidental consent, not only of those two, but also of a third; this endangereth the commonwealth, sometimes for want of consent to good laws; but most often for want of such nourishment, as is necessary to life, and motion. For although few perceive, that such government, is not government, but division of the commonwealth into three factions, and call it mixed monarchy; yet the truth is, that it is not one independent commonwealth, but three independent factions; nor one representative person, but three. In the kingdom of God, there may be three persons independent, without breach of unity in God that reigneth; but where men reign, that be subject to diversity of opinions, it cannot be so. And therefore if the king bear the person of the people, and the general assembly bear also the person of the people, and another assembly bear the person of a part of the people, they are not one person, nor one sovereign, but three persons, and three sovereigns.

To what disease in the natural body of man I may exactly compare this irregularity of a commonwealth, I know not. But I have seen a man, that had another man growing out of his side, with a head, arms, breast, and stomach, of his own; if he had had another man growing out of his other side, the comparison might then have been exact.

Hitherto, I have named such diseases of a commonwealth, as are of the greatest, and most present danger. There be other, not so great; which nevertheless are not unfit to be observed. At first, the difficulty of raising money, for the necessary uses of the commonwealth; especially in the approach of war. This difficulty ariseth from the opinion, that every subject hath a propriety in his lands and goods, exclusive of the sovereign's right to the use of the same. From whence it cometh to pass, that the sovereign power, which foreseeth the necessities and dangers of the commonwealth, (finding the passage of money to the public treasury obstructed, by the tenacity of the people) whereas it ought to extend itself, to encounter, and prevent such dangers in their beginnings, contracteth itself as long as it can, and when it cannot longer, struggles with the people by stratagems of law, to obtain little sums, which not sufficing, he is fain at last violently to open the way for present supply, or perish; and being put often to these extremities, at last reduceth the people to their due temper; or else the commonwealth must perish. Insomuch as we may compare this distemper very aptly to an ague; wherein, the fleshy parts being congealed, or by venomous matter obstructed, the veins which by their natural course empty themselves into the heart, are not (as they ought to be) supplied from the arteries, whereby there succeedeth at first a cold contraction, and trembling of the limbs; and afterward a hot, and strong endeavour of the heart, to force a passage for the blood; and before it can do that, contenteth itself with the small refreshments of such things as cool for a time, till (if nature be strong enough) it break at last the contumacy of the parts obstructed, and dissipateth the venom into sweat; or (if nature be too weak) the patient dieth.

Again, there is sometimes in a commonwealth, a disease, which resembleth the pleurisy; and that is, when the treasure of the commonwealth, flowing out of its due course, is gathered together in too much abundance, in one, or a few private men, by monopolies, or by farms of the public revenues; in the same manner as the blood in a pleurisy, getting into the membrane of the breast, breedeth there an inflammation, accompanied with a fever, and painful stitches.

Also, the popularity of a potent subject, (unless the commonwealth have very good caution of his fidelity) is a dangerous disease; because the people, (which should receive their motion from the authority of the sovereign) by the flattery, and by the reputation of an ambitious man are drawn away from their obedience to the laws, to follow a man, of whose virtues and designs they have no knowledge. And this is commonly of more danger in a popular government, than in a monarchy; because an army is of so great force, and multitude, as it may easily be made believe, they are the people. By this means it was, that Julius Caesar, who was set up by the people against the senate, having won to himself the affections of his army, made himself master, both of senate and people. And this proceeding of popular, and ambitious men, is plain rebellion; and may be resembled to the effects of witchcraft.

Another infirmity of a commonwealth, is the immoderate greatness of a town, when it is able to furnish out of its own circuit, the number, and expense of a great army: as also the great number of corporations; which are as it were many lesser commonwealths in the bowels of a greater, like worms in the entrails of a natural man. To which may be added, the liberty of disputing against absolute power, by pretenders to political prudence; which though bred for the most part in the lees of the people, yet animated by false doctrines, are perpetually meddling with the fundamental laws, to the molestation of the commonwealth; like the little worms, which physicians call *ascarides*.

We may further add, the insatiable appetite, or bulimia, of enlarging dominion; with the incurable *wounds* thereby many times received from the enemy; and the *wens*, of ununited conquests, which are many times a burthen, and with less danger lost, than kept; as also the *lethargy* of ease, and *consumption* of riot and vain expense.

Lastly, when in a war (foreign or intestine) the enemies get a final victory; so as (the forces of the commonwealth keeping the field no longer) there is no further protection of subjects in their loyalty; then is the commonwealth dissolved, and every man at liberty to protect himself by such courses as his own discretion shall suggest unto him. For the sovereign, is the public soul, giving life and motion to the commonwealth; which expiring, the members are governed by it no more, than the carcase of a man, by his departed (though immortal) soul. For though the right of a sovereign monarch cannot be extinguished by the act of another; yet the obligation of the members may. For he that wants protection, may seek it anywhere; and when he hath it, is obliged (without fraudulent pretence of having submitted himself out of fear) to protect his protection as long as he is able. But when the power of an assembly is once suppressed, the right of the same perisheth utterly, because the assembly itself is extinct; and consequently, there is no possibility for the sovereignty to re-enter.

CHAPTER 30

Of the Office of the Sovereign Representative

The office of the sovereign, (be it a monarch or an assembly) consisteth in the end, for which he was trusted with the sovereign power, namely the procuration of *the safety of the people*; to which he is obliged by the law of nature, and to render an account thereof to God, the author of that law, and to none but him. But by safety here, is not meant a bare preservation, but also all other contentments of life, which every man by lawful industry, without danger, or hurt to the commonwealth, shall acquire to himself.

And this is intended should be done, not by care applied to individuals, further than their protection from injuries, when they shall complain; but by a general providence, contained in public instruction, both of doctrine, and example; and in the making and executing of good laws, to which individual persons may apply their own cases.

And because, if the essential rights of sovereignty (specified before in the eighteenth chapter) be taken away, the commonwealth is thereby dissolved, and every man returneth into the condition, and calamity of a war with every other man, (which is the greatest evil that can happen in this life) it is the office of the sovereign, to maintain those rights entire; and consequently against his duty, first, to transfer to another, or to lay from himself any of them. For he that deserteth the means, deserteth the ends; and he deserteth the means, that being the sovereign, acknowledgeth himself subject to the civil laws; and renounceth the power of supreme judicature; or of making war or peace by his own authority; or of judging of the necessities of the commonwealth; or of levying money, and soldiers, when, and as much as in his own conscience he shall judge necessary; or of making officers and ministers both of war and peace; or of appointing teachers, and examining what doctrines are conformable or contrary to the defence, peace, and good of the people. Secondly, it is against his duty, to let the people be ignorant, or misinformed of the grounds and reasons of those his essential rights; because thereby men are easy to be seduced, and drawn to resist him, when the commonwealth shall require their use and exercise.

And the grounds of these rights, have the rather need to be diligently and truly taught; because they cannot be maintained by any civil law, or terror of legal punishment. For a civil law, that shall forbid rebellion, (and such is all resistance to the essential rights of the sovereignty) is not (as a civil law) any obligation, but by virtue only of the law of nature, that forbiddeth the violation of faith; which natural obligation if men know not, they cannot know the right of any law the sovereign maketh. And for the punishment, they take it but for an act of hostility; which when they think they have strength enough, they will endeavour by acts of hostility, to avoid.

As I have heard some say, that justice is but a word, without substance; and that whatsoever a man can by force, or art, acquire to himself, (not only in the condition of war, but also in a commonwealth) is his own, which I have already showed to be false: so there be also that maintain, that there are no grounds, nor principles of reason, to sustain those essential rights, which make sovereignty absolute. For if there were, they would have been found out in some place, or other; whereas we see, there has not hitherto been any commonwealth, where those rights have been acknowledged, or challenged. Wherein they argue as ill, as if the savage people of America, should deny there were any grounds, or principles of reason, so to build a house, as to last as long as the materials, because they never yet saw any so well built. Time, and industry, produce every day new knowledge. And as the art of well building, is derived from principles of reason, observed by industrious men, that had long studied the nature of materials, and the divers effects of figure, and proportion, long after mankind began (though poorly) to build: so, long time after men have begun to constitute commonwealths, imperfect, and apt to relapse into disorder, there may principles of reason be found out, by industrious meditation, to make their constitution (excepting by external violence) everlasting. And such are those which I have in this discourse set forth: which whether they come not into the sight of those that have power to make use of them, or be neglected by them, or not, concerneth my particular interests, at this day, very little. But supposing that these of mine are not such principles of reason; yet I am sure they are principles from authority of Scripture; as I shall make it appear, when I shall come to speak of the kingdom of God, (administered by Moses) over the Jews, his peculiar people by covenant.

But they say again, that though the principles be right, yet common people are not of capacity enough to be made to understand them. I should be glad, that the rich and potent subjects of a kingdom, or those that are accounted the most learned, were no less incapable than they. But all men know, that the obstructions to this kind of doctrine, proceed not so much from the difficulty of the matter, as from the interest of them that are to learn. Potent men digest hardly any thing that setteth up a power to bridle their affections; and learned men, any thing that discovereth their errors, and thereby lesseneth their authority: whereas the common people's minds, unless they be tainted with dependence on the potent, or scribbled over with the opinions of their doctors, are like clean paper, fit to receive whatsoever by public authority shall be imprinted in them. Shall whole nations be brought to *acquiesce* in the great mysteries of the Christian religion, which are above reason, and millions of men be made believe, that the same body may be in innumerable places, at one and the same time, which is against reason; and shall not men be able, by their teaching, and preaching, protected by the law, to make that received, which is so consonant to reason, that any unprejudicated man, needs no more to learn it, than to hear it? I conclude therefore, that in the instruction of the people in the essential rights (which are the natural, and fundamental laws) of sovereignty, there is no difficulty, (whilst a sovereign has his power entire) but what proceeds from his own fault, or the fault of those whom he trusteth in the administration of the commonwealth; and consequently, it is his duty, to cause them so to be instructed; and not only his duty, but his benefit also, and security, against the danger that may arrive to himself in his natural person from rebellion.

And (to descend to particulars) the people are to be taught, first, that they ought not to be in love with any form of government they see in their neighbour nations, more than with their own, nor (whatsoever present prosperity they behold in nations that are otherwise governed than they) to desire change. For the prosperity of a people ruled by an aristocratical or democratical assembly, cometh not from aristocracy, nor from democracy, but from the obedience, and concord of the subjects: nor do the people flourish in a monarchy, because one man has the right to rule them, but because they obey him. Take away in any kind of state, the obedience, (and consequently the concord of the people) and they shall not only not flourish, but in short time be dissolved. And they that go about by disobedience, to do no more than reform the Commonhealth, shall find they do thereby destroy it; like the foolish daughters of Peleus, (in the fable) which desiring to renew the youth of their decrepit father, did by the counsel of Medea, cut him in pieces, and boil him, together with strange herbs, but made not of him a new man. This desire of change, is like the breach of the first of God's commandments: for there God says, *Non habebis Deos alienos*; Thou shalt not have the Gods of other nations; and in another place concerning *kings*, that they are *Gods*.

Secondly, they are to be taught, that they ought not to be led with admiration of the virtue of any of their fellow-subjects, how high soever he stand, or how conspicuously soever he shine in the commonwealth; nor of any assembly, (except the sovereign assembly) so as to defer to them any obedience, or honour, appropriate to the sovereign only, whom (in their particular stations) they represent; nor to receive any influence from them, but such as is conveyed by them from the sovereign authority. For that sovereign, cannot be imagined to love his people as he ought, that is not jealous of them, but suffers them by the flattery of popular men, to be seduced from their loyalty, as they have often been, not only secretly, but openly, so as to proclaim marriage with them *in facie ecclesiae* by preachers; and by publishing the same in the open streets: which may fitly be compared to the violation of the second of the ten commandments.

Thirdly, in consequence to this, they ought to be informed, how great a fault it is, to speak evil of the sovereign representative, (whether one man, or an assembly of men) or to argue and dispute his power; or any way to use his name irreverently, whereby he may be brought into contempt with his people, and their obedience (in which the safety of the commonwealth consisteth) slackened. Which doctrine the third commandment by resemblance pointeth to.

Fourthly, seeing people cannot be taught this, nor when 'tis taught, remember it, nor after one generation past, so much as know in whom the sovereign power is placed, without setting apart from their ordinary labour, some certain times, in which they may attend those that are appointed to instruct them; it is necessary that some such times be determined, wherein they may assemble together, and (after prayers and praises given to God, the sovereign of sovereigns) hear those their duties told them, and the positive laws, such as generally concern them all, read and expounded, and be put in mind of the authority that maketh them laws. To this end had the Jews every seventh day, a sabbath, in which the law was read and expounded; and in the solemnity whereof they were put in mind, that their king was God; that having created the world in six days, he rested the seventh day; and by their resting on it from their labour, that that God was their king, which redeemed them from their servile, and painful labour in Egypt, and gave them a time, after they had rejoiced in God, to take joy also in themselves, by lawful recreation. So that the first table of the commandments, is spent all, in setting down the sum of God's absolute power; not only as God, but as king by pact (in peculiar) of the Jews; and may therefore give light, to those that have sovereign power conferred on them by the consent of men, to see what doctrine they ought to teach their subjects.

And because the first instruction of children, dependeth on the care of their parents; it is necessary that they should be obedient to them, whilst they are under their tuition; and not only so, but that also afterwards (as gratitude requireth) they acknowledge the benefit of their education, by external signs of honour. To which end they are to be taught, that originally the father of every man was also his sovereign lord, with power over him of life and death; and that the fathers of families, when by instituting a commonwealth, they resigned that absolute power, yet it was never intended, they should lose the honour due unto them for their education. For to relinquish such right, was not necessary to the institution of sovereign power; nor would there be any reason, why any man should desire to have children, or take the care to nourish and instruct them, if they were afterwards to have no other benefit from them, than from other men. And this accordeth with the fifth commandment.

Again, every sovereign ought to cause justice to be taught, which (consisting in taking from no man what is his) is as much as to say, to cause men to be taught not to deprive their neighbours, by violence, or fraud, of any thing which by the sovereign authority is theirs. Of things held in propriety, those that are dearest to a man are his own life, and limbs; and in the next degree, (in most men) those that concern conjugal affection; and after them, riches and means of living. Therefore the people are to be taught, to abstain from violence to one another's person, by private revenges; from violation of conjugal honour; and from forcible rapine, and fraudulent surreption of one another's goods. For which purpose also it is necessary they be showed the evil consequences of false judgment, by corruption either of judges or witnesses, whereby the distinction of propriety is taken away, and justice becomes of no effect: all which things are intimated in the sixth, seventh, eighth, and ninth commandments.

Lastly, they are to be taught, that not only the unjust facts, but the designs and intentions to do them, (though by accident hindered,) are injustice; which consisteth in the pravity of the will, as well as in the irregularity of the act. And this is the intention of the tenth commandment, and the sum of the second table; which is reduced all to this one commandment of mutual charity, *thou shalt love thy neighbour as thyself*: as the sum of the first table is reduced to *the love of God*; whom they had then newly received as thier king.

As for the means, and conduits, by which the people

may receive this instruction, we are to search, by what means so many opinions, contrary to the peace of mankind, upon weak and false principles, have nevertheless been so deeply rooted in them. I mean those, which I have in the precedent chapter specified: as that men shall judge of what is lawful and unlawful, not by the law itself, but by their own consciences; that is to say, by their own private judgment: that subjects sin in obeying the commands of the commonwealth, unless they themselves have first judged them to be lawful: that their propriety in their riches is such, as to exclude the dominion, which the commonwealth hath over the same: that it is lawful for subjects to kill such as they call tyrants: that the sovereign power may be divided, and the like; which come to be instilled into the people by this means. They whom necessity, or covetousness keepeth attent on their trades, and labour; and they, on the other side, whom superfluity or sloth carrieth after their sensual pleasures, (which two sorts of men take up the greatest part of mankind) being diverted from the deep meditation, which the learning of truth, not only in the matter of natural justice, but also of all other sciences necessarily requireth, receive the notions of their duty, chiefly from divines in the pulpit, and partly from such of their neighbours or familiar acquaintance, as having the faculty of discoursing readily and plausibly, seem wiser and better learned in cases of law, and conscience, than themselves. And the divines, and such others as make show of learning, derive their knowledge from the universities, and from the schools of law, or from the books, which by men, eminent in those schools and universities, have been published. It is therefore manifest, that the instruction of the people, dependeth wholly, on the right teaching of youth in the universities. But are not (may some man say) the universities of England learned enough already to do that? Or is it you, will undertake to teach the universities? Hard questions. Yet to the first, I doubt not to answer; that till towards the latter end of Henry the Eighth, the power of the Pope was always upheld against the power of the commonwealth, principally by the universities; and that the doctrines maintained by so many preachers, against the sovereign power of the king, and by so many lawyers, and others, that had their education there, is a sufficient argument, that though the universities were not authors of those false doctrines, yet they knew not how to plant the true. For in such a contradiction of opinions, it is most certain, that they have not been sufficiently instructed; and 'tis no wonder, if they yet retain a relish of that subtle liquor, wherewith they were first seasoned, against the civil authority. But to the latter question, it is not fit, nor needful for me to say either aye, or no: for any man that sees what I am doing, may easily perceive what I think.

The safety of the people, requireth further, from him or them that have the sovereign power, that justice be equally administered to all degrees of people; that is, that as well the rich and mighty, as poor and obscure persons, may be righted of the injuries done them; so as the great, may have no greater hope of impunity, when they do violence, dishonour, or any injury to the meaner sort, than when one of these, does the like to one of them: for in this consisteth equity; to which, as being a percept of the law of nature, a sovereign is as much subject, as any of the meanest of his people. All breaches of the law, are offences against the commonwealth: but there be some, that are also against private persons. Those that concern the commonwealth only, may without breach of equity be pardoned; for every man may pardon what is done against himself, according to his own discretion. But an offence against a private man, cannot in equity be pardoned, without the consent of him that is injured; or reasonable satisfaction.

The inequality of subjects, proceedeth from the acts of sovereign power; and therefore has no more place in the presence of the sovereign; that is to say, in a court of justice, than the inequality between kings, and their subjects, in the presence of the King of kings. The honour of great persons, is to be valued for their beneficence, and the aids they give to men of inferior rank, or not at all. And the violences, oppressions, and injuries they do, are not extenuated, but aggravated by the greatness of their persons; because they have least need to commit them. The consequences of this partiality towards the great, proceed in this manner. Impunity maketh insolence; insolence, hatred; and hatred, an endeavour to pull down all oppressing and contumelious greatness, though with the ruin of the commonwealth.

To equal justice, appertaineth also the equal imposition of taxes; the equality whereof dependeth not on the equality of riches, but on the equality of the debt, that every man oweth to the commonwealth for his defence. It is not enough, for a man to labour for the maintenance of his life; but also to fight, (if need be) for the securing of his labour. They must either do as the Jews did after their return from captivity, in re-edifying the temple, build with one hand, and hold the sword in the other; or else they must hire others to fight for them. For the impositions, that are laid on the people by the sovereign power, are nothing else but the wages, due to them that hold the public sword, to defend private men in the exercise of their several trades, and callings. Seeing then the benefit that every one receiveth thereby, is the enjoyment of life, which is equally dear to poor, and rich; the debt which a poor man oweth them that defend his life, is the same which a rich man oweth for the defence of his; saving that the rich, who have the service of the poor, may be debtors not only for their own persons, but for many more. Which considered, the equality of imposition, consisteth rather in the equality of that which is consumed, than of the riches of the persons that consume the same. For what reason is there, that he which laboureth much, and sparing the fruits of his labour, consumeth little, should be more charged, than he that living idly, getteth little, and spendeth all he gets; seeing the one hath no more protection from the commonwealth, than the other? But when the impositions, are laid upon those things which men consume, every man payeth equally for what he useth: nor is the commonwealth defrauded by the luxurious waste of private men.

And whereas many men, by accident inevitable, become unable to maintain themselves by their labour; they ought not to be left to the charity of private persons; but to be provided for, (as far forth as the necessities of nature require) by the laws of the commonwealth. For as it is uncharitableness in any man, to neglect the impotent; so it is in the sovereign of a commonwealth, to expose them to the hazard of such uncertain charity.

But for such as have strong bodies, the case is otherwise: they are to be forced to work; and to avoid the excuse of not finding employment, there ought to be such laws, as may encourage all manner of arts; as navigation, agriculture, fishing, and all manner of manufacture that requires labour. The multitude of poor, and yet strong people still increasing, they are to be transplanted into countries not sufficiently inhabited: where nevertheless, they are not to exterminate those they find there; but constrain them to inhabit closer together, and not to range a great deal of ground, to snatch what they find; but to court each little plot with art and labour, to give them their sustenance in due season. And when all the world is overcharged with inhabitants, then the last remedy of all is war; which provideth for every man, by victory, or death.

To the care of the sovereign, belongeth the making of good laws. But what is a good law? By a good law, I mean not a just law: for no law can be unjust. The law is made by the sovereign power, and all that is done by such power, is warranted, and owned by every one of the people; and that which every man will have so, no man can say is unjust. It is in the laws of a commonwealth, as in the laws of gaming: whatsoever the gamesters all agree on, is injustice to none of them. A good law is that, which is *needful*, for the *good of the people*, and withal *perspicuous*.

For the use of laws, (which are but rules authorised) is not to bind the people from all voluntary actions; but to direct and keep them in such a motion, as not to hurt themselves by their own impetuous desires, rashness or indiscretion; as hedges are set, not to stop travellers, but to keep them in their way. And therefore a law that is not needful, having not the true end of a law, is not good. A law may be conceived to be good, when it is for the benefit of the sovereign; though it be not necessary for the people; but it is not so. For the good of the sovereign and people, cannot be separated. It is a weak sovereign, that has weak subjects; and a weak people, whose sovereign wanteth power to rule them at his will. Unnecessary laws are not good laws; but traps for money: which where the right of sovereign power is acknowledged are superfluous; and where it is not acknowledged, unsufficient to defend the people.

The perspicuity, consisteth not so much in the words of the law itself, as in a declaration of the causes, and motives, for which it was made. That is it, that shows us the meaning of the legislator; and the meaning of the legislator known, the law is more easily understood by few, than many words. For all words, are subject to ambiguity; and therefore multiplication of words in the body of the law, is multiplication of ambiguity: besides it seems to imply, (by too much diligence) that whosoever can evade the words, is without the compass of the law. And this is a cause of many unnecessary processes. For when I consider how short were the laws of ancient times; and how they grew by degrees still longer; methinks I see a contention between the penners, and pleaders of the law; the former seeking to circumscribe the latter; and the latter to evade their circumscriptions; and that the pleaders have got the victory. It belongeth therefore to the office of a legislator, (such as is in all commonwealths the supreme representative, be it one man, or an assembly) to make the reason perspicuous, why the law was made; and the body of the law itself, as short, but in as proper, and significant terms, as may be.

It belongeth also to the office of the sovereign, to make a right application of punishments, and rewards. And seeing the end of punishing is not revenge, and discharge of choler; but correction, either of the offender, or of others by his example; the severest punishments are to be inflicted for those crimes, that are of most danger to the public; such as are those which proceed from malice to the government established; those that spring from contempt of justice; those that provoke indignation in the multitude; and those, which unpunished, seem authorised, as when they are committed by sons, servants, or favourites of men in authority: for indignation carrieth men, not only against the actors, and authors of injustice; but against all power that is likely to protect them; as in the case of Tarquin; when for the insolent act of one of his sons, he was driven out of Rome, and the monarchy itself dissolved. But crimes of infirmity; such as are those which proceed from great provocation, from great fear, great need, or from ignorance whether the fact be a great crime, or not, there is place many times for lenity, without prejudice to the commonwealth; and lenity, when there is such place for it, is required by the law of nature. The punishment of the leaders and teachers in a commotion, not the poor seduced people, when they are punished, can profit the commonwealth by their example. To be severe to the people, is to punish that ignorance, which may in great part be imputed to the sovereign, whose fault it was, they were no better instructed.

In like manner it belongeth to the office, and duty of the sovereign, to apply his rewards always so, as there may arise from them benefit to the commonwealth: wherein consisteth their use, and end; and is then done, when they that have well served the commonwealth, are with as little expense of the common treasure, as is possible, so well recompensed, as others thereby may be encouraged, both to serve the same as faithfully as they can, and to study the arts by which they may be enabled to do it better. To buy with money, or preferment, from a popular ambitious subject, to be quiet, and desist from making ill impressions in the minds of the people, has nothing of the nature of reward; (which is ordained not for disservice, but for service past) nor a sign of gratitude, but of fear: nor does it tend to the benefit, but to the damage of the public. It is a contention with ambition, like that of Hercules with the monster Hydra, which having many heads, for every one that was vanquished, there grew up three. For in like manner, when the stubbornness of one popular man, is overcome with reward, there arise many more (by the example) that do the same mischief, in hope of like benefit: and as all sorts of manufacture, so also malice increaseth by being vendible. And though sometimes a civil war, may be deferred, by such ways as that, yet the danger grows still the greater, and the public ruin more assured. It is therefore against the duty of the sovereign, to whom the public safety is committed, to reward those that aspire to greatness by disturbing the peace of their country, and not rather to oppose the beginnings of such men, with a little danger, than after a longer time with greater.

Another business of the sovereign, is to choose good counsellors; I mean such, whose advice he is to take in the government of the commonwealth. For this word counsel, *consilium*, corrupted from *considium*, is of a large signification, and comprehendeth all assemblies of men that sit together, not only to deliberate what is to be done hereafter, but also to judge of facts past, and of law for the present. I take it here in the first sense only: and in this sense, there is no choice of counsel, neither in a democracy, nor aristocracy; because the persons counselling are members of the person counselled. The choice of counsellors therefore is proper to monarchy; in which, the sovereign that endeavoureth not to make choice of those, that in every kind are the most able, dischargeth not his office as he ought to do. The most able counsellors, are they that have least hope of benefit by giving evil counsel, and most knowledge of those things that conduce to the peace, and defence of the commonwealth. It is a hard matter to know who expecteth benefit from public troubles; but the signs that guide to a just suspicion, is the soothing of the people in their unreasonable, or irremediable grievances, by men whose estates are not sufficient to discharge their accustomed expenses, and may easily be observed by any one whom it concerns to know it. But to know, who has most knowledge of the public affairs, is yet harder; and they that know them, need them a great deal the less. For to know, who knows the rules almost of any art, is a great degree of the knowledge of the same art; because no man can be assured of the truth of another's rules, but he that is first taught to understand them. But the best signs of knowledge of any art, are, much conversing in it, and constant good effects of it. Good counsel comes not by lot, nor by inheritance; and therefore there is no more reason to expect good advice from the rich, or noble, in matter of state, than in delineating the dimensions of a fortress; unless we shall think there needs no method in the study of the politics, (as there does in the study of geometry) but only to be lookers on; which is not so. For the politics is the harder study of the two. Whereas in these parts of Europe, it hath been taken for a right of certain persons, to have place in the highest council of state by inheritance; it is derived from the conquests of the ancient Germans; wherein many absolute lords joining together to conquer other nations, would not enter into the confederacy, without such privileges, as might be marks of difference in time following, between their posterity, and the posterity of their subjects; which privileges being inconsistent with the sovereign power, by the favour of the sovereign, they may seem to keep; but contending for them as their right, they must needs by degrees let them go, and have at last no further honour, than adhereth naturally to their abilities.

And how able soever be the counsellors in any affair, the benefit of their counsel is greater, when they give every one his advice, and the reasons of it, apart, than when they do it in an assembly, by way of orations; and when they have premeditated, than when they speak on the sudden; both because they have more time, to survey the consequences of action; and are less subject to be carried away to contradiction, though envy, emulation, or other passions arising from the difference of opinion.

The best counsel, in those things that concern not other nations, but only the ease, and benefit the subjects may enjoy, by laws that look only inward, is to be taken from the general informations, and complaints of the people of each province, who are best acquainted with their own wants, and ought therefore, when they demand nothing in derogation of the essential rights of sovereignty, to be diligently taken notice of. For without those essential rights, (as I have often before said) the commonwealth cannot at all subsist.

A commander of an army in chief, if he be not popular, shall not be beloved, nor feared as he ought to be by his army; and consequently, cannot perform that office with good success. He must therefore be industrious, valiant, affable, liberal and fortunate, that he may gain an opinion both of sufficiency, and of loving his soldiers. This is popularity, and breeds in the soldiers both desire, and courage, to recommend themselves to his favour; and protects the severity of the general, in punishing (when need is) the mutinous, or negligent soldiers. But this love of soldiers, (if caution be not given of the commander's fidelity) is a dangerous thing to sovereign power; especially when it is in the hands of an assembly not popular. It belongeth therefore to the safety of the people, both that they be good conductors, and faithful subjects, to whom the sovereign commits his armies.

But when the sovereign himself is popular; that is, reverenced and beloved of his people, there is no danger at all from the popularity of a subject. For soldiers are never so generally unjust, as to side with their captain, though they love him, against their sovereign, when they love not only his person, but also his cause. And therefore those, who by violence have at any time suppressed the power of their lawful sovereign, before they could settle themselves in his place, have been always put to the trouble of contriving their titles, to save the people from the shame of receiving them. To have a known right to sovereign power, is so popular a quality, as he that has it needs no more, for his own part, to turn the hearts of his subjects to him, but that they see him able absolutely to govern his own family: nor, on the part of his enemies, but a disbanding of their armies. For the greatest and most active part of mankind, has never hitherto been well contented with the present.

Concerning the offices of one sovereign to another, which are comprehended in that law, which is commonly called the *law of nations*, I need not say any thing in this place; because the law of nations, and the law of nature, is the same thing. And every sovereign hath the same right, in procuring the safety of his people, that any particular man can have, in procuring his own safety. And the same law, that dictateth to men that have no civil government, what they ought to do, and what to avoid in regard of one another, dictateth the same to commonwealths, that is, to the consciences of sovereign princes and sovereign assemblies; there being no court of natural justice, but in the conscience only; where not man, but God reigneth; whose laws, (such of them as oblige all mankind) in respect of God, as he is the author of nature, are *natural*; and in respect of the same God, as he is King of kings, are *laws*. But of the kingdom of God, as King of kings, and as King also of a peculiar people, I shall speak in the rest of this discourse.

CHAPTER 31

Of the Kingdom of God by Nature

That the condition of mere nature, that is to say, of absolute liberty, such as is theirs, that neither are sovereigns, nor subjects, is anarchy, and the condition of war: that the precepts, by which men are guided to avoid that condition, are the laws of nature: that a commonwealth, without sovereign power, is but a word without substance, and cannot stand: that subjects owe to sovereigns, simple obedience, in all things, wherein their obedience is not repugnant to the laws of God, I have sufficiently proved, in that which I have already written. There wants only, for the entire knowledge of civil duty, to know what are those laws of God. For without that, a man knows not, when he is commanded any thing by the civil power, whether it be contrary to the law of God, or not: and so, either by too much civil obedience, offends the Divine Majesty, or through fear of offending God, transgresses the commandments of the commonwealth. To avoid both these rocks, it is necessary to know what are the laws divine. And seeing the knowledge of all law, dependeth on the knowledge of the sovereign power; I shall say something in that which followeth, of the kingdom of God.

God is king, let the earth rejoice, saith the psalmist (97:1). And again, (Psalm 99:1) *God is king though the nations be angry; and he that sitteth on the cherubims, though the earth be moved.* Whether men will or not, they must be subject always to the divine power. By denying the existence, or providence of God, men may shake off their ease, but not their yoke. But to call this power of God, which extendeth itself not only to man, but also to beasts, and plants, and bodies inanimate, by the name of kingdom, is but a metaphorical use of the word. For he only is properly said to reign, that governs his subjects, by his word, and by promise of rewards to those that obey it, and by threatening them with punishment that obey it not. Subjects therefore in the kingdom of God, are not bodies inanimate, nor creatures irrational; because they understand no precepts as his: nor atheists; nor they that believe not that God has any care of the actions of mankind; because they acknowledge no word for his, nor have hope of his rewards or fear of his threatenings. They therefore that believe there is a God that governeth the world, and hath given precepts, and propounded rewards and punishments to mankind, are God's subjects; all the rest, are to be understood as enemies.

To rule by words, requires that such words be manifestly made known; for else they are no laws: for to the nature of laws belongeth a sufficient and clear promulgation, such as may take away the excuse of ignorance; which in the laws of men is but of one only kind, and that is, proclamation, or promulgation by the voice of man. But God declareth his laws three ways; by the dictates of *natural reason*, by *revelation*, and by the *voice* of some *man*, to whom by the operation of miracles, he procureth credit with the rest. From hence there ariseth a triple word of God, *rational*, *sensible*, and *prophetic*: to which correspondeth a triple hearing; *right reason*, *sense supernatural*, and *faith*. As for sense supernatural, which consisteth in revelation, or inspiration, there have not been any universal laws so given, because God speaketh not in that manner, but to particular persons, and to divers men divers things.

From the difference between the other two kinds of God's word, *rational*, and *prophetic*, there may be attributed to God, a twofold kingdom, *natural*, and *prophetic*: natural, wherein he governeth as many of mankind as acknowledge his providence, by the natural dictates of right reason; and prophetic, wherein having chosen out one peculiar nation (the Jews) for his subjects, he governed them, and none but them, not only by natural reason, but by positive laws, which he gave them by the mouths of his holy prophets. Of the natural kingdom of God I intend to speak in this chapter.

The right of nature, whereby God reigneth over men, and punisheth those that break his laws, is to be derived, not from his creating them, as if he required obedience as of gratitude for his benefits; but from his *irresistible power*. I have formerly shown, how the sovereign right ariseth from pact: to show how the same right may arise from nature, requires no more, but to show in what case it is never taken away. Seeing all men by nature had right to all things, they had right every one to reign over all the rest. But because this right could not be obtained by force, it concerned the safety of every one, laying by that right, to set up men (with sovereign authority) by common consent, to rule and defend them: whereas if there had been any man of power irresistible; there had been no reason, why he should not by that power have ruled, and defended both himself and them, according to his own discretion. To those therefore whose power is irresistible, the dominion of all men adhereth naturally by their excellence of power; and consequently it is from that power, that the kingdom over men, and the right of afflicting men at his pleasure, belongeth naturally to God Almighty; not as Creator, and gracious; but as omnipotent. And though punishment be due for sin only, because by that word is understood affliction for sin; yet the right of afflicting, is not always derived from men's sin, but from God's power.

This question, *why evil men often prosper, and good men suffer adversity*, has been much disputed by the ancient, and is the same with this of ours, *by what right God dispenseth the prosperities and adversities of this life*; and is of that difficulty, as it hath shaken the faith, not only of the vulgar, but of philosophers, and which is more, of the Saints, concerning the Divine Providence. *How good*, saith David, (Psalm 73:1, 2, 3) *is the God of Israel to those that are upright in heart; and yet my feet were almost gone, my treadings had well-nigh slipt; for I was grieved at the wicked, when I saw the ungodly in such prosperity.* And Job, how earnestly does he expostulate with God, for the many afflictions he suffered, notwithstanding his righteousness? This question in the case of Job, is decided by God himself, not by arguments derived from Job's sin, but his own power. For whereas the friends of Job drew their arguments from his affliction to his sin, and he defended himself by the conscience of his innocence, God himself taketh up the matter, and having justified the affliction by arguments drawn from his power, such as this, (Job 38:4) *Where wast thou, when I laid the foundations of the earth*? and the like, both approved Job's innocence, and reproved the erroneous doctrine of his friends. Conformable to this doctrine is the sentence of our Saviour, concerning the man that was born blind, in these words, *Neither hath this man sinned, nor his fathers; but that the works of God might be made manifest in him.* And though it be said, *that death entered into the world by sin*, (by which is meant, that if Adam had never sinned, he had never died, that is, never suffered any separation of his soul from his body) it follows not thence, that God could not justly have afflicted him, though he had not sinned, as well as he afflicteth other living creatures, that cannot sin.

Having spoken of the right of God's sovereignty, as grounded only on nature; we are to consider next, what are the Divine laws, or dictates of natural reason; which laws concern either the natural duties of one man to another, or the honour naturally due to our Divine Sovereign. The first are the same laws of nature, of which I have spoken already in the fourteenth and fifteenth chapters of this treatise; namely, equity, justice, mercy, humility, and the rest of the moral virtues. It remaineth therefore that we consider, what precepts are dictated to men, by their natural reason only, without other word of God, touching the honour and worship of the Divine Majesty.

Honour consisteth in the inward thought and opinion of the power and goodness of another: and therefore to honour God, is to think as highly of his power and goodness, as is possible. And of that opinion, the external signs appearing in the words and actions of men, are called *worship*; which is one part of that which the Latins understand by the word *cultus*. For *cultus* signifieth properly, and constantly, that labour which a man bestows on any thing, with a purpose to make benefit by it. Now those things whereof we make benefit, are either subject to us, and the profit they yield followeth the labour we bestow upon them, as a natural effect; or they are not subject to us, but answer our labour, according to their own wills. In the first sense the labour bestowed on the earth, is called *culture*; and the education of children, a *culture* of their minds. In the second sense, where men's wills are to be wrought to our purpose, not by force, but by complaisance, it signifieth as much as courting, that is, a winning of favour by good offices; as by praises, by acknowledging their power, and by whatsoever is pleasing to them from whom we look for any benefit. And this is properly *worship*: in which sense *Publicola*, is understood for a worshipper of the people; and *cultus Dei*, for the worship of God.

From internal honour, consisting in the opinion of power and goodness, arise three passions; *love*, which hath reference to goodness; and *hope*, and *fear*, that relate to power: and three parts of external worship; *praise*, *magnifying*, and *blessing*: the subject of praise, being goodness; the subject of magnifying and blessing, being power, and the effect thereof felicity. Praise and magnifying are signified both by words and actions: by words, when we say a man is good, or great: by actions, when we thank him for his bounty, and obey his power. The opinion of the happiness of another, can only be expressed by words.

There be some signs of honour, (both in attributes and actions) that be naturally so; as amongst attributes, *good*, *just*, *liberal*, and the like; and amongst actions, *prayers*, *thanks*, and *obedience*. Others are so by institution, or custom of men; and in some times and places are honourable; in others, dishonourable; in others, indifferent: such as are the gestures in salutation, prayer, and thanksgiving, in different times and places, differently used. The former is *natural*; the latter *arbitrary* worship.

And of arbitrary worship, there be two differences: for sometimes it is a *commanded*, sometimes a *voluntary* worship: commanded, when it is such as he requireth, who is worshipped: free, when it is such as the worshipper thinks fit. When it is commanded, not the words, or gesture, but the obedience is the worship. But when free, the worship consists in the opinion of the beholders: for if to them the words, or actions by which we intend honour, seem ridiculous, and tending to contumely, they are no worship, because no signs of honour; and no signs of honour, because a sign is not a sign to him that giveth it, but to him to whom it is made; that is, to the spectator.

Again, there is a *public*, and a *private* worship. Public, is the worship that a commonwealth performeth, as one person. Private, is that which a private person exhibiteth. Public, in respect of the whole commonwealth, is free; but in respect of particular men, it is not so. Private, is in secret free; but in the sight of the multitude, it is never without some restraint, either from the laws, or from the opinion of men; which is contrary to the nature of liberty.

The end of worship amongst men, is power. For where a man seeth another worshipped, he supposeth him powerful, and is the readier to obey him; which makes his power greater. But God has no ends: the worship we do him, proceeds from our duty, and is directed according to our capacity, by those rules of honour, that reason dictateth to be done by the weak to the more potent men, in hope of benefit, for fear of damage, or in thankfulness for good already received from them.

That we may know what worship of God is taught us by the light of nature, I will begin with his attributes. Where, first, it is manifest, we ought to attribute to him *existence*: for no man can have the will to honour that, which he thinks not to have any being.

Secondly, that those philosophers, who said the world, or the soul of the world was God, spake unworthily of him; and denied his existence: for by God, is understood the cause of the world; and to say the world is God, is to say there is no cause of it, that is, no God.

Thirdly, to say the world was not created, but eternal, (seeing that which is eternal has no cause) is to deny there is a God.

Fourthly, that they who attributing (as they think) ease to God, take from him the care of mankind; take from him his honour: for it takes away men's love, and fear of him; which is the root of honour.

Fifthly, in those things that signify greatness, and power; to say he is *finite*, is not to honour him: for it is not a sign of the will to honour God, to attribute to him less than we can; and finite, is less than we can; because to finite, it is easy to add more.

Therefore to attribute *figure* to him, is not honour; for all figure is finite:

Nor to say we conceive, and imagine, or have an *idea* of him, in our mind: for whatsoever we conceive is finite:

Nor to attribute to him *parts*, or *totality*; which are the attributes only of things finite:

Nor to say he is in this, or that *place*: for whatsoever is in place, is bounded, and finite:

Nor that he is *moved*, or *resteth*: for both these attributes ascribe to him place:

Nor that there be more Gods than one; because it implies them all finite: for there cannot be more than one infinite:

Nor to ascribe to him, (unless metaphorically, meaning not the passion but the effect) passions that partake of grief; as *repentance*, *anger*, *mercy*: or of want; as *appetite*, *hope*, *desire*; or of any passive faculty: for passion, is power limited by somewhat else.

And therefore when we ascribe to God a *will*, it is not to be understood, as that of man, for a *rational appetite*; but as the power, by which he effecteth every thing.

Likewise when we attribute to him *sight*, and other acts of sense; as also *knowledge*, and *understanding*; which in us is nothing else, but a tumult of the mind, raised by external things that press the organical parts of man's body: for there is no such thing in God; and being things that depend on natural causes, cannot be attributed to him.

He that will attribute to God, nothing but what is warranted by natural reason, must either use such negative attributes, as *infinite*, *eternal*, *incomprehensible*; or superlatives, as *most high*, *most great*, and the like; or indefinite, as *good*, *just*, *holy*, *creator*; and in such sense, as if he meant not to declare what he is, (for that were to circumscribe him within the limits of our fancy) but how much we admire him, and how ready we would be to obey him; which is a sign of humility, and of a will to honour him as much as we can: for there is but one name to signify our conception of his nature, and that is, I am: and but one name of his relation to us, and that is, *God*; in which is contained Father, King, and Lord.

Concerning the actions of divine worship, it is a most general precept of reason, that they be signs of the intention to honour God; such as are, first, *prayers*: for not the carvers, when they made images, were thought to make them gods; but the people that *prayed* to them.

Secondly, *thanksgiving*; which differeth from prayer in divine worship, no otherwise, than that prayers precede, and thanks succeed the benefit; the end, both of the one and the other, being to acknowledge God, for author of all benefits, as well past, as future.

Thirdly, *gifts*; that is to say, *sacrifices* and *oblations*, (if they be of the best) are signs of honour: for they are thanksgivings.

Fourthly, *not to swear by any but God*, is naturally a sign of honour: for it is a confession that God only knoweth the heart; and that no man's wit, or strength can protect a man against God's vengeance on the perjured.

Fifthly, it is a part of rational worship, to speak considerately of God; for it argues a fear of him, and fear, is a confession of his power. Hence followeth, that the name of God is not to be used rashly, and to no purpose; for that is as much, as in vain: and it is to no purpose, unless it be by way of oath, and by order of the commonwealth, no make judgments certain; or between commonwealths, to avoid war. And that disputing of God's nature is contrary to his honour: for it is supposed, that in this natural kingdom of God, there is no other way to know any thing, but by natural reason; that is, from the principles of natural science; which are so far from teaching us any thing of God's nature, as they cannot teach us our own nature, nor the nature of the smallest creature living. And therefore, when men out of the principles of natural reason, dispute of the attributes of God, they but dishonour him: for in the attributes which we give to God, we are not to consider the signification of philosophical truth; but the signification of pious intention, to do him the greatest honour we are able. From the want of which consideration, have proceeded the volumes of disputation about the nature of God, that tend not to his honour, but to the honour of our own wits, and learning; and are nothing else but inconsiderate and vain abuses of his sacred name.

Sixthly, in *prayers*, *thanksgivings*, *offerings*, and *sacrifices*, it is a dictate of natural reason, that they be every one in his kind the best, and most significant of honour. As for example, that prayers, and thanksgiving, be made in words and phrases, not sudden, nor light, nor plebeian; but beautiful, and well composed; for else we do not God as much honour as we can. And therefore the heathens did absurdly, to worship images for gods: but their doing it in verse, and with music, both of voice and instruments, was reasonable. Also that the beasts they offered in sacrifice, and the gifts they offered, and their actions in worshipping, were full of submission, and commemorative of benefits received, was according to reason, as proceeding from an intention to honour him.

Seventhly, reason directeth not only to worship God in secret; but also, and especially, in public, and in the sight of men: for without that, (that which in honour is most acceptable) the procuring others to honour him, is lost.

Lastly, obedience to his laws (that is, in this case to the laws of nature) is the greatest worship of all. For as obedience is more acceptable to God than sacrifice; so also to set light by his commandments, is the greatest of all contumelies. And these are the laws of that divine worship, which natural reason dictateth to private men.

But seeing a commonwealth is but one person, it ought also to exhibit to God but one worship; which then it doth, when it commandeth it to be exhibited by private men, publicly. And this is public worship; the property whereof, is to be *uniform*: for those actions that are done differently, by different men, cannot be said to be a public worship. And therefore, where many sorts of worship be allowed, proceeding from the different religions of private men, it cannot be said there is any public worship, nor that the commonwealth is of any religion at all.

And because words (and consequently the attributes of God) have their signification by agreement, and constitution of men, those attributes are to be held significative of honour, that men intend shall so be; and whatsoever may be done by the wills of particular men, where there is no law but reason, may be done by the will of the commonwealth, by laws civil. And because a commonwealth hath no will, nor makes no laws, but those that are made by the will of him or them that have the sovereign power; it followeth, that those attributes which the sovereign ordaineth, in the worship of God, for signs of honour, ought to be taken and used for such, by private men in their public worship.

But because not all actions are signs by constitution; but some are naturally signs of honour, others of contumely, these latter (which are those that men are ashamed to do in the sight of them they reverence) cannot be made by human power a part of Divine worship; nor the former (such as are decent, modest, humble behaviour) ever be separated from it. But whereas there be an infinite number of actions, and gestures, of an indifferent nature; such of them as the commonwealth shall ordain to be publicly and universally in use, as signs of honour, and part of God's worship, are to be taken and used for such by the subjects. And that which is said in the Scripture, *It is better to obey God than man*, hath place in the kingdom of God by pact, and not by nature.

Having thus briefly spoken of the natural kingdom of God, and his natural laws, I will add only to this chapter a short declaration of his natural punishments. There is no action of man in this life, that is not the beginning of so long a chain of consequences, as no human's providence is high enough, to give a man a prospect to the end. And in this chain, there are linked together both pleasing and unpleasing events; in such manner, as he that will do any thing for his pleasure, must engage himself to suffer all the pains annexed to it; and these pains, are the natural punishments of those actions, which are the beginning of more harm than good. And hereby it comes to pass, that intemperance is naturally punished with diseases; rashness, with mischances; injustice, with the violence of enemies; pride, with ruin; cowardice, with oppression; negligent government of princes, with rebellion; and rebellion, with slaughter. For seeing punishments are consequent to the breach of laws;

natural punishments must be naturally consequent to the breach of the laws of nature; and therefore follow them as their natural, not arbitrary effects.

And thus far concerning the constitution, nature, and right of sovereigns; and concerning the duty of subjects, derived from the principles of natural reason. And now, considering how different this doctrine is, from the practice of the greatest part of the world, especially of these western parts, that have received their moral learning from Rome, and Athens; and how much depth of moral philosophy is required, in them that have the administration of the sovereign power; I am at the point of believing this my labour as useless, as the commonwealth of Plato; for he also is of opinion that it is impossible for the disorders of state, and change of governments by civil war, ever to be taken away, till sovereigns be philosophers. But when I consider again, that the science of natural justice, is the only science necessary for sovereigns, and their principal ministers; and that they need not be charged with the sciences mathematical, (as by Plato they are) farther, than by good laws to encourage men to the study of them; and that neither Plato, nor any other philosopher hitherto, hath put into order, and sufficiently or probably proved all the theorems of moral doctrine, that men may learn thereby, both how to govern, and how to obey; I recover some hope, that one time or other, this writing of mine, may fall into the hands of a sovereign, who will consider it himself, (for it is short, and I think clear) without the help of any interested, or envious interpreter; and by the exercise of entire sovereignty, in protecting the public teaching of it, convert this truth of speculation, into the utility of practice.

SECOND TREATISE OF GOVERNMENT

CONTENTS

CHAPTER I

The Introduction

It having been shown in the foregoing discourse,

1. That Adam had not, either by natural right of fatherhood, or by positive donation from God, any such authority over his children, or dominion over the world, as is pretended:

2. That if he had, his heirs yet had no right to it:

3. That if his heirs had, there being no law of nature nor positive law of God that determines which is the right heir in all cases that may arise, the right of succession, and consequently of bearing rule, could not have been certainly determined:

4. That if even that had been determined, yet the knowledge of which is the eldest line of Adam's posterity being so long since utterly lost, that in the races of mankind and families of the world there remains not to one above another the least pretence to be the eldest house, and to have the right of inheritance:

All these premises having, as I think, been clearly made out, it is impossible that the rulers now on earth should make any benefit, or derive any the least shadow of authority from that, which is held to be the fountain of all power, 'Adam's private dominion and paternal jurisdiction;' so that he that will not give just occasion to think that all government in the world is the product only of force and violence, and that men live together by no other rules but that of beasts, where the strongest carries it, and so lay a foundation for perpetual disorder and mischief, tumult, sedition, and rebellion, (things that the followers of that hypothesis so loudly cry out against) must of necessity find out another rise of government, another original of political power, and another way of designing and knowing the persons that have it, than what Sir Robert Filmer hath taught us.

To this purpose, I think it may not be amiss to set down what I take to be political power; that the power of a magistrate over a subject may be distinguished from that of a father over his children, a master over his servants, a husband over his wife, and a lord over his slave. All which distinct powers happening sometimes together in the same man, if he be considered under these different relations, it may help us to distinguish these powers one from another, and show the difference betwixt a ruler of a commonwealth, a father of a family, and a captain of a galley.

Political power, then, I take to be a right of making laws with penalties of death, and consequently all less penalties, for the regulating and preserving of property, and of employing the force of the community, in the execution of such laws, and in the defence of the commonwealth from foreign injury; and all this only for the public good.

CHAPTER 2

Of the State of Nature

To understand political power right, and derive it from its original, we must consider what state all men are naturally in, and that is, a state of perfect freedom to order their actions and dispose of their possessions and persons, as they think fit, within the bounds of the law of nature; without asking leave, or depending upon the will of any other man.

A state also of equality, wherein all the power and jurisdiction is reciprocal, no one having more than another; there being nothing more evident than that creatures of the same species and rank, promiscuously born to all the same advantages of nature, and the use of the same faculties, should also be equal one amongst another without subordination or subjection; unless the Lord and Master of them all should, by any manifest declaration of his will, set one above another, and confer on him, by an evident and clear appointment, an undoubted right to dominion and sovereignty.

This equality of men by nature the judicious Hooker looks upon as so evident in itself, and beyond all question, that he makes it the foundation of that obligation to mutual love amongst men, on which he builds the duties we owe one another, and from whence he derives the great maxims of justice and charity. His words are, 'The like natural inducement hath brought men to know that it is no less their duty to love others than themselves; for seeing those things which are equal must needs all have one measure; if I cannot but wish to receive good, even as much at every man's hands as any man can wish unto his own soul, how should I look to have any part of my desire herein satisfied, unless myself be careful to satisfy the like desire, which is undoubtedly in other men, being of one and the same nature? To have any thing offered them repugnant to this desire must needs in all respects grieve them as much as me; so that, if I do harm, I must look to suffer, there being no reason that others should show greater measure of love to me than they have by me showed unto them: my desire therefore to be loved of my equals in nature, as much as possibly may be, imposeth upon me a natural duty of bearing to them-ward fully the like affection: from which relation of equality between ourselves and them that are as ourselves, what several rules and canons natural reason hath drawn, for direction of life, no man is ignorant.'

But though this be a state of liberty, yet it is not a state of licence: though man in that state have an uncontrollable liberty to dispose of his person or possessions, yet he has not liberty to destroy himself, or so much as any creature in his possession, but where some nobler use than its bare preservation calls for it. The state of nature has a law of nature to govern it, which obliges every one: and reason, which is that law, teaches all mankind, who will but consult it, that being all equal and independent, no one ought to harm another in his life, health, liberty, or possessions: for men being all the workmanship of one omnipotent and infinitely wise Maker; all the servants of one sovereign Master, sent into the world by his order, and about his business; they are his property, whose workmanship they are, made to last during his, not another's pleasure: and being furnished with like faculties, sharing all in one community of nature, there cannot be supposed any such subordination among us that may authorise us to destroy another, as if we were made for one another's uses, as the inferior ranks of creatures are for ours. Every one, as he is bound to preserve himself, and not to quit his station wilfully, so by the like reason, when his own preservation comes not in competition, ought he, as much as he can, to preserve the rest of mankind, and may not, unless it be to do justice to an offender, take away or impair the life, or what tends to the preservation of life, the liberty, health, limb, or goods of another. And that all men may be restrained from invading others' rights, and from doing hurt to one another, and the law of nature be observed, which willeth the peace and preservation of all mankind, the execution of the law of nature is, in that state, put into every man's hands, whereby every one has a right to punish the transgressors of that law to such a degree as may hinder its violation: for the law of nature would, as all other laws that concern men in this world, be in vain, if there were nobody that in the state of nature had a power to execute that law, and thereby preserve the innocent, and restrain offenders. And if any one in the state of nature may punish another for any evil he has done, every one may do so: for in that state of perfect equality, where naturally there is no superiority or jurisdiction of one over another, what any may do in prosecution of that law every one must needs have a right to do.

And thus, in the state of nature, 'one man comes by a power over another;' but yet no absolute or arbitrary power to use a criminal, when he has got him in his hands, according to the passionate heats or boundless extravagancy of his own will: but only to retribute to him, so far as calm reason and conscience dictate, what is proportionate to his transgression; which is so much as may serve for reparation and restraint: for these two are the only reasons why one man may lawfully do harm to another, which is that we call punishment. In transgressing the law of nature, the offender declares himself to live by another rule than that of reason and common equity, which is that measure God has set to the actions of men for their mutual security; and so he becomes dangerous to mankind, the tie, which is to secure them from injury and violence, being slighted and broken by him: which being a trespass against the whole species, and the peace and safety of it, provided for by the law of nature; every man upon this score, by the right he hath to preserve mankind in general, may restrain, or, where it is necessary, destroy things noxious to them, and so may bring such evil on any one, who hath transgressed that law, as may make him repent the doing of it, and thereby deter him, and by his example others, from doing the like mischief. And in this case, and upon this ground, 'every man hath a right to punish the offender, and be executioner of the law of nature.'

I doubt not but this will seem a very strange doctrine to some men: but, before they condemn it, I desire them to resolve me by what right any prince or state can put to death or punish an alien for any crime he commits in their country. It is certain their laws, by virtue of any sanction they receive from the promulgated will of the legislative, reach not a stranger: they speak not to him, nor, if they did, is he bound to hearken to them. The legislative authority, by which they are in force over the subjects of that commonwealth, hath no power over him. Those who have the supreme power of making laws in England, France, or Holland, are to an Indian but like the rest of the world, men without authority: and therefore, if by the law of nature every man hath not a power to punish offences against it, as he soberly judges the case to require, I see not how the magistrates of any community can punish an alien of another country; since, in reference to him, they can have no more power than what every man naturally may have over another.

Besides the crime which consists in violating the law, and varying from the right rule of reason, whereby a man so far becomes degenerate, and declares himself to quit the principles of human nature, and to be a noxious creature, there is commonly injury done to some person or other, and some other man receives damage by his transgression: in which case he who hath received any damage, has, besides the right of punishment common to him with other men, a particular right to seek reparation from him that has done it: and any other person, who finds it just, may also join with him that is injured, and assist him in recovering from the offender so much as may make satisfaction for the harm he has suffered.

From these two distinct rights, the one of punishing the crime for restraint, and preventing the like offence, which right of punishing is in every body; the other of taking reparation, which belongs only to the injured party; comes it to pass that the magistrate, who by being magistrate hath the common right of punishing put into his hands, can often, where the public good demands not the execution of the law, remit the punishment of criminal offences by his own authority, but yet cannot remit the satisfaction due to any private man for the damage he has received. That he who has suffered the damage has a right to demand in his own name, and he alone can remit: the damnified person has this power of appropriating to himself the goods or service of the offender, by right of self-preservation, as every man has a power to punish the crime, to prevent its being committed again, 'by the right he has of preserving all mankind,' and doing all reasonable things he can in order to that end: and thus it is that every man, in the state of nature, has a power to kill a murderer, both to deter others from doing the like injury, which no reparation can compensate, by the example of the punishment that attends it from every body; and also to secure men from the attempts of a criminal, who having renounced reason, the common rule and measure God hath given to mankind, hath, by the unjust violence and slaughter he hath committed upon one, declared war against all mankind; and therefore may be destroyed as a lion or a tiger, one of those wild savage beasts with whom men can have no society nor security: and upon this is grounded that great law of nature, 'Whoso sheddeth man's blood, by man shall his blood be shed.' And Cain was so fully convinced that every one had a right to destroy such a criminal, that, after the murder of his brother, he cries out, 'Every one that findeth me shall slay me;' so plain was it writ in the hearts of mankind.

By the same reason may a man in the state of nature punish the lesser breaches of that law. It will perhaps be demanded, with death? I answer, each transgression may be punished to that degree, and with so much severity, as will suffice to make it an ill bargain to the offender, give him cause to repent, and terrify others from doing the like. Every offence, that can be committed in the state of nature, may in the state of nature be also punished equally, and as far forth, as it may in a commonwealth: for though it would be beside my present purpose to enter here into the particulars of the law of nature, or its measures of punishment, yet it is certain there is such a law, and that too as intelligible and plain to a rational creature, and a studier of that law, as the positive laws of commonwealths; nay, possibly plainer, as much as reason is easier to be understood than the fancies and intricate contrivances of men, following contrary and hidden interests put into words; for so truly are a great part of the municipal laws of countries, which are only so far right, as they are founded on the law of nature, by which they are to be regulated and interpreted.

To this strange doctrine, viz. That 'in the state of nature every one has the executive power' of the law of nature, I doubt not but it will be objected, that it is unreasonable for men to be judges in their own cases, that self-love will make men partial to themselves and their friends: and, on the other side, that ill-nature, passion, and revenge will carry them too far in punishing others; and hence nothing but confusion and disorder will follow: and that therefore God hath certainly appointed government to restrain the partiality and violence of men. I easily grant, that civil government is the proper remedy for the inconveniencies of the state of nature, which must certainly be great, where men may be judges in their own case; since it is easy to be imagined, that he who was so unjust as to do his brother an injury, will scarce be so just as to condemn himself for it: but I shall desire those who make this objection to remember, that absolute monarchs are but men; and if government is to be the remedy of those evils, which necessarily follow from men's being judges in their own cases, and the state of nature is therefore not to be endured; I desire to know what kind of government that is, and how much better it is than the state of nature, where one man, commanding a multitude, has the liberty to be judge in his own case, and may do to all his subjects whatever he pleases, without the least liberty to any one to question or control those who execute his pleasure? And in whatsoever he doth, whether led by reason. mistake, or passion, must be submitted to? Much better it is in the state of nature, wherein men are not bound to submit to the unjust will of another: and if he that judges, judges amiss in his own, or any other case, he is answerable for it to the rest of mankind.

It is often asked, as a mighty objection, 'where are or ever were there any men in such a state of nature?' To which it may suffice as an answer at present, that since all princes and rulers of independent governments, all through the world, are in a state of nature, it is plain the world never was, nor ever will be, without numbers of men in that state. I have named all governors of independent communities, whether they are, or are not, in league with others: for it is not every compact that puts an end to the state of nature between men, but only this one of agreeing together mutually to enter into one community, and make one body politic; other promises and compacts men may make one with another, and yet still be in the state of nature. The promises and bargains for truck, &c. between the two men in the desert island, mentioned by Garcilasso de la Vega, in his history of Peru; or between a Swiss and an Indian, in the woods of America; are binding to them, though they are perfectly in a state of nature, in reference to one another: for truth and keeping of faith belongs to men as men, and not as members of society.

To those that say, there were never any men in the state of nature, I will not only oppose the authority of the judicious Hooker, *Eccl. Pol.*, lib. I, sect. 10, where he says, 'The laws which have been hitherto mentioned,' i.e. the laws of nature, 'do bind men absolutely, even as they are men, although they have never any settled fellowship, never any solemn agreement amongst themselves what to do, or not to do: but forasmuch as we are not by ourselves sufficient to furnish ourselves with competent store of things, needful for such a life as our nature doth desire, a life fit for the dignity of man; therefore to supply those defects and imperfections which are in us, as living singly and solely by ourselves, we are naturally induced to seek communion and fellowship with others. This was the cause of men's uniting themselves at first in politic societies.' But I moreover affirm, that all men are naturally in that state, and remain so, till by their own consents they make themselves members of some politc society; and I doubt not in the sequel of this discourse to make it very clear.

CHAPTER 3

Of the State of War

The state of war is a state of enmity and destruction: and therefore declaring by word or action, not a passionate and hasty, but a sedate, settled design upon another man's life, puts him in a state of war with him against whom he has declared such an intention, and so has exposed his life to the other's power to be taken away by him, or any one that joins with him in his defence, and espouses his quarrel; it being reasonable and just, I should have a right to destroy that which threatens me with destruction: for, by the fundamental law of nature, man being to be preserved as much as possible, when all cannot be preserved, the safety of the innocent is to be preferred: and one may destroy a man who makes war upon him, or has discovered an enmity to his being, for the same reason that he may kill a wolf or a lion; because such men are not under the ties of the common law of reason, have no other rule but that of force and violence, and so may be treated as beasts of prey, those dangerous and noxious creatures, that will be sure to destroy him whenever he falls into their power.

And hence it is, that he who attempts to get another man into his absolute power, does thereby put himself into a state of war with him; it being to be understood as a declaration of a design upon his life: for I have reason to conclude, that he who would get me into his power without my consent, would use me as he pleased when he got me there, and destroy me too when he had a fancy to it; for nobody can desire to have me in his absolute power, unless it be to compel me by force to that which is against the right of my freedom, i.e. make me a slave. To be free from such force is the only security of my preservation; and reason bids me look on him as an enemy to my preservation, who would take away that freedom which is the fence to it; so that he who makes an attempt to enslave me, thereby puts himself into a state of war with me. He that, in the state of nature, would take away the freedom that belongs to any one in that state, must necessarily be supposed to have a design to take away every thing else, that freedom being the foundation of all the rest; as he that, in the state of society, would take away the freedom belonging to those of that society or commonwealth, must be supposed to design to take away from them every thing else, and so be looked on as in a state of war.

This makes it lawful for a man to kill a thief, who has not in the least hurt him, nor declared any design upon his life, any farther than, by the use of force, so to get him in his power, as to take away his money, or what he please, from him; because using force, where he has no right, to get me into his power, let his pretence be what it will, I have no reason to suppose, that he who would take away my liberty, would not, when he had me in his power, take away every thing else. And therefore it is lawful for me to treat him as one who has put himself into a state of war with me, i.e. kill him if I can; for to that hazard does he justly expose himself, whoever introduces a state of war, and is aggressor in it.

And here we have the plain 'difference between the state of nature and the state of war;' which, however some men have confounded, are as far distant as a state of peace, good-will, mutual assistance and preservation, and a state of enmity, malice, violence, and mutual destruction, are one from another. Men living together according to reason, without a common superior on earth, with authority to judge between them, is properly the state of nature. But force, or a declared design of force, upon the person of another, where there is no common superior on earth to appeal to for relief, is the state of war: and it is the want of such an appeal gives a man the right of war even against an aggressor, though he be in society, and a fellow-subject. Thus a thief, whom I cannot harm, but by appeal to the law, for having stolen all that I am worth, I may kill, when he sets on me to rob me but of my horse or coat; because the law, which was made for my preservation, where it cannot interpose to secure my life from present force, which, if lost, is capable of no reparation, permits me my own defence, and the right of war, a liberty to kill the aggressor, because the aggressor allows not time to appeal to our common judge, nor the decision of the law, for remedy in a case where the mischief may be irreparable. Want of a common judge with authority puts all men in a state of nature: force without right, upon a man's person, makes a state of war, both where there is, and is not, a common judge.

But when the actual force is over, the state of war ceases between those that are in society, and are equally on both sides subjected to the fair determination of the law; because then there lies open the remedy of appeal for the past injury, and to prevent future harm: but where no such appeal is, as in the state of nature, for want of positive laws, and judges with authority to appeal to, the state of war once begun, continues with a right to the innocent party to destroy the other whenever he can, until the aggressor offers peace, and desires reconciliation on such terms as may repair any wrongs he has already done, and secure the innocent for the future; nay, where an appeal to the law, and constituted judges, lies open, but the remedy is denied by a manifest perverting of justice, and a barefaced wresting of the laws to protect or indemnify the violence or injuries of some men, or party of men; there it is hard to imagine any thing but a state of war: for wherever violence is used, and injury done, though by hands appointed to administer justice, it is still violence and injury, however coloured with the name, pretences, or forms of law, the end whereof being to protect and redress the innocent, by an unbiassed application of it to all who are under it; wherever that is not *bona fide* done, war is made upon the sufferers, who having no appeal on earth to right them, they are left to the only remedy in such cases, an appeal to Heaven.

To avoid this state of war (wherein there is no appeal but to Heaven, and wherein every the least difference is apt to end, where there is no authority to decide between the contenders) is one great reason of men's putting themselves into society, and quitting the state of nature: for where there is an authority, a power on earth, from which relief can be had by appeal, there the continuance of the state of war is excluded, and the controversy is decided by that power. Had there been any such court, any superior jurisdiction on earth, to determine the right between

Jephthah and the Ammonites, they had never come to a state of war: but we see he was forced to appeal to Heaven: 'The Lord the Judge (says he) be judge this day, between the children of Israel and the children of Ammon,' Judges 11:27; and then prosecuting, and relying on his appeal, he leads out his army to battle: and therefore in such controversies, where the question is put, who shall be judge? it cannot be meant, who shall decide the controversy; every one knows what Jephthah here tells us, that 'the Lord the Judge' shall judge. Where there is no judge on earth, the appeal lies to God in heaven. That question then cannot mean, who shall judge whether another hath put himself in a state of war with me, and whether I may, as Jephthah did, appeal to Heaven in it? Of that I myself can only be judge in my own conscience, as I will answer it, at the great day, to the supreme Judge of all men.

CHAPTER 4

Of Slavery

The natural liberty of man is to be free from any superior power on earth, and not to be under the will or legislative authority of man, but to have only the law of nature for his rule. The liberty of man, in society, is to be under no other legislative power, but that established, by consent, in the commonwealth; nor under the dominion of any will, or restraint of any law, but what that legislative shall enact, according to the trust put in it. Freedom, then, is not what Sir Robert Filmer tells us, O.A. 55, 'a liberty for every one to do what he lists, to live as he pleases, and not to be tied by any laws:' but freedom of men under government is, to have a standing rule to live by, common to every one of the society, and made by the legislative power erected in it; a liberty to follow my own will in all things, where the rule prescribes not; and not to be subject to the inconstant, uncertain, unknown, arbitrary will of another man: as freedom of nature is, to be under no other restraint but the law of nature.

This freedom from absolute, arbitrary power, is so necessary to, and closely joined with, a man's preservation. that he cannot part with it, but by what forfeits his preservation and life together: for a man, not having the power of his own life, cannot, by compact, or his own consent, enslave himself to any one, nor put himself under the absolute, arbitrary power of another, to take away his life when he pleases. Nobody can give more power than he has himself; and he that cannot take away his own life, cannot give another power over it. Indeed, having by his fault forfeited his own life, by some act that deserves death; he, to whom he has forfeited it, may (when he has him in his power) delay to take it, and make use of him to his own service, and he does him no injury by it: for, whenever he finds the hardship of his slavery outweigh the value of his life, it is in his power, by resisting the will of his master, to draw on himself the death he desires.

This is the perfect condition of slavery, which is nothing else but 'the state of war continued, between a lawful conqueror and a captive:' for, if once compact enter between them, and make an agreement for a limited power on the one side, and obedience on the other, the state of war and slavery ceases, as long as the compact endures: for, as has been said, no man can, by agreement, pass over to another that which he hath not in himself, a power over his own life.

I confess, we find among the Jews, as well as other nations, that men did sell themselves; but, it is plain, this was only to drudgery, not to slavery: for, it is evident, the person sold was not under an absolute, arbitrary, despotical power: for the master could not have power to kill him, at any time, whom, at a certain time, he was obliged to let go free out of his service; and the master of such a servant was so far from having an arbitrary power over his life, that he could not, at pleasure, so much as maim him, but the loss of an eye, or tooth, set him free, Exod. 21.

CHAPTER 5

Of Property

Whether we consider natural reason, which tells us, that men, being once born, have a right to their preservation, and consequently to meat and drink, and such other things as nature affords for their subsistence; or revelation, which gives us an account of those grants God made of the world to Adam, and to Noah and his sons; it is very clear that God, as King David says, Psalms 105:16, 'has given the earth to the children of men;' given it to mankind in common. But this being supposed, it seems to some a very great difficulty how any one should ever come to have a property in any thing: I will not content myself to answer, that if it be difficult to make out property, upon a supposition that God gave the world to Adam and his posterity in common, it is impossible that any man, but one universal monarch, should have any property, upon a supposition that God gave the world to Adam, and his heirs in succession, exclusive of all the rest of his posterity. But I shall endeavour to show how men might come to have a property in several parts of that which God gave to mankind in common, and that without any express compact of all the commoners.

God, who hath given the world to men in common, hath also given them reason to make use of it to the best advantage of life and convenience. The earth, and all that is therein, is given to men for the support and comfort of their being. And though all the fruits it naturally produces, and beasts it feeds, belong to mankind in common, as they are produced by the spontaneous hand of nature; and nobody has originally a private dominion, exclusive of the rest of mankind, in any of them, as they are thus in their natural state: yet being given for the use of men, there must of necessity be a means to appropriate them some way or other before they can be of any use, or at all beneficial to any particular man. The fruit, or venison, which nourishes the wild Indian, who knows no enclosure, and is still a tenant in common, must be his, or so his, i.e. a part of him, that another can no longer have any right to it, before it can do him any good for the support of his life.

Though the earth, and all inferior creatures, be common to all men, yet every man has a property in his own person: this nobody has any right to but himself. The labour of his body, and the work of his hands, we may say, are properly his. Whatsoever then he removes out of the state that nature hath provided, and left it in, he hath mixed his labour with, and joined to it something that is his own, and thereby makes it his property. It being by him removed from the common state nature hath placed it in, it hath by this labour something annexed to it that excludes the common right of other men. For this labour being the unquestionable property of the labourer, no man but he can have a right to what that is once joined to, at least where there is enough, and as good, left in common for others.

He that is nourished by the acorns he picked up under an oak, or the apples he gathered from the trees in the wood, has certainly appropriated them to himself. Nobody can deny but the nourishment is his. I ask then, when did they begin to be his? When he digested? Or when he ate? Or when he boiled? Or when he brought them home? Or when he picked them up? And it is plain, if the first gathering made them not his, nothing else could. That labour put a distinction between them and common: that added something to them more than nature, the common mother of all, had done; and so they became his private right. And will any one say, he had no right to those acorns or apples he thus appropriated, because he had not the consent of all mankind to make them his? Was it a robbery thus to assume to himself what belonged to all in common? If such a consent as that was necessary, man had starved, notwithstanding the plenty God had given him. We see in commons, which remain so by compact, that it is the taking any part of what is common, and removing it out of the state nature leaves it in, which begins the property; without which the common is of no use. And the taking of this or that part does not depend on the express consent of all the commoners. Thus the grass my horse has bit; the turfs my servant has cut; and the ore I have digged in any place, where I have a right to them in common with others, become my property, without the assignation or consent of any body. The labour that was mine, removing them out of that common state they were in, hath fixed my property in them.

By making an explicit consent of every commoner necessary to any one's appropriating to himself any part of what is given in common, children or servants could not cut the meat, which their father or master had provided for them in common, without assigning to every one his peculiar part. Though the water running in the fountain be every one's, yet who can doubt but that in the pitcher is his only who drew it out? His labour hath taken it out of the hands of nature, where it was common, and belonged equally to all her children, and hath thereby appropriated it to himself.

Thus this law of reason makes the deer that Indian's who hath killed it; it is allowed to be his goods who hath bestowed his labour upon it, though before it was the common right of every one. And amongst those who are counted the civilized part of mankind, who have made and multiplied positive laws to determine property, this original law of nature, for the beginning of property, in what was before common, still takes place; and by virtue thereof, what fish any one catches in the ocean, that great and still remaining common of mankind; or what ambergris any one takes up here, is by the labour that removes it out of that common state nature left it in made his property who takes that pains about it. And even amongst us, the hare that any one is hunting is thought his who pursues her during the chase: for being a beast that is still looked upon as common, and no man's private possession; whoever has employed so much labour about any of that kind, as to find and pursue her, has thereby removed her from the state of nature, wherein she was common, and hath begun a property.

It will perhaps be objected to this, that 'if gathering the acorns, or other fruits of the earth, &c. makes a right to them, then any one may engross as much as he will.' To which I answer, Not so. The same law of nature, that does by this means give us property, does also bound that property too. 'God has given us all things richly,' 1 Tim. 6:17, is the voice of reason confirmed by inspiration. But how far has he given it us? To enjoy. As much as any one can make use of to any advantage of life before it spoils, so much he may by his labour fix a property in: whatever is beyond this, is more than his share, and belongs to others. Nothing was made by God for man to spoil or destroy. And thus, considering the plenty of natural provisions there was a long time in the world, and the few spenders; and to how small a part of that provision the industry of one man could extend itself, and engross it to the prejudice of others; especially keeping within the bounds, set by reason, of what might serve for his use; there could be then little room for quarrels or contentions about property so established.

But the chief matter of property being now not the fruits of the earth, and the beasts that subsist on it, but the earth itself; as that which takes in, and carries with it all the rest; I think it is plain, that property in that too is acquired as the former. As much land as a man tills, plants, improves, cultivates, and can use the product of, so much is his property. He by his labour does, as it were, enclose it from the common. Nor will it invalidate his right, to say every body else has an equal title to it, and therefore he cannot appropriate, he cannot enclose, without the consent of all his fellow-commoners, all mankind. God, when he gave the world in common to all mankind, commanded man also to labour, and the penury of his condition required it of him. God and his reason commanded him to subdue the earth, i.e. improve it for the benefit of life, and therein lay out something upon it that was his own, his labour. He that, in obedience to this command of God, subdued, tilled, and sowed any part of it, thereby annexed to it something that was his property, which another had no title to, nor could without injury take from him.

Nor was this appropriation of any parcel of land, by improving it, any prejudice to any other man, since there was still enough, and as good left; and more than the yet unprovided could use. So that, in effect, there was never the less left for others because of his enclosure for himself: for he that leaves as much as another can make use of, does as good as take nothing at all. Nobody could think himself injured by the drinking of another man, though he took a good draught, who had a whole river of the same water left him to quench his thirst; and the case of land and water, where there is enough of both, is perfectly the same.

God gave the world to men in common; but since he gave it them for their benefit, and the greatest conveniencies of life they were capable to draw from it, it cannot be supposed he meant it should always remain common and uncultivated. He gave it to the use of the industrious and rational (and labour was to be his title to it), not to the fancy or covetousness of the quarrelsome and contentious. He that had as good left for his improvement as was already taken up, needed not complain, ought not to meddle with what was already improved by another's labour: if he did, it is plain he desired the benefit of another's pains, which he had no right to, and not the ground which God had given him in common with others to labour on, and whereof there was as good left as that already possessed, and more than he knew what to do with, or his industry could reach to.

It is true, in land that is common in England, or any other country, where there is plenty of people under government, who have money and commerce, no one can enclose or appropriate any part without the consent of all his fellow-commoners; because this is left common by compact, i.e. by the law of the land, which is not to be violated. And though it be common, in respect of some men, it is not so to all mankind, but is the joint property of this country, or this parish. Besides, the remainder, after such enclosure, would not be as good to the rest of the commoners as the whole was when they could all make use of the whole; whereas in the beginning and first peopling of the great common of the world it was quite otherwise. The law man was under was rather for appropriating. God commanded, and his wants forced him to labour. That was his property which could not be taken from him wherever he had fixed it. And hence subduing or cultivating the earth, and having dominion, we see are joined together. The one gave title to the other. So that God, by commanding to subdue, gave authority so far to appropriate: and the condition of human life, which requires labour and materials to work on, necessarily introduces private possessions.

The measure of property nature has well set by the extent of men's labour and the conveniencies of life: no man's labour could subdue, or appropriate all; nor could his enjoyment consume more than a small part; so that it was impossible for any man, this way, to intrench upon the right of another, or acquire to himself a property, to the prejudice of his neighbour, who would still have room for as good and as large a possession (after the other had taken out his) as before it was appropriated. This measure did confine every man's possession to a very moderate proportion, and such as he might appropriate to himself, without injury to any body, in the first ages of the world, when men were more in danger to be lost, by wandering from their company, in the then vast wilderness of the earth, than to be straitened for want of room to plant in. And the same measure may be allowed still without prejudice to any body, as full as the world seems: for supposing a man, or family, in the state they were at first peopling of the world by the children of Adam, or Noah; let him plant in some inland, vacant places of America, we shall find that the possessions he could make himself, upon the measures we have given, would not be very large, nor, even to this day, prejudice the rest of mankind, or give them reason to complain, or think themselves injured by this man's encroachment; though the race of men have now spread themselves to all the corners of the world, and do infinitely exceed the small number was at the beginning. Nay, the extent of ground is of so little value, without labour, that I have heard it affirmed, that in Spain itself a man may be permitted to plough, sow, and reap, without being disturbed, upon land he has no other title to, but only his making use of it. But, on the contrary, the inhabitants think themselves beholden to him, who, by his industry on neglected, and consequently waste land, has increased the stock of corn, which they wanted. But be this as it will, which I lay no stress on; this I dare boldly affirm, that the same rule of propriety, viz. that every man should have as much as he could make use of, would hold still in the world, without straitening any body; since there is land enough in the world to suffice double the inhabitants, had not the invention of money, and the tacit agreement of men to put a value on it, introduced (by consent) larger possessions, and a right to them; which, how it has done, I shall by and by show more at large.

This is certain, that in the beginning, before the desire of having more than man needed had altered the intrinsic value of things, which depends only on their usefulness to the life of man; or had agreed, that a little piece of yellow metal, which would keep without wasting or decay, should be worth a great piece of flesh, or a whole heap of corn; though men had a right to appropriate, by their labour, each one to himself, as much of the things of nature as he could use: yet this could not be much, nor to the prejudice of others, where the same plenty was still left to those who would use the same industry. To which let me add, that he who appropriates land to himself by his labour, does not lessen, but increase the common stock of mankind: for the provisions serving to the support of human life, produced by one acre of enclosed and cultivated land, are (to speak much within compass) ten times more than those which are yielded by an acre of land of an equal richness lying waste in common. And therefore he that encloses land, and has a greater plenty of the conveniences of life from ten acres, than he could have from an hundred left to nature, may truly be said to give ninety acres to mankind: for his labour now supplies him with provisions out of ten acres, which were by the product of an hundred lying in common. I have here rated the improved land very low, in making its product but as ten to one, when it is much nearer an hundred to one: for I ask, whether in the wild woods and uncultivated waste of America, left to nature, without any improvement, tillage, or husbandry, a thousand acres yield the needy and wretched inhabitants as many conveniencies of life as ten acres equally fertile land do in Devonshire, where they are well cultivated?

Before the appropriation of land, he who gathered as much of the wild fruit, killed, caught, or tamed, as many of the beasts, as he could; he that so employed his pains about any of the spontaneous products of nature, as any way to alter them from the state which nature put them in, by placing any of his labour on them, did thereby acquire a propriety in them: but if they perished, in his possession, without their due use; if the fruits rotted, or the venison putrefied, before he could spend it; he offended against the common law of nature, and was liable to be punished; he invaded his neighbour's share, for he had no right, farther than his use called for any of them, and they might serve to afford him conveniencies of life.

The same measures governed the possession of land too: whatsoever he tilled and reaped, laid up and made use of, before it spoiled, that was his peculiar right; whatsoever he enclosed, and could feed, and make use of, the cattle and product was also his. But if either the grass of his enclosure rotted on the ground, or the fruit of his planting perished without gathering and laying up; this part of the earth, notwithstanding his enclosure, was still to be looked on as waste, and might be the possession of any other. Thus, at the beginning, Cain might take as much ground as he could till, and make it his own land, and yet leave enough to Abel's sheep to feed on; a few acres would serve for both their possessions. But as families increased, and industry enlarged their stocks, their possessions enlarged with the need of them; but yet it was commonly without any fixed property in the ground they made use of, till they incorporated, settled themselves together, and built cities; and then, by consent, they came in time to set out the bounds of their distinct territories, and agree on limits between them and their neighbours; and by laws within themselves settled the properties of those of the same society: for we see that in that part of the world which was first inhabited, and therefore like to be best peopled, even as low down as Abraham's time, they wandered with their flocks, and their herds, which was their substance, freely up and down; and this Abraham did, in a country where he was a stranger. Whence it is plain, that at least a great part of the land lay in common; that the inhabitants valued it not, nor claimed property in any more than they made use of. But when there was not room enough in the same place for their herds to feed together, they by consent, as Abraham and Lot did, Gen. 13:5. separated and enlarged their pasture, where it best liked them. And for the same reason Esau went from his father, and his brother, and planted in mount Seir, Gen.36:6.

And thus, without supposing any private dominion and property in Adam, over all the world, exclusive of all other men, which can no way be proved, nor any one's property be made out from it; but supposing the world given, as it was, to the children of men in common, we see how labour could make men distinct titles to several parcels of it, for their private uses; wherein there could be no doubt of right, no room for quarrel.

Nor is it so strange, as perhaps before consideration it may appear, that the property of labour should be able to overbalance the community of land: for it is labour indeed that put the difference of value on every thing; and let any one consider what the difference is between an acre of land planted with tobacco or sugar, sown with wheat or barley, and an acre of the same land lying in common, without any husbandry upon it, and he will find, that the improvement of labour makes the far greater part of the value. I think it will be but a very modest computation to say, that of the products of the earth useful to the life of man, nine-tenths are the effects of labour: nay, if we will rightly estimate things as they come to our use, and cast up the several expenses about them, what in them is purely owing to nature, and what to labour, we shall find, that in most of them ninety-nine hundredths are wholly to be put on the account of labour.

There cannot be a clearer demonstration of any

thing, than several nations of the Americans are of this, who are rich in land, and poor in all the comforts of life; whom nature having furnished as liberally as any other people with the materials of plenty, i.e. a fruitful soil, apt to produce in abundance what might serve for food, raiment, and delight; yet, for want of improving it by labour, have not one-hundredth part of the conveniencies we enjoy: and a king of a large and fruitful territory there feeds, lodges, and is clad worse than a day-labourer in England.

To make this a little clear, let us but trace some of the ordinary provisions of life, through their several progresses, before they come to our use, and see how much of their value they receive from human industry. Bread, wine, and cloth, are things of daily use, and great plenty; yet notwithstanding, acorns, water, and leaves, or skins, must be our bread, drink, and clothing, did not labour furnish us with these more useful commodities: for whatever bread is more worth than acorns, wine than water, and cloth or silk than leaves, skins, or moss, that is wholly owing to labour and industry; the one of these being the food and raiment which unassisted nature furnishes us with; the other, provisions which our industry and pains prepare for us; which, how much they exceed the other in value, when any one hath computed, he will then see how much labour makes the far greatest part of the value of things we enjoy in this world: and the ground which produces the materials is scarce to be reckoned in as any, or, at most, but a very small part of it; so little, that even amongst us, land that is left wholly to nature, that hath no improvement of pasturage, tillage, or planting, is called, as indeed it is, waste; and we shall find the benefit of it amount to little more than nothing.

This shows how much numbers of men are to be preferred to largeness of dominions; and that the increase of lands, and the right of employing of them, is the great art of government: and that prince, who shall be so wise and godlike, as by established laws of liberty to secure protection and encouragement to the honest industry of mankind, against the oppression of power and narrowness of party, will quickly be too hard for his neighbours: but this by the by. To return to the argument in hand.

An acre of land, that bears here twenty bushels of wheat, and another in America, which, with the same husbandry, would do the like, are, without doubt, of the same natural intrinsic value: but yet the benefit mankind receives from the one in a year is worth 5l. and from the other possibly not worth a penny, if all the profit an Indian received from it were to be valued, and sold here; at least, I may truly say, not one thousandth. It is labour, then, which puts the greatest part of the value upon land, without which it would scarcely be worth any thing: it is to that we owe the greatest part of all its useful products; for all that the straw, bran, bread, of that acre of wheat, is more worth than the product of an acre of as good land, which lies waste, is all the effect of labour: for it is not barely the ploughman's pains, the reaper's and thresher's toil, and the baker's sweat, is to be counted into the bread we eat; the labour of those who broke the oxen, who digged and wrought the iron and stones, who felled and framed the timber employed about the plough, mill, oven, or any other utensils, which are a vast number, requisite to this corn, from its being seed to be sown to its being made bread, must all be charged on the account of labour, and received as an effect of that: nature and the earth furnished only the almost worthless materials, as in themselves. It would be a strange 'catalogue of things, that industry provided and made use of, about every loaf of bread,' before it came to our use, if we could trace them; iron, wood, leather, bark, timber, stone, bricks, coals, lime, cloth, dyeing, drugs, pitch, tar, masts, ropes, and all the materials made use of in the ship, that brought any of the commodities used by any of the workmen, to any part of the work: all which it would be almost impossible, at least too long, to reckon up.

From all which it is evident, that though the things of nature are given in common, yet man, by being master of himself, and 'proprietor of his own person, and the actions or labour of it, had still in himself the great foundation of property;' and that which made up the greater part of what he applied to the support or comfort of his being, when invention and arts had improved the conveniencies of life, was perfectly his own, and did not belong in common to others.

Thus labour, in the beginning, gave a right of property wherever any one was pleased to employ it upon what was common, which remained a long while the far greater part, and is yet more than mankind makes use of. Men, at first, for the most part, contented themselves with what unassisted nature offered to their necessities: and though afterwards, in some parts of the world, (where the increase of people and stock, with the use of money, had made land scarce, and so of some value) the several communities settled the bounds of their distinct territories, and by laws within themselves regulated the properties of the private men of their society, and so, by compact and agreement, settled the property which labour and industry began: and the leagues that have been made between several states and kingdoms, either expressly or tacitly disowning all claim and right to the land in the others' possession, have, by common consent, given up their pretences to their natural common right, which originally they had to those countries, and so have, by positive agreement, settled a property amongst themselves, in distinct parts and parcels of the earth; yet there are still great tracts of ground to be found, which (the inhabitants thereof not having joined with the rest of mankind in the consent of the use of their common money) lie waste, and are more than the people who dwell on it do or can make use of, and so still lie in common; though this can scarce happen amongst that part of mankind that have consented to the use of money.

The greatest part of things really useful to the life of man, and such as the necessity of subsisting made the first commoners of the world look after, as it doth the Americans now, are generally things of short duration; such as, if they are not consumed by use, will decay and perish of themselves: gold, silver, and diamonds, are things that fancy or agreement hath put the value on, more than real use, and the necessary support of life. Now of those good things which nature hath provided in common, every one had a right (as hath been said) to as much as he could use, and property in all that he could effect with his labour; all that his industry could extend to, to alter from the state nature had put it in, was his. He that gathered a hundred bushels of acorns or apples, had thereby a property in them; they were his goods as soon as gathered. He was only to look that he used them before they spoiled, else he took more than his share, and robbed others. And indeed it was a foolish thing, as well as dishonest, to hoard up more than he could make use of. If he gave away a part to any body else, so that it perished not uselessly in his possession, these he also made use of. And if he also bartered away plums, that would have rotted in a week, for nuts that would last good for his eating a whole year, he did no injury; he wasted not the common stock; destroyed no part of the portion of the goods that belonged to others, so long as nothing perished uselessly in his hands. Again, if he would give his nuts for a piece of metal, pleased with its colour; or exchange his sheep for shells, or wool for a sparkling pebble or a diamond, and keep those by him all his life, he invaded not the right of others; he might heap as much of these durable things as he pleased; the exceeding of the bounds of his just property not lying in the largeness of his possession, but the perishing of any thing uselessly in it.

And thus came in the use of money, some lasting thing that men might keep without spoiling, and that by mutual consent men would take in exchange for the truly useful, but perishable supports of life.

And as different degrees of industry were apt to give men possessions in different proportions, so this invention of money gave them the opportunity to continue and enlarge them: for supposing an island, separate from all possible commerce with the rest of the world, wherein there were but an hundred families, but there were sheep, horses, and cows, with other useful animals, wholesome fruits, and land enough for corn for a hundred thousand times as many, but nothing in the island, either because of its commonness, or perishableness, fit to supply the place of money; what reason could any one have there to enlarge his possessions beyond the use of his family and a plentiful supply to its consumption, either in what their own industry produced, or they could barter for like perishable, useful commodities with others? Where there is not something, both lasting and scarce, and so valuable, to be hoarded up, there men will not be apt to enlarge their possessions of land, were it ever so rich, ever so free for them to take: for I ask, what would a man value ten thousand, or an hundred thousand acres of excellent land, ready cultivated, and well stocked too with cattle, in the middle of the inland parts of America, where he had no hopes of commerce with other parts of the world, to draw money to him by the sale of the product? It would not be worth the enclosing, and we should see him give up again to the wild common of nature, whatever was more than would supply the conveniencies of life to be had there for him and his family.

Thus in the beginning all the world was America, and more so than that is now; for no such thing as money was any where known. Find out something that hath the use and value of money amongst his neighbours, you shall see the same man will begin presently to enlarge his possessions.

But since gold and silver, being little useful to the life of man in proportion to food, raiment, and carriage, has its value only from the consent of men, whereof labour yet makes, in great part, the measure;

it is plain, that men have agreed to a disproportionate and unequal possession of the earth; they having, by a tacit and voluntary consent, found out a way how a man may fairly possess more land than he himself can use the product of, by receiving, in exchange for the overplus, gold and silver, which may be hoarded up without injury to any one; these metals not spoiling or decaying in the hands of the possessor. This partage of things in an inequality of private possessions, men have made practicable out of the bounds of society, and without compact; only by putting a value on gold and silver, and tacitly agreeing in the use of money: for in governments, the laws regulate the right of property, and the possession of land is determined by positive constitutions.

And thus, I think, it is very easy to conceive, 'how labour could at first begin a title of property' in the common things of nature, and how the spending it upon our uses bounded it. So that there could then be no reason of quarrelling about title, nor any doubt about the largeness of possession it gave. Right and conveniency went together; for as a man had a right to all he could employ his labour upon, so he had no temptation to labour for more than he could make use of. This left no room for controversy about the title, nor for encroachment on the right of others; what portion a man carved to himself was easily seen: and it was useless, as well as dishonest, to carve himself too much, or take more than he needed.

CHAPTER 6

Of Paternal Power

It may perhaps be censured as an impertinent criticism, in a discourse of this nature, to find fault with words and names that have obtained in the world: and yet possibly it may not be amiss to offer new ones when the old are apt to lead men into mistakes, as this of paternal power probably has done; which seems so to place the power of parents over their children wholly in the father, as if the mother had no share in it: whereas, if we consult reason or revelation, we shall find she hath an equal title. This may give one reason to ask, whether this might not be more properly called parental power? for whatever obligation nature and the right of generation lays on children, it must certainly bind them equally to both concurrent causes of it. And accordingly we see the positive law of God everywhere joins them together, without distinction, when it commands the obedience of children: 'Honour thy father and thy mother,' Exod. 20:12. 'Whosoever curseth his father or his mother,' Lev. 20:9. 'Ye shall fear every man his mother and his father,' Lev. 19:5. 'Children, obey your parents,' &c. Eph. 6:1, is the style of the Old and New Testament.

Had but this one thing been well considered, without looking any deeper into the matter, it might perhaps have kept men from running into those gross mistakes they have made, about this power of parents; which, however it might, without any great harshness, bear the name of absolute dominion, and regal authority, when under the title of paternal power it seemed appropriated to the father, would yet have sounded but oddly, and in the very name shown the absurdity, if this supposed absolute power over children had been called parental; and thereby have discovered, that it belonged to the mother too: for it will but very ill serve the turn of those men who contend so much for the absolute power and authority of the fatherhood, as they call it, that the mother should have any share in it; and it would have but ill supported the monarchy they contend for, when by the very name it appeared that that fundamental authority, from whence they would derive their government of a single person only, was not placed in one, but two persons jointly. But to let this of names pass.

Though I have said above, chapter 2, 'that all men by nature are equal,' I cannot be supposed to understand all sorts of equality: age or virtue may give men a just precedency: excellency of parts and merit may place others above the common level: birth may subject some, and alliance or benefits others, to pay an observance to those whom nature, gratitude, or other respects, may have made it due: and yet all this consists with the equality which all men are in, in respect of jurisdiction or dominion one over another; which was the equality I there spoke of, as proper to the business in hand, being that equal right that every man hath to his natural freedom, without being subjected to the will or authority of any other man.

Children, I confess, are not born in this state of equality, though they are born to it. Their parents have a sort of rule and jurisdiction over them when they come into the world, and for some time after; but it is but a temporary one. The bonds of this subjection are like the swaddling-clothes they are wrapt up in, and supported by, in the weakness of their infancy: age and reason, as they grow up, loosen them, till at length they drop quite off, and leave a man at his own free disposal.

Adam was created a perfect man, his body and mind in full possession of their strength and reason, and so was capable from the first instant of his being to provide for his own support and preservation, and govern his actions according to the dictates of the law of reason which God had implanted in him. From him the world is peopled with his descendants, who are all born infants, weak and helpless, without knowledge or understanding: but to supply the defects of this imperfect state, till the improvement of growth and age hath removed them, Adam and Eve, and after them all parents were, by the law of nature, 'under an obligation to preserve, nourish, and educate the children' they had begotten; not as their own workmanship, but the workmanship of their own maker, the Almighty, to whom they were to be accountable for them.

The law that was to govern Adam was the same that was to govern all his posterity, the law of reason. But his offspring having another way of entrance into the world, different from him, by a natural birth, that produced them ignorant and without the use of reason, they were not presently under that law; for nobody can be under a law which is not promulgated to him; and this law being promulgated or made known by reason only, he that is not come to the use of his reason cannot be said to be under this law; and

Adam's children, being not presently as soon as born under this law of reason, were not presently free: for law, in its true notion, is not so much the limitation, as the direction of a free and intelligent agent to his proper interest, and prescribes no farther than is for the general good of those under that law: could they be happier without it, the law, as an useless thing, would of itself vanish; and that ill deserves the name of confinement which hedges us in only from bogs and precipices. So that, however it may be mistaken, the end of law is not to abolish or restrain, but to preserve and enlarge freedom: for in all the states of created beings capable of laws, 'where there is no law, there is no freedom;' for liberty is to be free from restraint and violence from others; which cannot be where there is not law: but freedom is not, as we are told, 'a liberty for every man to do what he lists:' (for who could be free, when every other man's humour might domineer over him?) but a liberty to dispose and order as he lists his person, actions, possessions, and his whole property, within the allowance of those laws under which he is, and therein not to be subject to the arbitrary will of another, but freely follow his own.

The power, then, that parents have over their children arises from that duty which is incumbent on them, to take care of their offspring during the imperfect state of childhood. To inform the mind, and govern the actions of their yet ignorant nonage, till reason shall take its place, and ease them of that trouble, is what the children want, and the parents are bound to: for God having given man an understanding to direct his actions, has allowed him a freedom of will, and liberty of acting, as properly belonging thereunto, within the bounds of that law he is under. But whilst he is in an estate wherein he has not understanding of his own to direct his will, he is not to have any will of his own to follow: he that understands for him, must will for him too; he must prescribe to his will, and regulate his actions; but when he comes to the estate that made his father a freeman, the son is a freeman too.

This holds in all the laws a man is under, whether natural or civil. Is a man under the law of nature? What made him free of that law? What gave him a free disposing of his property, according to his own will, within the compass of that law? I answer, a state of maturity, wherein he might be supposed capable to know that law, that so he might keep his actions within the bounds of it. When he has acquired that state, he is presumed to know how far that law is to be his guide, and how far he may make use of his freedom, and so comes to have it; till then, somebody else must guide him, who is presumed to know how far the law allows a liberty. If such a state of reason, such an age of discretion made him free, the same shall make his son free too. Is a man under the law of England? What made him free of that law? That is, to have the liberty to dispose of his actions and possessions according to his own will, within the permission of that law? A capacity of knowing that law, which is supposed by that law at the age of one-and-twenty years, and in some cases sooner. If this made the father free, it shall make the son free too. Till then we see the law allows the son to have no will, but he is to be guided by the will of his father or guardian, who is to understand for him. And if the father die, and fail to substitute a deputy in his trust;

if he hath not provided a tutor to govern his son during his minority, during his want of understanding, the law takes care to do it; some other must govern him, and be a will to him, till he hath attained to a state of freedom, and his understanding be fit to take the government of his will. But after that, the father and son are equally free as much as tutor and pupil after nonage; equally subjects of the same law together, without any dominion left in the father over the life, liberty, or estate of his son, whether they be only in the state and under the law of nature, or under the positive laws of an established government.

But if, through defects that may happen out of the ordinary course of nature, any one comes not to such a degree of reason wherein he might be supposed capable of knowing the law, and so living within the rules of it, he is never capable of being a free man, he is never let loose to the disposure of his own will, (because he knows no bounds to it, has not understanding, its proper guide) but is continued under the tuition and government of others, all the time his own understanding is incapable of that charge. And so lunatics and idiots are never set free from the government of their parents. 'Children, who are not as yet come unto those years whereat they may have; and innocents which are excluded by a natural defect from ever having; thirdly, mad men, which for the present cannot possibly have the use of right reason to guide themselves, have for their guide the reason that guideth other men which are tutors over them, to seek and procure their good for them,' says Hooker, *Eccl. Pol.*, lib. 1, sect. 7. All which seems no more than that duty which God and nature has laid on man, as well as other creatures, to preserve their offspring till they can be able to shift for themselves, and will scarce amount to an instance or proof of parents' regal authority.

Thus we are born free, as we are born rational; not that we have actually the exercise of either: age, that brings one, brings with it the other too. And thus we see how natural freedom and subjection to parents may consist together, and are both founded on the same principle. A child is free by his father's title, by his father's understanding, which is to govern him till he hath it of his own. The freedom of a man at years of discretion, and the subjection of a child to his parents, whilst yet short of that age, are so consistent, and so distinguishable, that the most blinded contenders for monarchy, by right of fatherhood, cannot miss this difference; the most obstinate cannot but allow their consistency: for were their doctrine all true, were the right heir of Adam now known, and by that title settled a monarch in his throne, invested with all the absolute unlimited power Sir Robert Filmer talks of; if he should die as soon as his heir were born, must not the child, notwithstanding he were ever so free, ever so much sovereign, be in subjection to his mother and nurse, to tutors and governors, till age and education brought his reason and ability to govern himself and others? The necessities of his life, the health of his body, and the information of his mind, would require him to be directed by the will of others, and not his own; and yet will any one think that this restraint and subjection were inconsistent with, or spoiled him of that liberty of sovereignty he had a right to, or gave away his empire to those who had the government of his nonage? This government over him only prepared him the better and sooner for it. If any body should ask me, when my son is of age to be free? I shall answer, just when his monarch is of age to govern. 'But at what time,' says the judicious Hooker, *Eccl. Pol.*, lib. I, sect. 6, 'a man may be said to have attained so far forth the use of reason, as sufficeth to make him capable of those laws whereby he is then bound to guide his actions: this is a great deal more easy for sense to discern than for any one by skill and learning to determine.'

Commonwealths themselves take notice of, and allow, that there is a time when men are to begin to act like freemen, and therefore till that time require not oaths of fealty or allegiance, or other public owning of, or submission to, the government of their countries.

The freedom then of man, and liberty of acting according to his own will, is grounded on his having reason, which is able to instruct him in that law he is to govern himself by, and make him know how far he is left to the freedom of his own will. To turn him loose to an unrestrained liberty, before he has reason to guide him, is not the allowing him the privilege of his nature to be free; but to thrust him out amongst brutes, and abandon him to a state as wretched, and as much beneath that of a man, as theirs. This is that which puts the authority into the parents' hands to govern the minority of their children. God hath made it their business to employ this care on their offspring, and hath placed in them suitable inclinations of tenderness and concern to temper this power, to apply it, as his wisdom designed it, to the children's good, as long as they should need to be under it.

But what reason can hence advance this care of the parents due to their offspring into an absolute arbitrary dominion of the father, whose power reaches no farther than, by such a discipline as he finds most effectual, to give such strengths and health to their bodies, such vigour and rectitude to their minds, as may best fit his children to be most useful to themselves and others; and, if it be necessary to his condition, to make them work, when they are able, for their own subsistence. But in this power the mother too has her share with the father.

Nay, this power so little belongs to the father by any peculiar right of nature, but only as he is guardian of his children, that when he quits his care of them, he loses his power over them, which goes along with their nourishment and education, to which it is inseparably annexed; and it belongs as much to the foster-father of an exposed child, as to the natural father of another. So little power does the bare act of begetting give a man over his issue, if all his care ends there, and this be all the title he hath to the name and authority of a father. And what will become of this paternal power in that part of the world where one woman hath more than one husband at a time? Or in those parts of America, where, when the husband and wife part, which happens frequently, the children are all left to the mother, follow her, and are wholly under her care and provision? If the father die whilst the children are young, do they not naturally everywhere owe the same obedience to their mother, during their minority, as to their father were he alive? and will any one say, that the mother hath a legislative power over her children? That she can make standing rules, which shall be of perpetual obligation, by which they ought to regulate all the concerns of their property, and bound their liberty all the course of their lives? Or can she enforce the observation of them with capital punishments? For this is the proper power of the magistrate, of which the father hath not so much as the shadow. His command over his children is but temporary, and reaches not their life or property: it is but a help to the weakness and imperfection of their nonage, a discipline necessary to their education: and though a father may dispose of his own possessions as he pleases, when his children are out of danger of perishing for want, yet his power extends not to the lives or goods, which either their own industry or another's bounty has made theirs; nor to their liberty neither, when they are once arrived to the enfranchisement of the years of discretion. The father's empire then ceases, and can from thenceforwards no more dispose of the liberty of his son than that of any other man: and it must be far from an absolute or perpetual jurisdiction, from which a man may withdraw himself, having licence from divine authority to 'leave father and mother, and cleave to his wife.'

But though there be a time when a child comes to be as free from subjection to the will and command of his father, as the father himself is free from subjection to the will of any body else, and they are each under no restraint but that which is common to them both, whether it be the law of nature, or municipal law of their country; yet this freedom exempts not a son from that honour which he ought, by the law of God and nature, to pay his parents. God having made the parents instruments in his great design of continuing the race of mankind, and the occasions of life to their children; as he hath laid on them an obligation to nourish, preserve, and bring up their offspring; so he has laid on the children a perpetual obligation of honouring their parents, which containing in it an inward esteem and reverence to be shown by all outward expressions, ties up the child from any thing that may ever injure or affront, disturb or endanger, the happiness or life of those from whom he received his; and engages him in all actions of defence, relief, assistance, and comfort of those by whose means he entered into being, and has been made capable of any enjoyments of life: from this obligation no state, no freedom, can absolve children. But this is very far from giving parents a power of command over their children, or authority to make laws and dispose as they please of their lives and liberties. It is one thing to owe honour, respect, gratitude, and assistance; another to require an absolute obedience and submission. The honour due to parents, a monarch in his throne owes his mother; and yet this lessens not his authority, nor subjects him to her government.

The subjection of a minor, places in the father a temporary government, which terminates with the minority of the child: and the honour due from a child, places in the parents perpetual right to respect, reverence, support, and compliance too, more or less, as the father's care, cost, and kindness in his education, have been more or less. This ends not with minority, but holds in all parts and conditions of a man's life. The want of distinguishing these two powers, viz. that which the father hath in the right of tuition, during minority, and the right of honour all his life, may perhaps have caused a great part of the mistakes about this matter: for, to speak properly of them, the first of these is rather the privilege of children, and duty of parents, than any prerogative of paternal power. The nourishment and education of their children is a charge so incumbent on parents for their children's good, that nothing can absolve them from taking care of it: and though the power of commanding and chastising them go along with it, yet God hath woven into the principles of human nature such a tenderness for their offspring, that there is little fear that parents should use their power with too much rigour; the excess is seldom on the severe side, the strong bias of nature drawing the other way. And therefore God Almighty, when he would express his gentle dealing with the Israelites, he tells them, that though he chastened them, 'he chastened them as a man chastens his son,' Deut. 8:5. *i.e.* with tenderness and affection, and kept them under no severer discipline than what was absolutely best for them, and had been less kindness to have slackened. This is that power to which children are commanded obedience, that the pains and care of their parents may not be increased, or ill rewarded.

On the other side, honour and support, all that which gratitude requires to return for the benefits received by and from them, is the indispensable duty of the child, and the proper privilege of the parents. This is intended for the parents' advantage, as the other is for the child's; though education, the parents' duty, seems to have most power, because the ignorance and infirmities of childhood stand in need of restraint and correction; which is a visible exercise of rule, and a kind of dominion. And that duty which is comprehended in the word honour requires less obedience, though the obligation be stronger on grown than younger children: for who can think the command, 'Children obey your parents,' requires in a man that has children of his own the same submission to his father, as it does in his yet young children to him; and that by this precept he were bound to obey all his father's commands, if, out of a conceit of authority, he should have the indiscretion to treat him still as a boy?

The first part then of paternal power, or rather duty, which is education, belongs so to the father, that it terminates at a certain season; when the business of education is over, it ceases of itself, and is also alienable before: for a man may put the tuition of his son in other hands; and he that has made his son an apprentice to another, has discharged him, during that time, of a great part of his obedience both to himself and to his mother. But all the duty of honour, the other part, remains nevertheless entire to them; nothing can cancel that: it is so inseparable from them both, that the father's authority cannot dispossess the mother of this right, nor can any man discharge his son from honouring her that bore him. But both these are very far from a power to make laws, and enforcing them with penalties that may reach estate, liberty, limbs, and life. The power of commanding ends with nonage; and though after that, honour and respect, support and defence, and whatsoever gratitude can oblige a man to, for the highest benefits he is naturally capable of, be always due from a son to his parents; yet all this puts no sceptre into the father's hand, no sovereign power of commanding. He has no dominion over his son's property, or actions; nor any right that his will should prescribe to his son's in all things; however it may become his son in many things, not very inconvenient to him and his family, to pay a deference to it.

A man may owe honour and respect to an ancient or wise man; defence to his child or friend; relief and support to the distressed; and gratitude to a benefactor, to such a degree, that all he has, all he can do, cannot sufficiently pay it: but all these give no authority, no right to any one, of making laws over him from whom they are owing. And it is plain, all this is due not only to the bare title of father; not only because, as has been said, it is owing to the mother too, but because these obligations to parents, and the degrees of what is required of children, may be varied by the different care and kindness, trouble and expense, which are often employed upon one child more than another.

This shows the reason how it comes to pass, that parents in societies, where they themselves are subjects, retain a power over their children, and have as much right to their subjection as those who are in the state of nature. Which could not possibly be, if all political power were only paternal, and that in truth they were one and the same thing: for then, all paternal power being in the prince, the subject could naturally have none of it. But these two powers, political and paternal, are so perfectly distinct and separate, are built upon so different foundations, and given to so different ends, that every subject, that is a father, has as much a paternal power over his children as the prince has over his: and every prince, that has parents, owes them as much filial duty and obedience as the meanest of his subjects do to theirs; and cannot therefore contain any part or degree of that kind of dominion which a prince or magistrate has over his subjects.

Though the obligation on the parents to bring up their children, and the obligation on children to honour their parents, contain all the power on the one hand, and submissions on the other, which are proper to this relation, yet there is another power ordinary in the father, whereby he has a tie on the obedience of his children; which though it be common to him with other men, yet the occasions of showing it almost constantly happening to fathers in their private families, and the instances of it elsewhere being rare, and less taken notice of, it passes in the world for a part of paternal jurisdiction. And this is the power men generally have to bestow their estates on those who please them best; the possession of the father being the expectation and inheritance of the children, ordinarily in certain proportions, according to the law and custom of each country; yet it is commonly in the father's power to bestow it with a more sparing or liberal hand, according as the behaviour of this or that child hath comported with his will and humour.

This is no small tie on the obedience of children: and there being always annexed to the enjoyment of land a submission to the government of the country, of which that land is a part; it has been commonly supposed, that a father could oblige his posterity to that government, of which he himself was a subject, and that his compact held them; whereas, it being only a necessary condition annexed to the land, and the inheritance of an estate which is under that government, reaches only those who will take it on that condition, and so is no natural tie or engagement, but a voluntary submission: for every man's children being by nature as free as himself, or any of his ancestors ever were, may, whilst they are in that freedom, choose what society they will join themselves to, what commonwealth they will put themselves under. But if they will enjoy the inheritance of their ancestors, they must take it on the same terms their ancestors had it, and submit to all the conditions annexed to such a possession. By this power indeed fathers oblige their children to obedience to themselves, even when they are past minority, and most commonly too subject them to this or that political power: but neither of these by any peculiar right of fatherhood, but by the reward they have in their hands to enforce and recompense such a compliance; and is no more power than what a Frenchman has over an Englishman, who, by the hopes of an estate he will leave him, will certainly have a strong tie on his obedience: and if, when it is left him, he will enjoy it, he must certainly take it upon the conditions annexed to the possession of land in that country where it lies, whether it be France or England.

To conclude then, though the father's power of commanding extends no farther than the minority of his children, and to a degree only fit for the discipline and government of that age; and though that honour and respect, and all that which the Latins called piety, which they indispensably owe to their parents all their lifetime, and in all estates, with all that support and defence which is due to them, gives the father no power of governing, *i.e.* making laws and enacting penalties on his children; though by all this he has no dominion over the property or actions of his son: yet it is obvious to conceive how easy it was, in the first ages of the world, and in places still, where the thinness of people gives families leave to separate into unpossessed quarters, and they have room to remove or plant themselves in yet vacant habitations, for the father of the family to become the prince* of it; he had been a ruler from the beginning of the infancy of his children: and since without some government it would be hard for them to live together, it was likeliest it should, by the express or tacit consent of the children when they were grown up, be in the father, where it seemed without any change barely to continue; when indeed nothing more was required to it than the permitting the father to exercise alone, in his family, that executive power of the law of nature, which every free man naturally hath, and by that permission resigning up to him a monarchical power, whilst they remained in it. But

* It is no improbable opinion, therefore, which the arch-philosopher was of, 'That the chief person in every household was always, as it were, a king: so when numbers of households joined themselves in civil societies together, kings were the first kind of governors amongst them, which is also, as it seemeth, the reason why the name of fathers continued still in them, who, of fathers, were made rulers: as also the ancient custom of governors to do as Melchizedeck, and being kings, to exercise the office of priests, which fathers did at the first, grew perhaps by the same occasion. Howbeit, this is not the only kind of regiment that has been received in the world. The inconveniencies of one kind have caused sundry others to be devised: so that, in a word, all public regiment, of what kind soever, seemeth evidently to have risen from the deliberate advice, consultation, and composition between men, judging it convenient and behoveful; there being no impossibility in nature considered by itself, but that man might have lived without any public regiment.' – Hooker's *Eccl. Pol.*, lib. 1, sect. 10.

that this was not by any paternal right, but only by the consent of his children, is evident from hence, that nobody doubts, but if a stranger, whom chance or business had brought to his family, had there killed any of his children, or committed any other fact, he might condemn and put him to death, or otherwise punish him, as well as any of his children: which it was impossible he should do by virtue of any paternal authority over one who was not his child, but by virtue of that executive power of the law of nature, which, as a man, he had a right to: and he alone could punish him in his family, where the respect of his children had laid by the exercise of such a power, to give way to the dignity and authority they were willing should remain in him, above the rest of his family.

Thus it was easy, and almost natural for children, by a tacit, and scarce avoidable consent, to make way for the father's authority and government. They had been accustomed in their childhood to follow his direction, and to refer their little differences to him; and when they were men, who fitter to rule them? Their little properties, and less covetousness, seldom afforded greater controversies; and when any should arise, where could they have a fitter umpire than he, by whose care they had every one been sustained and brought up, and who had a tenderness for them all? It is no wonder that they made no distinction betwixt minority and full age; nor looked after one-and-twenty, or any other age that might make them the free disposers of themselves and fortunes, when they could have no desire to be out of their pupilage: the government they had been under during it, continued still to be more their protection than restraint: and they could nowhere find a greater security to their peace, liberties, and fortunes, than in the rule of a father.

Thus the natural fathers of families by an insensible change became the politic monarchs of them too: and as they chanced to live long, and leave able and worthy heirs, for several successions, or otherwise; so they laid the foundations of hereditary, or elective kingdoms, under several constitutions and manners, according as chance, contrivance, or occasions happened to mould them. But if princes have their titles in their fathers' right, and it be a sufficient proof of the natural right of fathers to political authority, because they commonly were those in whose hands we find, *de facto*, the exercise of government: I say, if this argument be good, it will as strongly prove, that all princes, nay princes only, ought to be priests, since it is as certain, that in the beginning, 'the father of the family was priest, as that he was ruler in his own household.'

CHAPTER 7

Of political or civil Society

God having made man such a creature, that in his own judgment it was not good for him to be alone, put him under strong obligations of necessity, convenience, and inclination, to drive him into society, as well as fitted him with understanding and language to continue and enjoy it. The first society was between man and wife, which gave beginning to that between parents and children; to which, in time, that between master and servant came to be added: and though all these might, and commonly did meet together, and make up but one family, wherein the master or mistress of it had some sort of rule proper to a family; each of these, or all together, came short of political society, as we shall see, if we consider the different ends, ties, and bounds of each of these.

Conjugal society is made by a voluntary compact between man and woman; and though it consist chiefly in such a communion and right in one another's bodies as is necessary to its chief end, procreation; yet it draws with it mutual support and assistance, and a communion of interests too, as necessary not only to unite their care and affection, but also necessary to their common offspring, who have a right to be nourished and maintained by them, till they are able to provide for themselves.

For the end of conjunction between male and female being not barely procreation, but the continuation of the species; this conjunction betwixt male and female ought to last, even after procreation, so long as is necessary to the nourishment and support of the young ones, who are to be sustained by those that got them, till they are able to shift and provide for themselves. This rule, which the infinite wise Maker hath set to the works of his hands, we find the inferior creatures steadily obey. In those viviparous animals which feed on grass, the conjunction between male and female lasts no longer than the very act of copulation; because the teat of the dam being sufficient to nourish the young, till it be able to feed on grass, the male only begets, but concerns not himself for the female or young, to whose sustenance he can contribute nothing. But in beasts of prey the conjunction lasts longer: because the dam not being able well to subsist herself, and nourish her numerous offspring by her own prey alone, a more laborious, as well as more dangerous way of living, than by feeding on grass; the assistance of the male is necessary to the maintenance of their common family, which cannot subsist till they are able to prey for themselves, but by the joint care of male and female. The same is to be observed in all birds, (except some domestic ones, where plenty of food excuses the cock from feeding, and taking care of the young brood) whose young needing food in the nest, the cock and hen continue mates, till the young are able to use their wing, and provide for themselves.

And herein I think lies the chief, if not the only reason, 'why the male and female in mankind are tied to a longer conjunction' than other creatures, viz. because the female is capable of conceiving, and *de facto* is commonly with child again, and brings forth too a new birth, long before the former is out of a dependency for support on his parents' help, and able to shift for himself, and has all the assistance that is due to him from his parents: whereby the father, who is bound to take care for those he hath begot, is under an obligation to continue in conjugal society with the same woman longer than other creatures, whose young being able to subsist of themselves before the time of procreation returns again, the conjugal bond dissolves of itself, and they are at liberty, till Hymen at his usual anniversary season summons them again to choose new mates. Wherein one cannot but admire the wisdom of the great Creator, who having given to man foresight, and an ability to lay up for the future, as well as to supply the present necessity, hath made it necessary, that society of man and wife should be more lasting than of male and female amongst other creatures; that so their industry might be encouraged, and their interest better united, to make provision and lay up goods for their common issue, which uncertain mixture, or easy and frequent solutions of conjugal society, would mightily disturb.

But though these are ties upon mankind, which make the conjugal bonds more firm and lasting in man than the other species of animals; yet it would give one reason to inquire, why this compact, where procreation and education are secured, and inheritance taken care for, may not be made determinable, either by consent, or at a certain time, or upon certain conditions, as well as any other voluntary compacts, there being no necessity in the nature of the thing, nor to the ends of it, that it should always be for life; I mean, to such as are under no restraint of any positive law, which ordains all such contracts to be perpetual.

But the husband and wife, though they have but one common concern, yet having different understandings, will unavoidably sometimes have different wills too; it therefore being necessary that the last determination, *i.e.* the rule, should be placed somewhere; it naturally falls to the man's share, as the abler and the stronger. But this reaching but to the things of their common interest and property, leaves the wife in the full and free possession of what by contract is her peculiar right, and gives the husband no more power over her life than she has over his; the power of the husband being so far from that of an absolute monarch, that the wife has in many cases a liberty to separate from him, where natural right or their contract allows it; whether that contract be made by themselves in the state of nature, or by the customs or laws of the country they live in; and the children upon such separation fall to the father's or mother's lot, as such contract does determine.

For all the ends of marriage being to be obtained under politic government, as well as in the state of nature, the civil magistrate doth not abridge the right or power of either naturally necessary to those ends, viz. procreation and mutual support and assistance whilst they are together; but only decides any controversy that may arise between man and wife about them. If it were otherwise, and that absolute sovereignty and power of life and death naturally belonged to the husband, and were necessary to the society between man and wife, there could be no matrimony in any of those countries where the husband is allowed no such absolute authority. But the ends of matrimony requiring no such power in the husband, the condition of conjugal society put it not in him, it being not at all necessary to that state. Conjugal society could subsist and attain its ends without it; nay, community of goods, and the power over them, mutual assistance and maintenance, and other things belonging to conjugal society, might be varied and regulated by that contract which unites man and wife in that society, as far as may consist with procreation and the bringing up of children till they could shift for themselves; nothing being necessary to any society, that is not necessary to the ends for which it is made.

The society betwixt parents and children, and the distinct rights and powers belonging respectively to them, I have treated of so largely, in the foregoing chapter, that I shall not here need to say any thing of it. And I think it is plain, that it is far different from a politic society.

Master and servant are names as old as history, but given to those of far different condition; for a freeman makes himself a servant to another, by selling him, for a certain time, the service he undertakes to do, in exchange for wages he is to receive: and though this commonly puts him into the family of his master, and under the ordinary discipline thereof: yet it gives the master but a temporary power over him, and no greater than what is contained in the contract between them. But there is another sort of servants, which by a peculiar name we call slaves, who being captives taken in a just war, are by the right of nature subjected to the absolute dominion and arbitrary power of their masters. These men having, as I say, forfeited their lives, and with it their liberties, and lost their estates; and being in the state of slavery, not capable of any property; cannot in that state be considered as any part of civil society; the chief end whereof is the preservation of property.

Let us therefore consider a master of a family with all these subordinate relations of wife, children, servants, and slaves, united under the domestic rule of a family; which, what resemblance soever it may have in its order, offices, and number too, with a little commonwealth, yet is very far from it, both in its constitution, power, and end: or if it must be thought a monarchy, and the paterfamilias the absolute monarch in it, absolute monarchy will have but a very shattered and short power, when it is plain, by what has been said before, that the master of the family has a very distinct and differently limited power, both as to time and extent, over those several persons that are in it: for excepting the slave (and the family is as much a family, and his power as paterfamilias as great, whether there be any slaves in his family or no), he has no legislative power of life and death over any of them, and none too but what a mistress of a family may have as well as he. And he certainly can have no absolute power over the whole family, who has but a very limited one over every individual in it. But how a family, or any other society of men, differ from that which is properly political society, we shall best see by considering wherein political society itself consists.

Man being born, as has been proved, with a title to perfect freedom, and uncontrolled enjoyment of all the rights and privileges of the law of nature, equally with any other man, or number of men in the world, hath by nature a power, not only to preserve his property, that is, his life, liberty, and estate, against the injuries and attempts of other men; but to judge of and punish the breaches of that law in others, as he is persuaded the offence deserves, even with death itself, in crimes where the heinousness of the fact, in his opinion, requires it. But because no political society can be, nor subsist, without having in itself the power to preserve the property, and, in order thereunto, punish the offences of all those of that society; there and there only is political society, where every one of the members hath quitted this natural power, resigned it up into the hands of the community in all cases that exclude him not from appealing for protection to the law established by it. And thus all private judgment of every particular member being excluded, the community comes to be umpire, by settled standing rules, indifferent, and the same to all parties; and by men having authority from the community, for the execution of those rules, decides all the differences that may happen between any members of that society concerning any matter of right; and punishes those offences which any member hath committed against the society, with such penalties as the law has established: whereby it is easy to discern who are, and who are not, in political society together. Those who are united into one body, and have a common established law and judicature to appeal to, with authority to decide controversies between them, and punish offenders, are in civil society one with another: but those who have no such common appeal, I mean on earth, are still in the state of nature, each being, where there is no other, judge for himself, and executioner: which is, as I have before showed it, the perfect state of nature.

And thus the commonwealth comes by a power to set down what punishment shall belong to the several transgressions which they think worthy of it, committed amongst the members of that society, (which is the power of making laws) as well as it has the power to punish any injury done unto any of its members, by any one that is not of it, (which is the power of war and peace) and all this for the preservation of the property of all the members of that society, as far as is possible. But though every man who has entered into civil society, and is become a member of any commonwealth, has thereby quitted his power to punish offences against the law of nature, in prosecution of his own private judgment; yet with the judgment of offences, which he has given up to the legislative in all cases, where he can appeal to the magistrate, he has given a right to the commonwealth to employ his force, for the execution of the judgments of the commonwealth, wherever he shall be called to it; which indeed are his own judgments, they being made by himself, or his representative. And herein we have the original of the legislative and executive power of civil society, which is to judge by standing laws, how far offences are to be punished, when committed within the commonwealth; and also to determine, by occasional judgments founded on the present circumstances of the fact, how far injuries from without are to be vindicated; and in both these to employ all the force of all the members, when there shall be need.

Whenever therefore any number of men are so united into one society, as to quit every one his executive power of the law of nature, and to resign it to the public, there and there only is a political or civil society. And this is done, wherever any number of men, in the state of nature, enter into society to make one people, one body politic, under one supreme government; or else when any one joins himself to, and incorporates with any government already made: for hereby he authorizes the society, or, which is all one, the legislative thereof, to make laws for him, as the public good of the society shall require; to the execution whereof, his own assistance (as to his own degrees) is due. And this puts men out of a state of nature into that of a commonwealth, by setting up a judge on earth, with authority to determine all the controversies, and redress the injuries that may happen to any member of the commonwealth; which judge is the legislative, or magistrate appointed by it. And wherever there are any number of men, however associated, that have no such decisive power to appeal to, there they are still in the state of nature.

Hence it is evident, that absolute monarchy, which by some men is counted the only government in the world, is indeed inconsistent with civil society, and so can be no form of civil government at all: for the end of civil society being to avoid and remedy those inconveniencies of the state of nature which necessarily follow from every man being judge in his own case, by setting up a known authority, to which every one of that society may appeal upon any injury received, or controversy that may arise, and which every one of the society* ought to obey; wherever any persons are, who have not such an authority to appeal to, for the decision of any difference between them, there those persons are still in the state of nature; and so is every absolute prince, in respect of those who are under his dominion.

For he being supposed to have all, both legislative and executive power in himself alone, there is no judge to be found, no appeal lies open to any one, who may fairly and indifferently, and with authority decide, and from whose decision relief and redress may be expected of any injury or inconveniency, that may be suffered from the prince, or by his order: so that such a man, however entitled, czar, or grand seignior, or how you please, is as much in the state of nature, with all under his dominion, as he is with the rest of mankind: for wherever any two men are, who

* 'The public power of all society is above every soul contained in the same society; and the principal use of that power is, to give laws unto all that are under it, which laws in such cases we must obey, unless there be reason showed which may necessarily inforce, that the law of reason, or of God, doth enjoin the contrary.' Hooker, *Eccl. Pol.*, lib. I, sect. 16.

have no standing rule, and common judge to appeal to on earth, for the determination of controversies of right betwixt them, there they are still in the state of nature,* and under all the inconveniencies of it, with only this woeful difference to the subject, or rather slave of an absolute prince: that whereas in the ordinary state of nature he has a liberty to judge of his right, and, according to the best of his power, to maintain it; now, whenever his property is invaded by the will and order of his monarch, he has not only no appeal, as those in society ought to have, but, as if he were degraded from the common state of rational creatures, is denied a liberty to judge of, or to defend

* 'To take away all such mutual grievances, injuries, and wrongs,' *i.e.* such as attend men in the state of nature, 'there was no way but only by growing into composition and agreement amongst themselves by ordaining some kind of government public, and by yielding themselves subject thereunto, that unto whom they granted authority to rule and govern, by them the peace, tranquillity, and happy state of the rest might be procured. Men always knew that where force and injury was offered, they might be defenders of themselves; they knew that however men may seek their own commodity, yet if this were done with injury unto others, it was not to be suffered, but by all men, and all good means, to be withstood. Finally, they knew that no man might in reason take upon him to determine his own right, and according to his own determination proceed in maintenance thereof, inasmuch as every man is towards himself, and them whom he greatly affects, partial; and therefore that strifes and troubles would be endless, except they gave their common consent, all to be ordered by some, whom they should agree upon, without which consent there would be no reason that one man should take upon him to be lord or judge over another.' Hooker, *Eccl. Pol.*, lib. I, sect. 10.

his right: and so is exposed to all the misery and inconveniencies, that a man can fear from one, who being in the unrestrained state of nature, is yet corrupted with flattery, and armed with power.

For he that thinks absolute power purifies men's blood, and corrects the baseness of human nature, need read but the history of this, or any other age, to be convinced of the contrary. He that would have been insolent and injurious in the woods of America, would not probably be much better in a throne; where perhaps learning and religion shall be found out to justify all that he shall do to his subjects, and the sword presently silence all those that dare question it: for what the protection of absolute monarchy is, what kind of fathers of their countries it makes princes to be, and to what a degree of happiness and security it carries civil society, where this sort of government is grown to perfection; he that will look into the late relation of Ceylon may easily see.

In absolute monarchies indeed, as well as other governments of the world, the subjects have an appeal to the law, and judges to decide any controversies, and restrain any violence that may happen betwixt the subjects themselves, one amongst another. This every one thinks necessary, and believes he deserves to be thought a declared enemy to society and mankind who should go about to take it away. But whether this be from a true love of mankind and society, and such a charity as we all owe one to another, there is reason to doubt: for this is no more than what every man, who loves his own power, profit, or greatness, may and naturally must do, keep those animals from hurting or destroying one another, who labour and drudge only for his pleasure and advantage; and so are taken care of, not out of any love the master has for them, but love of himself, and the profit they bring him: for if it be asked, what security, what fence is there, in such a state, against the violence and oppression of this absolute ruler, the very question can scarce be borne. They are ready to tell you, that it deserves death only to ask after safety. Betwixt subject and subject, they will grant, there must be measures, laws, and judges, for their mutual peace and security: but as for the ruler, he ought to be absolute, and is above all such circumstances; because he has power to do more hurt and wrong, it is right when he does it. To ask how you may be guarded from harm, or injury, on that side where the strongest hand is to do it, is presently the voice of faction and rebellion: as if when men quitting the state of nature entered into society, they agreed that all of them but one should be under the restraint of laws, but that he should still retain all the liberty of the state of nature, increased with power, and made licentious by impunity. This is to think, that men are so foolish, that they take care to avoid what mischiefs may be done them by pole-cats, or foxes; but are content, nay think it safety, to be devoured by lions.

But whatever flatterers may talk to amuse people's understandings, it hinders not men from feeling; and when they perceive that any man, in what station soever, is out of the bounds of the civil society which they are of, and that they have no appeal on earth against any harm they may receive from him, they are apt to think themselves in the state of nature in respect of him whom they find to be so; and to take care, as soon as they can, to have that safety and security in civil society for which it was instituted, and for which only they entered into it. And therefore, though perhaps at first (as shall be showed more at large hereafter in the following part of this discourse), some one good and excellent man having got a pre-eminency amongst the rest, had this deference paid to his goodness and virtue, as to a kind of natural authority, that the chief rule, with arbitration of their differences, by a tacit consent devolved into his hands, without any other caution but the assurance they had of his uprightness and wisdom; yet when time, giving authority, and (as some men would persuade us) sacredness to customs, which the negligent and unforeseeing innocence of the first ages began, had brought in successors of another stamp; the people finding their properties not secure under the government as then it was (whereas government has no other end but the preservation of property),* could never be safe nor at rest, nor think themselves in civil society, till the legislature was placed in collective bodies of men, call them senate, parliament, or what you please. By which means every single person became subject, equally with other the meanest men, to those laws which he himself, as part of the legislative, had established; nor

* 'At the first, when some certain kind of regiment was once appointed, it may be that nothing was then farther thought upon for the manner of governing, but all permitted unto their wisdom and discretion, which were to rule, till by experience they found this for all parts very inconvenient, so as the thing which they had devised for a remedy did indeed but increase the sore which it should have cured. They saw that to live by one man's will became the cause of all men's misery. This constrained them to come into laws, wherein all men might see their duty beforehand, and know the penalties of transgressing them.' Hooker, *Eccl. Pol.*, lib. I, sect. 10.

could any one, by his own authority, avoid the force of the law when once made; nor by any pretence of superiority plead exemption, thereby to license his own, or the miscarriages of any of his dependents.* 'No man in civil society can be exempted from the laws of it': for if any man may do what he thinks fit, and there be no appeal on earth, for redress or security against any harm he shall do; I ask, whether he be not perfectly still in the state of nature, and so can be no part or member of that civil society; unless anyone will say the state of nature and civil society are one and the same thing, which I have never yet found any one so great a patron of anarchy as to affirm.

CHAPTER 8

Of the Beginning of Political Societies

Men being, as has been said, by nature all free, equal, and independent, no one can be put out of this estate, and subjected to the political power of another, without his own consent. The only way whereby any one divests himself of his natural liberty, and puts on the bonds of civil society, is by agreeing with other men to join and unite into a community, for their comfortable, safe, and peaceable living one amongst another, in a secure enjoyment of their properties, and a greater security against any that are not of it. This any number of men may do, because it

* 'Civil law, being the act of the whole body politic, doth therefore overrule each several part of the same body.' Hooker, *Eccl. Pol.*, lib. 1, sect. 10.)

injures not the freedom of the rest; they are left as they were in the liberty of the state of nature. When any number of men have so consented to make one community or government, they are thereby presently incorporated, and make one body politic, wherein the majority have a right to act and conclude the rest.

For when any number of men have, by the consent of every individual, made a community, they have thereby made that community one body, with a power to act as one body, which is only by the will and determination of the majority; for that which acts any community being only the consent of the individuals of it, and it being necessary to that which is one body to move one way, it is necessary the body should move that way whither the greater force carries it, which is the consent of the majority: or else it is impossible it should act or continue one body, one community, which the consent of every individual that united into it agreed that it should; and so every one is bound by that consent to be concluded by the majority. And therefore we see that in assemblies, empowered to act by positive laws, where no number is set by that positive law which empowers them, the act of the majority passes for the act of the whole, and of course determines; as having, by the law of nature and reason, the power of the whole.

And thus every man, by consenting with others to make one body politic under one government, puts himself under an obligation to every one of that society to submit to the determination of the majority, and to be concluded by it; or else this original compact, whereby he with others incorporate into one society, would signify nothing, and be no compact, if he be left free, and under no other ties than he was in before in the state of nature. For what appearance would there be of any compact? What new engagement, if he were no farther tied by any decrees of the society than he himself thought fit, and did actually consent to? This would be still as great a liberty as he himself had before his compact, or any one else in the state of nature hath, who may submit himself and consent to any acts of it if he thinks fit.

For if the consent of the majority shall not, in reason, be received as the act of the whole, and conclude every individual, nothing but the consent of every individual can make any thing to be the act of the whole: but such a consent is next to impossible ever to be had, if we consider the infirmities of health, and avocations of business, which in a number, though much less than that of a commonwealth, will necessarily keep many away from the public assembly. To which if we add the variety of opinions, and contrariety of interests which unavoidably happen in all collections of men, the coming into society upon such terms would be only like Cato's coming into the theatre, only to go out again. Such a constitution as this would make the mighty leviathan of a shorter duration than the feeblest creatures, and not let it outlast the day it was born in: which cannot be supposed, till we can think that rational creatures should desire and constitute societies only to be dissolved: for where the majority cannot conclude the rest, there they cannot act as one body, and consequently will be immediately dissolved again.

Whosoever therefore out of a state of nature unite into a community, must be understood to give up all the power necessary to the ends for which they unite into society, to the majority of the community, unless they expressly agreed in any number greater than the majority. And this is done by barely agreeing to unite into one political society, which is all the compact that is, or needs be, between the individuals that enter into, or make up a commonwealth. And thus that which begins and actually constitutes any political society, is nothing but the consent of any number of freemen capable of a majority, to unite and incorporate into such a society. And this is that, and that only, which did or could give beginning to any lawful government in the world.

To this I find two objections made.

First, 'that there are no instances to be found in story, of a company of men independent and equal one amongst another, that met together, and in this way began and set up a government.'

Secondly, 'it is impossible of right, that men should do so, because all men being born under government, they are to submit to that, and are not at liberty to begin a new one.'

To the first there is this to answer, that it is not at all to be wondered, that history gives us but a very little account of men that lived together in the state of nature. The inconveniencies of that condition, and the love and want of society, no sooner brought any number of them together, but they presently united and incorporated, if they designed to continue together. And if we may not suppose men ever to have been in the state of nature, because we hear not much of them in such a state, we may as well suppose the armies of Salmanasser or Xerxes were never children, because we hear little of them till they were men, and embodied in armies. Government is every where antecedent to records, and letters seldom come in amongst a people till a long continuation of civil society has, by other more necessary arts, provided for their safety, ease, and plenty: and then they begin to look after the history of their founders, and search into their original, when they have outlined the memory of it: for it is with commonwealths as with particular persons, they are commonly ignorant of their own births and infancies: and if they know any thing of their original, they are beholden for it to the accidental records that others have kept of it. And those that we have of the beginning of any politics in the world, excepting that of the Jews, where God himself immediately interposed, and which favours not at all paternal dominion, are all either plain instances of such a beginning as I have mentioned, or at least have manifest footsteps of it.

He must show a strange inclination to deny evident matter of fact, when it agrees not with his hypothesis, who will not allow, that the beginnings of Rome and Venice were by the uniting together of several men free and independent one of another, amongst whom there was no natural superiority or subjection. And if Josephus Acosta's word may be taken, he tells us, that in many parts of America there was no government at all. 'There are great and apparent conjectures,' says he, 'that these men, speaking of those of Peru, for a long time had neither kings nor commonwealths, but lived in troops, as they do this day in Florida, the Cheriquanas, those of Brasil, and many other nations, which have no certain kings, but as occasion is offered, in peace or war, they choose their captains as they please,' lib. 1, ch. 25. If it be said that every man there was born subject to his father, or the head of his family; that the subjection due from a child to a father took not away his freedom of uniting into what political society he thought fit, has been already proved. But be that as it will, these men, it is evident, were actually free; and whatever superiority some politicians now would place in any of them, they themselves claimed it not, but by consent were all equal, till by the same consent they set rulers over themselves. So that their politic societies all began from a voluntary union, and the mutual agreement of men freely acting in the choice of their governors and forms of government.

And I hope those who went away from Sparta with Palantus, mentioned by Justin, lib. 3, ch. 4, will be allowed to have been freemen, independent one of another, and to have set up a government over themselves, by their own consent. Thus I have given several examples out of history, of people free and in the state of nature, that being met together incorporated and began a commonwealth. And if the want of such instances be an argument to prove that governments were not, nor could not be so begun, I suppose the contenders for paternal empire were better let it alone than urge it against natural liberty: for if they can give so many instances out of history, of governments begun upon paternal right, I think (though at best an argument from what has been, to what should of right be, has no great force) one might, without any great danger, yield them the cause. But if I might advise them in the case, they would do well not to search too much into the original of governments, as they have begun *de facto*: lest they should find, at the foundation of most of them, something very little favourable to the design they promote, and such a power as they contend for.

But to conclude, reason being plain on our side, that men are naturally free, and the examples of history showing, that the governments of the world, that were begun in peace, had their beginning laid on that foundation, and were made by the consent of the people; there can be little room for doubt, either where the right is, or what has been the opinion or practice of mankind about the first erecting of governments.

I will not deny, that if we look back as far as history will direct us, towards the original of commonwealths, we shall generally find them under the government and administration of one man. And I am also apt to believe, that where a family was numerous enough to subsist by itself, and continued entire together, without mixing with others, as it often happens, where there is much land and few people, the government commonly began in the father: for the father having, by the law of nature, the same power with every man else to punish, as he thought fit, any offences against that law, might thereby punish his transgressing children, even when they were men, and out of their pupilage; and they were very likely to submit to his punishment, and all join with him against the offender in their turns, giving him thereby power to execute his sentence against any transgression, and so in effect make him the law-maker and governor over all that remained in conjunction with his family. He was fittest to be trusted; paternal affection secured their property and interest under his care; and the custom of obeying him in their childhood, made it easier to submit to him rather than to any other. If, therefore, they must have one to rule them, as government is hardly to be avoided amongst men that live together, who so likely to be the man as he that was their common father, unless negligence, cruelty, or any other defect of mind or body made him unfit for it? But when either the father died, and left his next heir, for want of age, wisdom, courage, or any other qualities, less fit for rule, or where several families met and consented to continue together, there it is not to be doubted but they used their natural freedom to set up him whom they judged the ablest, and most likely to rule well over them. Conformable hereunto, we find the people of America, who (living out of the reach of the conquering swords and spreading domination of the two great empires of Peru and Mexico, enjoyed their own natural freedom, though, *cæteris paribus*, they commonly prefer the heir of their deceased king; yet if they find him any way weak or incapable, they pass him by, and set up the stoutest and bravest man for their ruler.

Thus, though looking back as far as records give us any account of peopling the world, and the history of nations, we commonly find the government to be in one hand; yet it destroys not that which I affirm, viz. that the beginning of politic society depends upon the consent of the individuals, to join into and make one society; who, when they are thus incorporated, might set up what form of government they thought fit. But this having given occasion to men to mistake, and think that by nature government was monarchical, and belonged to the father; it may not be amiss here to consider, why people in the beginning generally pitched upon this form: which though perhaps the father's preeminency might, in the first institution of some commonwealth, give a rise to, and place in the beginning the power in one hand; yet it is plain that the reason that continued the form of government in a single person, was not any regard or respect to paternal authority; since all petty monarchies, that is, almost all monarchies, near this original, have been commonly, at least upon occasion, elective.

First then, in the beginning of things, the father's government of the childhood of those sprung from him, having accustomed them to the rule of one man, and taught them that where it was exercised with care and skill, with affection and love to those under it, it was sufficient to procure and preserve to men all the political happiness they sought for in society; it was no wonder that they should pitch upon, and naturally run into that form of government, which from their infancy they had been all accustomed to; and which, by experience, they had found both easy and safe. To which if we add, that monarchy being simple, and most obvious to men, whom neither experience had instructed in forms of government, nor the ambition or insolence of empire had taught to beware of the encroachments of prerogative, or the inconveniencies of absolute power, which monarchy in succession was apt to lay claim to, and bring upon them; it was not at all strange that they should not much trouble themselves to think of methods of restraining any exorbitancies of those to whom they had given the authority over them, and of balancing the power of government, by placing several parts of it in different hands. They had neither felt the oppression of tyrannical dominion, nor did the fashion of the age, nor their possessions, or way of living (which afforded little matter for covetousness or ambition), give them any reason to apprehend or provide against it; and therefore it is no wonder they put themselves into such a frame of government, as was not only, as I said, most obvious and simple, but also best suited to their present state and condition, which stood more in need of defence against foreign invasions and injuries, than of multiplicity of laws. The equality of a simple poor way of living, confining their desires within the narrow bounds of each man's small property, made few controversies, and so no need of many laws to decide them, or variety of officers to superintend the process, or look after the execution of justice, where there were but few trespasses, and few offenders. Since then those who liked one another so well as to join into society, cannot but be supposed to have some acquaintance and friendship together, and some trust one in another, they could not but have greater apprehensions of others than of one another: and therefore their first care and thought cannot but be supposed to be, how to secure themselves against foreign force. It was natural for them to put themselves under a frame of government which might best serve to that end, and choose the wisest and bravest man to conduct them in their wars, and lead them out against their enemies, and in this chiefly be their ruler.

Thus we see that the kings of the Indians in America, which is still a pattern of the first ages in Asia and Europe, whilst the inhabitants were too few for the country, and want of people and money gave men no temptation to enlarge their possessions of land, or contest for wider extent of ground, are little more than generals of their armies; and though they command absolutely in war, yet at home and in time of peace they exercise very little dominion, and have but a very moderate sovereignty; the resolutions of peace and war being ordinarily either in the people, or in a council. Though the war itself, which admits not of plurality of governors, naturally devolves the command into the king's sole authority.

And thus, in Israel itself, the chief business of their judges and first kings, seems to have been to be captains in war, and leaders of their armies; which (besides what is signified by 'going out and in before the people,' which was to march forth to war, and home again at the heads of their forces) appears plainly in the story of Jephthah. The Ammonites making war upon Israel, the Gileadites in fear send to Jephthah, a bastard of their family whom they had cast off, and article with him, if he will assist them against the Ammonites, to make him their ruler; which they do in these words, 'And the people made him head and captain over them,' Judg. 11:11. which was, as it seems, all one as to be judge. 'And he judged Israel,' Judg. 12:7, that is, was their captain-general, 'six years.' So when Jotham upbraids the Shechemites with the obligation they had to Gideon, who had been their judge and ruler, he tells them, 'He fought for you, and adventured his life far, and delivered you out of the hands of Midian,' Judg. 9:17. Nothing is mentioned of him but what he did as a general: and indeed that is all is found in his history, or in any of the rest of the judges. And Abimelech particularly is called king, though at most he was but their general. And when, being weary of the ill conduct of Samuel's sons, the children of Israel desired a king, 'like all the nations, to judge them, and to go out before them, and to fight their battles,' 1 Sam. 8:20, God, granting their desire, says to

Samuel, 'I will send thee a man, and thou shalt anoint him to be captain over my people Israel, that he may save my people out of the hands of the Philistines,' 9:16. As if the only business of a king had been to lead out their armies, and fight in their defence; and accordingly Samuel, at his inauguration, pouring a vial of oil upon him, declares to Saul, that 'the Lord had anointed him to be captain over his inheritance,' 10:1. And therefore those who, after Saul's being solemnly chosen and saluted king by the tribes of Mispeh, were unwilling to have him their king, made no other objection but this, 'How shall this man save us?' 5:27; as if they should have said, this man is unfit to be our king, not having skill and conduct enough in war to be able to defend us. And when God resolved to transfer the government to David, it is in these words, 'But now thy kingdom shall not continue: the Lord hath sought him a man after his own heart, and the Lord hath commanded him to be captain over his people,' 13:14. As if the whole kingly authority were nothing else but to be their general: and therefore the tribes who had stuck to Saul's family, and opposed David's reign, when they came to Hebron with terms of submission to him, they tell him, amongst other arguments they had to submit to him as to their king, that he was in effect their king in Saul's time, and therefore they had no reason but to receive him as their king now. 'Also (say they) in time past, when Saul was king over us, thou wast he that leddest out and broughtest in Israel, and the Lord said unto thee, Thou shalt feed my people Israel, and thou shalt be a captain over Israel.'

Thus, whether a family by degrees grew up into

a commonwealth, and the fatherly authority being continued on to the elder son, every one in his turn growing up under it, tacitly submitted to it; and the easiness and equality of it not offending anyone, everyone acquiesced, till time seemed to have confirmed it, and settled a right of succession by prescription: or whether several families, or the descendants of several families, whom chance, neighbourhood, or business brought together, uniting into society: the need of a general, whose conduct might defend them against their enemies in war, and the great confidence the innocence and sincerity of that poor but virtuous age, (such as are almost all those which begin governments, that ever come to last in the world) gave men of one another, made the first beginners of commonwealths generally put the rule into one man's hand, without any other express limitation or restraint, but what the nature of the thing and the end of government required: whichever of those it was that at first put the rule into the hands of a single person, certain it is that nobody was intrusted with it but for the public good and safety, and to those ends, in the infancies of commonwealths, those who had it, commonly used it. And unless they had done so, young societies could not have subsisted; without such nursing fathers, tender and careful of the public weal, all governments would have sunk under the weakness and infirmities of their infancy, and the prince and the people had soon perished together.

But though the golden age (before vain ambition, and *amor sceleratus habendi*, evil concupiscence, had corrupted men's minds into a mistake of true power and honour) had more virtue, and consequently better governors, as well as less vicious subjects; and there was then no stretching prerogative on the one side, to oppress the people; nor, consequently on the other, any dispute about privilege, to lessen or restrain the power of the magistrate; and so no contest betwixt rulers and people about governors or government: yet, when ambition and luxury in future ages* would retain and increase the power, without doing the business for which it was given; and, aided by flattery, taught princes to have distinct and separate interests from their people; men found it necessary to examine more carefully the original and rights of government, and to find out ways to restrain the exorbitancies, and prevent the abuses of that power, which they having intrusted in another's hands only for their own good, they found was made use of to hurt them.

Thus we may see how probable it is, that people that were naturally free, and by their own consent either submitted to the government of their father, or united together out of different families to make a government, should generally put the rule into one

* At first, when some certain kind of regiment was once approved, it may be nothing was then farther thought upon for the manner of governing, but all permitted unto their wisdom and discretion which were to rule, till by experience they found this for all parts very inconvenient, so as the thing which they had devised for a remedy, did indeed but increase the sore which it should have cured. They saw, that to live by one man's will, became the cause of all men's misery. This constrained them to come unto laws wherein all men might see their duty beforehand, and know the penalties of transgressing them.' Hooker, *Eccl. Pol.*, lib. I, sect. 10.

man's hands, and choose to be under the conduct of a single person, without so much as by express conditions limiting or regulating his power, which they thought safe enough in his honesty and prudence: though they never dreamed of monarchy being *jure divino*, which we never heard of among mankind, till it was revealed to us by the divinity of this last age; nor ever allowed paternal power to have a right to dominion, or to be the foundation of all government. And thus much may suffice to show, that, as far as we have any light from history, we have reason to conclude, that all peaceful beginnings of government have been laid in the consent of the people. I say peaceful, because I shall have occasion in another place to speak of conquest, which some esteem a way of beginning of governments.

The other objection I find urged against the beginning of politics, in the way I have mentioned, is this, viz.

'That all men being born under government, some or other, it is impossible any of them should ever be free, and at liberty to unite together, and begin a new one, or ever be able to erect a lawful government.'

If this argument be good, I ask, how came so many lawful monarchies into the world? For if any body, upon this supposition, can show me any one man in any age of the world free to begin a lawful monarchy, I will be bound to show him ten other free men at liberty at the same time to unite and begin a new government under a regal, or any other form; it being demonstration, that if any one, born under the dominion of another, may be so free as to have a right to command others in a new and distinct empire, every one that is born under the dominion of another may be so free too, and may become a ruler, or subject of a distinct separate government. And so by this their own principle, either all men, however born, are free, or else there is but one lawful prince, one lawful government in the world. And then they have nothing to do, but barely to show us which that is; which when they have done, I doubt not but all mankind will easily agree to pay obedience to him.

Though it be a sufficient answer to their objection, to show that it involves them in the same difficulties that it doth those they use it against; yet I shall endeavour to discover the weakness of this argument a little farther.

'All men, say they, are born under government, and therefore they cannot be at liberty to begin a new one. Every one is born a subject to his father or his prince, and is therefore under the perpetual tie of subjection and allegiance.' It is plain mankind never owned nor considered any such natural subjection that they were born in, to one or to the other, that tied them, without their own consents, to a subjection to them and their heirs.

For there are no examples so frequent in history, both sacred and profane, as those of men withdrawing themselves, and their obedience, from the jurisdiction they were born under, and the family or community they were bred up in, and setting up new governments in other places; from whence sprang all that number of petty commonwealths in the beginning of ages, and which always multiplied as long as there was room enough, till the stronger, or more fortunate, swallowed the weaker; and those great ones again breaking to pieces, dissolved into lesser dominions. All which are so many testimonies against paternal sovereignty, and plainly prove that it was not the natural right of the father descending to his heirs, that made governments in the beginning, since it was impossible, upon that ground, there should have been so many little kingdoms; all must have been but only one universal monarchy, if men had not been at liberty to separate themselves from their families and the government, be it what it will, that was set up in it, and go and make distinct commonwealths and other governments, as they thought fit.

This has been the practice of the world from its first beginning to this day; nor is it now any more hindrance to the freedom of mankind, that they are born under constituted and ancient polities, that have established laws and set forms of government, than if they were born in the woods, amongst the unconfined inhabitants that run loose in them: for those who would persuade us, that 'by being born under any government, we are naturally subjects to it,' and have no more any title or pretence to the freedom of the state of nature: have no other reason (bating that of paternal power, which we have already answered) to produce for it, but only because our fathers or progenitors passed away their natural liberty, and thereby bound up themselves and their posterity to a perpetual subjection to the government which they themselves submitted to. It is true, that whatever engagement or promises any one made for himself, he is under the obligation of them, but cannot, by any compact whatsoever, bind his children or posterity: for his son, when a man, being altogether as free as the father, any 'act of the father can no more give away the liberty of the son,' than it can of any else: he may indeed annex such conditions to the land he enjoyed as a subject of any commonwealth, as may oblige his son to be of that community, if he will enjoy those possessions which were his father's; because that estate being his father's property; he may dispose or settle it as he pleases.

And this has generally given the occasion to mistake in this matter; because commonwealths not permitting any part of their dominions to be dismembered, not to be enjoyed by any but those of their community, the son cannot ordinarily enjoy the possessions of his father, but under the same terms his father did, by becoming a member of the society; whereby he puts himself presently under the government he finds there established, as much as any other subject of that commonwealth. And thus, 'the consent of freemen, born under government, which only makes them members of it,' being given separately in their turns, as each comes to be of age, and not in a multitude together; people take no notice of it, and thinking it not done at all, or not necessary, conclude they are naturally subjects as they are men.

But it is plain governments themselves understand it otherwise; they claim 'no power over the son, because of that they had over the father;' nor look on children as being their subjects, by their fathers being so. If a subject of England have a child by an English woman in France, whose subject is he? Not the king of England's; for he must have leave to be admitted to the privileges of it: nor the king of France's; for how then has his father a liberty to bring him away, and breed him as he pleases? And who ever was judged as a traitor or deserter, if he left or warred against a country, for being barely born in it of parents that were aliens there? It is plain, then, by the practice of governments themselves, as well as by the law of right reason, that 'a child is born a subject of no country or government.' He is under his father's tuition and authority till he comes to age of discretion; and then he is a freeman, at liberty what government he will put himself under, what body politic he will unite himself to: for if an Englishman's son, born in France, be at liberty, and may do so, it is evident there is no tie upon him by his father's being a subject of this kingdom; nor is he bound up by any compact of his ancestors. And why then hath not his son, by the same reason, the same liberty, though he be born any where else? Since the power that a father hath naturally over his children is the same, wherever they be born, and the ties of natural obligations are not bounded by the positive limits of kingdoms and commonwealths.

Every man being, as has been showed, naturally free, and nothing being able to put him into subjection to any earthly power, but only his own consent; it is to be considered what shall be understood to be a sufficient declaration of a man's consent, to make him subject to the laws of any government. There is a common distinction of an express and a tacit consent, which will concern our present case. Nobody doubts but an express consent of any man entering into any society, makes him a perfect member of that society, a subject of that government. The difficulty is, what ought to be looked upon as a tacit consent, and how far it binds, *i.e.* how far any one shall be looked on to have consented, and thereby submitted to any government, where he has made no expressions of it at all. And to this I say, that every man, that hath any possessions, or enjoyment of any part of the dominions of any government, doth thereby give his tacit consent, and is as far forth obliged to obedience to the laws of that government, during such enjoyment, as any one under it; whether this his possession be of land, to him and his heirs for ever, or a lodging only for a week; or whether it be barely travelling freely on the highway; and, in effect, it reaches as far as the very being of any one within the territories of that government.

To understand this the better, it is fit to consider, that every man, when he at first incorporates himself into any commonwealth, he, by his uniting himself thereunto, annexes also, and submits to the community those possessions which he has, or shall acquire, that do not already belong to any other government: for it would be a direct contradiction for any one to enter into society with others for the securing and regulating of property, and yet to suppose his land, whose property is to be regulated by the laws of the society, should be exempt from the jurisdiction of that government, to which he himself, the proprietor of the land, is a subject. By the same act therefore, whereby any one unites his person, which was before free, to any commonwealth, by the same he unites his possessions, which were before free, to it also: and they become, both of them, person and possession, subject to the government and dominion of that commonwealth, as long as it hath a being. Whoever, therefore, from thenceforth, by inheritance, purchase, permission, or otherways, enjoys any part of the land so annexed to, and under the government of that commonwealth, must take it with the condition it is under; that is, of submitting to the government of the commonwealth, under whose jurisdiction it is, as far forth as any subject of it.

But since the government has a direct jurisdiction only over the land, and reaches the possessor of it (before he has actually incorporated himself in the society) only as he dwells upon, and enjoys that; the obligation any one is under, by virtue of such enjoyment, to 'submit to the government, begins and ends with the enjoyment:' so that whenever the owner, who has given nothing but such a tacit consent to the government, will, by donation, sale, or otherwise, quit the said possession, he is at liberty to go and incorporate himself into any other commonwealth; or to agree with others to begin a new one, in *vacuis locis*, in any part of the world they can find free and unpossessed: whereas he that has once, by actual agreement, and any express declaration, given his consent to be of any commonwealth, is perpetually and indispensably obliged to be, and remain unalterably a subject to it, and can never be again in the liberty of the state of nature; unless, by any calamity, the government he was under comes to be dissolved, or else by some public act cuts him off from being any longer a member of it.

But submitting to the laws of any country, living quietly, and enjoying privileges and protection under them, makes not a man a member of that society: this is only a local protection and homage due to and from all those who, not being in a state of war, come within the territories belonging to any government, to all parts whereof the force of its laws extends. But this no more makes a man a member of that society, a perpetual subject of that commonwealth, than it would make a man a subject to another, in whose family he found it convenient to abide for some time; though, whilst he continued in it, he were obliged to comply with the laws, and submit to the government he found there. And thus we see, that foreigners, by living all their lives under another government, and enjoying the privileges and protection of it, though they are bound, even in conscience, to submit to its administration, as far forth as any denison; yet do not thereby come to be subjects or members of that commonwealth. Nothing can make any man so, but his actually entering into it by positive engagement, and express promise and compact. This is that which I think concerning the beginning of political societies, and that consent which makes any one a member of any commonwealth.

CHAPTER 9

Of the Ends of Political Society and Government

If man in the state of nature be so free as has been said; if he be absolute lord of his own person and possessions, equal to the greatest, and subject to nobody, why will he part with his freedom, why will he give up this empire, and subject himself to the dominion and control of any other power? To which it is obvious to answer, that though in the state of nature he hath such a right, yet the enjoyment of it is very uncertain, and constantly exposed to the invasion of others; for all being kings as much as he, every man his equal, and the greater part no strict observers of equity and justice, the enjoyment of the property he has in this state is very unsafe, very unsecure. This makes him willing to quit a condition, which, however free, is full of fears and continual dangers: and it is not without reason that he seeks out, and is willing to join in society with others, who are already united, or have a mind to unite, for the mutual preservation of their lives, liberties, and estates, which I call by the general name property.

The great and chief end, therefore, of men's uniting into commonwealths, and putting themselves under government, is the preservation of their property. To which in the state of nature there are many things wanting.

First, there wants an established, settled, known law, received and allowed by common consent to be the standard of right and wrong, and the common measure to decide all controversies between them: for though the law of nature be plain and intelligible to all rational creatures; yet men being biased by their interest, as well as ignorant for want of studying it, are not apt to allow of it as a law binding to them in the application of it to their particular cases.

Secondly, in the state of nature there wants a known and indifferent judge, with authority to determine all differences according to the established law: for every one in that state being both judge and executioner of the law of nature, men being partial to themselves, passion and revenge is very apt to carry them too far, and with too much heat, in their own cases; as well as negligence and unconcernedness, to make them too remiss in other men's.

Thirdly, in the state of nature there often wants power to back and support the sentence when right, and to give it due execution. They who by any injustice offend, will seldom fail, where they are able, by force to make good their injustice; such resistance many times makes the punishment dangerous, and frequently destructive to those who attempt it.

Thus mankind, notwithstanding all the privileges of the state of nature, being but in an ill condition, while they remain in it, are quickly driven into society. Hence it comes to pass, that we seldom find any number of men live any time together in this state. The inconveniences that they are therein exposed to, by the irregular and uncertain exercise of the power every man has of punishing the transgressions of others, make them take sanctuary under the established laws of government, and therein seek the preservation of their property. It is this makes them so willingly give up every one his single power of punishing, to be exercised by such alone as shall be appointed to it amongst them; arid by such rules as the community, or those authorised by them to that purpose, shall agree on. And in this we have the original right of both the legislative and executive power, as well as of the governments and societies themselves.

For in the state of nature, to omit the liberty he has of innocent delights, a man has two powers.

The first is to do whatsoever he thinks fit for the preservation of himself and others within the permission of the law of nature: by which law, common to them all, he and all the rest of mankind are one community, make up one society, distinct from all other creatures. And, were it not for the corruption and viciousness of degenerate men, there would be no need of any other; no necessity that men should separate from this great and natural community, and by positive agreements combine into smaller and divided associations.

The other power a man has in the state of nature, is the power to punish the crimes committed against that law. Both these he gives up when he joins in a private, if I may so call it, or particular politic society, and incorporates into any commonwealth, separate from the rest of mankind.

The first power. viz. 'of doing whatsoever he thought fit for the preservation of himself' and the rest of mankind, he gives up to be regulated by laws made by the society, so far forth as the preservation of himself and the rest of that society shall require; which laws of the society in many things confine the liberty he had by the law of nature.

Secondly, The power of punishing he wholly gives up, and engages his natural force (which he might before employ in the execution of the law of nature, by his own single authority, as he thought fit), to assist the executive power of the society, as the law thereof shall require: for being now in a new state, wherein he is to enjoy many conveniencies, from the labour, assistance, and society of others in the same community, as well as protection from its whole strength; he is to part also with as much of his natural liberty, in providing for himself, as the good, prosperity, and safety of the society, shall require, which is not only necessary, but just, since the other members of the society do the like.

But though men, when they enter into society, give up the equality, liberty, and executive power they had in the state of nature, into the hands of the society, to be so far disposed of by the legislative as the good of the society shall require; yet it being only with an intention in every one the better to preserve himself, his liberty and property (for no rational creature can be supposed to change his condition with an intention to be worse); the power of the society, or legislative constituted by them, can never be supposed to extend farther than the common good; but is obliged to secure every one's property by providing against those three defects above-mentioned, that made the state of nature so unsafe and uneasy. And so whoever has the legislative or supreme power of any commonwealth, is bound to govern by established standing laws, promulgated and known to the people, and not by extemporary decrees; by indifferent and upright judges, who are to decide controversies by those laws; and to employ the force of the community at home, only in the execution of such laws; or abroad to prevent or redress foreign injuries, and secure the community from inroads and invasion. And all this to be directed to no other end but the peace, safety, and public good of the people.

CHAPTER 10

Of the Forms of a Commonwealth

The majority having, as has been showed, upon men's first uniting into society, the whole power of the community naturally in them, may employ all that power in making laws for the community from time to time, and executing those laws by officers of their own appointing; and then the form of the government is a perfect democracy: or else may put the power of making laws into the hands of a few select men, and their heirs or successors; and then it is an oligarchy: or else into the hands of one man, and then it is a monarchy: if to him and his heirs, it is an hereditary monarchy: if to him only for life, but upon his death the power only of nominating a successor to return to them, an elective monarchy. And so accordingly of these the community may make compounded and mixed forms of government, as they think good. And if the legislative power be at first given by the majority to one or more persons only for their lives, or any limited time, and then the supreme power to revert to them again; when it is so reverted, the community may dispose of it again anew into what hands they please, and so constitute a new form of government: for the form of government depending upon the placing the supreme power, which is the legislative (it being impossible to conceive that an inferior power should prescribe to a superior, or any but the supreme make laws), according as the power of making laws is placed, such is the form of the commonwealth.

By commonwealth, I must be understood all along to mean, not a democracy, or any form of government, but any independent community, which the Latins signified by the word *civitas*: to which the word which best answers in our language is commonwealth, and most properly expresses such a society of men, which community or city in English does not: for there may be subordinate communities in government; and city amongst us has a quite different notion from commonwealth: and therefore, to avoid ambiguity, I crave leave to use the word commonwealth in that sense, in which I find it used by King James I; and I take it to be its genuine signification; which if any body dislike, I consent with him to change it for a better.

CHAPTER II

Of the Extent of the legislative Power

The great end of men's entering into society being the enjoyment of their properties in peace and safety, and the great instrument and means of that being the laws established in that society; the first and fundamental positive law of all commonwealths is the establishing of the legislative power; as the first and fundamental natural law, which is to govern even the legislative itself, is the preservation of the society, and (as far as will consist with the public good) of every person in it. This legislative is not only the supreme power of the commonwealth, but sacred and unalterable in the hands where the community have once placed it; nor can any edict of any body else, in what form soever conceived, or by what power soever backed, have the force and obligation of a law, which has not its sanction from that legislative which the public has chosen and appointed: for without this the law could not have that which is absolutely necessary to its being a law,* the consent of the society; over whom nobody can have a power to make laws, but by their own consent, and by authority received from them. And therefore all the obedience, which by the most solemn ties any one can be obliged to pay, ultimately terminates in this supreme power, and is directed by those laws which it enacts: nor can any oaths to any foreign power whatsoever, or any domestic subordinate power, discharge any member of the society from his obedience to the legislative, acting pursuant to their trust; nor oblige him to any obedience contrary to the laws so enacted, or farther than they do allow; it being ridiculous to imagine one

* 'The lawful power of making laws to command whole politic societies of men, belonging so properly unto the same entire societies, that for any prince or potentate of what kind soever upon earth, to exercise the same of himself, and not by express commission immediately and personally received from God, or else by authority derived at the first from their consent, upon whose persons they impose laws, it is no better than mere tyranny. Laws they are not, therefore, which public approbation hath not made so.' Hooker, *Eccl. Pol.*, lib. I. sect. 10. 'Of this point therefore we are to note, that sith men naturally have no full and perfect power to command whole politic multitudes of men, therefore utterly without our consent, we could in such sort be at no man's commandment living. And to be commanded we do consent, when that society, whereof we be a part, hath at any time before consented, without revoking the same by the like universal agreement.

'Laws therefore human, of what kind soever, are available by consent.' *Ibid.*

can be tied ultimately to obey any power in the society which is not supreme.

Though the legislative, whether placed in one or more, whether it be always in being, or only by intervals, though it be the supreme power in every commonwealth; yet,

First, it is not, nor can possibly be absolutely arbitrary over the lives and fortunes of the people: for it being but the joint power of every member of the society given up to that person or assembly which is legislator; it can be no more than those persons had in a state of nature before they entered into society, and gave up to the community: for nobody can transfer to another more power than he has in himself; and nobody has an absolute arbitrary power over himself, or over any other, to destroy his own life, or take away the life or property of another. A man, as has been proved, cannot subject himself to the arbitrary power of another; and having in the state of nature no arbitrary power over the life, liberty, or possession of another, but only so much as the law of nature gave him for the preservation of himself and the rest of mankind; this is all he doth, or can give up to the commonwealth, and by it to the legislative power, so that the legislative can have no more than this. Their power, in the utmost bounds of it, is limited to the public good of the society. It is a power that hath no other end but preservation, and therefore can never* have a right to destroy,

* Two foundations there are which bear up public societies; the one a natural inclination, whereby all men desire sociable life and fellowship: the other an order, expressly or secretly agreed upon, touching the manner of their union in living together: the latter is that which we call the law of a commonweal, the very soul of a politic body, the parts

enslave, or designedly to impoverish the subjects. The obligations of the law of nature cease not in society, but only in many cases are drawn closer, and have by human laws known penalties annexed to them, to enforce their observation. Thus the law of nature stands as an eternal rule to all men, legislators as well as others. The rules that they make for other men's actions must, as well as their own and other men's actions be conformable to the law of nature, *i.e.* to the will of God, of which that is a declaration; and the 'fundamental law of nature being the preservation of mankind,' no human sanction can be good or valid against it.

Secondly,* the legislative or supreme authority

whereof are by law animated, held together, and set on work in such actions as the common good requireth. Laws politic, ordained for external order and regiment amongst men, are never framed as they should be, unless presuming the will of man to be inwardly obstinate, rebellious, and averse from all obedience to the sacred laws of his nature; in a word, unless presuming man to be, in regard to his depraved mind, little better than a wild beast, they do accordingly provide, notwithstanding, so to frame his outward actions, that they be no hindrance unto the common good, for which societies are instituted. Unless they do this, they are not perfect.' Hooker, *Eccl. Pol.*, lib. 1. sect. 10.

* 'Human laws are measures in respect of men whose actions they must direct, howbeit such measures they are as have also their higher rules to be measured by, which rules are two, the law of God, and the law of nature; so that laws human must be made according to the general laws of nature, and without contradiction to any positive law of scripture, otherwise they are ill made.' Hooker, *Eccl. Pol.*, lib. 3, sect. 9.

'To constrain men to any thing inconvenient doth seem unreasonable.' *Ibid.* lib. 1, sect. 10.

cannot assume to itself a power to rule by extemporary, arbitrary decrees; but is bound to dispense justice, and to decide the rights of the subject, by promulgated, standing laws, and known authorised judges. For the law of nature being unwritten, and so nowhere to be found, but in the minds of men, they who, through passion, or interest, shall miscite, or misapply it, cannot so easily be convinced of their mistake, where there is no established judge: and so it serves not, as it ought, to determine the rights, and fence the properties of those that live under it; especially where every one is judge, interpreter, and executioner of it too, and that in his own case: and he that has right on his side, having ordinarily but his own single strength, hath not force enough to defend himself from injuries, or to punish delinquents. To avoid these inconveniencies, which disorder men's properties in the state of nature, men unite into societies, that they may have the united strength of the whole society to secure and defend their properties, and may have standing rules to bound it, by which every one may know what is his. To this end it is that men give up all their natural power to the society which they enter into, and the community put the legislative power into such hands as they think fit; with this trust, that they shall be governed by declared laws, or else their peace, quiet, and property will still be at the same uncertainty as it was in the state of nature.

Absolute arbitrary power, or governing without settled standing laws, can neither of them consist with the ends of society and government, which men would not quit the freedom of the state of nature for, and tie themselves up under, were it not to preserve their lives, liberties, and fortunes, and by stated rules of right and property to secure their peace and quiet. It cannot be supposed that they should intend, had they a power so to do, to give any one, or more, an absolute arbitrary power over their persons and estates, and put a force into the magistrate's hand to execute his unlimited will arbitrarily upon them. This were to put themselves into a worse condition than the state of nature. Wherein they had a liberty to defend their right against the injuries of others, and were upon equal terms of force to maintain it, whether invaded by a single man, or many in combination. Whereas by supposing they have given up themselves to the absolute arbitrary power and will of a legislator, they have disarmed themselves, and armed him, to make a prey of them when he pleases; he being in a much worse condition, who is exposed to the arbitrary power of one man, who has the command of 100,000 than he that is exposed to the arbitrary power of 100,000 single men; nobody being secure that his will, who has such a command, is better than that of other men, though his force be 100,000 times stronger. And therefore, whatever form the commonwealth is under, the ruling power ought to govern by declared and received laws, and not by extemporary dictates and undetermined resolutions; for then mankind will be in a far worse condition than in the state of nature; if they shall have armed one or a few men with the joint power of a multitude, to force them to obey at pleasure the exorbitant and unlimited degrees of their sudden thoughts, or unrestrained, and till that moment unknown wills, without having any measures set down which may guide and justify their actions: for all the power the government has being only for the good of the society, as it ought not to be arbitrary and at pleasure, so it ought to be exercised by established and promulgated laws; that both the people may know their duty, and be safe and secure within limits of the law; and the rulers too kept within their bounds, and not be tempted, by the power they have in their hands, to employ it to such purposes, and by such measures, as they would not have known, and own not willingly.

Thirdly, the supreme power cannot take from any man part of his property without his own consent: for the preservation of property being the end of government, and that for which men enter into society, it necessarily supposes and requires, that the people should have property, without which they must be supposed to lose that, by entering into society, which was the end for which they entered into it: too gross an absurdity for any man to own. Men therefore in society having property, they have such right to the goods, which by the law of the community are theirs, that nobody hath a right to take their substance or any part of it from them, without their own consent: without this they have no property at all; for I have truly no property in that, which another can by right take from me, when he pleases, against my consent. Hence it is a mistake to think, that the supreme or legislative power of any commonwealth can do what it will, and dispose of the estates of the subject arbitrarily, or take any part of them at pleasure. This is not much to be feared in governments where the legislative consists, wholly or in part, in assemblies which are variable, whose members, upon the dissolution of the assembly, are subjects under the common laws of their country, equally with the rest. But in governments where the legislative is in one lasting assembly always in being, or in one man, as in absolute monarchies, there is danger still that they will think themselves to have a distinct interest from the rest of the community; and so will be apt to increase their own riches and power, by taking what they think fit from the people: for a man's property is not at all secure, though there be good and equitable laws to set the bounds of it between him and his fellow-subjects, if he who commands those subjects have power to take from any private man what part he pleases of his property, and use and dispose of it as he thinks good.

But government, into whatsoever hands it is put, being, as I have before showed, entrusted with this condition, and for this end, that men might have and secure their properties; the prince, or senate, however it may have power to make laws for the regulating of property between the subjects one amongst another, yet can never have a power to take to themselves the whole or any part of the subject's property without their own consent: for this would be in effect to leave them no property at all. And to let us see, that even absolute power, where it is necessary, is not arbitrary by being absolute, but is still limited by that reason, and confined to those ends, which required it in some cases to be absolute, we need look no farther than the common practice of martial discipline: for the preservation of the army, and in it of the whole commonwealth, requires an absolute obedience to the command of every superior officer, and it is justly death to disobey or dispute the most dangerous or unreasonable of them; but yet we see, that neither the serjeant, that could command a soldier to march up to the mouth of a cannon, or stand in a breach, where he is almost sure to perish, can command that soldier to give him one penny of his money; nor the general, that can condemn him to death for deserting his post, or for not obeying the most desperate orders, can yet, with all his absolute power of life and death, dispose of one farthing of that soldier's estate, or seize one jot of his goods; whom yet he can command any thing, and hang for the least disobedience; because such a blind obedience is necessary to that end for which the commander has his power, viz, the preservation of the rest; but disposing of his goods has nothing to do with it.

It is true, governments cannot be supported without great charge, and it is fit every one who enjoys his share of the protection, should pay out of his estate his proportion for the maintenance of it. But still it must be with his own consent, *i.e.* the consent of the majority, giving it either by themselves, or their representatives chosen by them: for if any one shall claim a power to lay and levy taxes on the people by his own authority, and without such consent of the people, he thereby invades the fundamental law of property, and subverts the end of government: for what property have I in that which another may by right take, when he pleases, to himself?

Fourthly, the legislative cannot transfer the power of making laws to any other hands: for it being but a delegated power from the people, they who have it cannot pass it over to others. The people alone can appoint the form of the commonwealth, which is by constituting the legislative, and appointing in whose hands that shall be. And when the people have said, we will submit to rules, and be governed by laws made by such men, and in such forms, nobody else can say other men shall make laws for them; nor can the people be bound by any laws but such as are enacted by those whom they have chosen, and authorised to make laws for them. The power of the legislative being derived from the people by a positive voluntary grant and institution, can be no other than what that positive grant conveyed, which being only to make laws, and not to make legislators, the legislative can have no power to transfer their authority of making laws and place it in other hands.

These are the bounds which the trust that is put in them by the society, and the law of God and nature, have set to the legislative power of every commonwealth, in all forms of government.

First, they are to govern by promulgated established laws, not to be varied in particular cases, but to have one rule for rich and poor, for the favourite at court, and the countryman at plough.

Secondly, these laws also ought to be designed for no other end ultimately, but the good of the people.

Thirdly, they must not raise taxes on the property of the people, without the consent of the people, given by themselves or their deputies. And this properly concerns only such governments where the legislative is always in being, or at least where the people have not reserved any part of the legislative to deputies, to be from time to time chosen by themselves.

Fourthly, the legislative neither must nor can transfer the power of making laws to any body else, or place it any where, but where the people have.

CHAPTER 12

Of the Legislative, Executive, and Federative Power of the Commonwealth

The legislative power is that, which has a right to direct how the force of the commonwealth shall be employed for preserving the community and the members of it. But because those laws which are constantly to be executed, and whose force is always to continue, may be made in a little time, therefore there is no need that the legislative should be always in being, not having always business to do. And because it may be too great a temptation to human frailty, apt to grasp at power, for the same persons who have the power of making laws, to have also in their hands the power to execute them; whereby they may exempt themselves from obedience to the laws they make, and suit the law, both in its making and execution, to their own private advantage, and thereby come to have a distinct interest from the rest of the community, contrary to the end of society and government: therefore in well ordered commonwealths, where the good of the whole is so considered, as it ought, the legislative power is put into the hands of divers persons, who, duly assembled, have by themselves, or jointly with others, a power to make laws; which when they have done, being separated again, they are themselves subject to the laws they have made; which is a new and near tie upon them, to take care that they make them for the public good.

But because the laws, that are at once, and in a short time made, have a constant and lasting force, and need a perpetual execution, or an attendance thereunto; therefore it is necessary there should be a power always in being, which should see to the execution of the laws that are made, and remain in force. And thus the legislative and executive power come often to be separated.

There is another power in every commonwealth, which one may call natural, because it is that which answers to the power every man naturally had before it entered into society: for though in a commonwealth, the members of it are distinct persons still in reference to one another, and as such are governed by the laws of the society; yet in reference to the rest of mankind, they make one body, which is, as every member of it before was, still in the state of nature with the rest of mankind. Hence it is, that the controversies that happen between any man of the society with those that are out of it, are managed by the public; and an injury done to a member of their body engages the whole in the reparation of it. So that, under this consideration, the whole community is one body in the state of nature, in respect of all other states of persons out of its community.

This therefore contains the power of war and peace, leagues and alliances, and all the transactions with all persons and communities without the commonwealth; and may be called federative, if any one pleases. So the thing be understood, I am indifferent as to the name.

These two powers, executive and federative, though they be really distinct in themselves, yet one comprehending the execution of the municipal laws of the society within itself, upon all that are parts of it; the other the management of the security and interest of the public without, with all those that it may receive benefit or damage from; yet they are almost always united. And though this federative power in the well or ill management of it be of great moment to the commonwealth, yet it is much less capable to be directed by antecedent, standing, positive laws, than the executive; and so must necessarily be left to the prudence and wisdom of those whose hands it is in, to be managed for the public good: for the laws that concern subjects one amongst another, being to direct their actions, may well enough precede them. But what is to be done in reference to foreigners, depending much upon their actions, and the variation of designs, and interests, must be left in great part to the prudence of those who have this power committed to them, to be managed by the best of their skill, for the advantage of the commonwealth.

Though, as I said, the executive and federative power of every community be really distinct in themselves, yet they are hardly to be separated, and placed at the same time in the hands of distinct persons: for both of them requiring the force of the society for their exercise, it is almost impracticable to place the force of the commonwealth in distinct, and not subordinate hands; or that the executive and federative power should be placed in persons that might act separately, whereby the force of the public would be under different commands; which would be apt some time or other to cause disorder and ruin.

CHAPTER 13

Of the Subordination of the Powers of the Commonwealth

Though in a constituted commonwealth, standing upon its own basis, and acting according to its own nature, that is, acting for the preservation of the community, there can be but one supreme power, which is the legislative, to which all the rest are and must be subordinate; yet the legislative being only a fiduciary power to act for certain ends, there remains still 'in the people a supreme power to remove or alter the legislative,' when they find the legislative act contrary to the trust reposed in them: for all power given with trust for the attaining an end, being limited by that end: whenever that end is manifestly neglected or opposed, the trust must necessarily be forfeited, and the power devolve into the hands of those that gave it, who may place it anew where they shall think best for their safety and security. And thus the community perpetually retains a supreme power of saving themselves from the attempts and designs of any body, even of their legislators, whenever they shall be so foolish, or so wicked, as to lay and carry on designs against the liberties and properties of the subject: for no man, or society of men, having a power to deliver up their preservation, or consequently the means of it, to the absolute will and arbitrary dominion of another; whenever any one shall go about to bring them into such a slavish condition, they will always have a right to preserve what they have not a power to part with; and to rid themselves of those who invade this fundamental, sacred, and unalterable law of self-preservation, for which they entered into society. And thus the community may be said in this respect to be always the supreme power, but not as considered under any form of government, because this power of the people can never take place till the government be dissolved.

In all cases, whilst the government subsists, the legislative is the supreme power: for what can give laws to another, must needs be superior to him; and since the legislative is no otherwise legislative of the society, but by the right it has to make laws for all the parts, and for every member of the society, prescribing rules to their actions, and giving power of execution, where they are transgressed; the legislative must needs be the supreme, and all other powers, in any members or parts of the society, derived from and subordinate to it.

In some commonwealths, where the legislative is not always in being, and the executive is vested in a single person, who has also a share in the legislative; there that single person in a very tolerable sense may also be called supreme; not that he has in himself all the supreme power, which is that of law-making; but because he has in him the supreme execution, from whom all inferior magistrates derive all their several subordinate powers, or at least the greatest part of them: having also no legislative superior to him, there being no law to be made without his consent, which cannot be expected should ever subject him to the other part of the legislative, he is properly enough in this sense supreme. But yet it is to be observed, that though oaths of allegiance and fealty are taken to him, it is not to him as supreme legislator, but as supreme executor of the law, made by a joint power of him with others: allegiance being nothing but an obedience according to law, which when he violates, he has no right to obedience, nor can claim it otherwise than as the public person invested with the power of the law; and so is to be considered as the image, phantom, or representative of the commonwealth, acted by the will of the society, declared in its laws; and thus he has no will, no power, but that of the law. But when he quits this representation, this public will, and acts by his own private will, he degrades himself, and is but a single private person without power, and without will, that has no right to obedience: the members owing no obedience but to the public will of the society.

The executive power, placed any where but in a person that has also a share in the legislative, is visibly subordinate and accountable to it, and may be at pleasure changed and displaced; so that it is not the supreme executive power that is exempt from subordination: but the supreme executive power vested in one, who having a share in the legislative, has no distinct superior legislative to be subordinate and accountable to, farther than he himself shall join and consent; so that he is no more subordinate than he himself shall think fit, which one may certainly conclude will be but very little. Of other ministerial and subordinate powers in a commonwealth we need not speak, they being so multiplied with infinite variety, in the different customs and constitutions of distinct commonwealths, that it is impossible to give a particular account of them all. Only thus much, which is necessary to our present purpose, we may take notice of concerning them, that they have no manner of authority, any of them, beyond what is by positive grant and commission delegated to them, and are all of them accountable to some other power in the commonwealth.

It is not necessary, no, nor so much as convenient, that the legislative should be always in being; but absolutely necessary that the executive power should; because there is not always need for new laws to be made, but always need of execution of the laws that are made. When the legislative hath put the execution of the laws they make into other hands, they have a power still to resume it out of those hands, when they find cause, and to punish for any maladministration against the laws. The same holds also in regard of the federative power, that and the executive being both ministerial and subordinate to the legislative, which, as has been showed, in a constituted commonwealth is the supreme. The legislative also in this case being supposed to consist of several persons, (for if it be a single person, it cannot but be always in being, and so will, as supreme, naturally have the supreme executive power, together with the legislative) may assemble, and exercise their legislature, at the times that either their original constitution, or their own adjournment, appoints, or when they please; if neither of these hath appointed any time, or there be no other way prescribed to convoke them: for the supreme power being placed in them by the people, it is always in them, and they may exercise it when they please, unless by their original constitution they are limited to certain seasons, or by an act of their supreme power they have adjourned to a certain time; and when that time comes, they have a right to assemble and act again.

If the legislative, or any part of it, be made up of representatives chosen for that time by the people, which afterwards return into the ordinary state of subjects, and have no share in the legislature but upon a new choice, this power of choosing must also be exercised by the people, either at certain appointed seasons, or else when they are summoned to it; and in this latter case the power of convoking the legislative is ordinarily placed in the executive, and has one of these two limitations in respect of time: that either the original constitution requires their assembling and acting at certain intervals, and then the executive power does nothing but ministerially issue directions for their electing and assembling according to due forms; or else it is left to his prudence to call them by new elections, when the occasions or exigencies of the public require the amendment of old, or making of new laws, or the redress or prevention of any inconveniences, that lie on, or threaten the people.

It may be demanded here, What if the executive power, being possessed of the force of the commonwealth, shall make use of that force to hinder the meeting and acting of the legislative, when the original constitution or the public exigencies require it? I say, using force upon the people without authority, and contrary to the trust put in him that does so, is a state of war with the people, who have a right to reinstate their legislative in the exercise of their power: for having erected a legislative, with an intent they should exercise the power of making laws, either at certain set times, or when there is need of it; when they are hindered by any force from what is so necessary to the society, and wherein the safety and preservation of the people consists, the people have a right to remove it by force. In all states and conditions, the true remedy of force without authority is to oppose force to it. The use of force without authority always puts him that uses it into a state of war, as the aggressor, and renders him liable to be treated accordingly.

The power of assembling and dismissing the legislative, placed in the executive, gives not the executive a superiority over it, but is a fiduciary trust placed in him for the safety of the people, in a case where the uncertainty and variableness of human affairs could not bear a steady fixed rule: for it not being possible that the first framers of the government should, by any foresight, be so much masters of future events as to be able to prefix so just periods of return and duration to the assemblies of the legislative, in all times to come, that might exactly answer all the exigencies of the commonwealth; the best remedy could be found for this defect was to trust this to the prudence of one who was always to be present, and whose business it was to watch over the public good. Constant frequent meetings of the legislative, and long continuations of their assemblies, without necessary occasion, could not but be burdensome to the people, and must necessarily in time produce more dangerous inconveniences, and yet the quick turn of affairs might be sometimes such as to need their present help; any delay of their convening might endanger the public; and sometimes too their business might be so great, that the limited time of their sitting might be too short for their work, and rob the public of that benefit which could be had only from their mature deliberation. What then could be done in this case to prevent the community from being exposed some time or other to eminent hazard, on one side or the other, by fixed intervals and periods, set to the meeting and acting of the legislative: but to intrust it to the prudence of some, who being present, and acquainted with the state of public affairs, might make use of this prerogative for the public good? And where else could this be so well placed as in his hands, who was intrusted with the execution of the laws for the same end? Thus supposing the regulation of times for the assembling and sitting of the legislative not settled by the original constitution, it naturally fell into the hands of the executive, not as an arbitrary power depending on his good pleasure, but with this trust always to have it exercised only for the public weal, as the occurrences of times and change of affairs might require. Whether settled periods of their convening, or a liberty left to the prince for convoking the legislative, or perhaps a mixture of both, hath the least inconvenience attending it, it is not my business here to inquire; but only to show, that though the executive power may have the prerogative of convoking and dissolving such conventions of the legislative, yet it is not thereby superior to it.

Things of this world are in so constant a flux, that nothing remains long in the same state. Thus people, riches, trade, power, change their stations, flourishing mighty cities come to ruin, and prove in time neglected desolate corners, whilst other unfrequented places grow into populous countries, filled with wealth and inhabitants. But things not always changing equally, and private interest often keeping up customs and privileges, when the reasons of them are ceased; it often comes to pass, that in governments, where part of the legislative consists of representatives chosen by the people, that in tract of time this representation becomes very unequal and disproportionate to the reasons it was at first established upon. To what gross absurdities the following of custom, when reason has left it, may lead, we may be satisfied, when we see the bare name of a town, of which there remains not so much as the ruins, where scarce so much housing as a sheepcote, or more inhabitants than a shepherd is to be found, sends as many representatives to the grand assembly of law-makers as a whole county, numerous in people, and powerful in riches. This strangers stand amazed at, and every one must confess needs a remedy; though most think it hard to find one; because the constitution of the legislative being the original and supreme act of the society, antecedent to all positive laws in it, and depending wholly on the people, no inferior power can alter it. And therefore the people, when the legislative is once constituted, having, in such a government as we have been speaking of, no power to act as long as the government stands; this inconvenience is thought incapable of a remedy.

Salus populi suprema lex, is certainly so just and fundamental a rule, that he who sincerely follows it, cannot dangerously err. If therefore the executive, who has the power of convoking the legislative, observing rather the true proportion than fashion of representation, regulates not by old custom, but true reason, the number of members in all places that have a right to be distinctly represented, which no part of the people, however incorporated, can pretend to, but in proportion to the assistance which it affords to the public; it cannot be judged to have set up a new legislative, but to have restored the old and true one, and to have rectified the disorders which succession of time had insensibly, as well as inevitably introduced; for it being the interest as well as intention of the people, to have a fair and equal representative; whoever brings it nearest to that, is an undoubted friend to, and establisher of the government, and cannot miss the consent and approbation of the community: prerogative being nothing but a power in the hands of the prince, to provide for the public good, in such cases, which depending upon unforeseen and uncertain occurrences, certain and unalterable laws could not safely direct; whatsoever shall be done manifestly for the good of the people, and the establishing the government upon its true foundations, is, and always will be, just prerogative. The power of erecting new corporations, and therewith new representatives, carries with it a supposition that in time the measures of representation might vary, and those places have a just right to be represented which before had none; and by the same reason, those cease to have a right, and be too inconsiderable for such a privilege, which before had it. It is not a change from the present state, which perhaps corruption or decay has introduced, that makes an inroad upon the government; but the tendency of it to injure or oppress the people, and to set up one part or party, with a distinction from, and an unequal subjection of the rest. Whatsoever cannot but be acknowledged to be of advantage to the society, and people in general, upon just and lasting measures, will always, when done, justify itself; and whenever the people shall choose their representatives upon just and undeniably equal measures, suitable to the original frame of the government, it cannot be doubted to be the will and act of the society, whoever permitted or caused them so to do.

CHAPTER 14

Of Prerogative

Where the legislative and executive power are in distinct hands, (as they are in all moderated monarchies and well-framed governments) there the good of the society requires, that several things should be left to the discretion of him that has the executive power: for the legislators not being able to foresee, and provide by laws, for all that may be useful to the community, the executor of the laws having the power in his hands, has by the common law of nature a right to make use of it for the good of the society, in many cases, where the municipal law has given no direction, till the legislative can conveniently be assembled to provide for it. Many things there are, which the law can by no means provide for; and those must necessarily be left to the discretion of him that has the executive power in his hands, to be ordered by him as the public good and advantage shall require: nay, it is fit that the laws themselves should in some cases give way to the executive power, or rather to this fundamental law of nature and government, viz. that, as much as may be, all the members of the society are to be preserved: for since many accidents may happen, wherein a strict and rigid observation of the laws may do harm (as not to pull down an innocent man's house to stop the fire, when the next to it is burning) and a man may come sometimes within the reach of the law, which makes no distinction of persons, by an action that may deserve reward and pardon; it is fit the ruler should have a power, in many cases, to mitigate the severity of the law, and pardon some offenders: for the end of government being the preservation of all, as much as may be, even the guilty are to be spared, where it can prove no prejudice to the innocent.

This power to act according to discretion for the public good, without the prescription of the law, and sometimes even against it, is that which is called prerogative: for since in some governments the law-making power is not always in being, and is usually too numerous, and so too slow for the despatch requisite to execution; and because also it is impossible to foresee, and so by laws to provide for all accidents and necessities that may concern the public, or to make such laws as will do no harm, if they are executed with an inflexible rigour on all occasions, and upon all persons that may come in their way; therefore there is a latitude left to the executive power, to do many things of choice which the laws do not prescribe.

This power, whilst employed for the benefit of the community, and suitably to the trust and ends of the government, is undoubted prerogative, and never is questioned; for the people are very seldom or never scrupulous or nice in the point; they are far from examining prerogative, whilst it is in any tolerable degree employed for the use it was meant; that is, for the good of the people, and not manifestly against it: but if there comes to be a question between the executive power and the people, about a thing claimed as a prerogative, the tendency of the exercise of such prerogative to the good or hurt of the people will easily decide that question.

It is easy to conceive, that in the infancy of governments, when commonwealths differed little from families in number of people, they differed from them too but little in number of laws: and the governors being as the fathers of them, watching over them for their good, the government was almost all prerogative. A few established laws served the turn, and the discretion and care of the ruler supplied the rest. But when mistake or flattery prevailed with weak princes to make use of this power for private ends of their own, and not for the public good, the people were fain by express laws to get prerogative determined in those points wherein they found disadvantage from it: and thus declared limitations of prerogative were by the people found necessary in cases which they and their ancestors had left, in the utmost latitude, to the wisdom of those princes who made no other but a right use of it: that is, for the good of their people.

And therefore they have a very wrong notion of government, who say, that the people have encroached upon the prerogative, when they have got any part of it to be defined by positive laws: for in so doing they have not pulled from the prince any thing that of right belonged to him, but only declare, that that power which they indefinitely left in his or his ancestors' hands, to be exercised for their good, was not a thing which they intended him when he used it otherwise: for the end of government being the good of the community, whatsoever alterations are made in it, tending to that end, cannot be an encroachment upon any body, since nobody in government can have a right tending to any other end: and those only are encroachments which prejudice or hinder the public good. Those who say otherwise, speak as if the prince had a distinct and separate interest from the good of the community, and was not made for it; the root and source from which spring almost all those evils and disorders which happen in kingly governments. And indeed, if that be so, the people under his government are not a society of rational creatures, entered into a community for their mutual good; they are not such as have set rulers over themselves, to guard and promote that good; but are to be looked on as an herd of inferior creatures under the dominion of a master, who keeps them and works them for his own pleasure or profit. If men were so void of reason, and brutish, as to enter into society upon such terms, prerogative might indeed, be, what some men would have it, an arbitrary power to do things hurtful to the people.

But since a rational creature cannot be supposed, when free, to put himself into subjection to another, for his own harm (though, where he finds a good and wise ruler, he may not perhaps think it either necessary or useful to set precise bounds to his power in all things), prerogative can be nothing but the people's permitting their rulers to do several things, of their own free choice, where the law was silent, and sometimes too against the direct letter of the law, for the public good; and their acquiescing in it when so done: for as a good prince, who is mindful of the trust put into his hands, and careful of the good of his people, cannot have too much prerogative, that is, power to do good; so a weak and ill prince, who would claim that power which his predecessors exercised without the direction of the law, as a prerogative belonging to him by right of his office, which he may exercise at his pleasure, to make or promote an interest distinct from that of the public; gives the people an occasion to claim their right, and limit that power, which, whilst it was exercised for their good, they were content should be tacitly allowed.

And therefore he that will look into the history of England, will find, that prerogative was always largest in the hands of our wisest and best princes; because the people, observing the whole tendency of their actions to be the public good, contested not what was done without law to that end: or, if any human frailty or mistake (for princes are but men, made as others) appeared in some small declinations from that end; yet it was visible, the main of their conduct tended to nothing but the care of the public. The people, therefore, finding reason to be satisfied with these princes, whenever they acted without, or contrary to the letter of the law, acquiesced in what they did, and, without the least complaint, let them enlarge their prerogative as they pleased; judging rightly, that they did nothing herein to the prejudice of their laws, since they acted conformably to the foundation and end of all laws, the public good.

Such God-like princes, indeed, had some title to arbitrary power by that argument, that would prove absolute monarchy the best government, as that which God himself governs the universe by; because such kings partook of his wisdom and goodness. Upon this is founded that saying, that the reigns of good princes have been always most dangerous to the liberties of their people: for when their successors, managing the government with different thoughts, would draw the actions of those good rulers into precedent, and make them the standard of their prerogative, as if what had been done only for the good of the people was a right in them to do for the harm of the people, if they so pleased; it has often occasioned contest, and sometimes public disorders, before the people could recover their original right, and get that to be declared not to be prerogative, which truly was never so: since it is impossible that any body in the society should ever have a right to do the people harm; though it be very possible and reasonable that the people should not go about to set any bounds to the prerogative of those kings or rulers, who themselves transgressed not the bounds of the public good; for 'prerogative is nothing but the power of doing public good without a rule.'

The power of calling parliaments in England, as to precise time, place, and duration, is certainly a prerogative of the king, but still with this trust, that it shall be made use of for the good of the nation, as the exigencies of the times, and variety of occasions shall require: for it being impossible to foresee which should always be the fittest place for them to assemble in, and what the best season, the choice of these was left with the executive power, as might be most subservient to the public good, and best suit the ends of parliaments.

The old question will be asked in this matter of prerogative, 'But who shall be judge when this power is made a right use of?' I answer: between an executive power in being, with such a prerogative, and a legislative that depends upon his will for their convening, there can be no judge on earth; as there can be none between the legislative and the people, should either the executive or the legislative, when they have got the power in their hands, design or go about to enslave or destroy them. The people have no other remedy in this, as in all other cases where they have no judge on earth, but to appeal to heaven: for the rulers, in such attempts, exercising a power the people never put into their hands (who can never be supposed to consent that any body should rule over them for their harm), do that which they have not a right to do. And where the body of the people, or any single man, is deprived of their right, or under the exercise of a power without right, and have no appeal on earth, then they have a liberty to appeal to heaven, whenever they judge the cause of sufficient moment. And therefore, though the people cannot be judge, so as to have, by the constitution of that society, any superior power to determine and give effective sentence in the case; yet they have, by a law antecedent and paramount to all positive laws of men, reserved that ultimate determination to themselves which belongs to all mankind, where there lies no appeal on earth, viz. to judge whether they have just cause to make their appeal to heaven. – And this judgment they cannot part with, it being out of a man's power so to submit himself to another, as to give him a liberty to destroy him; God and nature never allowing a man so to abandon himself, as to neglect his own preservation: and since he cannot take away his own life, neither can he give another power to take it. Nor let any one think this lays a perpetual foundation for disorder; for this operates not till the inconveniency is so great that the majority feel it, and are weary of it, and find a necessity to have it amended. But this the executive power, or wise princes, never need come in the danger of: and it is the thing, of all others, they have most need to avoid, as of all others the most perilous.

CHAPTER 15

Of Paternal, Political, and Despotical Power, considered together

Though I have had occasion to speak of these separately before, yet the great mistakes of late about government having, as I suppose, arisen from confounding these distinct powers one with another, it may not, perhaps, be amiss to consider them here together.

First, then, paternal or parental power is nothing but that which parents have over their children, to govern them for the children's good, till they come to the use of reason, or a state of knowledge, wherein they may be supposed capable to understand that rule, whether it be the law of nature, or the municipal law of their country, they are to govern themselves by: capable, I say, to know it, as well as several others, who live as freemen under that law. The affection and tenderness which God hath planted in the breast of parents towards their children, makes it evident, that this is not intended to be a severe arbitrary government, but only for the help, instruction, and preservation of their offspring.

But happen it as it will, there is, as I have proved, no reason why it should be thought to extend to life and death, at any time, over their children, more than over anybody else; neither can there be any pretence why this parental power should keep the child, when grown to a man, in subjection to the will of his parents, any farther than having received life and education from his parents, obliges him to respect, honour, gratitude, assistance, and support, all his life, to both father and mother. And thus, it is true, the paternal is a natural government, but not at all extending itself to the ends and jurisdictions of that which is political. The power of the father doth not reach at all to the property of the child, which is only in his own disposing.

Secondly, political power is that power which every man having in the state of nature, has given up into the hands of the society, and therein to the governors, whom the society hath set over itself, with this express or tacit trust, that it shall be employed for their good, and the preservation of their property: now this power, which every man has in the state of nature, and which he parts with to the society in all such cases where the society can secure him, is to use such means for the preserving of his own property as he thinks good, and nature allows him; and to punish the breach of the law of nature in others, so as (according to the best of his reason) may most conduce to the preservation of himself and the rest of mankind. So that the end and measure of this power, when in every man's hands in the state of nature, being the preservation of all of his society, that is, all mankind in general, it can have no other end or measure, when in the hands of the magistrate, but to preserve the members of that society in their lives, liberties, and possessions; and so cannot be an absolute arbitrary power over their lives and fortunes, which are as much as possible to be preserved; but a power to make laws, and annex such penalties to them, as may tend to the preservation of the whole, by cutting off those parts, and those only, which are so corrupt that they threaten the sound and healthy, without which no severity is lawful. And this power has its original only from compact and agreement, and the mutual consent of those who make up the community.

Thirdly, despotical power is an absolute, arbitrary power one man has over another, to take away his life whenever he pleases. This is a power, which neither nature gives, for it has made no such distinction between one man and another, nor compact can convey; for man not having such an arbitrary power over his own life, cannot give another man such a power over it; but it is the effect only of forfeiture, which the aggressor makes of his own life, when he puts himself into the state of war with another: for having quitted reason, which God hath given to be the rule betwixt man and man, and the common bond whereby human kind is united into one fellowship and society, and having renounced the way of peace which that teaches, and made use of the force of war, to compass his unjust ends upon another, where he has no right; and so revolting from his own kind to that of beasts, by making force, which is theirs, to be his rule of right; he renders himself liable to be destroyed by the injured person, and the rest of mankind, that will join with him in the execution of justice, as any other wild beast, or noxious brute, with whom mankind can have neither society nor security.* And thus captives, taken in a just and lawful war, and such only, are subject to a despotical power; which, as it arises not from compact, so neither is it capable of any, but is the state of war continufor what compact can be made with a man that is not master of his own life? What condition can he perform? And if he be once allowed to be master of his own life, the despotical arbitrary power of his master ceases. He that is master of himself, and his own life, has a right too to the means of preserving it; so that, as soon as compact enters, slavery ceases, and he so far quits his absolute power, and puts an end to the state of war, who enters into conditions with his captive.

Nature gives the first of these, viz. paternal power, to parents for the benefit of their children during their minority, to supply their want of ability and understanding how to manage their property. (By property I must be understood here, as in other places, to mean that property which men have in their persons as well as goods.) Voluntary agreement gives the second, viz. political power to governors for the benefit of their subjects, to secure them in the possession and use of their properties. And forfeiture gives the third despotical power to lords, for their own benefit, over those who are stripped of all property.

He that shall consider the distinct rise and extent, and the different ends of these several powers, will plainly see, that paternal power comes as far short of that of the magistrate, as despotical exceeds it; and that absolute dominion, however placed, is so far from

* Another copy, corrected by Mr Locke, has it thus, 'noxious brute that is destructive to their being.'

being one kind of civil society, that it is as inconsistent with it, as slavery is with property. Paternal power is only where minority makes the child incapable to manage his property; political, where men have property in their own disposal; and despotical, over such as have no property at all.

CHAPTER 16

Of Conquest

Though governments can originally have no other rise than that before-mentioned, nor politics be founded on any thing but the consent of the people; yet such have been the disorders ambition has filled the world with, that in the noise of war, which makes so great a part of the history of mankind, this consent is little taken notice of: and therefore many have mistaken the force of arms for the consent of the people, and reckon conquest as one of the originals of government. But conquest is as far from setting up any government, as demolishing a house is from building a new one in the place. Indeed, it often makes way for a new frame of a commonwealth, by destroying the former; but, without the consent of the people, can never erect a new one.

That the aggressor, who puts himself into the state of war with another, and unjustly invades another man's right, can, by such an unjust war, never come to have a right over the conquered, will be easily agreed by all men, who will not think that robbers and pirates have a right of empire over whomsoever they have force enough to master or that men are bound by promises which unlawful force extorts from them. Should a robber break into my house, and with a dagger at my throat make me seal deeds to convey my estate to him, would this give him any title? Just such a title, by his sword, has an unjust conqueror, who forces me into submission. The injury and the crime are equal, whether committed by the wearer of the crown or some petty villain. The title of the offender, and the number of his followers, make no difference in the offence, unless it be to aggravate it. The only difference is, great robbers punish little ones, to keep them in their obedience; but the great ones are rewarded with laurels and triumphs, because they are too big for the weak hands of justice in this world, and have the power in their own possession which should punish offenders. What is my remedy against a robber, that so broke into my house? Appeal to the law for justice. But perhaps justice is denied, or I am crippled and cannot stir, robbed and have not the means to do it. If God has taken away all means of seeking remedy, there is nothing left but patience. But my son, when able, may seek the relief of the law, which I am denied: he or his son may renew his appeal, till he recover his right. But the conquered, or their children, have no court, no arbitrator on earth to appeal to. Then they may appeal, as Jephthah did, to heaven, and repeat their appeal till they have recovered the native right of their ancestors, which was, to have such a legislative over them as the majority should approve, and freely acquiesce in. If it be objected, this would cause endless trouble; I answer, no more than justice does, where she lies open to all that appeal to her. He that troubles his neighbour without a cause, is punished for it by the justice of the court he appeals to; and he that appeals to heaven must be sure he has right on his side, and a right too that is worth the trouble and cost of the appeal, as he will answer at a tribunal that cannot be deceived, and will be sure to retribute to every one according to the mischiefs he hath created to his fellow-subjects; that is, any part of mankind: from whence it is plain, that he that 'conquers in an unjust war, can thereby have no title to the subjection and obedience of the conquered.'

But supposing victory favours the right side, let us consider a conqueror in a lawful war, and see what power he gets, and over whom.

First, it is plain he 'gets no power by his conquest over those that conquered with him.' They that fought on his side cannot suffer by the conquest, but must at least be as much freeman as they were before. And most commonly they serve upon terms, and on conditions to share with their leader, and enjoy a part of the spoil, and other advantages that attended the conquering sword; or at least have a part of the subdued country bestowed upon them. And 'the conquering people are not, I hope, to be slaves by conquest,' and wear their laurels only to show they are sacrifices to their leader's triumph. They that found absolute monarchy upon the title of the sword, make their heroes, who are the founders of such monarchies, arrant Drawcansirs, and forget they had any officers and soldiers that fought on their side in the battles they won, or assisted them in the subduing, or shared in possessing, the countries they mastered. We are told by some, that the English monarchy is founded in the Norman conquest, and that our princes have thereby a title to absolute dominion: which if it were true (as by the history it appears otherwise), and that William had a right to make war on this island, yet his dominion by conquest could reach no farther than to the Saxons and Britons, that were then inhabitants of this country. The Normans that came with him, and helped to conquer, and all descended from them, are freemen, and no subjects by conquest, let that give what dominion it will. And if I, or any body else, shall claim freedom, as derived from them, it will be very hard to prove the contrary; and it is plain the law, that has made no distinction between the one and the other, intends not there should be any difference in their freedom or privileges.

But supposing, which seldom happens, that the conquerors and conquered never incorporate into one people, under the same laws and freedom; let us see next 'what power a lawful conqueror has over the subdued:' and that I say is purely despotical. He has an absolute power over the lives of those who by an unjust war have forfeited them: but not over the lives or fortunes of those who engaged not in the war, nor over the possessions even of those who were actually engaged in it.

Secondly, I say then the conqueror gets no power but only over those who have actually assisted, concurred, or consented to that unjust force that is used against him: for the people having given to their governors no power to do an unjust thing, such as is to make an unjust war (for they never had such a power in themselves) they ought not to be charged as guilty of the violence and injustice that is committed in an unjust war, any farther than they actually abet it, no more than they are to be thought guilty of any violence or oppression their governors should use upon the people themselves, or any part of their fellow-subjects, they having empowered them no more to the one than to the other. Conquerors, it is true, seldom trouble themselves to make the distinction, but they willingly permit the confusion of war to sweep all together: but yet this alters not the right; for the conqueror's power over the lives of the conquered being only because they have used force to do, or maintain an injustice, he can have that power only over those who have concurred in that force; all the rest are innocent; and he has no more title over the people of that country, who have done him no injury, and so have made no forfeiture of their lives, than he has over any other, who, without any injuries or provocations, have lived upon fair terms with him.

Thirdly, the power a conqueror gets over those he overcomes in a just war, is perfectly despotical: he has an absolute power over the lives of those, who, by putting themselves in a state of war, have forfeited them; but he has not thereby a right and title to their possessions. This I doubt not but at first sight will seem a strange doctrine, it being so quite contrary to the practice of the world; there being nothing more familiar in speaking of the dominion of countries, than to say such an one conquered it; as if conquest, without any more ado, conveyed a right of possession. But when we consider, that the practice of the strong and powerful, how universal soever it may be, is seldom the rule of right, however it be one part of the subjection of the conquered, not to argue against the conditions cut out to them by the conquering sword.

Though in all war there be usually a complication of

force and damage, and the aggressor seldom fails to harm the estate, when he uses force against the persons of those he makes war upon; yet it is the use of force only that puts a man into the state of war: for whether by force he begins the injury, or else having quietly, and by fraud, done the injury, he refuses to make reparation, and by force maintains it (which is the same thing, as at first to have done it by force), it is the unjust use of force that makes the war: for he that breaks open my house, and violently turns me out of doors; or, having peaceably got in, by force keeps me out, does in effect the same thing; supposing we are in such a state that we have no common judge on earth whom I may appeal to, and to whom we are both obliged to submit; for of such I am now speaking. It is the 'unjust use of force then, that puts a man into the state of war' with another; and thereby he that is guilty of it makes a forfeiture of his life: for quitting reason, which is the rule given between man and man, and using force, the way of beasts, he becomes liable to be destroyed by him he uses force against, as any savage ravenous beast, that is dangerous to his being.

But because the miscarriages of the father are no faults of the children, and they may be rational and peaceable, notwithstanding the brutishness and injustice of the father; the father, by his miscarriages and violence, can forfeit but his own life, but involves not his children in his guilt or destruction. His goods, which nature, that willeth the preservation of all mankind as much as is possible, hath made to belong to the children to keep them from perishing, do still continue to belong to his children; for supposing them not to have joined in the war, either through infancy, absence, or choice, they have done nothing to forfeit them: nor has the conqueror any right to take them away, by the bare title of having subdued him that by force attempted his destruction; though perhaps he may have some right to them, to repair the damages he has sustained by the war, and the defence of his own right; which how far it reaches to the possessions of the conquered, we shall see by and by. So that he that by conquest has a right over a man's person to destroy him if he pleases, has not thereby a right over his estate to possess and enjoy it; for it is the brutal force the aggressor has used that gives his adversary a right to take away his life, and destroy him, if he pleases, as a noxious creature; but it is damage sustained that alone gives him title to another man's goods: for though I may kill a thief that sets on me in the highway, yet I may not (which seems less) take away his money and let him go: this would be robbery on my side. His force, and the state of war he put himself in, made him forfeit his life, but gave me no title to his goods. The right then of conquest extends only to the lives of those who joined in the war, not to their estates, but only in order to make reparation for the damages received, and the charges of the war; and that too with reservation of the right of the innocent wife and children.

Let the conqueror have as much justice on his side as could be supposed, he has no right to seize more than the vanquished could forfeit: his life is at the victor's mercy; and his service and goods he may appropriate to make himself reparation; but he cannot take the goods of his wife and children: they too had a title to the goods he enjoyed, and their shares in the estate he possessed: for example, I in the state of nature (and all commonwealths are in the state of nature one with another) have injured another man, and refusing to give satisfaction, it comes to a state of war, wherein my defending by force what I had gotten unjustly makes me the aggressor. I am conquered: my life, it is true, as forfeit, is at mercy, but not my wife's and children's. They made not the war, nor assisted in it. I could not forfeit their lives; they were not mine to forfeit. My wife had a share in my estate; that neither could I forfeit. And my children also, being born of me, had a right to be maintained out of my labour or substance. Here then is the case: the conqueror has a title to reparation for damages received, and the children have a title to their father's estate for their subsistence: for as to the wife's share, whether her own labour, or compact, gave her a title to it, it is plain her husband could not forfeit what was hers. What must be done in the case? I answer; the fundamental law of nature being, that all, as much as may be, should be preserved, it follows, that if there be not enough fully to satisfy both, viz. for the conqueror's losses, and children's maintenance, he that hath, and to spare, must remit something of his full satisfaction, and give way to the pressing and preferable title of those who are in danger to perish without it.

But supposing the charge and damages of the war are to be made up to the conqueror, to the utmost farthing; and that the children of the vanquished, spoiled of all their father's goods, are to be left to starve and perish; yet the satisfying of what shall, on this score, be due to the conqueror, will scarce give him a title to any country he shall conquer: for the damages of war can scarce amount to the value of any considerable tract of land, in any part of the world, where all the land is possessed, and none lies waste.

And if I have not taken away the conqueror's land, which, being vanquished, it is impossible I should; scarce any other spoil I have done him can amount to the value of mine, supposing it equally cultivated, and of an extent any way coming near what I have over-run of his. The destruction of a year's product or two (for it seldom reaches four or five) is the utmost spoil that usually can be done: for as to money, and such riches and treasures taken away, these are none of nature's goods, they have but a fantastical imaginary value: nature has put no such upon them: they are of no more account by her standard, than the wampompeke of the Americans to an European prince, or the silver money of Europe would have been formerly to an American. And five years product is not worth the perpetual inheritance of land, where all is possessed, and none remains waste, to be taken up by him that is disseized: which will be easily granted, if one do but take away the imaginary value of money, the disproportion being more than between five and five hundred; though, at the same time, half a year's product is more worth than the inheritance, where there being more land than the inhabitants possess and make use of, any one has liberty to make use of the waste: but there conquerors take little care to possess themselves of the lands of the vanquished. No damage, therefore, that men in the state of nature (as all princes and governments are in reference to one another) suffer from one another, can give a conqueror power to dispossess the posterity of the vanquished, and turn them out of that inheritance, which ought to be the possession of them and their descendants to all generations. The conqueror indeed will be apt to think himself master: and it is the very condition of the subdued not to be able to dispute their right. But if that be all, it gives no other title than what bare force gives to the stronger over the weaker: and, by this reason, he that is strongest will have a right to whatever he pleases to seize on.

Over those then that joined with him in the war, and over those of the subdued country that opposed him not, and the posterity even of those that did, the conqueror, even in a just war, hath, by his conquest, no right of dominion: they are free from any subjection to him, and if their former government be dissolved, they are at liberty to begin and erect another to themselves.

The conqueror, it is true, usually, by the force he has over them, compels them, with a sword at their breasts, to stoop to his conditions, and submit to such a government as he pleases to afford them; but the inquiry is, what right he has to do so? If it be said, they submit by their own consent, then this allows their own consent to be necessary to give the conqueror a title to rule over them. It remains only to be considered, whether promises extorted by force, without right, can be thought consent, and how far they bind. To which I shall say, they bind not at all; because whatsoever another gets from me by force, I still retain the right of, and he is obliged presently to restore. He that forces my horse from me, ought presently to restore him, and I have still a right to retake him. By the same reason, he that forced a promise from me, ought presently to restore it, *i.e.* quit me of the obligation of it; or I may resume it myself, *i.e.* choose whether I will perform it: for the law of nature laying an obligation on me only by the rules she prescribes, cannot oblige me by the violation of her rules: such is the extorting any thing from me by force. Nor does it at all alter the case to say, 'I gave my promise,' no more than it excuses the force, and passes the right, when I put my hand in my pocket and deliver my purse myself to a thief, who demands it with a pistol at my breast.

From all which it follows, that the government of a conqueror, imposed by force on the subdued, against whom he had no right of war, or who joined not in the war against him, where he had right, has no obligation upon them.

But let us suppose that all the men of that community, being all members of the same body politic, may be taken to have joined in that unjust war wherein they are subdued, and so their lives are at the mercy of the conqueror.

I say, this concerns not their children who are in their minority: for since a father hath not, in himself, a power over the life or liberty of his child, no act of his can possibly forfeit it. So that the children, whatever may have happened to the fathers, are freemen, and the absolute power of the conqueror reaches no farther than the persons of the men that were subdued by him, and dies with them: and should he govern them as slaves, subjected to his absolute arbitrary power, he has no such right or dominion over their children. He can have no power over them but by their own consent, whatever he may drive them to say or do; and he has no lawful authority, whilst force, and not choice, compels them to submission.

Every man is born with a double right: first, a right of freedom to his person, which no other man has a power over, but the free disposal of it lies in himself.

Secondly, a right, before any other man, to inherit with his brethren his father's goods.

By the first of these, a man is naturally free from subjection to any government, though he be born in a place under its jurisdiction; but if he disclaim the lawful government of the country he was born in, he must also quit the right that belonged to him by the laws of it, and the possessions there descending to him from his ancestors, if it were a government made by their consent.

By the second, the inhabitants of any country, who are descended, and derive a title to their estates from those who are subdued, and had a government forced upon them against their free consents, retain a right to the possession of their ancestors, though they consent not freely to the government, whose hard conditions were by force imposed on the possessors of that country: for, the first conqueror never having had a title to the land of that country, the people who are the descendants of, or claim under those who were forced to submit to the yoke of a government by constraint, have always a right to shake it off, and free themselves from the usurpation or tyranny which the sword hath brought in upon them, till their rulers put them under such a frame of government as they willingly and of choice consent to. Who doubts but the Grecian Christians, descendants of the ancient possessors of that country, may justly cast off the Turkish yoke, which they have so long groaned under, whenever they have an opportunity to do it? For no government can have a right to obedience from a people who have not freely consented to it; which they can never be supposed to do, till either they are put in a full state of liberty to choose their government and governors, or at least till they have such standing laws, to which they have by themselves or their representatives given their free consent; and also till they are allowed their due property, which is so to be proprietors of what they have, that nobody can take away any part of it without their own consent, without which, men under any government are not in the state of freemen, but are direct slaves under the force of war.

But granting that the conqueror in a just war has a right to the estates, as well as power over the persons of the conquered; which, it is plain, he hath not: nothing of absolute power will follow from hence, in the continuance of the government; because the descendants of these being all freemen, if he grants them estates and possessions to inhabit his country, (without which it would be worth nothing) whatsoever he grants them, they have, so far as it is granted, property in – the nature whereof is, that 'without a man's own consent, it cannot be taken from him.'

Their persons are free by a native right, and their properties, be they more or less, are their own, and at their own dispose, and not at his; or else it is no property. Supposing the conqueror gives to one man a thousand acres, to him and his heirs for ever; to another he lets a thousand acres for his life, under the rent of 50l. or 500l. per ann.: has not the one of these a right to his thousand acres for ever, and the other during his life, paying the said rent? And hath not the tenant for life a property in all that he gets over and above his rent, by his labour and industry during the said term, supposing it to be double the rent? Can any one say, the king, or conqueror, after his grant, may by his power of conqueror take away all, or part of the land from the heirs of one, or from the other during his life, he paying the rent? Or can he take away from either the goods or money they have got upon the said land, at his pleasure? If he can, then all free and voluntary contracts cease, and are void in the world; there needs nothing to dissolve them at any time, but power enough; and all the grants and promises of men in power are but mockery and collusion: for can there be any thing more ridiculous than to say, I give you and yours this for ever, and that in the surest and most solemn way of conveyance can be devised; and yet it is to be understood, that I have right, if I please, to take it away from you again tomorrow?

I will not dispute now, whether princes are exempt from the laws of their country; but this I am sure, they owe subjection to the laws of God and nature. Nobody, no power, can exempt them from the obligations of that eternal law. Those are so great, and so strong, in the case of promises, that omnipotency itself can be tied by them. Grants, promises, and oaths, are bonds that hold the Almighty: whatever some flatterers say to princes of the world, who all together, with all their people joined to them, are in comparison of the great God, but as a drop of the bucket, or a dust on the balance, inconsiderable, nothing.

The short of the case in conquest is this: the conqueror, if he have a just cause, has a despotical right over the persons of all that actually aided, and concurred in the war against him, and a right to make up his damage and cost out of their labour and estates, so he injure not the right of any other. Over the rest of the people, if there were any that consented not to the war, and over the children of the captives themselves, or the possessions of either, he has no power; and so can have, by virtue of conquest, no lawful title himself to dominion over them, or derive it to his posterity; but is an aggressor, if he attempts upon their properties, and thereby puts himself in a state of war against them: and has no better a right of principality, he, nor any of his successors, than Hingar or Hubba, the Danes, had here in England; or Spartacus, had he conquered Italy, would have had; which is to have their yoke cast off, as soon as God shall give those under their subjection courage and opportunity to do it. Thus, notwithstanding whatever title the kings of Assyria had over Judah, by the sword, God assisted Hezekiah to throw off the dominion of that conquering empire. 'And the Lord was with Hezekiah, and he prospered; wherefore he went forth, and he rebelled against the king of Assyria; and served him not,' 2 Kings 18:7. Whence it is plain, that shaking off a power, which force, and not right, hath set over any one, though it hath the name of rebellion, yet is no offence before God, but is that which he allows and countenances, though even promises and covenants, when obtained by force, have intervened: for it is very probable, to any one that reads the story of Ahaz and Hezekiah attentively, that the Assyrians subdued Ahaz, and deposed him, and made Hezekiah king in his father's lifetime; and that Hezekiah by agreement had done him homage, and paid him tribute all this time.

CHAPTER 17

Of Usurpation

As conquest may be called a foreign usurpation, so usurpation is a kind of domestic conquest; with this difference, that an usurper can never have right on his side, it being no usurpation but where one is got into the possession of what another has right to. This, so far as it is usurpation, is a change only of persons, but not of the forms and rules of the government: for if the usurper extend his power beyond what of right belonged to the lawful princes or governors of the commonwealth, it is tyranny added to usurpation.

In all lawful governments, the designation of the persons who are to bear rule, is as natural and necessary a part as the form of the government itself; and is that which had its establishment originally from the people: the anarchy being much alike to have no form of government at all, or to agree that it shall be monarchical, but to appoint no way to design the person that shall have the power, and be the monarch – hence all commonwealths, with the form of government established, have rules also of appointing those who are to have any share in the public authority, and settled methods of conveying the right to them: for the anarchy is much alike to have no form of government at all, or to agree that it shall be monarchical, but to appoint no way to know or design the person that shall have the power, and be the monarch. Whoever gets into the exercise of any part of the power, by other ways than what the laws of the community have prescribed, hath no right to be obeyed, though the form of the commonwealth be still preserved; since he is not the person the laws have appointed, and consequently not the person the people have consented to. Nor can such an usurper, or any deriving from him, ever have a title, till the people are both at liberty to consent, and have actually consented to allow, and confirm in him the power he hath till then usurped.

CHAPTER 18

Of Tyranny

As usurpation is the exercise of power, which another hath a right to, so tyranny is the exercise of power beyond right, which nobody can have a right to. And this is making use of the power any one has in his hands, not for the good of those who are under it, but for his own private, separate advantage – when the governor, however entitled, makes not the law, but his will, the rule; and his commands and actions are not directed to the preservation of the properties of his people, but the satisfaction of his own ambition, revenge, covetousness, or any other irregular passion.

If one can doubt this to be truth or reason, because it comes from the obscure hand of a subject, I hope the authority of a king will make it pass with him. King James the First, in his speech to the parliament, 1603, tells them thus: 'I will ever prefer the weal of the public, and of the whole commonwealth, in making of good laws and constitutions, to any particular and private ends of mine; thinking ever the wealth and weal of the commonwealth to be my greatest weal and worldly felicity; a point wherein a lawful king doth directly differ from a tyrant: for I do acknowledge, that the special and greatest point of difference that is between a rightful king and an usurping tyrant is this, that whereas the proud and ambitious tyrant doth think his kingdom and people are only ordained for satisfaction of his desires and unreasonable appetites, the righteous and just king doth, by the contrary, acknowledge himself to be ordained for the procuring of the wealth and property of his people.' And again, in his speech to the parliament, 1609, he hath these words: 'The king binds himself by a double oath to the observation of the fundamental laws of his kingdom; tacitly, as by being a king, and so bound to protect as well the people, as the laws of his kingdom; and expressly, by his oath at his coronation; so as every just king, in a settled kingdom, is bound to observe that paction made to his people by his laws, in framing his government agreeable thereunto, according to that paction which God made with Noah after the deluge. Hereafter, seed-time and harvest, and cold and heat, and summer and winter, and day and night, shall not cease while the earth remaineth. And therefore a king governing in a settled kingdom, leaves to be a king, and degenerates into a tyrant, as soon as he leaves off to rule according to his laws.' And a little after, 'Therefore all kings that are not tyrants, or perjured, will be glad to bound themselves within the limits of their laws; and they that persuade them the contrary, are vipers, and pests both against them and the commonwealth.' Thus that learned king, who well understood the notions of things, makes the difference betwixt a king and a tyrant to consist only in this, that one makes the laws the bounds of his power, and the good of the public the end of his government; the other makes all give way to his own will and appetite.

It is a mistake to think this fault is proper only to monarchies; other forms of government are liable to it, as well as that: for wherever the power that is put in any hands for the government of the people, and the preservation of their properties, is applied to other ends, and made use of to impoverish, harass, or subdue them to the arbitrary and irregular commands of those that have it; there it presently becomes tyranny, whether those that thus use it are one or many. Thus we read of the Thirty Tyrants at Athens, as well as one at Syracuse; and the intolerable dominion of the Decemviri at Rome was nothing better.

Wherever law ends, tyranny begins, if the law be transgressed to another's harm; and whosoever in authority exceeds the power given him by the law, and makes use of the force he has under his command, to compass that upon the subject which the law allows not, ceases in that to be a magistrate; and, acting without authority, may be opposed as any other man who by force invades the right of another. This is acknowledged in subordinate magistrates. He that hath authority to seize my person in the street, may be opposed as a thief and a robber if he endeavours to break into my house to execute a writ, notwithstanding that I know he has such a warrant, and such a legal authority as will impower him to arrest me abroad. And why this should not hold in the highest, as well as in the most inferior magistrate,

I would gladly be informed. Is it reasonable that the eldest brother, because he has the greatest part of his father's estate, should thereby have a right to take away any of his younger brother's portions? Or that a rich man, who possessed a whole country, should from thence have a right to seize, when he pleased, the cottage and garden of his poor neighbour? The being rightfully possessed of great power and riches, exceedingly beyond the greatest part of the sons of Adam, is so far from being an excuse, much less a reason, for rapine and oppression, which the endamaging another without authority is, that it is a great aggravation of it: for the exceeding the bounds of authority is no more a right in a great, than in a petty officer; no more justifiable in a king than a constable; but is so much the worse in him, in that he has more trust put in him, has already a much greater share than the rest of his brethren, and is supposed, from the advantages of his education, employment, and counsellors, to be more knowing in the measures of right and wrong.

'May the commands then of a prince be opposed? May he be resisted as often as any one shall find himself aggrieved, and but imagine he has not right done him? This will unhinge and overturn all politics, and, instead of government and order, leave nothing but anarchy and confusion.'

To this I answer, that force is to be opposed to nothing but to unjust and unlawful force; whoever makes any opposition in any other case, draws on himself a just condemnation both from God and man; and so no such danger or confusion will follow, as is often suggested: for, first, as in some countries, the person of the prince by the law is sacred; and so, whatever he commands or does, his person is still free from all question or violence, not liable to force, or any judicial censure or condemnation; but yet opposition may be made to the illegal acts of any inferior officer, or other commissioned by him, unless he will, by actually putting himself into a state of war with his people, dissolve the government, and leave them to that defence which belongs to every one in the state of nature: for of such things who can tell what the end will be? And a neighbour kingdom has showed the world an odd example. In all other cases the sacredness of the person exempts him from all inconveniences, whereby he is secure, whilst the government stands, from all violence and harm whatsoever; than which there cannot be a wiser constitution: for the harm he can do in his own person not being likely to happen often, nor to extend itself far; nor being able by his single strength to subvert the laws, nor oppress the body of the people; should any prince have so much weakness and ill-nature as to be willing to do it, the inconveniency of some particular mischiefs that may happen sometimes, when a heady prince comes to the throne, are well recompensed by the peace of the public, and security of the government, in the person of the chief magistrate, thus set out of the reach of danger: it being safer for the body, that some few private men should be sometimes in danger to suffer, than that the head of the republic should be easily, and upon slight occasions, exposed.

Secondly – but this privilege belonging only to the king's person, hinders not, but they may be questioned, opposed, and resisted, who use unjust force, though they pretend a commission from him, which the law authorises not; as is plain in the case of him that has the king's writ to arrest a man, which is a full commission from the king; and yet he that has it cannot break open a man's house to do it, nor execute this command of the king upon certain days, nor in certain places, though this commission have no such exception in it; but they are the limitations of the law, which if any one transgress, the king's commission excuses him not; for the king's authority being given him only by the law, he cannot empower any one to act against the law, or justify him, by his commission, in so doing; the commission or command of any magistrate, where he has no authority, being so void and insignificant as that of any private man; the difference between the one and the other being that the magistrate has some authority so far, and to such ends, and the private man has none at all: for it is not the commission, but the authority, that gives the right of acting; and against the laws there can be no authority. But, notwithstanding such resistance, the king's person and authority are still both secured, and so no danger to governor or government.

Thirdly – supposing a government wherein the person of the chief magistrate is not thus sacred: yet this doctrine of the lawfulness of resisting all unlawful exercises of his power, will not upon every slight occasion endanger him, or embroil the government: for where the injured party may be relieved, and his damages repaired by appeal to the law, there can be no pretence for force, which is only to be used where a man is intercepted from appealing to the law: for nothing is to be accounted hostile force, but where it leaves not the remedy of such an appeal; and it is such force alone that puts him that uses it into a state of war, and makes it lawful to resist him. A man with a sword in his hand demands my purse in the highway, when perhaps I have not twelve-pence in my pocket: this man I may lawfully kill. To another I deliver £100 to hold only whilst I alight, which he refuses to restore me, when I am got up again, but draws his sword to defend the possession of it by force, if I endeavour to retake it. The mischief this man does me is an hundred, or possibly a thousand times more than the other perhaps intended me (whom I killed before he really did me any); and yet I might lawfully kill the one, and cannot so much as hurt the other lawfully. The reason whereof is plain; because the one using force, which threatened my life, I could not have time to appeal to the law to secure it; and when it was gone, it was too late to appeal. The law could not restore life to my dead carcase, the loss was irreparable: which to prevent, the law of nature gave me a right to destroy him, who had put himself into a state of war with me, and threatened my destruction. But in the other case, my life not being in danger, I may have the benefit of appealing to the law, and have reparation for my £100 that way.

Fourthly – but if the unlawful acts done by the magistrate be maintained (by the power he has got), and the remedy which is due by law be by the same power obstructed, yet the right of resisting, even in such manifest acts of tyranny, will not suddenly, or on slight occasions, disturb the government: for if it reach no farther than some private men's cases, though they have a right to defend themselves, and to recover by force what by unlawful force is taken from them; yet the right to do so will not easily engage them in a contest, wherein they are sure to perish; it being as impossible for one, or a few oppressed men to disturb the government, where the body of the people do not think themselves concerned in it, as for a raving madman, or heady malcontent, to overturn a well-settled state; the people being as little apt to follow the one as the other.

But if either these illegal acts have extended to the majority of the people, or if the mischief and oppression has lighted only on some few, but in such cases, as the precedent and consequences seem to threaten all; and they are persuaded in their consciences, that their laws, and with them their estates, liberties, and lives are in danger, and perhaps their religion too; how they will be hindered from resisting illegal force, used against them, I cannot tell. This is an inconvenience, I confess, that attends all governments whatsoever, when the governors have brought it to this pass, to be generally suspected of their people; the most dangerous state which they can possibly put themselves in; wherein they are less to be pitied, because it is so easy to be avoided; it being as impossible for a governor, if he really means the good of his people, and the preservation of them, and their laws together, not to make them see and feel it, as it is for the father of a family not to let his children see he loves and takes care of them.

But if all the world shall observe pretences of one kind, and actions of another; arts used to elude the law, and the trust of prerogative (which is an arbitrary power in some things left in the prince's hand to do good, not harm to the people) employed contrary to the end for which it was given: if the people shall find the ministers and subordinate magistrates chosen suitable to such ends, and favoured, or laid by, proportionably as they promote or oppose them: if they see several experiments made of arbitrary power, and that religion underhand favoured (though publicly proclaimed against), which is readiest to introduce it; and the operators in it supported, as much as may be; and when that cannot be done, yet approved still, and liked the better: if a long train of actions show the councils all tending that way, how can a man any more hinder himself from being persuaded in his own mind which way things are going; or from casting about how to save himself, than he could from believing the captain of the ship he was in, was carrying him, and the rest of the company, to Algiers, when he found him always steering that course, though cross winds, leaks in his ship, and want of men and provisions did often force him to turn his course another way for some time, which he steadily returned to again, as soon as the wind, weather, and other circumstances would let him?

CHAPTER 19

Of the Dissolution of Government

He that will with any clearness speak of the dissolution of government, ought in the first place to distinguish between the dissolution of the society and the dissolution of the government. That which makes the community, and brings men out of the loose state of nature into one politic society, is the agreement which every one has with the rest to incorporate, and act as one body, and so be one distinct commonwealth. The usual, and almost only way whereby this union is dissolved, is the inroad of foreign force making a conquest upon them: for in that case (not being able to maintain and support themselves as one entire and independent body), the union belonging to that body which consisted therein, must necessarily cease, and so every one return to the state he was in before, with a liberty to shift for himself, and provide for his own safety, as he thinks fit, in some other society. Whenever the society is dissolved, it is certain the government of that society cannot remain. Thus conquerors' swords often cut up governments by the roots, and mangle societies to pieces, separating the subdued or scattered multitude from the protection of, and dependence on, that society which ought to have preserved them from violence. The world is too well instructed in, and too forward to allow of, this way of dissolving of governments, to need any more to be said of it; and there wants not much argument to prove, that where the society is dissolved, the government cannot remain; that being as impossible, as for the frame of a house to subsist when the materials of it are scattered and dissipated by a whirlwind, or jumbled into a confused heap by an earthquake.

Besides this overturning from without, governments are dissolved from within.

First, when the legislative is altered. Civil society being a state of peace, amongst those who are of it from whom the state of war is excluded by the umpirage, which they have provided in their legislative, for the ending all differences that may arise amongst any of them; it is in their legislative, that the members of a commonwealth are united, and combined together into one coherent living body. This is the soul that gives form, life, and unity to the commonwealth: from hence the several members have their mutual influence, sympathy, and connexion: and therefore, when the legislative is broken or dissolved, dissolution and death follows: for, the essence and union of the society consisting in having one will, the legislative, when once established by the majority, has the declaring, and as it were keeping of that will. The constitution of the legislative is the first and fundamental act of society, whereby provision is made for the continuation of their union, under the direction of persons, and bonds of laws, made by persons authorized thereunto, by the consent and appointment of the people; without which no one man, or number of men, amongst them, can have authority of making laws that shall be binding to the rest. When any one, or more, shall take upon them to make laws, whom the people have not appointed so to do, they make laws, whom the people have not appointed so to do, they make laws without authority, which the people are not therefore bound to obey; by which means they come again to be out of subjection, and may constitute to themselves a new legislative, as they think best, being in full liberty to resist the force of those, who without authority would impose any thing upon them. Every one is at the disposure of his own will, when those who had, by the delegation of the society, the declaring of the public will, are excluded from it, and others usurp the place, who have no such authority or delegation.

This being usually brought about by such in the commonwealth who misuse the power they have, it is hard to consider it aright, and know at whose door to lay it, without knowing the form of government in which it happens. Let us suppose then the legislative placed in the concurrence of three distinct persons.

A single hereditary person, having the constant, supreme, executive power, and with it the power of convoking and dissolving the other two, within certain periods of time.

An assembly of hereditary nobility.

An assembly of representatives chosen, *pro tempore*, by the people. Such a form of government supposed, it is evident, first, tthat when such a single person, or prince, sets up his own arbitrary will in place of the laws, which are the will of the society, declared by the legislative, then the legislative is changed: for that being in effect the legislative, whose rules and laws are put in execution, and required to be obeyed; when other laws are set up, and other rules pretended, and enforced, than what the legislative, constituted by the society, have enacted, it is plain that the legislative is changed. Whoever introduces new laws, not being thereunto authorised by the fundamental appointment of the society, or subverts the old, disowns and overturns the power by which they were made, and so sets up a new legislative.

Secondly, when the prince hinders the legislative from assembling in its due time, or from acting freely, pursuant to those ends for which it was constituted, the legislative is altered: for it is not a certain number of men, no, nor their meeting, unless they have also freedom of debating, and leisure of perfecting, what is for the good of the society, wherein the legislative consists: when these are taken away or altered, so as to deprive the society of the due exercise of their power, the legislative is truly altered: for it is not names that constitute governments, but the use and exercise of those powers that were intended to accompany them; so that he, who takes away the freedom, or hinders the acting of the legislative in its due seasons, in effect takes away the legislative, and puts an end to the government.

Thirdly, when, by the arbitrary power of the prince, the electors, or ways of election, are altered, without the consent, and contrary to the common interest of the people, there also the legislative is altered: for if others than those whom the society hath authorised thereunto, do choose, or in another way than what the society hath prescribed, those chosen are not the legislative appointed by the people.

Fourthly. The delivery also of the people into the subjection of a foreign power, either by the prince or by the legislative, is certainly a change of the legislative, and so a dissolution of the government: for the end why people entered into society being to be preserved one entire, free, independent society, to be governed by its own laws; this is lost, whenever they are given up into the power of another.

Why, in such a constitution as this, the dissolution of the government in these cases is to be imputed to the prince, is evident; because he, having the force, treasure, and offices of the state to employ, and often persuading himself, or being flattered by others, that as supreme magistrate he is uncapable of control; he alone is in a condition to make great advances toward such changes, under pretence of lawful authority, and has it in his hands to terrify or suppress opposers, as factious, seditious, and enemies to the government: whereas no other part of the legislative, or people, is capable by themselves to attempt any alteration of the legislative, without open and visible rebellion, apt enough to be taken notice of; which, when it prevails, produces effects very little different from foreign conquest. Besides, the prince in such a form of government having the power of dissolving the other parts of the legislative, and thereby rendering them private persons, they can never in opposition to him, or without his concurrence, alter the legislative by a law, his consent being necessary to give any of their decrees that sanction. But yet, so far as the other parts of the legislative any way contribute to any attempt upon the government, and do either promote, or not (what lies in them) hinder such designs; they are guilty, and partake in this, which is certainly the greatest crime men can be guilty of one towards another.

There is one way more whereby such a government may be dissolved, and that is, when he who has the supreme executive power, neglects and abandons that charge, so that the laws already made can no longer be put in execution. This is demonstratively to reduce all to anarchy, and so effectually to dissolve the government: for laws not being made for themselves, but to be, by their execution, the bonds of the society, to keep every part of the body politic in its due place and function; when that totally ceases, the government visibly ceases, and the people become a confused multitude, without order or connexion. Where there is no longer the administration of justice, for the securing of men's rights, nor any remaining power within the community to direct the force, or provide for the necessities of the public; there certainly is no government left. Where the laws cannot be executed, it is all one as if there were no laws; and a government without laws is, I suppose, a mystery in politics, inconceivable to human capacity, and inconsistent with human society.

In these and the like cases, when the government is dissolved, the people are at liberty to provide for themselves, by erecting a new legislative, differing from the other, by the change of persons, or form, or both, as they shall find it most for their safety and good: for the society can never, by the fault of another, lose the native and original right it has to preserve itself; which can only be done by a settled legislative, and a fair and impartial execution of the laws made by it. But the state of mankind is not so miserable that they are not capable of using this remedy, till it be too late to look for any. To tell people they may provide for themselves, by erecting a new legislative, when by oppression, artifice, or being delivered over to a foreign power, their old one is gone, is only to tell them, they may expect relief when it is too late, and the evil is past cure. This is in effect no more than to bid them first be slaves, and then to take care of their liberty; and when their chains are on, tell them they may act like freemen. This, if barely so, is rather mockery than relief; and men can never be secure from tyranny, if there be no means to escape it till they are perfectly under it; and therefore it is, that they have not only a right to get out of it, but to prevent it.

There is therefore, secondly, another way whereby governments are dissolved, and that is, when the legislative, or the prince, either of them, act contrary to their trust.

First, the legislative acts against the trust reposed in them, when they endeavour to invade the property of the subject, and to make themselves, or any part of the community, masters, or arbitrary disposers of the lives, liberties, or fortunes of the people.

The reason why men enter into society is the preservation of their property; and the end why they choose and authorise a legislative is, that there may be laws made, and rules set, as guards and fences to the properties of all the members of the society: to limit the power, and moderate the dominion, of every part and member of the society: for since it can never be supposed to be the will of the society that the legislative should have a power to destroy that which every one designs to secure by entering into society, and for which the people submitted themselves to legislators of their own making; whenever the legislators endeavour to take away and destroy the property of the people, or to reduce them to slavery under arbitrary power, they put themselves into a state of war with the people, who are thereupon absolved from any farther obedience, and are left to the common refuge, which God hath provided for all men, against force and violence. Whensoever therefore the legislative shall transgress this fundamental rule of society; and either by ambition, fear, folly, or corruption, endeavour to grasp themselves, or put into the hands of any other, an absolute power over the lives, liberties, and estates of the people; by this breach of trust they forfeit the power the people had put into their hands for quite contrary ends, and it devolves to the people, who have a right to resume their original liberty, and, by the establishment of a new legislative, (such as they shall think fit) provide for their own safety and security, which is the end for which they are in society. What I have said here, concerning the legislative in general, holds true also concerning the supreme executor, who having a double trust put in him, both to have a part in the legislative, and the supreme execution of the law, acts against both, when he goes about to set up his own arbitrary will as the law of the society. He acts also contrary to his trust, when he either employs the force, treasure, and offices of the society to corrupt the representatives, and gain them to his purposes; or openly pre-engages the electors, and prescribes to their choice, such whom he has, by solicitations, threats, promises, or otherwise, won to his designs; and employs them to bring in such, who have promised beforehand what to vote, and what to enact. Thus to regulate candidates and electors, and new-model the ways of election, what is it but to cut up the government by the roots, and poison the very fountain of public security? For the people having reserved to themselves the choice of their representatives, as the fence to their properties, could do it for no other end, but that they might always be freely chosen, and so chosen, freely act, and advise, as the necessity of the commonwealth and the public good should, upon examination and mature debate, be judged to require. This, those who give their votes before they hear the debate, and have weighed the reasons on all sides, are not capable of doing. To prepare such an assembly as this, and endeavour to set up the declared abettors of his own will, for the true representatives of the people, and the law-makers of the society, is certainly as great a breach of trust, and as perfect a declaration of a design to subvert the government, as is possible to be met with. To which if one shall add rewards and punishments visibly employed to the same end, and all the arts of perverted law made use of, to take off and destroy all that stand in the way of such a design, and will not comply and consent to betray the liberties of their country, it will be past doubt what is doing. What power they ought to have in the society, who thus employ it contrary to the trust that went along with it in its first institution, is easy to determine; and one cannot but see, that he who has once attempted any such thing as this, cannot any longer be trusted.

To this perhaps it will be said, that the people being ignorant, and always discontented, to lay the foundation of government in the unsteady opinion and uncertain humour of the people, is to expose it to certain ruin; and no government will be able long to subsist, if the people may set up a new legislative, whenever they take offence at the old one. To this I answer, quite the contrary. People are not so easily got out of their old forms, as some are apt to suggest. They are hardly to be prevailed with to amend the acknowledged faults in the frame they have been accustomed to. And if there be any original defects, or adventitious ones introduced by time, or corruption; it is not an easy thing to get them changed, even when all the world sees there is an opportunity for it. This slowness and aversion in the people to quit their old constitutions, has in the many revolutions, which have been seen in this kingdom, in this and former ages, still kept us to, or, after some interval of fruitless attempts, still brought us back again to, our old legislative of king, lords, and commons: and whatever provocations have made the crown be taken from some of our princes' heads, they never carried the people so far as to place it in another line.

But it will be said, this hypothesis lays a ferment for frequent rebellion. To which I answer, first, no more than any other hypothesis: for when the people are made miserable, and find themselves exposed to the ill usage of arbitrary power, cry up their governors as much as you will, for sons of Jupiter; let them be sacred and divine, descended, or authorised from heaven; give them out for whom or what you please, the same will happen. The people generally illtreated, and contrary to right, will be ready upon any occasion to ease themselves of a burden that sits heavy upon them. They will wish, and seek for the opportunity, which in the change, weakness, and accidents of human affairs, seldom delays long to offer itself. He must have lived but a little while in the world, who has not seen examples of this in his time; and he must have read very little, who cannot produce examples of it in all sorts of governments in the world.

Secondly, I answer, such revolutions happen not upon every little mismanagement in public affairs. Great mistakes in the ruling part, many wrong and inconvenient laws, and all the slips of human frailty, will be born by the people without mutiny or murmur. But if a long train of abuses, prevarications, and artifices, all tending the same way, make the design visible to the people, and they cannot but feel what they lie under, and see whither they are going; it is not to be wondered, that they should then rouse themselves, and endeavour to put the rule into such hands which may secure to them the ends for which government was at first erected; and without which, ancient names, and specious forms, are so far from being better, that they are much worse, than the state of nature, or pure anarchy; the inconveniencies, being all as great and as near, but the remedy farther off and more difficult.

Thirdly, I answer, that this doctrine of a power in the people of providing for their safety anew, by a new legislative, when their legislators have acted contrary to their trust by invading their property, is the best fence against rebellion, and the probablest means to hinder it: for rebellion being an opposition, not to persons, but authority, which is founded only in the constitutions and laws of the government: those, whoever they be, who by force break through, and by force justify their violation of them, are truly and properly rebels: for when men, by entering into society and civil government, have excluded force, and introduced laws for the preservation of property, peace, and unity amongst themselves; those who set up force again in opposition to the laws, do *rebellare*, that is, bring back again the state of war, and are properly rebels: which they who are in power (by the pretence they have to authority, the temptation of force they have in their hands, and the flattery of those about them) being likeliest to do; the properest way to prevent the evil is to show them the danger and injustice of it, who are under the greatest temptation to run into it.

In both the fore-mentioned cases, when either the legislative is changed, or the legislators act contrary to the end for which they were constituted, those who are guilty are guilty of rebellion: for if any one by force takes away the established legislative of any society, and the laws by them made pursuant to their trust, he thereby takes away the umpirage, which every one had consented to, for a peaceable decision of all their controversies, and a bar to the state of war amongst them. They who remove, or change the legislative, take away this decisive power, which nobody can have but by the appointment and consent of the people; and so destroying the authority which the people did, and nobody else can set up, and introducing a power which the people hath not authorised, they actually introduce a state of war, which is that of force without authority; and thus, by removing the legislative established by the society (in whose decisions the people acquiesced and united, as to that of their own will) they untie the knot, and expose the people anew to the state of war. And if those, who by force take away the legislative, are rebels, the legislators themselves, as has been shown, can be no less esteemed so; when they, who were set up for the protection and preservation of the people, their liberties and properties, shall by force invade and endeavour to take them away; and so they putting themselves into a state of war with those who made them the protectors and guardians of their peace, are properly, and with the greatest aggravation, *rebellantes*, rebels.

But if they, who say, 'it lays a foundation for rebellion,' mean that it may occasion civil wars, or intestine broils, to tell the people they are absolved from obedience when illegal attempts are made upon their liberties or properties, and may oppose the unlawful violence of those who were their magistrates, when they invade their properties contrary to the trust put in them; and that therefore this doctrine is not to be allowed, being so destructive to the peace of the world: they may as well say, upon the same ground, that honest men may not oppose robbers or pirates, because this may occasion disorder or bloodshed. If any mischief come in such cases, it is not to be charged upon him who defends his own right, but on him that invades his neighbour's. If the innocent honest man must quietly quit all he has, for peace sake, to him who will lay violent hands upon it, I desire it may be considered, what a kind of peace there will be in the world, which consists only in violence and rapine; and which is to be maintained only for the benefit of robbers and oppressors. Who would not think it an admirable peace betwixt the mighty and the mean, when the lamb, without resistance, yielded his throat to be torn by the imperious wolf? Polyphemus' den gives us a perfect pattern of such a peace, and such a government, wherein Ulysses and his companions had nothing to do, but quietly to suffer themselves to be devoured. And no doubt Ulysses, who was a prudent man, preached up passive obedience, and exhorted them to a quiet submission, by representing to them of what concernment peace was to mankind; and by showing the inconveniencies might happen, if they should offer to resist Polyphemus, who had now the power over them.

The end of government is the good of mankind: and which is best for mankind, that the people should be always exposed to the boundless will of tyranny; or that the rulers should be sometimes liable to be opposed, when they grow exorbitant in the use of their power, and employ it for the destruction, and not the preservation of the properties of their people?

Nor let any one say, that mischief can arise from hence, as often as it shall please a busy head, or turbulent spirit, to desire the alteration of the government. It is true, such men may stir, whenever they please; but it will be only to their own just ruin and perdition: for till the mischief be grown general, and the ill designs of the rulers become visible, or their attempts sensible to the greater part, the people, who are more disposed to suffer than right themselves by resistance, are not apt to stir. The examples of particular injustice or oppression, of here and there an unfortunate man, moves them not. But if they universally have a persuasion, grounded upon manifest evidence, that designs are carrying on against their liberties, and the general course and tendency of things cannot but give them strong suspicions of the evil intention of their governors, who is to be blamed for it? Who can help it, if they, who might avoid it, bring themselves into this suspicion? Are the people to be blamed, if they have the sense of rational creatures, and can think of things no otherwise than as they find and feel them? And is it not rather their fault, who put things into such a posture, that they would not have them thought to be as they are? I grant, that the pride, ambition, and turbulency of private men have sometimes caused great disorders in commonwealths, and factions have been fatal to states and kingdoms. But whether the mischief hath oftener begun in the people's wantonness, and a desire to cast off the lawful authority of their rulers, or in the rulers' insolence, and endeavours to get and exercise an arbitrary power over their people; whether oppression, or disobedience, gave the first rise to the disorder; I leave it to impartial history to determine. This I am sure, whoever, either ruler or subject, by force goes about to invade the rights of either prince or people, and lays the foundation for overturning the constitution and frame of any just government, is highly guilty of the greatest crime, I think, a man is capable of; being to answer for all those mischiefs of blood, rapine, and desolation, which the breaking to pieces of governments bring on a country. And he who does it, is justly to be esteemed the common enemy and pest of mankind, and is to be treated accordingly.

That subjects or foreigners, attempting by force on the properties of any people, may be resisted with force, is agreed on all hands. But that magistrates, doing the same thing, may be resisted, hath of late been denied: as if those who had the greatest privileges and advantages by the law, had thereby a power to break those laws, by which alone they were set in a better place than their brethren: whereas their offence is thereby the greater, both as being ungrateful for the greater share they have by the law, and breaking also that trust, which is put into their hands by their brethren.

Whosoever uses force without right, as every one does in society, who does it without law, puts himself into a state of war with those against whom he so uses it; and in that state all former ties are cancelled, all other rights cease, and every one has a right to defend himself, and to resist the aggressor. This is so evident, that Barclay himself, that great assertor of the power and sacredness of kings, is forced to confess, that it is lawful for the people, in some cases, to resist their king; and that too in a chapter, wherein he pretends to show, that the divine law shuts up the people from all manner of rebellion. Whereby it is evident, even by his own doctrine, that, since they may in some cases resist, all resisting of princes is not rebellion. His words are these.

Quod siquis dicat, ergone populus tyrannicae crudelitati et furori jugulum semper praebebit? Ergone multitudo civitates suas fame, ferro, et flamma vastari, seque, conjuges, et liberos fortunae ludibrio et tyranni libidini exponi, inque omnia vitae pericula omnesque miserias et molestias a rege deduci patientur? Num illis quod omni animantium generi est a natura tributum, denegari debet, ut sc. vim vi repellant, seseque ab injuria tueantur? Huic breviter responsum sit, Populo universo negari defensionem, quæ juris naturalis est, neque ultionem quae praeter naturam est adversus regem concedi debere. Quapropter si rex non in singulares tantum personas aliquot privatum odium exerceat, sed corpus etiam reipublicae, cujus ipse caput est, *i.e.* totum populum, vel insignem aliquam ejus partem immani et intoleranda sævitia seu tyrannide divexet; populo quidem hoc casu resistendi ac tuendi se ab injuria potestas competit; sed tuendi se tantum, non enim in principem invadendi: et restituendae injuriae illatae, non recedendi à debita reverentia; propter acceptam injuriam. Praesentem denique impetum propulsandi non vim praeteritam ulciscendi jus habet. Horum enim alterum a natura est, ut vitam scilicet corpusque tueamur. Alterum vero contra naturam, ut inferior de superiori supplicium sumat. Quod itaque populus malum, antequam factum sit, impedire potest, ne fiat; id postquam factum est, in regem authorem sceleris vindicare non potest: populus igitur hoc amplius quam privatus quispiam habet: quod huic, vel ipsis adversariis judicibus, excepto Buchanano, nullum nisi in patientia remedium superest. Cum ille si

> intolerabilis tyrannus est (modicum enim ferre omnino debet) resistere cum reverentia possit. – Barclay *contra Monarchom.*, lib. 3, ch. 8.

In English thus:

> But if any one should ask, Must the people then always lay themselves open to the cruelty and rage of tyranny? Must they see their cities pillaged and laid in ashes, their wives and children exposed to the tyrant's lust and fury, and themselves and families reduced by their king to ruin, and all the miseries of want and oppression; and yet sit still? Must men alone be debarred the common privilege of opposing force with force, which nature allows so freely to all other creatures for their preservation from injury? I answer: Self-defence is a part of the law of nature; nor can it be denied the community, even against the king himself: but to revenge themselves upon him, must by no means be allowed them; if being not agreeable to that law. Wherefore if the king should show an hatred, not only to some particular persons, but sets himself against the body of the commonwealth, whereof he is the head, and shall, with intolerable ill usage, cruelly tyrannise over the whole, or a considerable part of the people, in this case the people have a right to resist and defend themselves from injury: but it must be with this caution, that they only defend themselves, but do not attack their prince: they may repair the damages received, but must not for any provocation exceed the bounds of due reverence and respect. They may repulse the present attempt, but must not revenge past violences: for it is natural for us to defend life and limb; but that an inferior should

> punish a superior, is against nature. The mischief which is designed them the people may prevent before it be done: but when it is done, they must not revenge it on the king, though author of the villany. This therefore is the privilege of the people in general, above what any private person hath; that particular men are allowed by our adversaries themselves (Buchanan only excepted) to have no other remedy but patience; but the body of the people may with reverence resist intolerable tyranny; for, when it is but moderate, they ought to endure it.

Thus far that great advocate of monarchical power allows of resistance.

It is true, he has annexed two limitations to it, to no purpose:

First, he says, it must be with reverence.

Secondly, it must be without retribution, or punishment; and the reason he gives is, 'Because an inferior cannot punish a superior.'

First, how to resist force without striking again, or how to strike with reverence, will need some skill to make intelligible. He that shall oppose an assault only with a shield to receive the blows, or in any more respectful posture, without a sword in his hand, to abate the confidence and force of the assailant, will quickly be at an end of his resistance, and will find such a defence serve only to draw on himself the worse usage. This is as ridiculous a way of resisting, as Juvenal thought it of fighting; 'ubi tu pulsas, ego vapulo tantum.' And the success of the combat will be unavoidably the same he there describes it:

> Libertas pauperis haec est:
> Pulsatus rogat, et pugnis concisus, adorat,
> Ut liceat paucis cum dentibus inde reverti.

This will always be the event of such an imaginary resistance, where men may not strike again. He therefore who may resist, must be allowed to strike. And then let our author, or any body else, join a knock on the head, or a cut on the face, with as much reverence and respect as he thinks fit. He that can reconcile blows and reverence, may, for aught I know, deserve for his pains a civil, respectful cudgelling, wherever he can meet with it.

Secondly, as to his second, 'An inferior cannot punish a superior;' that is true, generally speaking, whilst he is his superior. But to resist force with force, being the state of war that levels the parties, cancels all former relation of reverence, respect, and superiority: and then the odds that remains, is that he, who opposes the unjust aggressor, has this superiority over him, that he has a right, when he prevails, to punish the offender, both for the breach of the peace, and all the evils that followed upon it. Barclay therefore, in another place, more coherently to himself, denies it to be lawful to resist a king in any case. But he there assigns two cases, whereby a king may unking himself. His words are.

> Quid ergo, nulline casus incidere possunt quibus populo sese erigere atque in regem impotentius dominantem arma capere et invadere jure suo suaque authoritate liceat? Nulli certe quamdiu rex manet. Semper enim ex divinis id obstat, Regem honorificato; et qui potestati resistit, Dei ordinationi resistit: non alias igitur in eum populo potestas est

quam si id committat propter quod ipso jure rex esse desinat. Tunc enim se ipse principatu exuit atque in privatis constituit liber: hoc modo populus et superior efficitur, reverso ad eum sc. jure illo quod ante regem inauguratum in interregno habuit. At sunt paucorum generum commissa ejusmodi quae hunc effectum pariunt. At ego cum plurima animo perlustrem, duo tantam ínvenio, duos, inquam, casus quibus rex ipso facto ex rege non regem se facit et omni honore et dignítate regali atque in subditos potestate destituit; quorum etiam meminit Winzerus. Horum unus est, si regnum disperdat, quemadmodum de Nerone fertur, quod is nempe senatum populumque Romanum, atque adeo urbem ipsam ferro flammaque vastare, ac novas sibi sedes quaerere, decrevisset. Et de Caligula, quod palam denunciarit se neque civem neque principem senatui amplius fore, inque animo habuerit interempto utriusque ordinis electissimo quoque Alexandriam commigrare, ac ut populum uno ictu interimeret, unam ei cervicem optavit. Talia cum rex aliquis meditatur et molitur serio, omnem regnandi curam et animum ilico abjicit, ac proinde imperium in subditos amittit, ut dominus servi pro derelicto habiti dominium.'

Alter casus est, si rex in alicujus clientelam se contulit, ac regnum quod liberum a majoribus et populo traditum accepit, alienae ditioni mancipavit. Nam tunc quamvis forte non ea mente id agit populo plane ut incommodet: tamen quia quod praecipuum est regiae dignitatis amisit, ut summus scilicet in regno secundum Deum sit, et solo Deo inferior, atque populum etiam totum ignorantem vel invitum, cujus libertatem sartam et tectam

> conservare debuit, in alterius gentis ditionem et potestatem dedidit; hac velut quadam regni ab alienatione efficit, ut nec quod ipse in regno imperium habuit retineat, nec in eum cui collatum voluit, juris quicquam transferat; atque ita eo facto liberum jam et suæ potestatis populum relinquit, cujus rei exemplum unum annales Scotici suppeditant. – Barclay *contra Monarchom.*, lib. 3, ch. 16.

Which in English runs thus:

> What then, can there no case happen wherein the people may of right, and by their own authority, help themselves, take arms, and set upon their king, imperiously domineering over them? None at all, whilst he remains a king. Honour the king, and he that resists the power, resists the ordinance of God, are divine oracles that will never permit it. The people therefore can never come by a power over him, unless he does something that makes him cease to be a king: for then he divests himself of his crown and dignity, and returns to the state of a private man, and the people become free and superior, the power which they had in the interregnum, before they crowned him king, devolving to them again. But there are but few miscarriages which bring the matter to this state. After considering it well on all sides, I can find but two. Two cases there are, I say, whereby a king, *ipso facto*, becomes no king, and loses all power and regal authority over his people; which are also taken notice of by Winzerus.
>
> The first is, if he endeavour to overturn the government, that is, if he have a purpose and design to ruin the kingdom and commonwealth; as

it is recorded of Nero, that he resolved to cut off the senate and people of Rome, lay the city waste with fire and sword, and then remove to some other place – and of Caligula, that he openly declared, that he would be no longer a head to the people or senate, and that he had it in his thoughts to cut off the worthiest men of both ranks, and then retire to Alexandria; and he wished that the people had but one neck, that he might despatch them all at a blow – such designs as these, when any king harbours in his thoughts, and seriously promotes, he immediately gives up all care and thought of the commonwealth; and consequently forfeits the power of governing his subjects, as a master does the dominion over his slaves whom he hath abandoned.'

The other case is, when a king makes himself the dependent of another, and subjects his kingdom which his ancestors left him, and the people put free into his hands, to the dominion of another: for however perhaps it may not be his intention to prejudice the people, yet because he has hereby lost the principal part of regal dignity, viz. to be next and immediately under God supreme in his kingdom; and also because he betrayed or forced his people, whose liberty he ought to have carefully preserved, into the power and dominion of a foreign nation. By this, as it were, alienation of his kingdom he himself loses the power he had in it before, without transferring any the least right to those on whom he would have bestowed it; and so by this act sets the people free, and leaves them at their own disposal. One example of this is to be found in the Scottish Annals.

In these cases, Barclay, the great champion of absolute monarchy, is forced to allow that a king may be resisted, and cease to be a king. That is, in short, not to multiply cases, in whatsoever he has no authority, there he is no king, and may be resisted: for wheresoever the authority ceases, the king ceases too, and becomes like other men who have no authority. And these two cases he instances differ little from those above-mentioned to be destructive to governments, only that he has omitted the principle from which his doctrine flows; and that is, the breach of trust, in not preserving the form of government agreed on, and in not intending the end of government itself, which is the public good and preservation of property. When a king has dethroned himself, and put himself in a state of war with his people, what shall hinder them from prosecuting him who is no king, as they would any other man, who has put himself into a state of war with them; Barclay and those of his opinion would do well to tell us. This farther I desire may be taken notice of out of Barclay, that he says, 'The mischief that is designed, them, the people may prevent before it be done:' whereby he allows resistance when tyranny is but in design. 'Such designs as these (says he) when any king harbours in his thoughts and seriously promotes, he immediately gives up all care and thought of the commonwealth;' so that, according to him, the neglect of the public good is to be taken as an evidence of such design, or at least for a sufficient cause of resistance. And the reason of all he gives in these words, 'Because he betrayed or forced his people, whose liberty he ought carefully to have preserved.' What he adds, 'into the power and dominion of a foreign nation,' signifies nothing, the fault and forfeiture lying in the loss of their liberty, which he ought to have preserved, and not in any distinction of the persons to whose dominion they were subjected. The people's right is equally invaded, and their liberty lost, whether they are made slaves to any of their own, or a foreign nation; and in this lies the injury, and against this only have they the right of defence. And there are instances to be found in all countries, which show that it is not the change of nations in the persons of their governors, but the change of government, that gives the offence. Bilson, a bishop of our church, and a great stickler for the power and prerogative of princes, does, if I mistake not, in his treatise of Christian subjection, acknowledge that princes may forfeit their power, and their title to the obedience of their subjects; and if there needed authority in a case where reason is so plain, I could send my reader to Bracton, Fortescue, and the author of the Mirror, and others, writers that cannot be suspected to be ignorant of our government, or enemies to it. But I thought Hooker alone might be enough to satisfy those men, who relying on him for their ecclesiastical polity, are by a strange fate carried to deny those principles upon which he builds it. Whether they are herein made the tools of cunninger workmen, to pull down their own fabric, they were best look. This I am sure, their civil policy is so new, so dangerous, and so destructive to both rulers and people, that as former ages never could bear the broaching of it; so it may be hoped those to come, redeemed from the impositions of these Egyptian under-taskmasters, will abhor the memory of such servile flatterers, who, whilst it seemed to serve their turn, resolved all government into absolute tyranny, and would have all men born to, what their mean souls fitted them for, slavery.

Here, it is like, the common question will be made, 'Who shall be judge, whether the prince or legislative act contrary to their trust?' This, perhaps, ill-affected and factious men may spread amongst the people, when the prince only makes use of his due prerogative. To this I reply, 'The people shall be judge;' for who shall be judge whether his trustee or deputy acts well, and according to the trust reposed in him, but he who deputes him, and must, by having deputed him, have still a power to discard him, when he fails in his trust? If this be reasonable in particular cases of private men, why should it be otherwise in that of the greatest moment, where the welfare of millions is concerned, and also where the evil, if not prevented, is greater, and the redress very difficult, dear, and dangerous?

But farther, this question ('Who shall be judge?') cannot mean, that there is no judge at all: for where there is no judicature on earth, to decide controversies amongst men, God in heaven is judge. He alone, it is true, is judge of the right. But every man is judge for himself, as in all other cases, so in this, whether another hath put himself into a state of war with him, and whether he should appeal to the supreme Judge, as Jephthah did.

If a controversy arise betwixt a prince and some of the people, in a matter where the law is silent or doubtful, and the thing be of great consequence, I should think the proper umpire, in such a case, should be the body of the people: for in cases where the prince hath a trust reposed in him, and is dispensed from the common ordinary rules of the law; there, if any men find themselves aggrieved, and think the prince acts contrary to, or beyond that trust, who so proper to judge as the body of the people, (who at first lodged that trust in him) how far they meant it should extend? But if the prince, or whoever they be in the administration, decline that way of determination, the appeal then lies nowhere but to Heaven; force between either persons, who have no known superior on earth, or which permits no appeal to a judge on earth, being properly a state of war, wherein the appeal lies only to Heaven; and in that state the injured party must judge for himself, when he will think fit to make use of that appeal, and put himself upon it.

To conclude, the power that every individual gave the society, when he entered into it, can never revert to the individuals again, as long as the society lasts, but will always remain in the community; because without this there can be no community, no commonwealth, which is contrary to the original agreement: so also when the society hath placed the legislative in any assembly of men, to continue in them and their successors, with direction and authority for providing such successors, the legislative can never revert to the people whilst that government lasts; because, having provided a legislative with power to continue for ever, they have given up their political power to the legislative, and cannot resume it. But if they have set limits to the duration of their legislative, and made this supreme power in any person, or assembly, only temporary; or else, when by the miscarriages of those in authority it is forfeited; upon the forfeiture, or at the determination of the time set, it reverts to the society, and the people have a right to act as supreme, and continue the legislative in themselves; or erect a new form, or under the old form place it in new hands, as they think good.